THE
SUCCESSFUL
MARKETING
PLAN

SECOND EDITION

THE
SUCCESSFUL
MARKETING
PLAN

SECOND EDITION

*A Disciplined and
Comprehensive Approach*

ROMAN G. HIEBING, JR.
SCOTT W. COOPER

NTC Business Books
a division of NTC/CONTEMPORARY PUBLISHING GROUP
Lincolnwood, Illinois USA

Library of Congress Cataloging-in-Publication Data

Hiebing, Roman G.
 The successful marketing plan : a disciplined and comprehensive
approach / Roman Hiebing, Jr., Scott W. Cooper.—2nd ed.
   p. cm.
 Includes index.
 ISBN 0-8442-3202-5; 0-8442-3203-3 (pbk.)
  1. Marketing—Planning. I. Cooper, Scott W. II. Title.
 HF5415.13.H523 1996
 658.8'02—dc20
             96-28253
             CIP

ISBN: 0-8442-3203-3 (softbound)
ISBN: 0-8442-3202-5 (hardbound)

Published by NTC Business Books,
a division of NTC/Contemporary Publishing Group, Inc.,
4255 West Touhy Avenue,
Lincolnwood (Chicago), Illinois 60646-1975 U.S.A.
19 18 17 16 15 14 13 12 11 10 9 8 7 6 5 4

FOREWORD

I knew Roman and Scott had a winner with their first text published in 1990, but they have exceeded that successful text with this new edition. This new edition includes not only updated, real business experiences that relate to rapidly changing market environments, but an easier-to-use and expanded marketing background section. Further, the authors' disciplined marketing planning approach includes a new and proven method for quantitatively locking projected sales to target market behavior and to communication throughout the entire plan. This provides focus on what needs to be accomplished, and helps insure that the marketing plan you developed actually fulfills the sales objectives.

For those of you who have not been exposed to Roman and Scott's work before, I want to say I know the authors well. They've worked on projects for my brands, and I've guest lectured for their business classes at the University of Wisconsin. So I speak from firsthand experience when I say readers of this book will get the real thing: straight from the shoulder, straight from real business life, this is how you do it! What Scott and Roman show you how to do in this book is exactly what they do for their own clients every day. And it works. This book gives you the information base, the insights, and the methodology to write a solid marketing plan that, properly executed, will get results.

I've been exposed to many marketing plans, not only at Kimberly-Clark, but previously in running my own small business, managing multimillion dollar Procter & Gamble brands, and a stint managing retail, package goods, and franchise accounts for one of the country's largest advertising agencies. This edition is the best all-around marketing planning tool I've seen, because it speaks to the needs of both the entrepreneur and the director of a traditional, structured marketing department.

But the best part of this book is its practical yet comprehensive approach. It doesn't just talk about what your marketing plan should include, it literally takes you by the hand and walks you through it, step by step. It takes what can seem an overwhelmingly complex process and breaks the task into manageable parts, providing an easy-to-follow path to completion of your successful marketing plan.

I believe that with this book as a guide, any intelligent, persevering person—regardless of experience level—can write an effective marketing plan. Even with my 25 years of marketing planning experience behind me, this book gives me

ideas for innovative but executable marketing methods. In fact, the authors'
Chinese translation is a great asset to my Chinese-fluent marketing people.

Paul Geisler
President
Asia and Pacific
Kimberly-Clark Corporation

PREFACE

Reasons and Goals for This Book

While we never could have imagined the success of our first text, we have nonetheless decided not to rest on our good fortune, but to improve continually upon what we began—making this text more comprehensive, easier to use, and more responsive by providing a proven, interlocking marketing planning method. This data-based method systematically gathers the background data to interface directly with marketing plan preparation. The plan itself quantitatively locks objectives, strategies, and tactics together so that it can be effectively executed, accurately evaluated, and, most importantly, achieve up-front sales objectives.

With nearly half of this edition being new or updated material, we believe we have enhanced this book as one definitive source that explains clearly, simply, and pragmatically *how to* prepare a marketing plan in a *disciplined* and *comprehensive* manner. This book is a source that can be used as a planning guide by the inexperienced marketer and as a reference on planning by the experienced marketer. This major rewrite of our text meets the ever-changing and more demanding business environment for quantifiable results from an organization's marketing efforts.

This "how to" on marketing planning is not meant to be a scholarly piece (although we believe in academia, and teach part-time in the School of Business at the University of Wisconsin). It is meant to be an easy-to-use, actionable resource from which to write a marketing plan that really does work. A marketing plan developed using the methodology in this book works because the disciplined planning process is based on proven marketing principles and many years of actual experience. We believe in the book's marketing methodology not just because we are the authors of the book, but because we use the same planning methods every day in our firm to help market our clients' products and services and in our own personal entrepreneurial endeavors. And it works because this approach forces us to do it the right way. You will find, as we have, if you do it by this book, your marketing plan with the proper execution will dramatically increase the level of success for your product and service.

While the vast majority of what is presented in this book is based on hard factual data, we've included personal experiences, observations, and opinions. For these we take full responsibility. Likewise, any errors are our own.

Acknowledgments

From Both of Us

We would first like to thank all those wonderful people not specifically mentioned here who had a hand in making this book a reality. A big thank you to our fellow staff members at The Hiebing Group, particularly our partners, for their support and understanding as we ran a business with them while writing a book.

Individually, we would like to acknowledge the following staff members for their support as we wrote this book:

- Our partners Barry Callen, Marion Michaels, Chris Schell, Patrick Warczak, and Sandy Weisberger who provided valuable assistance in writing portions of this text.

- We want to thank former staff members Michael Rothschild, Emily Child, Marilyn Gardner, Karen Sullivan, and Angie Wichmann who made key contributions to this edition.

We would like to thank the following practitioners for taking time from their busy schedules to read earlier versions of this text and give valuable feedback in the preparation of subsequent drafts and of the finished product. Their varied experiences with different types and sizes of organizations especially helped make this book a practical resource for everyone with an interest in, or need for, marketing planning methods.

Marshall Doney, Director of Marketing, Automobile Club of New York

Ron Fromm, Executive Vice President, Famous Footwear

Paul Geisler, President—Asia & Pacific, Kimberly-Clark

Tom O'Shea, Former Vice President, Kimberly-Clark, and now a successful entrepreneur

John Tuerff, Vice President of Planning and Market Development, Beatrice Cheese, Inc.

We also want to thank Andy Winston of NTC Business Books for providing encouragement, support, and valuable suggestions in subsequent drafts of the manuscript.

We also cannot overlook saying thank you to our students with whom we first tested our original book, and the subsequent versions of this edition, giving us the opportunity to improve its usefulness in the classroom. Their many suggestions improved its worth as a teaching tool. Likewise, the participants in our many marketing planning seminars, especially those of the University of Wisconsin Management Institute, provided valuable insight and feedback.

Finally, we want to thank all our clients who believed in us over the years and gave us the opportunity to apply again and again (in whole or part) our marketing methodology to their organizations. They provided us with valuable learning experiences and continually challenged us to develop innovative marketing programs that delivered results.

From Scott

There are many people to thank for their assistance in this book, both with the first edition and the current rewrite and update. First and foremost I thank my family. My wife, Liz, who encouraged me to undertake this project when Roman and I were first offered the opportunity, pushed me when I didn't feel like writing and throughout the past 18 years has remained my very best friend and confidant. To our four sons, Seth, Birk, Reed, and Cale, for giving me the excuse to grow up all over again, keep my enthusiasm, and see the world in an entirely different light. To my favorite in-laws who bailed me out time and time again during the initial drafts by coming to help Liz when I was writing and working virtually around the clock. And finally, to my parents who have always encouraged but never pushed (well, all right, sometimes, but always for the right reasons).

A special thanks goes to Margaret Hiebing. On some of those long days with Roman, writing, discussing, writing, and rewriting some more, Margaret's upbeat attitude and fantastic cooking were definitely the most positive experiences I had.

A big thanks to Mike Rothschild, Jack Nevin, and Neil Ford, who all at one time or the other as Marketing Department heads, have hired me to teach and lecture at the University of Wisconsin Business School. The combination of real-world agency business experience coupled with the teaching and writing has helped me improve all three endeavors. With each class I try to give back some small part that the University of Wisconsin has given me throughout my life, both as an undergraduate student and as a resident of the community. I'll never be able to repay the debt.

Thanks to Miami University (Oxford, Ohio) for a great graduate school experience.

Finally, a huge thanks goes to Roman Hiebing. I have had the opportunity to work closely with Roman for the past 15 years. I've known few people who are as smart, hard-working, and caring. Roman's childlike belief in honesty and his appreciation for each person's talents has created an environment which allows individuals to live up to their potential. I consider Roman a teacher, my mentor, a pain in the ass, one of my best friends, and business partner. Above all, he's the one person I know who is crazy enough to take this much time to write a book and still think it was one of the best experiences of his life.

From Roman

I have many friends, colleagues, and family members to thank for helping me over the years, and who directly or indirectly had a hand in making our first edition, and now this book, possible.

Thank you to my two mentors. First, to Harry Dean Wolfe (now deceased), who was my major professor in graduate school at the University of Wisconsin, from whom I learned that theory and practice are *both* necessary. Harry was instrumental in my taking a first job out of school with the Leo Burnett advertising agency in Chicago. And thanks to Rogers W. Zarling, entrepreneur extraordinaire, who from my boyhood to adulthood taught me business by what he called the best school, "the school of hard knocks."

Thank you to the Leo Burnett agency for instilling in me true advertising ideals and the quest for the best.

Thank you to all the McDonald's people that I have worked with over the years for what they taught me and for the confidence they placed in me, specifically Kathy Henry, now in England, handling the marketing for McDonald's Systems of Europe.

Thank you to Brian Cook, a friend, and president of Famous Footwear, who helped us complete the first edition of this book by continually badgering me, asking, "When are you going to get that damn book done?" And for helping us on the subsequent *One Day Marketing Plan.*

Thank you to my brothers, Al and Dick, former partners with me in a group of restaurants, for giving me the opportunity to try new things. In most cases they had to make the new ideas work and pay for them.

Thank you to my parents who were here in mind and spirit to see completion of the first text. To my father, Roman (now deceased), for teaching me to "finish what

I started" and that "if you are going to do something, make sure you do it right the first time." To my mother, Charlotte (now in a nursing home with Alzheimer's disease), for encouraging me to "go for it" and to take the chance to try something new. I am forever in their debt, and they're in my thoughts always.

Thank you to my wife, Margaret, for her understanding and constant support, who has sacrificed many vacations and weekends because she (thank God) accepts my need for a continual challenge.

A side note regarding Margaret and myself. Just after our first text was published, I used the same methodology of that text to write a plan targeted to birth mothers and referrals. The objective of the marketing plan was to adopt a child because Margaret and I were not having much luck producing our own, even with the help of modern science. In the plan, the timeline called for the objective to be achieved within a two-year window. However, to our pleasant surprise, the plan, along with excellent execution by Margaret, delivered in just two months a beautiful baby girl named Laura Rose who just turned six as this preface was written.

Finally, thank you to Scott, my friend, partner (now president of our firm), and the best co-author anyone could ever have, whose wife, Liz, encouraged him while he pushed me to do our first text which was the catalyst for our other texts and this edition. And we did it. Because we know there is a better way.

CONTENTS

Chapter 10—PRICING   **242**

INTRODUCTION

The purpose of this book is to provide you with a practical and proven, step-by-step guide for preparing your own marketing plan. This is not a discussion of marketing theory, but a text with real world answers to help you meet specific marketing challenges head-on, whatever your level of marketing expertise or the size and type of your organization. In addition to providing a realistic guide to preparing a marketing plan, this book is also a very useful reference resource that will help you find marketing solutions on an everyday basis.

WHAT THE READER CAN EXPECT

This book provides not only a disciplined and comprehensive approach to writing a marketing plan, but an integrated and interlocking, tested method that follows a disciplined planning process—from describing what background information is necessary and how to analyze it, to writing the marketing plan specifics and evaluating the results of the plan.

Whatever the marketing challenge, this how-to approach will have direct application because it is based on proven marketing principles and hundreds of real business experiences. A wide variety of actual examples, drawn from the authors' experiences, have been included to help the reader understand the marketing principles and the step-by-step marketing plan development process. Further, you will also find that this book will keep you on track, eliminate wasted effort, and most importantly, help you utilize a planning process that has achieved results for companies both large and small—from Fortune 500 to entrepreneurial start-up companies.

This book focuses primarily on the most important part of any marketing program—the preparation of a marketing plan, not the implementation. It includes helpful planning and research tools; it does not dwell on specific execution.

The authors have found that if a marketer takes the necessary time and makes the required effort to prepare an effective marketing plan, arriving at the actual executional elements is the easy part, as they flow naturally from the strategic framework of the marketing plan. In our opinion, marketing failures are far too often the result of marketing executions that were *not* rooted in a well thought-out disciplined marketing plan.

The authors might add that they believe it has been their recommended disciplined approach that has made the original edition of this text, a condensed version, and its translations a success not only in this country, but worldwide. Based on thorough investigation and continual application in today's marketplace, this second edition has been improved with a newly organized and updated marketing background section that is easier to apply directly to the writing of the marketing plan itself. It has been improved with a tested, interlocking method that helps ensure sales objectives are met and with the addition of new, but proven, marketing methods designed to meet the fast changing and competitive marketing environment of today. Finally, many recent, real-world marketing experiences have been added to this text that will help demonstrate how to prepare your own marketing plan.

DISCIPLINED MARKETING PLANNING

The key to writing an effective marketing plan is disciplined marketing planning. However, before defining disciplined marketing planning, it is necessary to first describe what a *marketing plan* is. We will describe a marketing plan as an arranged structure to guide the process of determining the target market for your product or service, detailing the target market's needs and wants, and then fulfilling these needs and wants better than the competition.

Next, we define *disciplined marketing planning* as a comprehensive, sequential, interlocking, step-by-step decision and action process. In using this disciplined approach, you follow a 10-step, prescribed but logical process that allows you to define issues, answer questions correctly, and make decisions. Each major step, as depicted by a box on the disciplined marketing planning chart in Exhibit 1, should be completed before going on to the next. Further, the major steps, such as marketing background and planning, are broken down into individual, ordered steps, providing a clear and efficient road map for preparing an effective marketing plan.

The 10-step, disciplined marketing planning method is built on a four-block foundation.

I. The *marketing background* includes the information base from which the marketing plan is developed.

II. The *marketing plan* provides direction for the execution in the marketplace.

III. The *marketing execution* is the actual interaction with the target market and is responsible for generating the projected sales and profits.

IV. The *marketing evaluation* measures the level of success of the plan's execution and provides learning that is incorporated in the marketing background section developed for the next year's marketing plan.

The disciplined approach, although initially more time consuming, dramatically increases the chances of your product's or service's success, because the marketing plan prepared in this manner is just that—totally planned. It is a data-based plan that is very encompassing, yet feasible to execute.

Why do we say employing this disciplined marketing planning methodology increases your chances of success in marketing your product or service? Because this method of marketing planning is:

1. *Disciplined:* To truly integrate marketing tools, one needs a very set methodology to sort out and interface these many overlapping elements. Integrating can become very complicated and, in some instances, overwhelming. Accord-

Exhibit 1 Ten Steps to Disciplined Marketing Planning

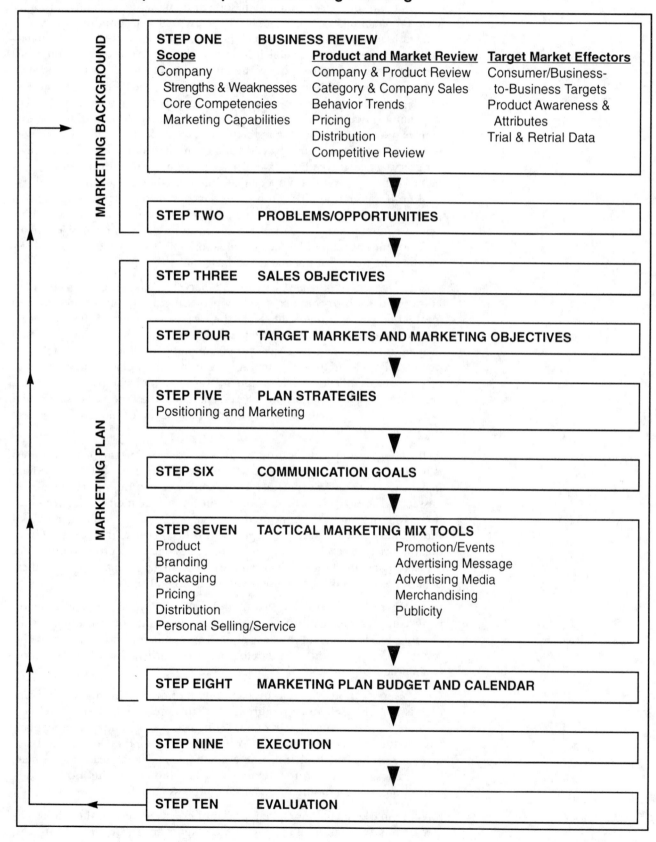

ingly, disciplined marketing planning employs a sequential, step-by-step system that asks for consideration of all tools and takes the marketing through a clear incremental building process. The sequential steps put the various planning tasks in a logical order so you do not get ahead of yourself (i.e., putting together an advertising and publicity campaign before clearly defining the heavy user target or failing to consider the interfacing of the promotion and merchandising tools with the advertising and publicity tools). Further, because so much of marketing is not easy to quantify and evaluate, disciplined marketing planning demands that measurable objectives are incorporated throughout your marketing plan. Starting at the top of the marketing plan, there are objectives for sales, marketing objectives and communication goals, and objectives for every tactical marketing mix tool, such as promotion, advertising, and publicity. Each objective is very specific and quantifiable. For example, increase trial by 10 percent at current average purchase rates, increase advertising awareness to 30 percent, or generate 300 inches of editorial space for a publicity program. If it is not quantifiable and measurable, it is not an objective. Finally, we end the plan with specific evaluation objectives in order to accurately measure the impact of the marketing program.

2. *Interlocking, not just integrated:* Disciplined marketing takes the integrated marketing approach to the next level by providing a sequential, step-by-step methodology that numerically locks the various elements of the marketing plan together. Each element and marketing mix tool is quantifiably integrated to meet the up-front sales objectives of the plan. No longer should the supporting plan elements and communication tools be woefully inadequate to meet the sales objectives. This happens, for example, when the target market(s) is too small to support the sales objectives or when the advertising media weight is half the amount necessary to generate the level of awareness to affect the target's attitude.

As the above example demonstrates, the sequence of how the plan is ordered is important, because what comes *after* in the order of the plan is, in effect, making what comes *before* possible. For example, generating advertising awareness for the message is made possible by the amount of media weight put into the marketplace to communicate the message. Likewise, certain elements of the plan are placed directly next to each other because they have a direct quantitative tie to each other. For example, sales objectives proceed the target market(s) and are directly reliant on the size of the target market(s) and their behavior as detailed in the subsequent marketing objectives.

In summary, this interlocking methodology goes beyond integration by directly tying each element of the marketing plan to fulfill the sales objectives and interlocking many of the tactical marketing mix tools to each other. The result of this interlocking methodology is the effective and efficient execution of a marketing plan.

3. *Comprehensive:* Another important component of disciplined marketing planning is the comprehensive requirement of this methodology. This includes not only the major components of marketing background and marketing plan, but also the actual execution in the marketplace, where the successes and failures take place. Finally, there is the evaluation step, which leads to the marketing background step for next year's plan and closes the loop on this continuous and comprehensive planning process (Exhibit 1).

Effective marketing cannot take place until every element of the marketing mix is considered and all appropriate elements are incorporated into the marketing plan. Further, because each tactical tool has communication value, each tool must be considered when preparing an integrated communication program. For example, price is not usually considered a marketing communication tool, yet the price charged for a product communicates something about the product image to the potential purchaser. It has been shown that a substantially higher competitive price charged for a product usually connotes a greater quality image for that product. Accordingly, it takes a comprehensive planning effort to make sure that the communication value of each tactical tool is taken into account and is correctly presented to the customer.

You will note that each step of the marketing planning process is comprehensive. Beginning with the business review portion of the marketing background section, you will see all the background information that must be gathered, reviewed, and analyzed in order to prepare a marketing plan and execute a communications program. Likewise, the summation of the marketing plan in the form of a final marketing plan calendar and budget is very detailed, ensuring that all necessary elements have been included, properly funded, and described so that there is proper execution in the marketplace. Finally, the evaluation component is very comprehensive to ensure that there is a clear understanding of the effectiveness of the overall plan and the individual components. This allows you to determine what did and didn't work and also learn how to improve on next year's plan by incorporating and reviewing the evaluation data in the business review for next year's planning process.

In summary, to be comprehensive not only means extra effort, but it also means leaving nothing or very little to chance. The net result is that marketing programs developed from comprehensive marketing plans are far more successful when implemented in the marketplace.

THE TEN STEPS TO DISCIPLINED MARKETING PLANNING

To bring order and efficiency to the difficult task of marketing planning, we have broken down the process into ten steps that we believe need to be addressed when developing a disciplined marketing plan. All too often companies think of marketing as only one or two components, rather than as an interlocking, step-by-step, comprehensive process. Following are the ten steps of disciplined marketing planning employed by the authors.

Step 1
Business Review

As part of the marketing background component (Exhibit 1), the business review includes the marketing database commonly referred to as the situation analysis.

To develop a marketing database there first needs to be an understanding of the scope of your business followed by a comprehensive analysis of the company product, and marketplace relevant to the target market and competitive situation. This is accomplished through secondary research (company records, data analysis, and existing industry reports) and very often, primary research, including surveys and focus group information. The business review provides a qualitative and quantitative decision-making base for the subsequent marketing plan and a rationale for all strategic marketing decisions within the plan.

Step 2
Problems and
Opportunities

The problems and opportunities step is a summary of the challenges that emerge from the marketing database. In this step the data collected from the business review is distilled into meaningful summary points that form the basis of the marketing plan.

Step 3
Quantifiable Sales Objectives

Sales objectives represent projected levels of goods or services to be sold. Setting sales objectives is critical because it is the first task of the marketing plan development and it sets the tone of the entire marketing plan. Everything that follows in the plan is designed to meet the sales objectives, from defining the size of the specific target market and establishing marketing objectives, to determining the amount of advertising and promotional dollars to be budgeted, to the actual hiring of marketing and sales personnel, to the number and kinds of distribution channels/stores utilized, and, very importantly, to the amount of product produced or inventoried.

Step 4
Target Markets and Marketing Objectives

We put the target market and marketing objective steps together because of their critical link to one another.

- *Target Markets* Once you have developed sales objectives, you must determine to whom you will be selling your product. Making this determination is really defining a target market—a group of people with a set of common characteristics. Target marketing concentrates marketing efforts towards a portion of the population with similar purchasing needs and buying habits.

- *Marketing Objectives* Marketing objectives clearly define what behavior you want from the target markets; they are measurable ends that need to be achieved. In this step you will quantitatively lock the required behavior in the marketing objectives to a quantified target market that will fulfill the sales objectives.

Step 5
Overall Plan Strategies

The overall plan strategies include the positioning strategy for the image of your product and the marketing strategies needed to fulfill the marketing objectives.

- *Positioning* Once you have defined your target market(s) and have established marketing objectives, you must develop a market positioning for your product. By positioning, we mean creating the desired perception of your product within your target market relative to the competition. The positioning strategy provides overall direction for the specific marketing strategies and a singular focus for the tactical marketing mix tools.

- *Marketing Strategies* A marketing strategy is a statement detailing how an individual marketing objective will be achieved. While marketing objectives are specific, quantifiable, and measurable, marketing strategies are descriptive. They explain how the measurable objectives will be met. In our planning methodology, we outline 18 strategic considerations that should be addressed in most marketing plans. The marketing strategies also guide the development of the tactical marketing mix tools (Step 7) and provide direction in setting communication contribution values for each tactical tool.

Step 6
Communication Goals

These goals set the target market awareness and attitudes necessary to deliver positioning and fulfill the marketing objectives, as well as provide direction for what is to be accomplished by each tactical tool in terms of communication value.

Step 7
Tactical Marketing Mix Tools

This step of disciplined marketing planning develops tactical plans. The tactical plans incorporate marketing executions that, when implemented, will allow you to meet your marketing objectives and fulfill the overall marketing strategies and communication guidelines established earlier. Each marketing mix tool should have its own objectives, strategies, and where appropriate, executional specifics.

The following marketing mix tools are included in the tactical planning process.

- *Product* The product is the tangible object that is marketed to the target market for consumer goods, retail, and business-to-business companies. For service businesses, the product is a future benefit or future promise.

- *Branding* Branding is the naming of the product, service, or company. A brand or name is the label that consumers associate with your product. For this reason, a brand or name should help communicate the product's positioning and its inherent drama for the consumer.

- *Packaging* For manufacturers, packaging holds and protects the product and assists in communicating the product's attributes and image. For retailers and service firms, packaging is the inside and outside environment that houses and dispenses the product/services (stores, offices, etc.), and it helps communicate the company's attributes and image.

- *Pricing* Price is the monetary value of the product. The monetary value is usually governed by what the target market or buyer will pay for the product and what the seller or company must receive for the product in order to defray costs and generate a profit.

- *Personal Selling/Service* Personal selling for retail and service firms, often referred to as operations, involves all functions related to selling and service in the store, office, or other environments, such as door-to-door solicitation, in-home selling, and telemarketing. This includes hiring and managing sales personnel, stocking inventory, preparing the product for sale, presenting and maintaining the facility, and follow-up service to the customers.

  For business-to-business and package goods firms, personal selling relates to the manufacturers' selling and servicing of its products to the trade and/or intermediate markets (various buyers of the product within the distribution channel from original producer to ultimate user).

- *Distribution* We define distribution as the transmission of goods and services from the producer or seller to the user. Distribution must ensure that product is accessible to the target market.

- *Promotion/Events* Promotion provides added incentive, encouraging the target market to perform some incremental behavior. The incremental behavior results in either increased short-term sales and/or an association with the product (e.g., product usage or an event-oriented experience). In addition, promotion is more short term in focus. For the purposes of this book, we will define promotion as an activity offering added incentive to stimulate incremental purchase or association with the product over the short run, for a reason that goes beyond just the product's inherent attributes and benefits.

- *Advertising Message* Communication which informs and persuades through paid media (television, radio, magazine, newspaper, outdoor, and direct mail) constitutes the advertising message.

- *Advertising Media* Advertising media are paid carriers of advertising, not at the point of purchase. While the advertising message is *what* is being communicated, the advertising media is *how* it is delivered.

- *Merchandising* Merchandising is non-media communication of the company and/or product to the target market. This is the method used to communicate product and promotional information. Merchandising makes a visual and/or written statement about your company through an environment other than paid media, with or without one-on-one personal communication. Merchandising includes brochures, sell sheets, product displays, video presentations, banners, trade show exhibits, shelf talkers, table tents, or any other non-media tools that can be used to communicate product attributes, positioning, pricing, or promotion information.

- *Publicity* Publicity is any non-paid media communication which helps build target market awareness and positively affects attitudes for your product or firm. Publicity provides your firm or product with a benefit not found in any other marketing mix tool. Since publicity utilizes non-commercial communication, it adds a dimension of legitimacy that can't be found in advertising.

  You should also be aware that publicity—editorial space and time for your product—are only one part of public relations. Public relations deals with creating goodwill for an organization, not just for the short term, but also regarding long-term public opinion issues.

Step 8
Budget, Calendar,
Payback Analysis

- *Budget* The budget is the cumulative monetary cost of implementing the plan.

- *Calendar* The calendar is a schedule of the marketing plan's tactical executions.

- *Payback Analysis* An analysis of whether the marketing plan and its specific marketing programs, as well as executions within the plan, will generate the projected revenues in excess of expenses constitutes the payback analysis.

Step 9
Execution

The tactical execution both for and in the marketplace is developed once the marketing plan is prepared. This is where it all happens—getting your product, service, or store ready for the market and executing the marketing mix tools, such as seasonal selling, the promotion, advertising, merchandising, and publicity. Finally, execution includes staying on top of all the execution detail in the marketplace. All that you have done will now face the ultimate test of marketplace acceptance. Will the target market buy your product?

Step 10
Evaluation

The methodology used to help determine the level of success of the overall marketing plan and its specific elements is part of evaluation. We have also included the research and testing components in this step. Research is included because it is a means to evaluation, and testing is a component of this step because it is a learning experience. For example, you might evaluate the effectiveness of a single plan element, such as advertising, or the entire plan in test markets on a limited scale before full implementation.

While evaluation is the last step in the process, it signals a new beginning to the whole disciplined approach, as evaluation findings become a major part of the marketing background section in the preparation of next year's marketing plan. Evaluation is one of the most important steps, because it is a learning tool which will lead to improved marketing plans and execution of marketing programs in the future.

HOW TO USE THIS BOOK IN YOUR MARKETING PLANNING

Before you begin writing your marketing plan, we recommend that you read through the entire book to understand the complete process and all that goes into preparing a comprehensive marketing plan. Next, as you actually prepare your own marketing plan, go through each chapter again and very diligently attempt to follow the step-by-step disciplined marketing planning process.

Adapt the Process to Fit Your Business

As you use the disciplined marketing planning process, keep in mind that, while you should understand the basic marketing principles provided throughout this book and follow the recommended methodology, you can adapt the review and planning process to best fit your product or marketing situation. The point to remember is that you want to be open-minded and innovative, but also methodical and consistent as you prepare the marketing background section and write the marketing plan.

Keep Track of Your Ideas

As you go through the whole process, you will come up with all types of ideas for different areas of the marketing plan that might not relate to the specific section of the plan you are currently writing. Don't lose these ideas, because they will be very helpful when you prepare the particular section to which they apply. As you prepare the background section and the marketing plan itself, have separate sheets of paper handy with headings of problems, opportunities, and each step of the marketing plan (including a separate sheet of paper for each marketing mix tool) under which you can jot down relevant ideas as they occur to you. Don't evaluate the worth of each idea as you think of it. Evaluate its application as you actually write the section of the marketing plan to which it pertains.

Apply to Your Own Marketing Situation

Also keep in mind that many of the principles, procedures, and examples provided in this book will have application to your particular marketing situation, even though it has not been written just for your specific product or service. In fact, this book is written for broad application by the marketer of a consumer/package goods product, business-to-business product, service, or retail outlet(s) with a private, public, or nonprofit organization. For simplicity and brevity, however, the word "product" is usually used throughout this book in generic planning discussions for whatever is to be marketed. When there is specific reference to consumer or business-to-business products, services, or retail, it will be singled out accordingly.

Use Idea Starters

While this book does not deal directly with execution in terms of preparing a newspaper ad or buying a radio schedule, you will find an "Idea Starters by Marketing Situation" grid in Appendix A. This unique marketing idea grid includes hundreds of business-building idea starters, categorized by most common marketing situations and presented separately for each marketing mix tool—from product, branding, and packaging to advertising, merchandising, and publicity. This grid section can be of major assistance to the reader who is beginning to develop the actual marketing plan and its executions.

Allow Sufficient Time to Prepare and Modify Your Plan

Writing a comprehensive marketing plan based on a thorough marketing background is a time-consuming project, particularly if it has not been done before. Therefore, it is wise to begin the disciplined marketing planning process far enough in advance of when the plan is due. It seems to take twice the time originally estimated to prepare a complete marketing plan. To do it right, you can estimate 50 to 100 hours or more to prepare the marketing background section and half this number of hours to prepare the first draft of the marketing plan section. Although the background section is usually the most demanding, without this database you have no real objective source from which to make your current and future marketing decisions.

As a side note, you will find that updating this background data and revising a marketing plan year to year is considerably less time consuming and easier than gathering the initial background information and writing the first marketing plan. This is particularly true if the initial marketing background section is prepared in a thorough and comprehensive manner. Once you have completed the background section, you will be continually revising the marketing plan as you write the first draft, reworking elements in the marketing plan so they effectively interface with each other.

Once the plan is written, you must allow adequate time to review the plan, make major changes, and rework the fine points. The time and rewriting are necessary to arrive at a marketing plan that is comprehensive, understandable, supportable, implementable, and in the end, successful.

PART ONE

MARKETING BACKGROUND

Step One   Business Review

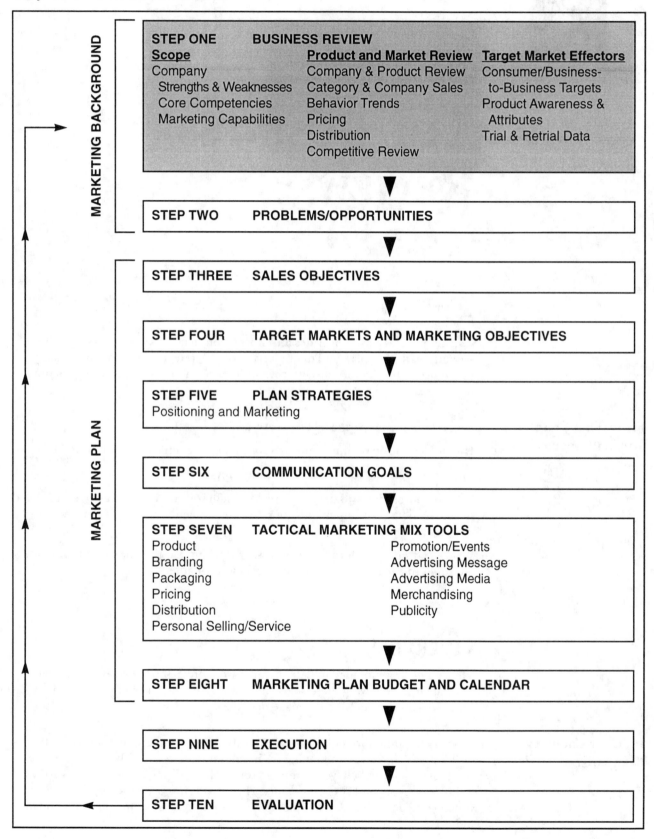

MARKETING BACKGROUND

STEP ONE   BUSINESS REVIEW

Scope	Product and Market Review	Target Market Effectors
Company	Company & Product Review	Consumer/Business-
Strengths & Weaknesses	Category & Company Sales	to-Business Targets
Core Competencies	Behavior Trends	Product Awareness &
Marketing Capabilities	Pricing	Attributes
	Distribution	Trial & Retrial Data
	Competitive Review	

STEP TWO   PROBLEMS/OPPORTUNITIES

MARKETING PLAN

STEP THREE   SALES OBJECTIVES

STEP FOUR   TARGET MARKETS AND MARKETING OBJECTIVES

STEP FIVE   PLAN STRATEGIES
Positioning and Marketing

STEP SIX   COMMUNICATION GOALS

STEP SEVEN   TACTICAL MARKETING MIX TOOLS

Product	Promotion/Events
Branding	Advertising Message
Packaging	Advertising Media
Pricing	Merchandising
Distribution	Publicity
Personal Selling/Service	

STEP EIGHT   MARKETING PLAN BUDGET AND CALENDAR

STEP NINE   EXECUTION

STEP TEN   EVALUATION

THE BUSINESS REVIEW

The business review provides an information decision-making base for the subsequent marketing plan and the rationale for all strategic marketing decisions within the plan. Most importantly, it provides for a consumer and customer orientation to your marketing communications.

From This Chapter You Will Learn

Suggestions for preparing a business review.

How to develop an outline to use as a road map for completing your business review.

The steps necessary to complete a business review.

How to utilize primary data (developed through your own company's research) and secondary data (existing in trade journals, government publications, etc.) in the development of your business review.

Where to find the information necessary to complete the charts and answer the questions in each step of the business review in Chapter 2.

OVERVIEW

This summary is intended to help organize work on the business review you develop in Chapter 2. Following these suggestions will save time and help create a more effective database from which to make decisions.

Industry Category Comparisons

It is very important to look not only inward at your company, but outside to the industry in which you are competing for insights into marketing planning direction. A business review will help you compare trends within your company to those of your industry category and key competitors. The *industry category* is the overall business in which you compete. For example, Sub Zero Freezers is in the kitchen appliance industry.

Consumers Versus Customers

Throughout the business review chapters we use the terms "consumers" and "customers." In order to analyze company trends, we need to investigate the behavior of company *customers*, those people who have purchased a company's product. If we are to compare company trends to industry category and key competitor trends, we also need to look at the purchase behavior of *consumers*, people who have purchased the industry category product, a subset of which is company customers. For business to business companies, think of customers as *business* customers and consumers as *business* consumers.

WHY MARKET INFORMATION IS IMPORTANT

Today, consumers have more product choices than ever before. They also have more information about the choices. The combination of more competition (from small niche marketers to large dominant category killers such as Toys 'R Us) and a bombardment of communication from the many competitive alternatives means marketers have to work much harder to affect target market behavior in today's environment. Thus it is more important now than at any time in the history of marketing to really understand your target market and to let this understanding drive not only your marketing decisions, but the entire decision-making framework of the company.

It is our opinion that many of the business successes of the past ten years have come about not because of great business management, but because of individuals with tremendous consumer insight—insight developed through a deep understanding of the target market, the business environment, and the competition. It was the genius of people like Steve Jobs, who understood the impact of the personal computer first on businesspeople and then on home consumers. Jobs started Apple Computer from his garage, igniting the computer revolution. It was Sam Walton's insight that determined that the rural consumer was underserved from a retail standpoint. Mr. Walton built his business on the concept that the rural consumer would travel much farther than the normal retail trading area distance to shop at a store which offered a one-stop shop with good value on its products. While the standard doctrine of the day said that there had to be 100,000 people within a 10-mile trading area to support large general merchandise stores such as Wal-Mart, Mr. Walton put his stores in small towns such a Viroqua, Wisconsin. He succeeded because consumers in rural areas were willing to drive much greater distances to avail themselves of the deep selection of merchandise and reasonable prices that in the past could only be found in the larger cities. One final example would be Famous Footwear. In an era of flat retail footwear sales, the fast-growing footwear retailer realized that Nike, Reebok, Keds, Rockport, Naturalizer, etc., were building the demand for brand-name shoes. What a retailer could do best was to provide the brands for less. Famous Footwear targeted the heavy female purchaser with children and provided that consumer value—not the best prices, not the best quality, not the biggest selection, but value. The best price on popular brand-name shoes for the entire family. In all of these examples, companies used their insight into their target markets to provide products, communication programs, and sales programs that made individuals in the target markets think they were talking directly to them.

Much of the target market innovation in today's marketing environment is coming from retailers, service firms, package goods companies, and business-to-business firms who are interacting with their target markets with a new level of urgency. Technological innovations in the retail industry, such as "smart cash registers," increased use of research, and marketing databases have provided marketers a wealth of customer information. The more successful business-to-business firms are spending less time selling what they have and more time defining their customers' needs. And package goods companies faced with parity of product and a sales promotion environment are exploring new ways to build brand equity and value-added with their products. Marketers who are on the front lines, engaging in dialog with the consumer on a daily basis, are the ones who are often closest to the consumer and target market demands. This "closeness" is bringing about a change in the way many marketing-oriented companies are doing business.

These marketing-oriented companies are now in a position to define specific segments based upon unique needs or consumption behavior and then realistically set marketing objectives to affect the segment's behavior. For example, companies now have the ability to know whether product repurchase rates are different for new versus old customers or by demographic age segment. They have the ability to determine exactly how many customers there are for each unique purchasing segment, and they know what the average expenditure per purchase and the average number of purchases is for the segments. With this type of target market information, the marketing-oriented company is able to set objectives to affect consumer behavior. As a result, the marketers writing the plan know they have a good chance of achieving the goals, because these objectives have been set with the consumer's needs in mind. For example, setting an objective which increases the repeat purchase rate might be developed due to a knowledge that the consumer has the desire and the ability to purchase more if the company made some basic changes in the way it does business. This might require changing the product to satisfy shortcomings in important attributes in order to stimulate increased repurchase. It might mean changing the packaging to allow for easier storage, or it might mean adjusting price to encourage multiple purchases. And, it might mean improving customer service to increase after-sale purchases and repurchases. While all these involve strategic decisions, it is consumer insights which provide the marketer the confidence to set obtainable marketing objectives and to determine the appropriate strategy for achieving them.

The premise of disciplined marketing planning as outlined in this text is that marketing plans focus on the needs of the target market. The business review is the place where the marketer develops a broad understanding of target market insights. Schultz, Tannenbaum, and Lauterborn argue in their text *Integrated Marketing Communications*[1] that Kotler's "Four P's"—product, price, place, and promotion (the foundations of most business reviews)—are a thing of the past. Instead, Lauterborn's "Four C's" rule the day. We've used this thinking as the framework for demonstrating below how the Four P's were manufacturer- or company-oriented, while the Four C's are target market-oriented. The change from the inner (company) focus of the Four P's to the outer (target market) focus of the Four C's is a critical concept in identifying target markets. The Four P's were driven by the product. A company developed a product and then sold it. The Four C's, as described below, are driven by the consumer—they are target market driven, not product and sales driven. The end result is a marketing orientation and business review format which revolves around the consumer's needs. (The consumer in this context may be the end consumer, an intermediary, or a business-to-business consumer.)

The Four C's

1. *Understand* **Consumer Wants And Needs** *instead of* **Product.** All marketers should spend a great deal of time studying trends in consumer purchasing.

[1]Lauterborn, Robert, Don Schultz and Stanely Tannenbaum. *Integrated Marketing Communications; Pulling It Together & Making It Work*, NTC Business Books, 1993, Lincolnwood, IL: pp. 12–13.

What is the consumer purchasing? At what times of year? How much and how often? What factors go into the decision process? Marketers can't just sell what they have; they can sell only what the consumer wants. People or businesses never buy anything (at least not twice) that fails to fulfill a personal need. Coffee is purchased because of its taste. Research tells us that shoes are purchased because they look good or feel comfortable on the feet. Diaper Geni (a disposable diaper dispenser) is purchased because it solves the odor problem of the traditional diaper pail for moms and dads. Kerry's spray-dried ingredients are purchased because of the efficiency of using the spray-dried technology in food processing and Kerry Ingredients' (previously Beatreme Foods) ability to provide a consistent product that meets food manufacturers' specifications. As in all these cases, marketing successes occur when the marketer brings the target market a product or service which solves a problem or fulfills a need.

2. *Understand the* **Consumer's Cost** *to satisfy that want or need instead of the* **Price** *of the product.* There is a need to understand not just the price of a product or service, but also the cost involved to the consumer. Costs such as the time it takes to purchase the product, the cost of the product failing, the ease of the service or after-sale agreement, and the cost of purchasing a product which says something about the owner of that product (whether it be environmentally correct or links the purchaser with a certain lifestyle to which he or she is aspiring) all play an important role in marketing to the consumer.

3. *Think* **Consumer Convenience** *to buy instead of* **Place.** It used to be that distribution, or how the product reached the consumer from the manufacturer, was the manufacturer's decision. In today's competitive environment, it is rare that any one marketer has a unique, successful product monopoly without someone else bringing a similar product to market. The differentiating factor is often the channel method, or effectiveness of the distribution. Many times products in a competitive situation gain a differential advantage because they are available through more convenient channels. While a food product might be found in only one size at the traditional grocery store, it can be found in bulk size at the discount warehouse store. In fact, with toll-free numbers and all-night shopping channels on cable, consumers don't have to go anywhere to purchase products.

4. *Think* **Consumer Communication** *instead of* **Promotion.** No longer should marketers think in terms of just promotion or advertising, which were mostly seen as costs in the past. Communication is a far broader term. Communication has as an underlying premise the concept of investment, the building of a consumer franchise. Communication includes the entire scope of tactics that were once thought of as individual disciplines—tactics such as advertising, promotion, personal selling, or merchandising. The tactical executions can be narrow in scope, through direct mail, or broad, via mass media. The common denominator is that all the tactics focus on select target markets that the company has chosen to serve. The communication should be focused not only on generating short-term sales, but also on developing a long-term relationship with the consumer. This means responding to the target market's media habits, understanding the target market by communicating solutions to their problems via your product, and building a long-term brand image or identity for your product. It also means using two-way communication tools (customer service, personal selling, research) to promote interaction and repeated contacts with your customers and to determine their feelings about your products relative to the competition. Contacts include getting consumers to talk to companies via the "800" number, to fill out warranty cards, to ask for additional product

information, or to receive newsletters; encouraging use of after-sale service; and even encouraging the communication of complaints.

A good example of a company developing a target market orientation consistent with the Four C's is WinterSilks. WinterSilks is a successful direct mail firm which markets silk products to a lifestyle target market consisting of, primarily, females 45+ and, secondarily, males 45+ who have an active outdoor lifestyle or who live in areas with winter and are interested in warmth. The following demonstrates how WinterSilks has gone from a Four P's orientation to a Four C's marketing philosophy.

Four P's

Product	Strong long underwear orientation. Very basic.
Price	Strong value orientation.
Place	Distribution through direct mail.
Promotion	Catalog copy straight to the point.

Four Consumer C's

Consumer Wants and Needs versus Product	Focus groups show need for more feminine lingerie, more varied colors in the silk apparel, and patterns in silk blouses. As a result, WinterSilks broadened product line.
Consumer's Cost versus Price	Continued with a value orientation. However, WinterSilks further stressed reliability, satisfaction guarantee, and special value buys throughout the catalog.
Consumer Convenience To Buy versus Place	Realized that WinterSilks was not just a direct mail company, but a company with a target market which was being marketed to via direct mail. WinterSilks is now testing alternative ways to reach the target via integrated communications such as home shopping networks, retail outlets, television direct response, etc.
Consumer Communication versus Promotion	Changed catalog copy to more closely identify with the lifestyle of the target audience. Initiated consumer research to determine preferences for catalog covers, product, and communication effectiveness. Initiated a counter-seasonal product line targeting WinterSilks more youthful target audience.

Marketing is a broad discipline in which multiple decisions must be made—decisions such as which customers should be targeted, through what specific combination of product features, with what price, through what distribution channels, with what type of service, and via what type of communication. However, these decisions cannot be made without a systematic review of all known facts affecting the customer. The business review provides these facts so that sound decision making can be achieved.

PRIMARY ELEMENTS OF THE BUSINESS REVIEW

A well-developed business review should be utilized as a daily reference source. Your business review should be updated each year to reflect the most recent changes in your industry and company. Therefore, if this is your first business review, don't be overwhelmed. If you don't have time to complete all sections, work on those that most affect your business. Then, next year, update those sections and further complete some of the others for which you didn't previously have time.

Completing the business review can be more than a one-person job. Request assistance from other people in your company to help compile the information. The step-by-step process of completing the business review in Chapter 2 allows for a marketer to more easily manage the information-gathering process.

There are three sections to a business review:

I.   Scope
II.   Product and Market Review
III.   Target Market Effectors

Section I
Scope

- Strengths and Weaknesses

- Core competencies

- Marketing capabilities

Section I, Scope, helps define your core business—it identifies what business or businesses you are in and, subsequently, the product or business area of emphasis for which the marketing plan will be developed. This area of emphasis will then direct your information search in the business review.

Often included in strategic business plans, this section will serve as a bridge from your strategic plan to the marketing plan. If you do not have a strategic business plan which has addressed this issue, you will need to do so in the scope section of the business review. Without this first section, you won't have parameters to guide your information search. For example, a company like Famous Footwear might pull information on athletic wear trends and footwear trends. While Famous Footwear only sells shoes, many competitors also sell athletic wear. However, the decision of whether or not to also carry athletic wear should be determined before the marketing department starts its planning process by collecting data. If the scope of the business is not decided in a systematic and disciplined manner, the business review can quickly become too broad and very unfocused. Worse yet, the availability and mere collection of data can be a self-fulfilling prophecy that impacts later decision making.

However, keep in mind as you prepare the next two sections of this business review, if you uncover a business opportunity that is out of the original scope of the business but has tremendous value, we would recommend you keep it in the business review. It might become part of a new product segment in your marketing plan.

Section II
Product and Market Review

- Corporate philosophy/description of company/analysis of product

- Category and company sales trends

- Consumer behavior trends

- Pricing

- Distribution

- Competitive review

Section II, Product and Market Review, examines the first layer of consumer and customer behavior. The aggregate behavior and demand of consumers and customers is identified through a comparison of the industry category, specific competitors, and your company in the areas of product, sales, distribution, pricing, and communications. This section also provides a historical perspective on the industry, company, and product development. It details pertinent consumer behavior trends which will influence future purchasing habits. Finally, this section includes a competitive review comparing your company's and/or product's performance to the competition.

Section III
Target Market Effectors

- Target Market

- Awareness

- Attitude

- Trial

- Retrial

Section III, Target Market Effectors, shifts the focus from the overall aggregate industry and company product trends to exploring consumer and customer segments which drive the trends in Section II. With the past sections, the business was defined in terms of products. This was a necessary first step in terms of insight into the consumer because product performance is a macro view of the consumer's habits. Now, by defining a business in terms of basic consumer and customer segment needs and wants, the business review will become fertile ground for creative decision making later in the planning process.

By breaking our Target Market Effectors analysis into the steps consumers take when purchasing—awareness of a product, the formation of attitudes, and if these attributes are favorable, product trial and retrial—we can identify areas of concentration later in the marketing plan. For example, there might be a situation with a large target market segment which has minimal awareness, yet for those that are aware, there are positive attitudes with strong trial and retrial. Thus, the goal is to increase awareness. Focus would be given to marketing mix tools which could help in this area. Similarly, you can look to determine, in other situations, if the target market segments are too small, if there is a drop in positive attitudes (those that are aware think poorly of the product), or if the customers who try the product don't try it again. Each scenario would require a different marketing solution.

Target Market

The first task is to define the target market segments (such as type of business or demographic category) for the highest volume products identified in Section II.

Awareness

Once the target segments have been defined, the awareness for your company or product is measured relative to the competition in each of the segments.

Attitude

Similarly, the attributes which determine purchase are identified. Then, your company or product is ranked in terms of how each segment feels you perform on those attributes relative to the competition.

Trial and Retrial Behavior

Finally, trial, first purchase of your product, and retrial, subsequent purchase of your product, are measured for each segment. The average number of purchases, dollar per purchase, and the trial to retrial rate is calculated (the number of customers who are repeat purchasers).

PREPARING THE BUSINESS REVIEW

Task 1

Prepare an Outline

It is important to understand that the business review, as presented in this book, is broad and at least attempts to be all-encompassing. You must tailor the business review to your specific needs and situation, both in terms of the information you gather and the format in which you provide it. For example, an auto parts manufacturer might include business-to-business information (sales, target market descriptors, etc.) and consumer information if their product has both an OEM and aftermarket component. A packaged goods manufacturer, by contrast, may only include the consumer market analysis. Further, availability and quality of information may dictate the ultimate form of your business review. The outline gives you a framework for gathering the information. Expect the business review to evolve as you go on.

Always start your business review by developing a written outline. The outline should be as specific as possible, covering each major area of the business review. The outline helps you stay focused and ensures that critical data needed for actionable marketing plans will be obtained in a disciplined and sequential process. It also serves as an overview for what is presented in Chapter 2. Each section is a step with topical points discussed and explained so that the reader has a full understanding of how to gather and organize this information for use in the marketing plan. The following is an example of an outline for a business review. The first task that you must undertake is an outline tailored to your business and industry.

Step 1: Scope

A.   Overall strengths and weaknesses of your company

B.   Core competencies of your company

C.   Marketing capabilities of your company

Step 2: Product and Market Review

A.   Corporate philosophy/description of the company

    1.   Corporate goals and objectives

    2.   General company history

    3.   Organizational chart

B.   Product analysis

    1.   Identify products sold in the industry category or within the scope of your business

    2.   Description of company product/company product strengths and weaknesses

    3.   Competitive strengths and weaknesses

    4. Product trends

C. Category and company sales trends
    1. Sales/Transactions/Profit Analysis
        a. Industry category sales
        b. Company sales
            i) Compared to overall industry
            ii) Compared to major competitors
        c. Market share
        d. Store-for-store for retailers
        e. Seasonality
        f. Sales by geographic territory

D. Consumer behavior trends
    1. Demographic trends
    2. Geographic trends
    3. Social/Consumer trends
    4. Technological trends
    5. Media viewing trends

E. Distribution
    1. Retail
        a. Channel type/trends
        b. Geography
        c. Penetration
    2. Packaged goods
        a. Channel types/trends
        b. Market coverage/all commodity volume percentage
        c. Shelf space
        d. Geography
        e. Sales method
    3. Business-to-business
        a. Channel type/trends
        b. Geography
        c. Personal selling method
    4. Service firms
        a. Type of office
        b. Geography
        c. Penetration
    5. Distribution strengths and weaknesses

F. Pricing review
    1. Price of your product relative to the industry or competition
    2. Distribution of sales by price point relative to the competition
    3. Price elasticity of your product
    4. Cost structure
    5. Company pricing strengths and weaknesses

G. Competitive review
    1. Competitive review of your product and the key competition
    2. Summary of strengths and weaknesses

   a. Market share
   b. Target market
   c. Marketing objectives/strategies
   d. Positioning
   e. Product/branding/packaging
   f. Pricing
   g. Distribution
   h. Personal selling
   i. Customer service
   j. Promotion
   k. Advertising
   l. Media
   m. Merchandising
   n. Publicity
   o. Testing/marketing research and development
   p. Summary of strengths and weaknesses

Step 3: Target Market Effectors

A. Target market: consumer
   1. Volume versus concentration
   2. Demographic measures: Industry category versus company target market
   3. Customer tenure segmentation
   4. Demographic segmentation (description and size)
      a. Sex
      b. Age
      c. Income
      d. Education
      e. Occupation
      f. Family/household size
      g. Region/Geography
   5. Product usage segmentation
   6. Psychographic/lifestyle segmentation
   7. Attribute segmentation
   8. Heavy user segmentation

B. Target market: business-to-business
   1. Standard Industrial Classification (SIC) segmentation
   2. Other methods of segmenting
      a. Dollar size segmentation
      b. Employee size segmentation
      c. Heavy usage segmentation
      d. Product application/use segmentation
      e. Organizational structure segmentation
      f. New versus repeat buyer segmentation
      g. Geographic location segmentation
      h. Decision maker and influencer segmentation
      i. Channel use segmentation

C. Awareness
   1. Unaided awareness (first mention and total awareness)

2. Aided awareness
3. Awareness by segments

D. Product attributes
1. Attribute importance by segment
2. Attribute ranking by segment
3. Product life cycle
   a. Introduction
   b. Growth
   c. Maturity

E. Trial behavior
1. Buying habits
2. Purchase rates of the industry product category and your company's product by geographic markets
   a. Category Development Index (CDI)
   b. Brand Development Index (BDI)
3. Trading areas
4. Brand loyalty

F. Retrial behavior
1. Trial to retrial behavior

Task 2
Develop Questions

List questions which need to be answered for each section of the business review outline. The questions will provide direction in determining what specific information you need to accumulate.

Task 3
Develop Data Charts

Develop data charts with headings to help structure your search for relevant information. When completed, the charts should enable you to answer the major questions pertaining to each section of the business review outline.

Organize the headings and columns of the charts first in order to determine what information needs to be found prior to the data search. This forces you to look for data and numbers that will provide meaningful information. Remember, if you look for data before developing your charts, you may tend to construct the charts around what is easy to find, not what should be found.

Task 4
Develop Reference Points for Comparisons

Always develop charts that have reference points for comparison so that the data are actionable. For example, when you analyze sales growth for your company, compare this against the sales growth for the industry. In this manner, the company's sales growth can be judged against a reference point. And, remember, a business review should always provide reference points of comparison within the company (past year trends), between the company and the industry category, and between the company and its key competitors. Whenever possible, include five-year trend information so that the current year's performance can be judged relative to past years' performance.

The following provide some basic reminders which are applicable throughout the business review and pertain to the collection and organization of the data you collect.

Compare 5-year Trends

It is important to review trends whenever analyzing data that will direct marketing decisions. This allows the marketer to determine not only increases and decreases from year-to-year, but also shifts in the marketplace over a period of time. For example, while any given product or target market segment may account for the greatest sales volume in one year, a review of five year's worth of data might show that the leader has had flat sales and that another product or target segment will soon dominate the category if the trends continue. Therefore, it is important to look beyond a static one-year number to get a feeling for the fluid nature of data over a period of time.

Trends Within the Company

The marketer must be aware of the trends within the company. For example, what customer segment accounts for the most volume? Is this same company segment growing, flat, or declining in volume over the past five years? Is there another company segment which is growing faster and will be the dominant target market in the future? If you have a large company, it is also very insightful to compare regions of the company to the overall company system. This regional review is helpful when determining different local target markets or marketing objectives versus *company system* target markets or marketing objectives.

Company to Industry Comparisons

It is also important to compare the company to the industry category. Are the target markets responsible for the most company product volume the same target segments responsible for the most industry category volume? Is your company's sales trending comparable, above, or below the industry category across products with the highest sales volume, transaction volume, and profit potential? What is your company's market share trends (your share of sales or transaction volume relative to the industry) overall and among various target market segments?

Competitive Comparisons

Finally, the marketer must also take into consideration the competitive environment and any changes or trends that will make it harder or easier to capture market share against identified target market segments. For example, there might be an increase in the total number of competitors, or a competitor may have developed a product or manufacturing innovation resulting in a price or product attribute advantage.

Benchmark Marketing

Although the concept of comparing relative points of data started in the retail industry, we apply the principles to all business types—retail, package goods, service, and business-to-business firms. One way benchmarking is successfully utilized today is with businesses that have multiple locations or geographic markets. The concept is to find departments, product lines, stores, or markets with similar characteristics, such as product mix and sales potential, and then compare results. In order to accomplish this, many firms designate their markets into A, B, and C markets, with each broad market designation demonstrating similar characteristics. In this manner, sales by store, sales by product, customer counts, sales per transactions, purchase ratios, profits, and expenses can be compared. With this benchmark across a marketer's system, strong and weak performances can be identified and management can take necessary actions based upon exceptions to the average.

Another way benchmarking is used is by comparing target market segment performance. For the American Automobile Association (AAA) we looked at the performance of customer segments based upon age, length of membership, and product use. For example, renewal was considerably lower among members of five years or less than for members of greater than five years. And users of specific AAA products had greater cross-sell into the range of AAA products than others. Again, establishing averages and then comparing target segments to the averages allowed us to do two things:

1. Identify target segments or products not performing to expectations or company averages with the objective of increasing past performance.

2. Focus on targets or products that were meeting company averages but that had inherent strengths that would allow them to perform significantly better into the future.

We use the concept of benchmark marketing in developing a comparison between relative points of data. Although in the past management used the comparisons as reasons for hiring and firing, we use the comparison data as a way to uncover opportunities and focus on solving problems. Therefore, we refer to comparing relative points of data not as the deadly parallel, but as benchmark marketing. A single piece of data is really of no use to any marketer. The fact that a company experienced a 10% sales growth means very little unless compared to some other benchmark, such as the industry category. If the industry category increased 15%, the company actually lost market share. Suddenly, the 10% sales growth doesn't look so good.

In summary, providing comparisons within your company and comparing your company to the industry category provides the following:

1. Allows you to identify products and/or target markets which are performing below or above the company average, thus providing insight to further exploit strengths or solve weaknesses.

   For example, with an accounting firm marketing to other businesses, we discovered that specific SICs (industry segments identified by Standard Industry Classification codes) had far greater sales, profits, and growth potential than other SICs. Thus, the marketing plan focused on target market segments which were prioritized based upon historical potential for the firm.

2. Allows you to identify shifts in target market and product trends within the industry.

   For example, AAA's strongest product, emergency road service, was relatively flat in terms of sales, yet the category had experienced strong growth. Upon investigation, the reasons were clear. AAA's target market skewed to consumers 55+. This was fairly consistent with the overall traditional road service category. However, the industry growth had come from another channel, the MMPs or Manufacturer Membership Programs (emergency road service provided by automobile manufacturers) and non-traditional sources such as credit card companies. Thus, the growth in the category of emergency road service was coming from non-traditional business-to-business channel competitors and non-traditional target markets for AAA.

3. Allows you to compare or benchmark your firm to your industry, thus providing insight into how you are actually performing versus your competition.

In a final example, you may find that your company's target market for a strong industry product category is far younger than the average industry category target market for the same product. This is true of Famous Footwear, which is far stronger among 18–24 and 25–34 year olds when compared to the target market of the overall shoe category.

Does this mean that Famous Footwear needs to start targeting older customers. No, because, upon further investigation, the skew towards 18–34 year olds points out the strength of Famous with athletic shoes. Athletic shoes have a younger target audience than other shoe categories. Athletic shoes were also the volume leaders in the 80s and into the early 90s. Thus, the numbers served to provide a confirmation of a Famous Footwear strength and identify an area where the company was strong in terms of target audience and corresponding product sales relative to its competition.

Task 5
Conduct Data Search

Institute a disciplined data search. Stay focused on what needs to be found by constantly reviewing your outline. This will allow you to feel confident that you have compiled all of the existing data necessary to complete your charts.

Task 6
Write Summary Statements

After the charts have been completed, write brief statements summarizing the major findings and answering the questions you developed in Task 2. Include a summary rationale when needed. Keep the summary objective by strictly reporting the findings; don't provide solutions at this point. The business review is not for developing objectives and strategies; it is for providing facts from which to develop a marketing plan and the supporting rationale. However, as mentioned in the introduction, jot down your thoughts and ideas as you prepare your business review to potentially use later when writing your marketing plan.

Organizing the Business Review

The sections of the final written business review should follow the same sequence as the steps developed in your outline. Each section should include summary statements followed by completed, detailed data charts.

Finally, write the marketing background and plan in the third person, being as objective as possible. Do not interject personal feelings that cannot be documented by fact. Write in a very clear, concise manner so that there can be no misinterpretation of what is presented. And don't assume that everyone who reads the plan will have the same base of information as the writer. Include all available information pertinent to the issues being discussed so that everyone reading the plan will have the same frame of reference.

CONDUCTING RESEARCH

In preparing your business review, data can be obtained through both primary and secondary research. If you employ a research firm, a marketing communications firm that conducts research, or an in-house research department, primary research is the most effective way of obtaining data specific to your market, your product, and your competitors. If you do not have access to a professional researcher, however, we recommend that you do not try to do primary research yourself, but rather, rely on secondary research, data compiled by outside sources.

The business review examples presented in Chapter 2 rely heavily on secondary research and your own company sales and marketing data to provide you with a marketing information base. However, we strongly recommend that, if possible, both secondary and primary research be utilized in preparing a marketing database and business review.

Primary Research

Original research compiled to meet your specific data requirements is broken down into two categories, quantitative and qualitative.

Quantitative Research

Data and information are usually obtained through surveys, with results gathered from a representative random sample of a given universe. The samples are large enough to make inferences that are statistically significant. We refer to two types of quantitative research methods most often throughout this book. One is customer based research, which provides information about a company's own customers. The other is market-wide research, which is used to provide information about the overall category user/purchaser base.

Qualitative Research

Research methods that do not statistically represent the target market universe provide qualitative data. Qualitative research typically involves small groups of consumers, such as focus groups, who are asked to provide insights into their likes and dislikes of a particular product and why and how they purchase or use one type of product versus another. Qualitative research is also used to gain insights into the strengths and weaknesses of advertising and other forms of communication.

Qualitative research is used to add depth and richness to quantitative findings. For example, quantitative research may determine that a company has a perceived customer service problem relative to the competition. Qualitative research can be used to help further explain what consumers feel customer service entails in the company's particular industry and what specifically is lacking in the company's customer service as compared to that of other companies.

Qualitative research is commonly used in what is referred to as "exploratory research," in which the facts and implications of a particular situation or marketing problem are explored. Such exploration is useful prior to quantitative research, as it can help determine the key issues to include in the study. Particularly if there has been no previous research, a company may want to utilize a focus group to provide added insights into consumer thinking prior to formulating a quantitative study. The information and insights gained from initial qualitative research can then be verified through quantitative, statistical research. Qualitative exploratory research can also be used following a quantitative study to further explore issues brought up in the quantitative research.

Finally, a word of caution. Used by itself, qualitative research can be very misleading. It is not statistically based; a roomful of 10 people is often a poor representation of what the marketplace really thinks. Qualitative research is most valuable when used to enrich quantitatively-defined observations.

Secondary Research

Secondary research, which may also be quantitative or qualitative, is not specifically compiled for your company; it is existing information that is available through outside sources. An example of a secondary research source is census information. Just as with primary research, combining this type of secondary research information with your company's data will allow you to develop insights into your customers, your market, and the problems and opportunities facing your company. The only

Exhibit 1.1 Indexing Example

Age Category	Home Ownership*	Index
18 to 24	20%	33
25 to 34	48	80
35 to 44	60	100
45 to 54	74	123
55 to 64	70	117
65 to 74	50	83
Average—all ages	60	100

*These numbers are used only for example. They do not reflect current home ownership rates.

difference is that primary research is conducted to answer specific questions a company might have. To answer these questions with secondary research you may have to dig a little more and be willing to analyze multiple studies to find your answers. Even then, you may not be able to answer all of your questions, so you will have to rely on judgment. Of course, secondary research is also typically less expensive than primary research. In most cases, a mix of both primary and secondary research is appropriate. A secondary search should be completed first, with primary research conducted to fill the voids of the existing data where possible.

Indexing

Indexing, used extensively in the business review, is a process that presents a number or group of numbers in relation to an average, or base. It is a method of showing a relationship between two sets of numbers or percentages. Indexing is based upon an average of 100. Anything over 100 means the index represents something greater than the average; anything below 100 is less than the average.

When indexing, a base number is established and all other numbers are compared to it. For example, assume 60 percent of the population owns a home and home ownership is further broken down by age category as shown in Exhibit 1.1. Since 60 percent is the average percentage of home ownership, it becomes the base number from which to measure any subset of the population. For example, among 18 to 24 year olds, only 20 percent own homes, so 20 percent divided by 60 percent equals .33. (For purposes of clarity and easier communications, the decimal is then multiplied by 100 to give a round number—.33 × 100 equals an index of 33. From this point on in the book we will not explicitly show the multiplication by 100.) Thirty-three is substantially below 100; thus, 18 to 24 year olds own homes at one-third the average across all ages.

In another example, 30 percent of a national company's consumers live in Chicago. With that, you would expect them to consumer 30 percent of the product (30 divided by 3 equals an index of 100, or average). But if Chicago consumers consume 60 percent of the company's product, they are consuming at a rate of 60 percent, divided by the base of 30 percent, for an index of 200. Thus, the Chicago market would compare at twice the national average, or 100 points above the expected consumption pattern.

We usually consider an index meaningful if it is plus or minus 10 from 100. In other words, we look for number 110 and above or 90 and below. If all age groups index between 95 and 105 in terms of consumption, we determine that our target market is flat across all age groups. However, if the 25 to 34 and 35 to 44 age groups indexed at 115 and 180, respectively, and all other age groups were at or below average (or below 100), then we would determine that those two age groups consumed at significantly higher levels.

Sources of Secondary Information

The following are commonly used sources of information available to most any marketer. They will help you obtain the necessary data to complete the business review portion of your marketing plan. Though this is by no means an exhaustive list of information sources, it is one that can be utilized by most marketing professionals without incurring large costs. Many of the sources listed can be found in a public or university library, can be obtained free, or can be purchased at a reasonable cost. Addresses and information on where to find the reference are provided for each listing.

Product User Characteristics/Size of Market/Demographics

Mediamark Research, Inc. (MRI)
708 Third Avenue
New York, NY 10017
212-599-0444

Simmons Market Research Bureau, Inc. (SMRB)
420 Lexington Avenue
New York, NY 10170
212-916-8900

MRI and SMRB provide information on the demographics, size, and media habits of the user and purchaser groups for various products, product categories, and brands. Available information includes:

Demographics and size of demographic groups using product

Heavy user/light user by demographic break

Brand loyalty measures

Media usage by demographic break

Approximate market share by brand

Where to Find: Advertising agency

Scarborough
The Arbitron Company
142 West 57th Street
New York, New York 10019
212-887-1300

Local market demographic/product usage profiles and media usage reports developed for the largest markets. Some key pieces of information include:

Local market target audience profile

Market share

Target audience media usage

Where to Find: Advertising agency, library

Standard Rate and Data Service (SRDS)
1700 West Higgins Road
Des Plaines, IL 60018
708-375-5000

Newspaper Rates and Data provides population, income, and general household expenditures for individual states, counties, and metro areas. Available information includes:

Population and households

Income per household

Household expenditures across eight categories

Number of passenger cars

Black and Spanish population

Where to Find: Library, advertising agency

Dun's Marketing Services (a company of the Dun and Bradstreet Corporation)

Dun's Marketing Services is a business list company that provides relatively accurate direct mail lists as well as information pertaining to the number and size of businesses within specific Standard Industrial Classification (SIC) categories and geographic territories. Available information includes:

Number of businesses by SIC by territory

Dollar size of businesses by SIC by territory

Employee size of businesses by SIC by territory

Listing of businesses within specific SIC, size, and territory parameters; trending of sales per employee; address; phone number; and listing of key personnel

Where to Find: Phone book in major U.S. cities

Dun's Million Dollar Directory

The directory provides a listing of businesses $.5 million in net worth and larger.

Where to Find: 1-800-526-0651 or phone book under Dun's Marketing Services in major U.S. cities

Nielsen DMA Test Market Profiles
A.C. Nielsen Company
299 Park Avenue
New York, NY 10171
212-707-7500

Contains demographic, retail sales, and media information for each DMA. Available information includes:

Demographics

Circulation of magazines, newspapers

Limited TV audience data

Retail purchasing rates

Households by county

Where to Find: Advertising agency

Fairchild Fact Files
Fairchild Books
7 West 34th Street
New York, NY 10001
212-630-3880

Each fact file provides sales, market trend, and buying habit information for product categories. The information is based on the U.S. Bureau of the Census, financial reports, *Sales and Marketing Management Survey of Buying Power,* and other trade publications and government studies specific to the product category. Available information includes:

Market trends

Production/unit volume

Sales

Sales by price range

Sales by geography

Sales by distribution method/outlet type

Margins/financial information

Advertising expenditures

Consumer expenditures/spending data/buying habits

Demographic profiles

Where to Find: Advertising agency; library

Sales and Marketing Management Survey of Buying Power
Sales and Marketing Management
355 Park Avenue South
New York, NY 10010
212-592-6300

Published in July of each year, the *Survey of Buying Power* details buying power by product category on a market-by-market basis. The data are divided into national and regional summaries and market rankings. Metromarket data by states and county/city data by states are also available. Available information includes:

Income

Buying power index

Sales by merchandise line/product category

Population by people/households

Retail sales

Where to Find: Library

Government Publications

No one collects more data on business than the government. The Department of Commerce has reference libraries in more than 40 field offices in major cities throughout the United States. The Small Business Administration can also help with information questions and is located in over 80 cities throughout the country. Examples of some of the government sources available are:

County and City Data Book. Provides a variety of statistical information for counties, cities, standard metropolitan statistical areas, incorporated places, and urbanized areas.

County Business Patterns. Details summary of number, dollar size, and employment size of businesses by county, state, and country. Breaks information into Standard Industrial Classification (SIC) categories.

Census Data. Includes census data on agriculture, housing, general population characteristics, social and economic characteristics, retail trade, manufacturing, wholesale trade, etc.

Where to Find: Library

Trade and Consumer Publications

Multiple trade publications with research departments are waiting to help. SRDS business, trade, and consumer publication issues have listings of those applicable to your industry.

Where to Find: Library, Standard Rate and Data Service, Inc.

Lifestyle Segmentation Information

Values and Lifestyles (VALS™) Program
SRI International
333 Ravenswood Avenue
Menlo Park, CA 94025-3493
415-859-3032

The Values and Lifestyles™ program segments American consumers into eight distinct lifestyle groups for the purpose of predicting consumer behavior. The segments are based upon the following:

Education

Income

Self-confidence

Health

Eagerness to buy

Intelligence

Energy level

Self-orientation

PRIZM

Claritas, Inc.
1525 Wilson Blvd.
Suite 1000
Arlington, VA 22209-2411
1-800-234-5973

PRIZM is a market segmentation system which defines U.S. neighborhoods into 62 lifestyle clusters and 15 larger social groups based on product, media, and lifestyle preferences. PRIZM can also cluster along industry and client-specific lines. The clustering information can be used for:

Defining and targeting consumer market segments

Strategic planning

Direct mailing

Site analysis

Media planning

ClusterPlus 2000
Strategic Mapping, Inc.
Corporate Headquarters
3135 Kifer Rd.
Santa Clara, CA 95051-0827
1-800-472-6277

ClusterPlus 2000 combines census, demographics, media habits, and consumer purchasing data to classify American consumers into 50 distinct segments and 9 larger classification groups. Geographically, it targets consumers from 5-digit ZIPs to the block level. Segmentation can be used for:

Product positioning
Promotion evaluation
Product mix designs
Cross-sell opportunities
Distribution strategies

MicroVision
Equifax National Decision Systems
1979 Lakeside Parkway
Tucker, GA 30084-5847
770-496-7171

MicroVision combines consumer and census data to classify American consumers into 50 distinct segments and 9 larger classification groups. Information can be provided in general, industry-specific, or custom form, and geographically it targets consumers down to the zip+4 level. This system is useful for:

Customer profiling

Product and service demand

Market analysis

Media selection

Direct marketing

Media Spending Data/Competitive Data

Leading National Advertisers (LNA)
11 West 42nd Street
11th Floor
New York, NY 10036
212-789-1400

LNA provides competitive spending data by medium, including a summary of national advertising expenditures by brand and industry category (class). Information is available on network TV, spot TV, magazines (consumer only), newspaper supplements, network radio, and outdoor.

Where to Find: Advertising agency

Rome Report
11 West 42nd Street
11th Floor
New York, NY 10036
212-789-1400

The *Rome Report* provides business-to-business and trade advertising expenditures.

Where to Find: Advertising agency

Media Representatives
Media representatives serve as valuable sources of competitive spending information. Contact local print, radio, television, and outdoor representatives.

Where to Find: Telephone book

Radio TV Reports, Inc.
317 Madison Avenue
New York, NY 10017
212-309-1400

This service provides copies of competitive radio and television ads. It will monitor specific industry categories or specific competitors.

Where to Find: Advertising agency

In addition, many advertising agencies have access to *Media Records* for newspaper information, *Broadcast Advertisers' Report* for network and spot television information, and *Publishers' Information Bureau* for consumer magazine information.

Association and Trade Show
Encyclopedia of Associations
Gale Research Company
835 Penobscot Building
Detroit, MI 48226-4094
1-800-877-4523

The *Encyclopedia of Associations* covers over 2,500 subjects and details over 19,500 national associations. It provides contacts to develop leads on how to find difficult information specific to a certain industry and customer groups. Available information includes:

  19,500 national organizations

  2,000 international organizations

  4,000 consultants, research centers, information services

Where to Find: Library

Trade Shows and Professional Exhibits Directory
Gale Research Company
835 Penobscot Building
Detroit, MI 48226-4094
1-800-877-4523

This directory serves as a guide to conferences, conventions, trade and industrial shows, merchandise marts, and expositions.

Where to Find: Library

Management Information Guides
Gale Research Company
835 Penobscot Building
Detroit, MI 48226-4094
1-800-877-4523

Each volume includes books, dictionaries, encyclopedias, film strips, government and institutional reports, periodical articles, and recordings on the featured subject. Guides are available from this series in almost every field.

Where to Find: Library

Information USA
Viking and Penguin Books
Viking Penguin, Inc.
375 Hudson Street
New York, NY 10014
212-366-2000

Billed as the "ultimate source of information on earth," this reference is a guide for direct access to government experts. It is a reference book for all the information you can obtain free or almost free from the government, including department of commerce data, census information, and information from individual committees and agencies.

Where to Find: Library

Media and Production Costs/Availability

Standard Rate and Data Service Publications
1700 West Higgins Road
Des Plaines, IL 60018
708-375-5000

These publications provide information required by advertisers for buying media and print production. The following source books are available:

Consumer Magazine and Farm Publication Rates and Data

Direct Mail Lists Rates and Data

Network Rates and Data (National TV and Radio Rates)

Newspaper Rates and Data

Spot Radio Rates and Data

Spot Television Rates and Data

Transit Advertising Rates and Data

Business Publication Rates and Data

Business Publication Rates and Data: Classified

Community Publication Rates and Data

Print Media Production Rates and Data

Where to Find: Library

The Circulation Book
P.O. Box 994
22619 Pacific Coast Highway
Malibu, CA 90265

This resource shows circulation and penetration by county, metro area, and TV viewing area for every daily newspaper, Sunday paper, all regional sales groups, national newspaper supplements, and leading magazines.

Where to Find: Ad agency, library

Additional Sources and Tips

In addition to the above sources, many additional references exist that will help you complete a business review consistent with the outline you establish. We suggest the following methodology to help you find additional information sources that pertain to your specific industry.

1. Go through the SRDS (Standard Rate and Data Service) and write down all trade and consumer publications pertaining to your industry.

2. Contact each trade publication, talk to the research department, and ask what information is available. Send them copies of your outline and charts. Ask for the specific information required for completion of your business review as detailed in your outline and charts. Ask about other available sources. Many times trade publications' research departments are aware of other studies that may help you. One publication told us about a consultant who has made it her life's work to learn about the plumbing and sink business. She saved us many days of searching by referring us to timely studies that helped us fulfill required data needs as specified in our outline for a national sink manufacturer.

3. Call the library and have them do a subject search, pulling all available reference materials. Utilize your local public library and the nearest college library. Many public universities have special reference services dedicated to compiling secondary research for private industry.

4. Dig, dig, and dig some more.

2

HOW TO PREPARE A BUSINESS REVIEW

T he business review is fundamental to the success of your marketing plan. Good data, organized in a meaningful and disciplined manner, will provide tremendous insights to your target customers and their purchase behavior. As outlined, the business review process provides for direct links from the data you organize to the marketing decisions made later in the plan.

From This Chapter You Will Learn

The data requirements and the material that needs to be analyzed in each of the three business review steps.

The key marketing issues and questions which need to be answered in each step of the business review.

How to write succinct summary statements describing the findings.

OVERVIEW

Now that you have an understanding of what is involved in a business review and how it is used, you are ready to work through each step of the review process. Each of the business review steps contain three main components.

1. A general *background discussion* that details each area covered in the step.

2. *Marketing questions* that must be answered in order to provide an adequate quantitative database for each section.

3. *Charts* to help you organize your information in a disciplined, efficient manner, so you will be able to answer the marketing questions accurately.

The charts can be easily adapted to your own situation. Worksheets for each of these charts are provided in Appendix B, located at the end of the book. Information on where data can be found to complete the charts is included on each worksheet.

The charts are intended to help you organize your data search. They are not exhaustive and cover only the major topical areas. Therefore, it is not intended that all the questions at the end of each business review section will have a corresponding chart. Many of the charts provide multiple pieces of information when completed. For example, one of the sales charts provides sales trending for the industry and for your company, demonstrates differences in industry growth compared to your company's growth, and provides company market share data.

Charts can also be used as support for business review conclusions during presentations. In addition, you may want to consider transferring the information in the charts onto graphs for presentation purposes. Graphs provide a better visual interpretation than charts, which tend to get very busy with numbers. Finally, please note that while we have provided charts for all three steps and most of the tasks within each step, there are some topics that either don't require charts or that warrant more company-specific or tailored charts. In these cases, charts are not provided.

STEP 1: SCOPE

The first step in developing a business review is to determine the overall scope of your business. The purpose of the scope section is to define your core business or businesses. You need to define your business in terms of the products you will be selling. In turn, the products help define the target markets you will be serving and the competitors against which you will be competing.

A warning: The business scope is very different from the communication positioning you will develop later in the plan. Communication positioning defines the overriding benefit that makes your product desirable to the marketplace; that benefit might be the best value, some service attribute, quality, business relationships, product availability, strong local sales force, or a superior product attribute such as softness, value, quality, etc. Don't make the mistake of thinking your business scope is defined by your communication benefit. Scope answers the question, "What business are you in?" Once this question is answered, you will have a greater degree of focus in terms of developing the rest of your business review. Without answering the question, a business review can become unnecessarily broad, unfocused, and inefficient in terms of gathering data.

The American Automobile Association told us their business was peace of mind. We asked in response, "Peace of mind in what?" Peace of mind could pertain to any number of combinations of businesses—banking, insurance, securities, moving company, a travel agency, an automobile club, and many more. Peace of mind is a communication positioning, not the scope of your business.

In summary, the scope section is a critical first step in establishing focus for your business review. The scope:

- defines what business the organization is in and the strategic leverage it will use to compete.

- defines product areas where the organization will grow and concentrate its business efforts.

- helps shape the positioning, marketing strategies, and communication sections later in the plan.

- drives where the organization seeks growth and where it does not seek growth. Thus, it determines the boundaries of the business review.

A Scope Case Study

The best way to review scope is to look at an example. The following example is structured after some work we did within the motor club industry. We will focus the example as it might apply to any of the larger motor clubs with multiple product areas and business lines. Within the case we will demonstrate the methodology for determining your business' scope. In order to give you a little background into the case and to further your insight into the methodology as we go through this section, the following provides a brief background on the motor club industry. Motor clubs typically provide towing service for members. Other services vary by club, but they often include travel services, insurance, and financial services such as credit cards.

The motor club industry is facing the following problems:

- Existing membership of motor clubs is significantly older than the overall U.S. population.

- Many motor clubs have tremendous potential to increase use of their products and services (travel services, insurance, credit cards) among the membership. However, most clubs are still primarily used for auto-related towing and services, with a weaker cross-sell to other club product offerings.

- Most motor clubs are mass marketers and have not segmented. They sell products to mass consumers—adults—without targeting specific interests, buying habits, or lifestyles of smaller customer segments within the club.

- Competition has increased. Traditional channels are seeing new entries, and there has been a growth of non-traditional channels where the road clubs have traditionally not been a market factor. For example, most car manufacturers offer road assistance programs through purchase, and insurance companies are offering road assistance with their car insurance policies.

- Towing, the traditional motor club product, is a mature market. Also, it is more of a generic commodity product with heavy price competition. Based on this situation, our hypothetical motor club will be utilized below as an example for developing the scope.

The following three tasks provide the framework for developing your business scope.

Task 1
Provide An Overview of Company Strengths and Weaknesses

Identify the strengths and weaknesses of your company across target market needs, product, operations, distribution, pricing, and communication programs.

Use the following definition of strength and weakness when developing this section. A chart for you to fill in with information pertinent to your own business appears in Appendix B.

Strength: Capability or resource that the organization has which could be used to improve its competitive position (share of market or size of market) or improve its financial performance.

Weakness: Exists in any capability or resource that may cause your organization to have a less competitive position or poorer financial performance.

Questions to Be Addressed

List your organization's strengths and weaknesses across the following categories:

- What are your advantages due to *target market needs, wants, and consumption trends?* (For example, there is a trend toward short trips, so many motor club companies attract the short-trip target market and use products such as maps as an advantage in marketing short trips.)

- What are your advantages due to the *value* the organization brings the target markets?

- What are the competitor's *product and technological advantages* relative to target market needs?

- What are the advantages due to *operational efficiencies* which make dealing with the organization a superior experience for the member/customer?

- What are the *distribution efficiencies* or advantages which make the organization unique?

- What are the *pricing advantages* which the organization can offer the customer?

- What are your *promotion/marketing communication advantages* over the competition?

Example Strengths

The following type of statements might be developed for a motor club based upon the above parameters.

- The motor club has a dedicated staff and strong belief in the service concept. Research shows small gaps between service expectations and service fulfillment.

- The club has the ability to provide a total travel solution at a value. This means planning the trip, reservations, protection from breakdown, maps, insurance, and credit cards.

- There is a strong loyalty among the membership as demonstrated by the high renewal rate.

- There is a skew towards older membership; older adults travel more frequently.

Example Weaknesses

Based on this example, the following statements might be developed for a motor club:

- Membership skews old, with younger members renewing at lower rates than older members.

- There is a falling value perception. Research shows people leave because of non-use and the feeling that the price is too high when very few services are used. Since the majority of the use is road service, people may feel the price is too high if they don't use the club because their car doesn't break down. In addition, many car manufacturers are offering roadside assistance programs which directly compete with independent motor clubs.

- There is a low membership awareness of products outside of emergency road service.

- There is a low membership usage of most products outside of emergency road service.

Task 2
Identify the Organization's Core Competencies

Core competencies represent the consolidation of firm-wide technologies and skills into a coherent thrust. A company's core competency is the trunk of the tree, while its products are the branches; one may not recognize the strength of a competitor by looking only at its end products and failing to examine the strength of its core reason for being. The key to strategic management can be the management of core competencies rather than business units. A core competency makes a business unit unique to the target market and competitively superior. A chart for you to fill in information pertinent to your own business appears in Appendix B.

A core competency becomes the focus of an organization relative to both the target market and the competition, enabled by underlying strengths of the organization in functional areas. A core competency must

- make a significant contribution to the perceived customer benefit of the end product.

- be difficult for competitors to imitate.

Question to Be Addressed

- What are your business's core competencies?

  A core competency is found by grouping a number of similar strengths together or by identifying underlying reasons for a particular strength.

  In our case study, the hypothetical motor club recorded the following conclusions in terms of its core competencies.

  Conclusion: The motor club's core competency is in consumer road travel and as a member travel organization.

  This core competency was enabled by the following functional areas, identified as strengths:

  —Full service of travel-related offerings

  —Breadth of potential land packages and road travel capability

  —Potential public relations tying motor club to the motorist

  —Breadth of all travel information

  —Branch offices

  The core competency moves the definition of the organization from motor club to a member travel organization. Thus, it begins to define the club's scope.

Task 3
Identifying Marketing Capabilities

Marketing capabilities are a second tier of scope factors below the core competencies. Marketing capabilities are those things which specifically link the business to the consumer, such as high awareness, strong distribution capabilities, a superior customer service ability, or a large customer base. Some businesses do not have a core competency, and must focus on marketing capabilities when developing scope. An example would be the company that has high awareness for a specific category of products. While it is not an advantage that can't be duplicated (a competitor with a significantly larger communications budget could, over time, dominate awareness), marketing capabilities are a significant factor in choosing the business focus or scope. A chart for you to fill in information pertinent to your business appears in Appendix B.

Marketing capabilities must

- constitute a unique ability to provide access to target markets versus the competition.

Question to Be Addressed

- What are your firm's marketing capabilities?

  Continuing with our case study, the motor club recorded the following conclusion in terms of its marketing capabilities.

  Conclusion: The organization's marketing capabilities include:

  —Highly regarded brand name

  —Large membership

  —National organization with local presence

  —Ability to relate one-on-one with member via branches and the sales organization

  —Strong retention

  —Regularly-published magazine for members

Task 4
Development and Analysis of Potential Business Scope Options

Based upon the work so far, develop alternative scope options. In this example, three were developed. Exhibit 2.1 represents three potential business scopes for any of the major motor club organizations. Examples of potential strategy ramifications follow so you can see not only how the business review would be affected, but also the strategic direction of the subsequent marketing plan. A chart for you to develop scope options pertinent to your business appears in Appendix B.

Scope Option 1—Membership Organization

The membership organization concept takes the membership card and makes it the focal point of the organization.

The approach to the business would be:

- Present the motor club as a membership organization that provides multiple products and product categories at a value. The product categories may be unrelated.

  —Emergency motor club

  —Insurance

  —Financial services

  —Travel agency

  —Other product categories as they are developed

- Develop a broad business review that identifies unrelated product categories in which the various membership segments would be interested.

Exhibit 2.1 Example of Business Scope Alternatives

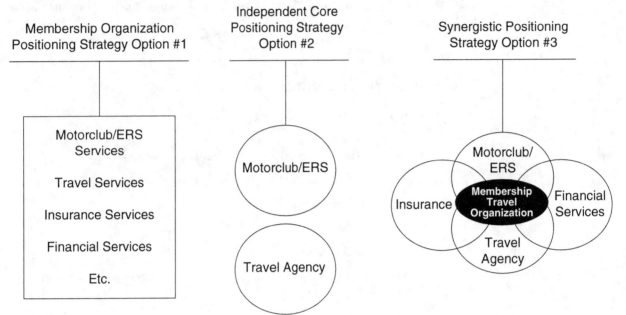

Example strategy ramifications of this approach would be:

Branding: Emphasize "membership" versus the automobile.

Product: Provide membership clubs and product offerings consistent with target market segment needs, similar to what AARP does. Also, focus on testing new product offerings consistent with membership needs across a broad range of categories.

Operations: Focus on identifying and bringing new products to the organization. Focus on individual products in terms of operations and marketing.

Publicity: Emphasize membership benefits instead of the identity as the "motorist's friend."

Communications: Focus on value of membership in terms of added value and savings on product offerings.

Scope Option 2—Independent Core Product Concept

The independent core product concept maintains the existing road club culture and operational orientation. It allows business lines to develop unique cultures and operational orientations consistent with the unique competitive environment of each business line.

The approach to the business would be:

- Take the two strongest core business categories and exploit them individually as separate business entities—emergency motor club and travel agency.

- Increase market share in the emergency motor club category through a separate emergency motor club marketing effort and operational staff.

  —Compete against all forms of emergency motor club competition.

  —Compete in both consumer and business channels (as retail/service organization and through ties with manufacturers).

- Increase travel agency market share through a separate travel agency marketing effort and operational staff.

  —Compete against multiple travel agency segments (personal and business).

- Prepare separate business reviews for road service and travel agency business entities.

Example strategy ramifications would be:

Branding: Use potentially distinct business brand names, one for each core business.

Product: Develop product segments consistent with motor club competitive environment—a consumer/retail club product and a product for car manufacturers which would be unbundled from the club.

Operations: Maintain operational autonomy between the motor club and the other existing business lines.

Publicity: Focus public affairs efforts separately against each of the business lines.

Communications: Communicate emergency motor club and the other business lines separately. Focus on unique benefits of each with individual programs.

Scope Option 3—Synergistic Product Concept

The synergistic product concept focuses on the synergy between strengths in various areas of the organization. A motor club with this scope has the potential to be a uniquely competitive, superior travel organization due to the ability to bundle previously autonomous products and services.

The approach to the business would be:

- Develop a Member Travel Organization bundling strategy.

  —Build on motor club's strengths as perceived by members and nonmembers.

  —Create a strong competitive strategy based on unique value-added products and services versus price orientation.

  —Take advantage of uniqueness pertaining to the motor club's breadth of products and organizational diversity.

- Compete as a unified entity against unbundled emergency motor club competitors.

- Compete against "Mom and Pop" travel agencies—distributors of unbundled travel services.

- Use emergency road service, the organization's major business strength, as a fundamental component of the synergistic travel organization positioning.

- Concentrate the business review on products which overlap into the member travel organization scope. Identify product categories which have the greatest chance of being cross-sold. Many product categories will not receive priority focus, such as any insurance product not connected to travel (maintain car insurance, eliminate life insurance) and any financial service not connected to travel (maintain credit cards, eliminate investment services).

Example strategy ramifications would be:

Branding: Place less emphasis on road service and automobile (as is common with most motor club names).

Product: Develop membership levels and benefits focusing on a value-added member travel organization rather than on road service benefits. Membership levels might include road travel and world travel options.

Operations: Develop programs to encourage cross-sell opportunities. Programs such as a cross-sell from maps (a standard feature of many motor clubs) to travel agency would be feasible. Strategies would delineate how cross-sell is facilitated and encouraged between business functions.

Publicity: Utilize Public Affairs to communicate a full travel-organization story, not just a motor club image, to the public.

Communications: Tie each new and existing product to the travel organization benefit. An example would be the VISA card. Its benefit to the member might be communicated as a travel card which would accumulate travel credits every time the member used the card. Rather than being marketed as a credit card with a low fee, its advantages would be directly tied to travel. If a motor club added a home security system to its line of products, the system would not be marketed as a stand-alone product, but as a way to protect the home when traveling.

Task 5
Analysis of Your Options

In order to complete the analysis of the options presented above, the following steps need to be accomplished:

- For each scope positioning option, list what is needed for your organization to succeed.

- Determine whether each need fits a strength or weakness of your organization.

- Identify the core competency needed to succeed with each scope option. Then determine if the core competency needed matches your organization's core competency.

- Identify the market capabilities needed to succeed with each scope option. Then determine if the marketing capabilities needed match your organization's marketing capabilities.

- Analyze the competitive set with each scope option. List the strengths and weaknesses of each competitor as they pertain to the core competencies and marketing capabilities needed to succeed. Compare the competitors to your company.

- Determine the risks and opportunities for each strategic positioning.

The following is an example of how this analysis would be implemented using the motor club case we have developed thus far using scope option #1. While we have not provided examples, the same would be done for scope option #2 and #3. A positioning would be chosen by comparing the analysis of all three positionings in this type of exercise. A chart for you to develop an analysis of your business' scope options appears in Appendix B.

Example Analysis of Scope Option #1: Membership Organization

What's Needed to Succeed	*Motor Club Rank*
■ Strong ability to market to segments within overall target market	Weakness
■ Effective communications with members—strong awareness of multiple products	Weakness
■ Strong ability to cross-sell between products	Weakness
■ Competitive point of entry to attract new members/value across entry products	Weakness
■ Ability to continually source and develop new products	Weakness

Core Competency Needed to Succeed	*Correlation to Motor Club's Core Competency*
■ The ability to generate margin dollars through high quantity of sales at low margin—providing members cost efficiencies	No

Marketing Capabilities Needed to Succeed	*Correlation to Motor Club's Marketing Capabilities*
■ Large membership	Yes
■ High retention	Yes
■ Perceived quality of products	Yes

Competitors

   —AARP

   —AAA

   —Credit Unions

   —USAA

   —AMOCO

   —Allstate

   —Focused/professional membership organizations such as AICPA (American Institute of Certified Public Accountants)

Risks and Opportunities

■ This is a very fractured organization with no focus and no real tie to the target market except on price. Competitors who succeed, such as AARP and USSA, have a strong affinity to a specific target market (AARP to elderly, USSA to military).

■ The club will not establish a long-term area of expertise; it will continually have to rely on new products and hot sellers to define its business to its customers. There will always be businesses with greater expertise in any given product area.

■ This strategic position puts emphasis on developing a premiere selling organization which takes advantage of the fact that the motor club has an established membership which trusts the motor club. If the membership trusts it for road service and has a long-term relationship with the club (renewal is extremely high), then there is the potential that this relationship will translate to selling other services.

■ This focus allows the club to sell products which are hot and in demand instead of constraining it with a more narrow focus.

Questions to Be Addressed

■ What are the business scope options for your firm?

■ What would be needed for your organization to succeed with each scope option?

■ Is what is needed a strength or weakness of your organization?

■ What is the core competency needed to succeed with each strategic scope option?

■ Does the core competency needed for each option's success match your core competencies?

■ What are the marketing capabilities needed to succeed with each scope option?

■ Do your company's marketing capabilities match those needed to succeed for any of the options?

■ What is the competitive set with each scope option? What are the strengths and weaknesses of your competitors as they pertain to the core competencies and marketing capabilities needed to succeed?

■ What are the risks and opportunities for each scope option?

STEP 2: PRODUCT AND MARKET REVIEW

The purpose of this step is fourfold:

1. To review the history of the industry, category, company, and product.

2. To review company, product, and industry category performance in terms of sales, distribution, and pricing.

3. To review how consumer behavior trends may affect future industry, category, company, or product performance.

4. To review company or product performance in the context of a formal competitive review.

<table>
<tr><td valign="top">

Task 1
_____
**Corporate Philosophy/
Description of the
Company**

</td><td>

Corporate Goals and Objectives

Different companies are unique in the ways they do business, their historical backgrounds, and their organizational structures—all of which have some level of impact on the development of a marketing plan. Before you begin, it is important to briefly describe predetermined corporate objectives, pertinent company and product history, and current product information and organizational parameters. By considering the culture and aspirations of the organization prior to writing the marketing plan, you stand a better chance of developing a plan that will be effectively implemented throughout the organization.

The marketer should have an understanding of existing sales goals, profit goals, and marketing expectations prior to the development of a marketing plan. The marketer should also review the operating budget to gain an understanding of each product's margins, costs, and potential profit contributions.

If your company does not yet have a mission statement or company philosophy, it is important to provide a written description of your company's overall business philosophy as it relates to marketing, growth, and business goals. All companies are different. If the marketing plan does not consider the company's basic philosophy, its chances for success are slim.

In stating corporate objectives and philosophies up front, the marketer will have a base to build upon when determining future marketing objectives and strategies. More importantly, through a thorough review of the market and company in the latter steps of the business review, the marketing manager will be able to judge whether the original overall business goals and philosophies are realistic and consistent with consumers' wants and needs. In this manner, the marketer is making himself or herself responsible for determining the feasibility of achieving the corporate goals given the market conditions and vice versa (achieving marketing goals given company conditions). A chart for filling in your company's goals and objectives appears in Appendix B.

Questions to Be Addressed

- What are the long-term and short-term goals, mission, and objectives of the company? Are there existing sales goals, profit goals, and marketing expectations?

- What is the operating budget for the company? What are the margins and planned profit contributions of each product?

- Is there a corporate philosophy on how to do business? What are the principles of the business in regard to working with customers, developing and selling product, and internal management?

General Company History

This section can provide many insights into the inherent drama of your industry and company. Include a historical and evolutionary perspective of your company, and summarize your company's results to date. A discussion of the history of your company along with the industries in which it competes is necessary. Provide as much pertinent information as possible, particularly as it relates to the specific product area or

</td></tr>
</table>

scope defined in step 1. Understanding the history of the company helps in understanding why certain strategies have evolved, and more importantly, this knowledge can be used later in the positioning and communications portions of the plan. Remember, there are no dull companies or products, only dull copywriters and salespeople. Steep & Brew, a coffee roaster, was started by an individual who had a passion for coffee houses as a way of providing alternative entertainment to bars. We successfully used his quest for a quality, alternative social setting as a way to position the company and communicate the Steep & Brew difference to grocery stores and ultimate consumers in the Midwest.

Along with a review of the company from a historical perspective, an analysis of future trends also serves to establish guidelines. It helps to understand both where a company has been and what its potential may be before you develop plans for its future. This trend analysis can provide insight as to what the future may hold in terms of marketing, operations, and technological innovation for your company and the total industry or product category. A chart for you to fill in pertinent to your company's history appears in Appendix B.

Questions to Be Addressed

- What is the history of your industry? Why was it started, how did it grow, and why is it successful?

- How did the company get into the market for the particular product around which this plan is based? What has the company's approach to this business been historically? How has the company marketed previously?

- What have been the most significant changes to your company and/or the industry in which your company competes over the past 5, 10, or 20 years?

- What are the critical strategies which have driven your company?

- What have been your company's biggest mistakes?

- What single thing does your company want to be known for? What are you best at? Why do consumers purchase from you?

- Where has your company succeeded and failed? Why?

- What future trends (marketing, product, technological, operations, distribution) will affect your company's performance?

Organizational Structure

Organizational structure tells a great deal about a company and its chance for successful marketing. Study your company's organizational chart. Analyze whether the marketing department is set up to develop and implement marketing plans efficiently. Determine where your marketing department fits in relation to the rest of the business. Determine with whom you have to work and who makes the final decisions regarding marketing direction or the company's marketing policies.

It is extremely important that you understand how the marketing department interfaces with the rest of the organization. Our feeling is that all areas of the marketing mix should be the direct responsibility of the marketing director, brand manager or target market director, and that this person should report directly to the president of the company. This means that the marketing director has decision-making impact on the sales, product, pricing, distribution, advertising, media, promotion, publicity, and merchandising functions. If this situation does not exist, there is less of a chance for cohesive implementation of the marketing plan; marketing strategies that should affect sales, product, pricing, and advertising might be interpreted and executed differently. This diminishes the synergistic effect of the marketing tools working together to achieve the company-wide sales and marketing objectives established in the marketing plan.

Later, you may want to develop a plan to reorganize your department or to improve communication with other departments in the company so your department has more positive impact. If the individual responsible for marketing does not have access to key decision makers in merchandising or operations, create a structure that forces this.

You won't change the way your department communicates and has input into corporate decision-making overnight. The purpose of reviewing the organizational structure is to make you aware of the ability of your department to provide marketing direction. You must develop a plan to make sure that marketing has the ability not only to formulate marketing plans and get them approved, but also to work with the rest of the company to effectively implement them and assure their success. A chart to help you describe your organizational structure appears in Appendix B.

Questions to Be Addressed

- Is your marketing department sufficiently organized to develop and execute a disciplined marketing plan? Do you have enough resources to plan, implement, and analyze results?

- To what degree is the company committed to marketing? Where does marketing fit in your overall organizational structure? Do you have a marketing director? Does she or he report directly to the president?

- Does your marketing department have the ability to communicate with and have a positive impact on other departments within the company?

- Does your marketing department have influence over all the marketing tools and the decisions made regarding sales, product, pricing, distribution, advertising, media, promotion, publicity, and merchandising?

- Is the company driven by operations, finance, merchandise, product, sales, or marketing? In other words, what area of the company is most responsible for the company's success? Will that be true in the future? How does the marketing department fit in? How will this affect your ability to develop and implement effective marketing plans?

Task 2
Product Analysis

An analysis of the product is important at this time, as it will be the first key in determining consumer behavior. In this Product and Market review, we'll look at product sales as an initial measure of customer and consumer demand. Later, in the Target Market Effectors step, we can further analyze customer and consumer segments of products with the greatest sales or most significant potential for sales growth in the future. A chart to help you fill in information for the following topics, pertinent to your own company, appears in Appendix B.

Identify Products Within Determined Scope of Your Business

In Section 1, you determined or reviewed the scope of your business. You now need to list the products sold in the industry category and the products sold by your company under the determined scope. For example, if you determined that the scope of your business is insurance, you would list the different insurance products sold in the industry (life, auto, home, etc.). You would then list the insurance products your company currently sells. This activity prevents you from defining the market by your company's experience. Rather, you analyze the whole range of competitive product offerings from a sales standpoint, including the subset which are your company's products.

Questions to Be Addressed

- What are the products sold in the industry category(ies) within the scope of your business?

- What products does your company sell under each industry category within the scope of your business?

Description of Company Products, History, Strengths and Weaknesses

Now that the products that fit within the scope of your marketing plan have been identified—both from an industry and company standpoint—we need to describe your company's product in the following terms:

- Manufacturing process (if applicable)

- Description and appearance

- Advantages/strengths in the marketplace

- Disadvantages/weaknesses in the marketplace

Apply the above descriptions to your particular industry and company. For example, your product may be providing accounting services. Describe the way you work and the different service areas you offer, and then analyze how you provide those services differently from the competition.

Think about how products or services are used together, at the same time, or in the same manner by your customer. The business review can start shaping your thinking, forcing you to take a critical look at how your customers use your products and to analyze natural groupings of services or products for later marketing efforts.

Describe the history of your product as you did the history of your company. Often, information about how a product evolved is still a core reason for its attraction today.

Identify plans for growth and expansion among existing product categories if they exist within your company. Describe plans for growth into new product categories if they exist.

Questions to Be Addressed

- How would you describe your company's products or services? What benefit do they provide your customer?

- Does your company provide groupings of products or services which are used together, in the same manner, or at the same time by your customer or their end customer?

- Do the products your company manufactures or sells have any potential manufacturing or service/operational problems? Are specialized parts, labor, or manufacturing processes necessary? Are the products vulnerable to shortages or other consumer, environmental, technological, or economic factors? If so, how?

- What are your company's product strengths?

- What are your company's product weaknesses?

- What is the history of your products? Have they always been successful? Why were they first marketed? Over the years, how have your products changed?

- What are the plans for growth and expansion among new product categories?

Description of Competitive Product Strengths and Weaknesses

Describe your competitor's products. How are they manufactured as compared to your products? What services do they offer and how do they differ from yours? As you did with your own company's products, describe your competitor's products in terms of:

- Manufacturing process

- Description and appearance

- Advantages in the marketplace

- Weaknesses in the marketplace

Now describe your competitor's strengths and weaknesses as they relate to your products. Describe the history of your competitor's products. Identify any plans you are aware of for growth and expansion among current lines or for growth plans into new product categories.

Questions to Be Addressed

- Describe your competitor's products or services. What benefit do they provide your customer?

- What are your competitor's product's strengths?

- What are your competitor's product's weaknesses?

- Does your competitor's product have any potential manufacturing, environmental, technological, or economic constraints which your product does not have?

- What are the growth and expansion plans for your competitor's product?

Product Trends

Highlight trends within your product category in terms of innovation, technological advantages, manufacturing process, appearance, how the product is used by the consumer, distribution, pricing, and marketing.

Questions to Be Addressed

- How has your product category done in terms of growth nationally?

- What are the trends over the past five years in terms of product innovation, marketing, distribution, pricing, and merchandising?

- What are the product trends in terms of appearance and technological and manufacturing capabilities?

- Are there product usage or consumer trends that might drive changes in the future?

Task 3
Category and
Company Sales Trends

Sales/Transactions/Profit Analysis

As stated previously, we start to learn a great deal about consumer behavior through the analysis of sales data. Sales are the most broad indicator of consumer demand. In working with Fort Howard in a series of marketing planning seminars, we looked at the napkin category. While dominant in printed lunch napkins with the Mardi Gras brand, the company had little presence in luncheon white or dinner napkins. In looking at sales trends, luncheon napkin sales dominate the napkin category in terms of both units and dollar volume. At the time of our work, within the luncheon category, printed napkins had increased over 20 percent and luncheon whites had decreased over 20 percent in sales during the past five years. This data matched Fort Howard's strengths in printed luncheon napkins. However, dinner napkins, though not the dominant napkin category, had shown double-digit increases in sales over a five-year period. As stated earlier, at the time of the seminar, the dinner napkins were not a Mardi Gras strength.

This information by itself does not necessarily drive any one decision. But later, during the planning process, if there are reasons to expand product offerings, dinner napkins could be an area worth investigating for the Mardi Gras brand from a sales volume standpoint.

The sales analysis allows the marketer to establish a clear picture of the sales trends for the industry, competitors, the company, and its products. A comparison may find that the industry is doing well, yet the category is doing poorly, or the findings may determine that, while the individual company is doing quite well, the industry growth is minimal or declining. Each situation would take the marketer in vastly different directions in the development of marketing objectives and strategies.

Industry Category Sales

Capture the industry category's sales growth over the past five years. Is it growing, flat, or shrinking? Next, list the largest sales volume and fastest growth products from the category. Provide sales trends, profit trends (gross margin if available), transactions, and percent of total category sales figures for these high volume, fast growing products.

Company Sales

Capture the overall company sales over the past five years. Is it growing, flat, or shrinking? Now, provide sales, transactions, profit, and percent of total category sales figures and trends for the largest sales volume and fastest growing company products. Does the company picture match that of the industry? They don't need to be the same, but the difference may be quite telling. If you are not strong against the largest volume or fastest growth products, you are running counter to the category and are most likely servicing a smaller niche target market segment.

The sales analysis should provide market share information. What percent of the market does your company have? Is it growing, shrinking, or stable? What is the

Exhibit 2.2 Industry Sales Compared to Company Sales

Year	Total Industry Sales (M)	Change	Total Company Sales (M)	Change	Your Company's Market Share
1996	$100,000	— %	$4,500	— %	4.5%
1995	110,000	10	5,500	22	5.0
1994	120,000	9	7,000	27	5.8
1993	130,000	8	8,000	14	6.2
1992	150,000	15	9,000	13	6.0

Estimated Sales by Competitor	Sales 1996 (M)	Market Share	Sales 1995 (M)	Market Share	Sales 1994 (M)	Market Share	Sales 1993 (M)	Market Share	Sales 1992 (M)	Market Share
Competitor A	$6,500	6.5%	$7,500	6.8%	$9,500	7.9%	$11,000	8.5%	$12,000	8.0%
Competitor B	3,000	3.0	4,000	3.6	7,000	5.8	8,000	6.2	9,000	6.0
Competitor C	7,500	7.5	8,000	7.3	9,000	7.5	10,000	7.7	10,000	6.7
Total Market Sales		100 %		100 %		100 %		100 %		100 %

market share for key growth or volume products? Market share information is used to help you develop a point of reference from which you can evaluate and plan your future marketing efforts.

Market share is your product's sales as a percent of the total market or category's sales. Market share can relate *total company dollar* sales as a percent of total market or category dollar sales; *total unit* sales as a percent of total market or category unit sales; or *individual product* sales as a percent of individual market product or category sales. Market share is a measure that quickly tells you how well your company or product is performing from a sales standpoint relative to the competition.

The chart in Exhibit 2.2 demonstrates industry performance and percent change in growth relative to your company's performance. The result is a market share figure for your company. The worksheet in Appendix B also allows you to compare the market share growth of your company with the estimated market share growth of your major competitors. Note that the chart could also be utilized for individual products, departments, or product categories. In addition, company profit could also be included in the same manner as sales.

Store-for-Store Sales By Retailers

Total retail sales for a company often reflect growth resulting from the opening of additional outlets rather than from increases from individual stores. Sales need to be monitored on a store-for-store (or same store) basis in order to determine the relative health of each unit/outlet as well as the total system of stores. The chart in Exhibit 2.3 shows total sales and per store averages (see Appendix B for worksheet). Charts would be developed on an annual basis over a five-year period for comparison.

Seasonality of Sales

It is important to ascertain the strength of the industry, the company, and each individual brand or department on a monthly basis (and even a weekly and daily basis

Exhibit 2.3 Store-for-Store Sales

Market	Sales Volume (M)	Change from Previous Year	Number of Stores	Per Store Average (M)	Change from Previous Year	Per Store Average Indexed to System Average ($569.2M)
Tulsa	$2,202.7	+12%	2	$1,001.4	+12%	$176
Minneapolis	6,147.5	+54*	8	768.4	+35*	135†
Milwaukee						
Atlanta						
Tampa						

*The percent change for total sales volume is higher than per store average volume due to a decrease in per store averages and an addition of stores. For example, this would be evident if there were a chart showing seven stores versus eight in the Minneapolis market the previous year.

†Minneapolis stores do 35 points better on a per store basis than the system average, which is $569.2M.

Break-even per store average for total system: $500,000. (Include this figure as another comparison point to be utilized when analyzing market performance.)

Note: Make sure your year-to-year analysis of per store averages includes comparable stores that have been open for the full year.

Exhibit 2.4 Sales Seasonality by Month

Month	Company Percent of Sales	Company Index to Average (8.33)	Industry Percent of Sales	Industry Index to Average (8.33)
January	10%*	120*	8%*	96*
February				
March				
April				
May				
June				
July				
August				
September				
October				
November				
December				

*10 percent of the company's sales occur in January. If sales are equal each month, 8.33 percent of the sales would occur in January (10/8.33 = 120); January was above average for sales. The industry index of 96 was slightly below average, demonstrating that company sales for the month of January are substantially above the norm when compared to industry sales. Another way to do this would be to take *total* sales and divide by 12 to get an average. Use this average as the base and divide each month's sales by the base to get an index.

Exhibit 2.5 Brand Seasonality by Month

	Base*	November		December		Etc.
		Percent of Total Dollars	Index to Total Year	Percent of Total Dollars	Index to Total Year	
Company Brand X	38.2%†	41.9%†	110†			
Company Brand Y	18.5	22.8	123			
Company Brand Z	6.2	11.2	181			

Base equals total figures for the year. Brand X accounts for 38.2 percent of the total company business.

†Brand X accounts for 38.2 percent of the sales volume during the year. During November, Brand X accounts for 41.9 percent (41.9 percent/38.2 percent = 110). This means that Brand X does better than it normally does throughout the year during the month of November, while accounting for 41.9 percent of the company's total business.

for retailers). This provides the marketer with a description of which months are typically strong-selling months and which are weaker-selling. The chart in Exhibit 2.4 tracks seasonality of industry sales as compared to company sales. The chart shown in Exhibit 2.5 demonstrates performance of individual brands or departments within your company on a monthly basis. The chart provides seasonality of sales by month for each brand or department. It is helpful to develop five-year trends of these charts to compare and identify any significant movement or changes in the seasonality from year to year. See Appendix B for worksheets to complete with information specific to your company.

The sales analysis provides answers to seasonality questions regarding sales performance by time of the year. This type of data is used to determine how you will budget on a monthly basis and when specific products will receive marketing emphasis.

Sales by Geographic Territory

Finally, sales by geographic markets should be analyzed. This can be done by region of the country, i.e., East, West, South, and North; by state; by SMSA (Standard Metropolitan Statistical Area); by city; or by any other geographic segmentation appropriate for your industry.

Questions to Be Addressed

Industry Category Sales

- If your industry category is made up of multiple products, what is the percentage of the total industry category of each product?

- Is the overall industry product category strong? Is it growing or declining? What are industry sales, transactions, and profit margins for the past five years? What is the percent increase over that period?

- Which products have the highest industry category
  —sales?
  —growth rates?
  —profit margins and/or total contributions to profits?
  —total number of transactions or highest purchase rates?

Company Sales

- What are the total company sales, transactions, and profit levels for the past five years? What has been the growth rate over the past five years?

- Which products have the highest company
  —sales?
  —growth rates?
  —profit margins and/or total contributions to profits?
  —total number of transactions or highest purchase rates?

- Do your high volume products correlate to the industry's high volume products? If not, why not?

- What is the market share for your total company sales within your industry category? Have you been gaining or losing share over the past five years?

- What is the market share for your company's high volume, high profit margin, and high growth products? Are you gaining or losing market share? Why?

- Are market sales likely to expand or shrink in the next 2, 5, or 10 years? Why? How will this affect your company?

- What competitors have gained or lost market share? Why?

Store-for-Store Sales for Retailers

- What are store-for-store sales over the past five years? Have they been increasing or decreasing? How do they compare to total sales?

- Is there a certain per-store sales average that must be met to break even?

- Which markets are above the break-even point and which are below?

- Which stores/markets are above or below budgeted sales and profits?

Seasonality of Sales

- Which products sell during certain times of the year? Does demand vary by season, business conditions, location, or weather?

- How does the seasonality of your company sales differ from that of the total category? Is there a time of the year in which you don't do as well or in which you outperform the industry as a whole? What is the seasonality of your company's product and the product category as a whole?

- Do specific products have strong seasonal selling periods that differ from the category nationally?

- For retailers, what are the weekly and daily seasonality trends of your product? Which days of the week are strong in sales relative to others? Which weeks are strong in sales relative to others?

Sales by Geographic Territory

- Are there areas of the country that provide more total sales and profits and/or sales per capita than others? Why? Consider the following:
  —Total sales
  —Sales by product line
  —Average sales per transaction or per customer
  —Average sales per store for retailers

Task 4
Behavior Trends

Consumer behavior is the process and activities people are involved in as they move through the purchase decision-making process. Consumers and consumer segments behave in certain ways and change their behavior over time due to many social, personal, geographic, and psychographic trends. Since the business review's purpose is to collect actionable data on the industry, company, overall industry category consumer, and company consumer, the consumer behavior trends are an important part of the process. It is important to review both the consumer behavior situation as it exists and to note trends which will affect its change into the future.

We analyze the following aspects of consumer behavior because we feel they are the most actionable in terms of determining target markets and developing strategies later in the plan. Use only sections applicable to your business. While most examples of behavior trends pertain to consumer products and services, behavior trends can also apply to business marketing as well, such as the trends toward downsizing and outsourcing.

- Demographic/psychographic trends

- Geographic trends

- Society trends

- Technology trends

- Media trends

Charts to gather and organize information for each of the above appear in Appendix B.

Demographic Trends

In this section we start by analyzing data from the U.S. census, among other sources, to note trends affecting the company's business.

Typically, we analyze the demographic trends listed below. We then compare national averages with product category averages to determine unique differences between the general population trends and the product category trends.

Consumer Products

- Median age

- Shifts in the percentage of total product usage accountable to age segments

- Percent of consumers in the labor force (male and female breaks)

    —Number and percentage

    —Types of jobs/job classifications

    —Percentage who own businesses

- Education levels for different age segments

- Income trends and averages/medians for different age segments

    —Gaps between poor and affluent

- Family composition

    —Percentage traditional family

    —Percentage female-headed

    —Percentage unmarried households with children

    —Percentage households with married couples with children

    —Percentage households with married couples with no children

- Ethnic minorities

Business-to-business firms

- Segment (SIC or other) competition

- Shifts in percentage of total product usage by size of firm (small, medium, large)

As an example of how we use this information, we developed marketing plans for two very different clients—a local realtor and a national manufacturer of a disposable diaper pail. In both situations the business review data outlining the median age of women and men was very helpful in analyzing demand potential and product strategies later in the plan. National Census Data, as reported in the business review, noted the following:

- From 1992 to 2000, as the baby boom population ages, the median age of women will increase from 34.8 to 37.6 years and the median age for men will increase from 32.6 to 35.2.

- The under-five group will decrease 7–8 percent as birthrates decrease.

- The 25–44 group will decrease 13.4 percent by the year 2000.

Disposable Diaper Pail Strategy Ramifications

The strategy examples derived from the above findings are fairly obvious. The disposable diaper pail company needed to explore secondary target markets and alternative product uses such as:

- Travel/car models

- Older adult incontinence products

In addition, it was necessary to review media and communication needs for increasing emphasis against secondary targets and stealing share within existing markets.

Realtor Strategy Ramifications

The realtor also had strategic ramifications from this business review data. It needed to place more emphasis against second homes (trade-ups) and retirement housing (condominiums).

Questions to Be Addressed

For each of the following, delineation of national averages and product category averages is useful for comparison purposes.

- What are the age trends in terms of usage, and how will they affect your business?

    —Median age of usage

    —Shifts in total product usage accountable by each age segment

- What percent of the consumers are in the labor force, and how will this affect your business?

- What are the educational levels for the different age segments, and how will this affect your business?

- What are the income trends for the different age segments, and how will this affect your business?

- What are the trends in terms of composition of the family, and how will this affect your business?

- What are the minority trends in terms of population as a whole and for your product category, and how will this affect your business?

- What are the trends in business buying, such as downsizing and outsourcing?

■ What growth changes are affecting key segments? Describe the segments by SIC code, industry type, firm make-up, etc.

Geographic Trends

The following information should be noted from the census and other geographic trend sources. Similar to the demographic information, national figures and product category figures should be compared where applicable.

■ Geographic population growth

Example of Comparing National Data To Your Product Category Data: Nationally, the West may be first in population growth, but among users of your product category, the South may be first.

■ Geographic differences in the percentage of the population in each age segment

■ Geographic differences of men and women in the labor force

—Number and percentage

—Types of jobs/job classifications

—Percentage who own businesses

■ Geographic differences in education levels

■ Geographic differences in income levels

■ Geographic differences in family composition

■ Geographic differences in ethnic minorities

As an example of how we use the above information later in the planning process, we noted that the West was projected to be the fastest growing U.S. region, with the South second, the Midwest Third, and the East last. The implications of this to our client Famous Footwear were as follows:

■ Store expansion plans need to take into account this shifting of population to the West.

■ Product strategies need to take into account the generally more casual Western lifestyle and dress.

■ From a merchandise perspective, take into consideration that trends in shoe styles increasingly originate in the West (and East) and spread inward to other major population centers.

Questions to Be Addressed

For each of the following, delineation of national trends and consumer trends in the company's product category is useful for comparison purposes.

■ What are the population growth trends by geographic region, and how will they affect your business?

■ What are the geographic differences in the percentage of the population in each age segment, and how will they affect your business?

- What are the geographic differences in education levels, and how will they affect your business?

- What are the geographic differences in income levels, and how will they affect your business?

- What are the geographic differences in family composition, and how will they affect your business?

- What are the geographic differences in ethnic minorities, and how will they affect your business?

- Are there geographic differences in terms of how the product is used or how much the product is used?

Social/Consumer Trends

Social trends affect how we will use products in the future. They include trends that influence how we live in our homes, what activities people become involved in, economic trends that predict "disposable" income availability, health concerns, environmental concerns, clothing, etc.

One place to look for social trends is in books and published reports by biometric technicians such as John Naisbitt and Faith Popcorn. Both Naisbitt and Popcorn study population trends and current socioeconomic trends to predict the future. Naisbitt's firm, the Naisbitt Group, gathers and analyzes information from 6,000 newspapers a month to identify social trends based upon common occurrence and frequency of similar stories.

Faith Popcorn, in her book *The Popcorn Report,* identifies ten key trends for marketers to look to in the 21st century.[1] The following two examples will serve to demonstrate the type of information found in sources such as *The Popcorn Report* and highlight potential strategy ramifications which could be developed from this information.

1. *Fantasy Adventure.* As we spend more time in our cocoons (homes), we will make the time outside of it more special, yet our basic increased level of risk adversity will lead us to fantasize about adventure more than actually live it. For example, we will drive our Jeep in the city as a way to get the emotional high of off-roading without the risk; or we will shop at Banana Republic rather than actually go on safari. Consumerism and shopping will need to be more recreational, as technology makes it easier to stay in our cocoons and do more mundane shopping. In addition to value, products will increasingly have to fit the mood of the consumer. And, since we will be out and about less and in with our own thoughts and moods more, fashions will matter less.

   Potential Strategy Implications for Later in the Plan:

   —Increasingly, the lifestyle image (not just the prestige value) of products, brands, and retail stores will need to be considered.

   —Consider ways of making shopping more of an experience; this could be as an actual in-store experience or via a direct response opportunity. Mer-

---

[1]Popcorn, Faith. *The Popcorn Report.* (Doubleday Publishers; New York, New York. 1991.)

chandising and products will need to take into account these would-be adventures as well.

2. *Purchase Trends/Small Indulgences.* Popcorn sees increased emphasis on small material rewards for getting through the week, month, etc.—an "emotional fix" or "ego boost." It's about choosing one small category in your life and buying the best you can afford in that area. Examples are Victoria's Secret, Godiva chocolates, and Häagen-Dazs ice cream. While we may never lease another BMW, we can still treat ourselves to these small indulgences. Product quality will be key, because you can't reward yourself with something that will fall apart soon. There will be a perceived value in just having gotten the best deal, above and beyond the product itself. Small indulgences will be even more crucial vis-a-vis kids, as the emerging MOBYs and DOBYs (Mommy/Daddy Older, Baby Younger) set will tend to indulge their "trophy children." They will be able to indulge, as they will have fewer children and will be older and more affluent when they become parents.

Potential Strategy Implications for Later in the Plan:

—Develop products and communicate product use in a manner consistent with indulgences.

Questions to Be Addressed

- What are the social trends affecting the population as a whole and specifically those in your product category, and how will they affect your business? Consider the following:

  —Home trends

  —Activity trends

  —Purchase trends

  —Economic trends

  —Attitudes toward aging and youth

  —Health trends

  —Consumerism

  —Time pressures

  —Environmental concerns

  —New generational trends

  —Clothing

  —Spending power

  —Activities

Technology Trends

This section is different for every business. It forces you to look at how technology is changing and will serve to point out both problems and opportunities later in the planning sections. Technology is accelerating in all areas of business, making what used to be impossible the norm today.

The following areas should be considered for study:

■ How does the ability to capture transaction and customer data affect your business environment?

—For our retail and service customers, technology such as scanning equipment at the point-of-sale has led to database capabilities and relationship marketing opportunities with the customer.

—For our consumer goods manufacturing customers, it means the retailers have sophisticated information regarding productivity and product turn per square foot of shelf space. Therefore, marketing efforts to the retailer have to address these primary concerns.

—For our business-to-business customers, it means the ability to segment customers and to track their purchases, purchase cycles, and order requirements, resulting in a more personalized selling effort.

■ New product development and capabilities

■ Competitive products which have superior competitive advantages

■ Predictions of how new technology will alter consumer behavior

■ Manufacturing trends that will fuel your industry

Questions to Be Addressed

■ What are the major trends in information gathering, and how will they affect your business?

■ What are the new product developments and capabilities in your industry, and how will they affect your business?

■ How will new technologies (just introduced or on the future horizon) affect consumer behavior?

Media Trends

The last consumer behavior trends area we look at is media. Media trends directly affect how your customer (whether consumer or business-to-business) receives their information. Information sources such as *Advertising Age, Direct Marketing, American Demographics,* and *Nielsen* provide insights into this area.

We typically look at the following categories:

1. *Trends in traditional media.* We discern trends in television, radio, newspaper, direct mail, magazine, and outdoor. For example, we concluded the following in a business review for a national retailer.

Estimated Distribution of the Average U.S. Adult's Daily Time Spent With The Four Major Media

	Time Spent With Media				
	TV	Radio	Magazines	Newspapers	Total
Mid-1940s:	—	3.2	.3	.9	4.4
Mid-1950s:	2.4	2.8	.3	.9	6.4
Mid-1960s:	3.6	2.8	.3	.6	7.3
Mid-1970s:	3.7	3.0	.3	.6	7.6
Mid-1980s:	4.0	3.2	.4	.5	8.1
Mid-1990s:	4.4	3.1	.4	.6	8.5

Source: *TV Dimensions '95*

—Time spent with television continues to increase.

—Time spent with the four major media in general continues to increase.

2. *Trends within each of the traditional media.* For example:

—Trends in time spent with radio format segments (country western versus soft rock versus golden oldies versus progressive rock, etc.)

—Trends in viewing cable versus network programming

3. *Trends in non-traditional media.* Two examples include:

—It is predicted that 40 percent of U.S. homes will have interactive television by early in the twenty-first century. This will create a new definition of direct marketing—the use of a chosen medium to get the target prospect to respond to a message. In the past this message has been provided almost exclusively through direct mail, but virtual reality technology will enable direct marketing to provide simulated "sample experiences" to get the prospect to respond.

—Computer interactive systems currently offer a range of services, including stock market information, weather reports, Associated Press news services, banking services, and airline ticket purchases. A home personal computer user hooks up to national services, such as CompuServe and Prodigy, via a modem to access this information. Currently, over three million subscribers tap into these services, and companies such as JC Penney, Lands' End, and BMW are advertising on them. Often the consumer can order products or additional information by simply hitting a key on the computer. With the introduction of services by cable companies and with fiber optics, the information flow by the end of the decade will be much faster and will have better graphics.

Questions to Be Addressed

■ For business-to-business firms, what are the trends in trade publication readership? Are certain publications or formats gaining greater acceptance or dominance among certain target audiences?

■ What are the consumer viewing trends within traditional media (TV, radio, newspaper, magazines, and outdoor)? Which medium is increasing in terms of viewership and which is decreasing? How do these trends affect your business?

■ What are the consumer trends within each of the traditional media? How do these trends affect your business? For example:

—radio listenership by day part

—radio listenership by program format

—TV programming trends

—cable penetration

—cable viewership versus network viewership

—type of cable programming which is most popular

—viewership profiles to different programming alternatives

—most popular magazine segments

—most popular newspaper formats

—most innovative direct mail applications

■ What are the trends in non-traditional media? How do these trends affect your business? For example:

—interactive TV

—PC services

—home shopping alternatives

—other

Task 5
Distribution

Distribution is the method of delivering the product to the consumer. In the business review, your job is to determine which method of distribution is used most successfully by the industry, your company, and your competitors. However, the concept of distribution varies depending upon the type of business category.

Retail

Retailers need to be aware of how and where their product is sold in relation to the industry. There are many unique ways to distribute the product to the consumer, and retailers should be aware of which distribution methods are increasing or decreasing in their industry and the advantages and disadvantages of the different methods.

Channel Type/Trends

The retailer has to determine and review the optimum outlet category or categories for the product being sold and the consumer who is purchasing. Common retail distribution outlet categories include mass merchandise, discount, off-price, department stores, specialty shops, chain stores, and direct mail. Each is a unique distribution method that a retailer can use to sell the product to the consumer. To determine the optimum outlet category, it helps to analyze the current channel trends. The business review may determine that the two fastest growing methods of distribution for your product category are smaller, single-line specialty shops and direct mail. If you were not currently using these channels, you would need to address the industry's shift in emphasis toward these alternative methods of distribution in the marketing plan. This could be done by adapting some of the strengths of specialty store retailing to your channel environment or by experimenting with direct mail. The chart in Exhibit 2.6 details dollar sales and unit sales by outlet type (see Appendix B for worksheet).

Geography

The geographical distribution of outlets should be studied. Try to grade the location of your stores relative to your competitors. Is your firm located in the optimal trading areas of the market? Are they easy to get to and do they have good access? Are they on or near thoroughfares of high traffic counts and other thriving retail locations? Are there markets or specific trading areas within markets that have large numbers of purchases per person and/or household and low levels of competition where you should be doing business?

Penetration

Optimum penetration levels (number of stores per *market*) should be calculated to determine if more distribution outlets are needed. Note that in the broadest sense we

Exhibit 2.6 Purchases by Outlet Type (5-Year Trend)

	Percent of Total Sales				Points Change 1996 to 2000	
	1992		1996			
Distribution Outlet*	Units	Dollars	Units	Dollars	Units	Dollars
Specialty store	36.2%†	48.4%†	43.1%†	51.2%†	6.9%†	3.8%†
Department store						
National chain						
Discount store						
Direct mail						
Other						

*The chart for retailers could easily be modified for appropriate use by package good or business-to-business firms by changing distribution outlets to reflect the industry. For example, a package good firm might want to look at sales by chain grocery stores, independent grocery stores, convenience food stores, delis, and specialty grocery stores.

†36.2 percent of the units and 48.4 percent of the dollars were sold through specialty stores in 1992 versus 43.1% and 51.2% in 1996. There was a 6.9 percent increase in units and a 3.8 percent increase in dollars between 1996 and 2000.

define markets as DMAs—Designated Market Areas or Television Coverage Areas—but markets can be defined in terms of a DMA, SMSA (Standard Metropolitan Statistical Area), county, or city/metro trading area. Penetration levels are evaluated on three issues:

1. The total number of competing outlets a market can support.

2. The number of your stores a market can support before cannibalization (stealing of customers from one of your stores by another) occurs.

3. The number of stores that are required in order for mass media such as newspapers, television, and radio to be efficiently leveraged, making the media affordable for your company from a percent-of-market sales or sales-per-store standpoint.

We provide two methods for determining optimum store penetration levels for each market (see Appendix B for worksheets to use in developing information for your company).

The chart in Exhibit 2.7 shows a method for determining the number of stores needed for Group 1 markets. In this example, Group 1 markets are under-penetrated and thus have not received the type of advertising support as the stores in Group 2. Because of this, Group 2 stores have a stronger sales performance than Group 1 stores.

In essence, this methodology assumes that if Group 1 markets are more fully penetrated with additional stores, the markets will be able to afford more advertising and the individual store sales figures will increase. Though it would be unrealistic to expect Group 1 stores to equal Group 2 stores in sales in the near future, ideals are established—the average sales per household and per store of the weaker Group 1 markets and the stronger Group 2 markets.

The number of stores needed is calculated by first multiplying the estimated TV market households by the average sales per household figure of the weaker Group 1 markets and the stronger Group 2 markets. Then, the end result of this multiplication is divided by the average per store sales for the Group 1 and Group 2 markets to produce a realistic penetration figure.

Exhibit 2.7 Store Penetration Analysis I

					Current Advertising Plans		Future Advertising Plans			
	Number of Stores	Sales Last Year (M)	Estimated Number of TV HH's (M)	Sales per HH	5% of Sales (M)	W18–49 GRP Media Weight Level*	Average Sales per HH	Number of Stores Needed	5% of Sales (M)	W18–49 GRP Media Weight Level*
Group 1 Markets (Weaker Markets)										
A	7	$ 3,233.5	1,229.6	$ 2.63	$ 161.7	1,587	$4.26	8.22	$ 261.9	2,567
B	9	4,508.9	1,662.1	2.71	225.4	1,896	4.26	11.12	354.0	2,978
C	6	2,292.1	708.9	3.23	114.6	1,983	4.26	4.74	151.0	2,613
D	2	1,597.6	868.2	1.84	79.9	1,535	4.26	5.80	184.9	3,552
E	4	2,079.9	2,518.0	.83	104.0	512	4.26	16.84	536.3	2,641
F	4	2,122.1	602.7	3.52	106.1	1,901	4.26	4.03	128.4	2,301
Subtotal	32	$15,834.1	7,589.5	$ 2.09	$ 791.7	1,358	$4.26	50.75	$1,916.5	2,770
Group 2 Markets (Stronger Markets)										
G	22	$13,487.1	3,016.8	$ 4.47	$ 674.4	3,148				
H	15	10,746.9	992.9	10.82	537.3	5,055				
I	5	4,350.4	703.7	6.18	217.5	3,191				
J	3	2,407.8	209.5	11.49	120.4	4,391				
K	5	4,323.6	694.9	6.22	216.2	3,947				
L	14	10,004.4	1,156.6	8.65	500.2	4,023				
Subtotal	64	$45,320.2	6,774.4	$ 6.69	$2,266.0	3,704				
Totals/Averages Groups 1 & 2	96	$61,154.3	14,363.9	$ 4.26	$3,057.7	2,461				

Average per store sales groups 1 and 2 $637.02 M ($61,154.3/96)
*⅔ weight in TV, ⅓ weight in newspaper.

The calculations for Market A in Group 1 are:

New sales goal based upon expected potential

Estimated TV HHs in Market A 1,229.6	×	Average sales per HH in Groups 1 and 2 $4.26	=	New sales goal for Market A $5,238.09M

Optimum projected stores for Market A

New sales goal for Market A $5,238.09	Per-store average of Groups 1 and 2 $637.02	Ideal number of stores required for optimum penetration 8.22 stores

This method should be applied to all markets, as the chart in Exhibit 2.7 indicates. In addition, Exhibit 2.8 provides an advertising comparison in the form of gross rating points (GRPs; see Chapter 15, Advertising Media, for definition) that could be achieved given a 5 percent advertising budget from the new projected sales and store penetration. Continuing with the examples, Market A will have a new sales goal of $5,238M from eight stores. Five percent of $5,238M equals $261.9M, which equals a media weight level of 2,567 GRPs.

Exhibit 2.8 Store Penetration Analysis II

	Existing Stores						Penetration of 1 Store per 100M HHs		
	Number of Stores	Existing Stores per 100M HHs	Total Sales Last Year (M)	Advertising Budget 5% of Sales (M)	Estimated 1 Week Cost	Estimated Number of Advertising Weeks*	Minimum Stores 1/100M HHs	Advertising Budget 5% of Sales (M)	New Estimated Number of Advertising Weeks
A	7	.569	$ 3,233.5	$ 161.7	$24.6	6–7	12.3	$284.1	11–12
B	9	.541	4,508.9	225.4	27.6	8	16.6	415.8	15
C	6	.846	2,292.1	114.6	13.8	8	7.1	135.6	10
D	2	.230	1,597.6	79.9	11.4	7	8.7	347.5	30
E	4	.159	2,079.9	104.0	48.6	2	25.2	655.2	13
F	4	.664	2,122.1	106.1	13.8	7–8	6.0	159.2	12
G	22	.729	13,487.1	674.4	49.6	13–14	30.2	925.7	19
H	15	1.511	10,746.9	537.3	27.0	20	10.0	358.2	13
I	5	.711	4,350.4	217.5	17.0	12–13	7.0	304.5	18
J	3	1.432	2,407.8	120.4	7.2	16–17	2.1	84.3	12
K	5	.720	4,323.6	216.2	13.0	16–17	6.9	298.3	23
L	14	1.210	10,004.4	500.2	31.6	15–16	11.6	414.5	13
All Stores	146	.536	$96,445.5	$4,822.3	—	—	272.4	—	—

*200 W18–49 GRPs TV: 30's

The chart in Exhibit 2.8 shows yet another way to calculate estimated penetration requirements. As with Exhibit 2.7, this chart takes a group of stores seen as optimum and uses their performance as the standard. Through this analysis, it was determined that the best performing markets from a sales standpoint have approximately one store per 100,000 households. This was accomplished by reviewing sales of those markets meeting sales and profit expectations. Column 7 shows how many stores would be needed in each market to match this goal.

In addition, this chart looks at how many weeks of television the markets could currently sustain, given the advertising goal of 5 percent of sales. This is then compared to the number of advertising weeks which could be afforded, given the optimum penetration level of one store per 100M households and the subsequent increase (or decrease) in sales this would create in any given market. For example, Market A currently has a per-store average of $461.9M ($3,233M divided by 7). With a projection of 12.3 stores (one store per 100M households), the new market sales figure becomes $5,681.7M (12.3 × $461.9M). A 5 percent advertising budget, given the fully-penetrated projected market sales of $5,681.7M, is $284.1M.

Questions to Be Addressed

- Where do consumers shop for products in your category? Where do they shop for your company's product? What channel or outlet type do consumers use most when purchasing?

- What is the importance of department stores, supermarkets, specialty stores, chain stores, independents, direct mail, discount stores, or other types of outlets that sell your product category or product? What are the 5-year sales trends of each outlet type used by your product category?

- What channels or methods of distribution are receiving increased use by the industry? Are new channels emerging? What trends are noticeable in the stores that dominate the sales for your product category?

- What channels or methods of distribution does your competition use? If they use different channels from you, why?

- Do you have adequate penetration of outlets to maximize sales in any given market?

- Does expansion into new territories make sense? Are there additional areas of the country in which you should be doing business?

- Does your product require mass, selective, or exclusive distribution? Why? Does it require a combination of distribution methods? Who can best provide this type of distribution? Do your competitors' products require mass, selective, or exclusive distribution?

Package Goods

A package or consumer goods company views distribution differently from a retailer. Package goods companies sell to outlets, which in turn sell to consumers. A cereal company sells to grocery stores, who in turn sell to consumers. Unlike retailers, package goods companies don't own the channel of distribution; thus, more emphasis is placed on making sure the package goods product is accepted and sold into the channel and that it receives proper shelf space and merchandising support relative to competitors' products.

Channel Type/Trends

The package goods marketer has to determine the type of channel(s) best suited for the product. For example, it may be chain grocery stores, independent grocery stores, mass merchandisers, specialty stores, or convenience stores.

Market Coverage

As with retailing, you need to determine the number of outlets required to cover a trading area efficiently. However, since the package goods firm doesn't own the outlets, there is less concern with over-penetration. In some cases, the goal is to reach 100 percent market coverage of grocery store outlets in a given market. At the other extreme, some manufacturers offer exclusive distribution to a chain in return for greater sales and merchandising support. In still other situations, the product is distributed on a more limited basis to outlets that are consistent with the image of the product.

In most cases, package goods marketers do not refer to distribution coverage in terms of total stores. Distribution is referred to as the percent of total grocery store dollar volume that the stores carrying the marketer's product account for in all grocery commodities, or all commodity volume (ACV). Thus, the term 65 percent ACV means that the marketer's brand is carried by grocery stores accounting for 65 percent of all commodity grocery store volume.

The chart in Exhibit 2.9 provides information detailing market coverage. This process is used primarily by manufacturers. The example is for a package goods firm, but it could easily be adapted to business-to-business. (A similar chart would be created for each business-to-business segment, such as an SIC classification.) From this chart you would determine that your product was represented in eight of the nine major outlets but that those outlets accounted for only 60 percent of the total product category business in the market.

Exhibit 2.9 Market Coverage Chart—Rockford

	Coverage for Your Product	Percent of Total Product Business in Market (% ACV)	Percent of Shelf Space Given Your Product in Store	Percent of Shelf Space for Main Competitors in Product Category	
				Competitor 1	Competitor 2
Outlet A	x*	10%*	10%*	15%*	10%*
Outlet B	x	20	15	15	10
Outlet C		40	N/A	20	10
Outlet D	x	5	10	10	10
Outlet E	x	5	15	15	15
Outlet F	x	5	15	20	10
Outlet G	x	5	20	20	10
Outlet H	x	5	10	15	10
Outlet I	x	5	10	15	5

Note: An identical chart would be created for each key market.
*Outlet A sells this company's product. Outlet A accounts for 10 percent of the product category's business in Rockford. The company receives 10 percent of the shelf space given the product category in Outlet A while the major competitors receive 15 and 10 percent, respectively.

Shelf Space

The amount of shelf space a product receives is critical to how well the product will do from a sales standpoint. Limited shelf space or facings and poor positioning on the shelf are both reasons for concern and need to be corrected. An average shelf space figure for your company could be calculated and included in your market coverage chart, as shown in Exhibit 2.9. The percent shelf space number can be compared to the shelf space percentages of your major competitors and can help you establish future shelf space goals (see Appendix B for worksheet).

Geography

As with retail, the package good marketer should analyze the geographic territories of the firm's distribution to determine if there are markets that should be further penetrated or new markets that should be entered.

Personal Selling Method

An integral part of package goods distribution is the personal selling method. Some companies choose to use an in-house sales force, others use independent sales representatives and brokers, and still others use distributors or wholesalers. You should analyze your current method as well as what your competitors use and then decide the best method or combination of methods for your company.

Another issue that needs to be explored is the selling programs your company has in place to sell the trade. The questions are designed to establish the importance of trade deals, co-op advertising, and other allowances in your marketplace.

Questions to Be Addressed

■ Where do consumers shop for products in your category? Where do they shop for your company's product? What channel or outlet type do consumers use most when purchasing?

- What is the importance of department stores, supermarkets, specialty stores, chain stores, independents, direct mail, discount stores, or other types of outlets that sell your product category or product? What are the 5-year sales trends of each outlet type used by your product category?

- What channels or methods of distribution are receiving increased use by the industry? Are new channels emerging? What trends are noticeable in the stores that dominate the sales of your product category?

- What channels or methods of distribution does your competition use? If they use different channels from you, why?

- Do you have enough market coverage to maximize sales in any given market?

- What is the ACV in each of your company's markets? What is the ACV for each of your major competitors in those same markets?

- Is the percent of shelf space your product receives in major outlets greater, the same, or lower than your competitors?

- Does expansion into new territories make sense? Are there additional areas of the country where you should be doing business?

- Does your product require mass, selective, or exclusive distribution? Why? Does it require a combination of distribution methods? Who can best provide this type of distribution? Do your competitors' products require mass, selective, or exclusive distribution?

- How many potential dealers, wholesalers, distributors, brokers, or retail outlets are there? What are their distribution trading areas geographically?

- How do you sell your product to the retail trade or other businesses? Do you use in-house sales staff, independent reps, wholesalers, or distributors? What is the most efficient method of selling to distributors, wholesalers, or the retail trade?

- What is the importance of your product to the retail stores and/or distribution channel that sell it? Do you need the channel's services more than they need your product? Who has the channel power? How important is your product to the channel in terms of profit and volume (units and dollars)? Does your product help build or sustain traffic? Is it prestigious? Does it help sell other goods? How do these points differ from your competition?

- How do retailers or other distributors sell or market your product? Does your product receive aggressive sales support, or does your product have to sell itself? Does your product receive prominent display relative to the competition? Does your product get promoted in-store or to the ultimate purchaser by the distribution channel? Does your product receive the same merchandising and promotion support (more or less) relative to the competition? Does your product receive other promotion, advertising, or merchandising support?

- How established is your product with the trade? How well is it known and accepted by the trade? Is it important to them? Do you receive cooperation from the channels to which you sell? How does your competition rate in these areas?

- What is the minimum order size you require of your customers/channels? Is this standard in your industry? What are the payment terms? How often is restocking needed?

- Do storage, price marking, packaging, or accounting practices help sell the trade or create problems?

- Do quantity discounts, cooperative advertising, promotion allowances, price discounts, trade promotions, or other deals play a large role in the selling of your product category to the trade? How? Does your company have the same programs as your competitors?

- What is the customary markup of your product by the trade? Does this affect your marketing to the trade or the acceptance of your product by the end consumer?

- Are retail sales or sales to the trade subject to taxes or legal restrictions?

- What are the stocking requirements of the trade? How does your company make allocation decisions? Who gets the best fill rates and why? How are out-of-stock situations handled?

- When, how often, and by whom are the orders placed?

Business to Business

Business-to-business firms sell directly to other businesses and/or sell through channels such as wholesalers or distributors.

Channel Types/Trends

The business-to-business firm must decide the most efficient and effective channel method for the company. We did a business review for a national manufacturer of sinks and disposals that clearly demonstrated the growing trend of do-it-yourselfers to install their own sinks and disposals. Further study demonstrated that a shift in purchasing patterns had accompanied the strength of do-it-yourselfers in the marketplace; home centers and lumberyards were now selling more of this type of product than traditional plumbing channels. Thus, because of the channel trend section of the business review, selling emphasis was placed against home centers and lumberyards, establishing a new channel of distribution for the manufacturer.

Geography

The same issues that were discussed in the package goods section need to be addressed here.

Personal Selling Method

As with package goods firms, business-to-business companies must decide how to sell the product through distribution channels. Company sales representatives, independent sales representatives, or wholesalers/distributors all have advantages and disadvantages. These are detailed in Chapter 12, Personal Selling/Service. Remember, in the business review your job is to analyze which method is used most successfully within the industry, as well as by your company and your competitors.

As with the package goods section, the business-to-business firm must also address the issues of sales programs to the channels. The importance of deals, allowances, co-op advertising, and other sales program issues are detailed in the questions.

Questions to Be Addressed

- What channels or methods of distribution are receiving increased use by the industry? Are new channels emerging? What trends are noticeable?

■ What channels or methods of distribution does your competition use? If they use different channels from you, why?

■ Do you have enough market coverage to maximize sales in any given market?

■ Does expansion into new territories make sense? Are there additional areas of the country where you should be doing business?

■ Does your product require mass, selective, or exclusive distribution? Why? Does it require a combination of distribution methods? Who can best provide this type of distribution? Do your competitors' products require mass, selective, or exclusive distribution?

■ How many potential dealers, wholesalers, distributors, or retail outlets are there? What are their distribution trading areas geographically?

■ How do you sell your product to the retail trade or other businesses? Do you use in-house sales staff, independent reps, wholesalers, or distributors? What is the most efficient method of selling to distributors, wholesalers, or the retail trade?

■ What is the importance of your product to the retail stores and/or distribution channel that sell it? Do you need the channel's services more than they need your product? Who has the channel power? How important is your product to the channel in terms of profit, volume (units and dollars)? Does your product help build or sustain traffic? Is it prestigious? Does it help sell other goods? How do these points differ from your competition?

■ How do retailers or other distributors sell or market your product? Does your product receive aggressive sales support, or does your product have to sell itself? Does your product get promoted to the ultimate purchaser by the distribution channel? Does your product receive the same merchandising and promotion support (less or more) relative to the competition? Does your product receive other promotion, advertising, or merchandising support?

■ How established is your product with the trade? How well is it known and accepted by the trade? Is it important to them? Do you receive cooperation from the channels to which you sell? How does your competition rate in these areas?

■ What is the minimum order size you require of your customers/channels? Is this standard in your industry? What are the payment terms? How often is restocking needed?

■ Do storage, price marking, packaging, or accounting practices help sell the trade or create problems?

■ Do quantity discounts, cooperative advertising, promotion allowances, price discounts, trade promotions, or other deals play a large role in the selling of your product category to the trade? How? Does your company have the same programs as your competitors?

■ What is the customary markup of your product by the trade? Does this affect your marketing to the trade or the acceptance of your product by the end consumer? Are sales subject to taxes or legal restrictions?

■ What are the stocking requirements of the trade? How does your company make allocation decisions? Who gets the best fill rates and why? How are out-of-stock situations handled?

■ When, how often, and by whom are the orders placed? Are there many decision makers? What is the decision criteria and sequence?

Service Firms

The service industry's method of distribution is much like the retailer's. It encompasses the business's office and how the service is sold to customers.

Type of Office

Of consideration for the service business is the type of office used to sell the service. For a service company, one of the only tangible things associated with the company is the actual office. Therefore, the office becomes an important representation of the more intangible service being sold. For many services, the service itself is sold or delivered out of the office. In this case, how and where the service is sold and delivered must be closely analyzed.

Geography

An important decision is where to locate an office or offices within a given market. When The Hiebing Group first began operation, we wanted to be close to Madison's Capitol Square because of the positive image associated with being downtown, adjacent to the center of state government, and close to the University of Wisconsin. When we outgrew our first location, we decided to stay close to downtown and the university, while maintaining a positive creative image. We found an historic old mansion overlooking Lake Mendota, and then later, as we continued to grow, converted an old Christian Science Church close to downtown, achieving our goals and creating an office environment and image consistent with that of the agency.

Another issue which must be addressed is the number of markets in which you do business. What markets seem ripe for geographic expansion, and which ones are not currently profitable and may need to be abandoned?

Penetration

As with retailers, proximity is also important to firms providing service. Accordingly, service companies also have to decide how many locations and sales and/or service people are needed to cover any given market effectively and efficiently.

Questions to Be Addressed

- Where do consumers of services in your category shop?

- What are the current methods of delivery used for services in your category? Are new methods of delivery emerging? Are there noticeable trends among the firms that dominate your service category?

- How does your competition deliver their services? If they use different delivery methods than you, why?

- Does expansion into new territories make sense? Are there additional areas of the country where you should be doing business?

- Does your product require mass, selective, or exclusive distribution? Why? Does it require a combination of delivery methods? Who can best provide this new method of delivery? Do your competitors require different methods of delivery?

- Is there a best way to deliver your service through company-owned offices, franchises, or dealerships?

Exhibit 2.10 Price of Your Company's Product Relative to the Competition During Key Selling Periods

	Price November/December	Price March/April	Price August/September
Your Company	$15.50	$15.50	$15.50
Competitor A	20.00	22.00	18.00
Competitor B	12.00	13.00	12.00
Competitor C	15.00	15.00	15.00
Competitor D	17.00	19.00	15.00

- As with retail, what is the physical exposure of the office and its signage to passing potential customers. This exposure can have a dramatic effect on the awareness of the company's name.

- What type of office is most consistent with your company's image? Describe the office interiors/exteriors of your competitors; are they similar to or different from yours? Where, when, and how is your service best sold to consumers?

Distribution Strengths and Weaknesses

Finally, analyze your company's strengths and weaknesses and compare them to your competitors.

- What are your company's strengths and weaknesses as compared to those of your competitors?

Task 6
Pricing

Price is a prominent part of the marketing decision-making process. A price that is too high may discourage purchase of the product and encourage competition in the form of lower price and more entries into the product category. Alternatively, a price that is too low may be a deterrent to reaching profit and sales goals.

The business review section on pricing is designed to provide pricing data regarding the competition, changes in the marketplace price structure, and strengths of consumer demand. This information will provide a reference and help guide your pricing objectives and strategies in the subsequent marketing plan.

The business review should provide you with four major insights on pricing:

1. The price of your product/brands relative to the competition

2. The distribution of sales by price point relative to the competition

3. The price elasticity of demand for your product

4. The cost structure of the product category

Price of Your Product

Changes in a competitor's price structure often cause reactive price strategies in the marketplace. Frequent competitive price checks should be made by the marketing department in order to track historical pricing patterns of the competition. To a large degree, competitive pricing information allows you to determine market supply and demand and provides accurate yardsticks from which to make timely pricing decisions of your own.

The chart in Exhibit 2.10 provides your company's prices relative to the competition during key selling periods of the year. It also allows the marketer to determine the pricing policies of the competition. Note that competitors A and D raise their

Exhibit 2.11 Distribution of Sales by Price Point (5-Year Trend)

	Price Range Industry Category		Price Range Company's Product	
	Percent of Sales	Percent of Items	Percent of Sales	Percent of Items
1996				
$0–$10	5	5	0	0
11–$20	5	10	5	5
21–$30	35	25	5	5
31–$40	25	25	15	15
41–$50	10	15	15	10
51–$60	10	10	25	30
61–$70	5	5	25	25
71+	5	5	10	10
1995				
$0–$10				
11–20				
21–30				
31–40				
41–50				
51–60				
61–70				
71+				
1994				
$0–$10				
11–$20				
21–$30				
31–$40				
41–$50				
51–$60				
61–$70				
71+				
1993, etc.				
1992, etc.				

prices during the spring and lower them in the August/September period. If this happened year after year, it would become evident it was a planned policy created in response to demand. You may also determine periods where competitors typically lower prices and use this knowledge when developing competitive pricing and promotion strategies.

Distribution of Sales by Price Point

In figuring the distribution of sales by price range relative to the competition, you determine what percent of the product category purchases are at each price level (low, medium, and high). Then compare your product's price category to the distribution of category sales by price point. You might be surprised to find that your major price category accounts for a small percentage of category sales or that there has been increased sales growth in your product's price category. This information will allow you to judge the potential impact of your pricing decisions later in the marketing plan (see Appendix B for worksheets to use in developing information specific to your company).

The chart in Exhibit 2.11 provides details of the percent of sales and percent of items sold by price range for the product category and your company. The chart allows for a trend comparison of sales by price over three years for both the category and the company. It also provides for comparison of pricing between the company and the category as a whole. From Exhibit 2.11, one can easily see the company's sales come from higher priced items compared to the industry category. This pricing should be consistent with an upscale target market and a positioning based on quality. Appendix B contains a chart that you can complete with information pertinent to your business.

Price Elasticity

Consumer purchase behavior responds directly to price changes. The effect and extent of price changes on consumer demand for a product is measurable in terms of price elasticity. Demand for a product is considered to be price elastic if sales go down when the price is raised and sales go up if the price is lowered. Demand for a product is considered to be price inelastic if demand is not significantly affected by changes in price.

Actual price elasticity can be determined in two ways. One method is through simulation research; the other method is through actual price changes in test markets. However, the way many marketers determine or estimate price elasticity is by monitoring competitive price changes and price changes on their own products and then noting the resulting effects on sales. This can be done by obtaining market share figures through secondary sources; by talking to consumers of your product, sales representatives, buyers, and wholesalers; or by shopping your competitors to determine the results of various price changes.

Cost Structure

The cost structure of your product relative to the selling price should be reviewed. This information will need to be available when you establish your pricing segment later in the plan. The following should be included:

- Fixed and variable costs associated with the selling of your product

- Cost of goods sold

- Margin and profit

- Gross price or gross sales figure

Questions to be Addressed
Price of Your Product

- What is the pricing structure for the product category? Are there price point products, brands, or stores that sell for more or less than yours? Is there a range from premium to off-price/discount pricing in your industry?

- What is the pricing structure for your product relative to the competition? Does the relationship of your product's price to that of the competition change during different selling seasons? Has it changed over a period of years?

- In addition to pure price, are discounts, credit, promotional allowances, return policies, restocking charges, shipping policies, etc., important to the ultimate sale of your product?

Distribution of Sales by Price Point

- What is the distribution of sales by price point for your industry and your company (five-year trend)? Do the majority of sales fall in one price category, or can consumers or businesses be segmented by price point?

- What has been the trend in pricing (five-year trend)? Are there price segments that are growing or shrinking?

Price Elasticity

- How price elastic is your product category? When you raise and/or lower the price, how does it affect demand? Are consumers price sensitive to your product category?

- Where is your product priced in relation to your major competitors? Why is it priced where it is?

Pricing Strengths and Weaknesses

- Finally, based upon the above analysis, what are your company's strengths and weaknesses as compared to your competitors?

Task 7
Competitive Review

This competitive analysis section is designed to provide you with a summary of how your company is performing in comparison to the competition across key marketing and communication variables. This step forces you to consider strategic and tactical differences and similarities in product marketing between your company and the competition. An analysis of your company's marketing activities in relation to the competition can provide benchmark information necessary to prepare your marketing plan. This knowledge will provide insights into potential defensive or offensive strategies which you can include in the marketing plan to curtail or exploit a major competitor's strength or weakness. In addition, by thoroughly studying your past marketing efforts and those of the competition, you may look at successes and failures in a new light. There might be ways to modify some of your competitors' more successful programs and make them your own, or there might be changes that can be made to successful programs that will make them even better.

How to Organize and Analyze Competitive Information

You should review your company and your competitors in terms of sales, target market, positioning, marketing objectives and strategies, positioning, product/branding/packaging, pricing, distribution, personal selling techniques, promotion strategies and expenditures, customer service, merchandising, and publicity. Make sure to review the previous two years and, if possible, project competitive activity into the future. Past years' successes and failures for both your company and your competitors can be great learning tools.

You should also consider the results of your marketing testing and research and development program. Did you introduce any new products, line extensions, services, merchandise, or store concepts? Did you test different approaches in your advertising message? Did you test the use of new and/or investment spending? Did you test various promotional offers? What can you learn from past tests that can be

Exhibit 2.12 Annual Competitive Spending Analysis

				Television			Newspaper		
Institution	Total Dollar Expenditures	Share of Spending: Total Expenditures	Change From Last Year	Total Dollar Expenditures	Percent	Change from Last Year	Total Dollar Expenditures	Percent	Change from Last Year
City S&L	$200,000	11%	+10%	$100,000	20%	+20%	$50,000	10%	−10%
First Bank									
State Bank									
Farmer's Bank									
United S&L									

Note: The above information should also be obtained on a quarterly basis to track seasonality of spending. If available, total dollars for each category should also be obtained.

translated into future success? If you have been doing the same things year after year, you should explore new uses of your marketing tools to ensure a competitive edge that will help guarantee increased sales and profits year after year.

Competitive analyses are not easy to complete because it is often difficult to obtain specific information about competitors. However, you can use secondary sources, some of which are listed in Chapter 1 and on the worksheets in Appendix B. We also encourage you to attend trade shows and shop your competition by purchasing your competitors' products.

In addition, there is a lot to be learned from media representatives regarding the media expenditures of your competitors. Exhibit 2.12 provides a review of competitive spending as compared to your company. The example utilizes banks in a given market and traces share of voice or media spending by dollar amount over a two year period (see Appendix B for worksheet).

Finally, one of the best ways to obtain competitive information is through awareness, attitude, and behavior primary research. If your company uses market tracking surveys, you can determine trends of the following:

- Awareness levels of competitors relative to your company

- Ranking of product attributes and consumers' rating of key product attributes for your company relative to the competition

- Market share estimates for competitors relative to your company

- Purchase ratios/trial and repeat purchases for your product relative to the competition

- Shopping habits for your product versus the competition (normally shop first, etc.)

Summary of Strengths and Weaknesses

Review your past marketing strategies and those of your competitors by answering the questions to be addressed and then completing the competitive analysis summary in Exhibit 2.13. The chart provides a brief competitive summary in graphic form for quick reference and comparison purposes. A worksheet is provided in Appendix B for you to complete with information specific to your company.

Exhibit 2.12 continued

Magazine			Radio			Outdoor		
Total Dollar Expenditures	Percent	Change from Last Year	Total Dollar Expenditures	Percent	Change from Last Year	Total Dollar Expenditures	Percent	Change from Last Year
$10,000	15%	—%	$30,000	15%	+4%	$10,000	12%	–30%

After a thorough review of your company and the competition, summarize your findings by developing a list of strengths and weaknesses across all marketing categories for your company and the competition.

Questions to Be Addressed

Market Share

- What is the trend in your company's market share and sales relative to key competitors? What is the market share growth/decline for your company or product over the past five years? What is the competitive set and relative market share overall, in your primary geographic area, and from market to market?

Target Market

- What is your primary target market? What percent of sales does it account for? How does this compare to the industry and your key competition?

- Is the description of your heavy users the same as that of the industry's or your key competitors?

Marketing Objectives/Strategies

- What are your company's marketing objectives and strategies? How do they appear to differ from your key competitors?

Whenever possible, develop answers for the past two years and project activity for the upcoming year.

Positioning

- What is the positioning of your company and your competitors? Is your positioning preemptive? Do you have a strong positioning relative to your competitors?

- Is your positioning dominating a strong attribute that is important to your target market?

Product

- What are your product's strengths and weaknesses relative to the competition?

Exhibit 2.13 Competitive Analysis

	Your Company	Competitor A	Competitor B	Competitor C	Competitor D
Market Share/Sales					
Current	15%/175MM	19%/225MM	26%/300MM	11%/125MM	8%/90MM
Growth/Decline past 5 years	+2 pts./+4%	+10 pts./+12%	−5 pts./−8%	+5 pts./+5%	−10 pts./−15%
Target Market					
Primary	Female 18 to 34 with kids	Female 25 to 45 with kids	Female 18 to 34 without kids	Female 35+ with older kids	Female 18 to 34 without kids
	Income $35M+	Income $20M+	Income $40M+	Income $50M+	Income $35M+
Secondary	Female 35 to 54	Female 25 to 54 Male 25 to 54	Female 35 to 54 Male 35 to 54	Female 35+	Female 35 to 54

Marketing Objectives/Strategies

Positioning

Product/Branding/Packaging
Strengths
Weaknesses

Pricing Strategies/Pricing Structure

**Distribution/Store Penetration/
Market Coverage Strategy**
Geographic sales territory
Store/Outlet locations and description
  of locations (e.g., for retailers strip
  center, mall, etc.)

Personal Selling Strategies

Customer Service Policies

Promotion Strategies

Advertising Message

Media Strategies and Expenditures
TV
Radio
Newspaper
Outdoor
Direct mail
Other

Merchandising Strategies

Publicity Strategies

**Testing/Research &
Development Strategies**

**Summary of Strengths and
Weaknesses**

Pricing

- Are your prices the same, lower, or higher than the competition?

Distribution/Store Penetration/Market Coverage Strategy

- How does your distribution strategy differ from that of your competitors?

Personal Selling

- What was your sales performance last year? Did you meet your goals?

- How does your company's selling philosophy differ from that of your competitors? Are there different methods that you may want to consider in the future? If so, why?

Customer Service Policies

- What are your company's customer service policies? Do they differ from the competition's? If so, how?

Promotion

- Do you rely more, the same, or less on promotion as compared to your competition?

- What were the results of your company's promotions and those of your competitors last year? What was successful or unsuccessful? Why? How does your company's promotions differ from those of your competitors?

- What promotions does your competition execute that are particularly successful?

Advertising Message

- How does your advertising compare to that of your competitors? Is it similar or different? What is the message of your advertising as compared to your major competitors?

- How successful has your advertising been relative to your competitors' advertising? Based not just on your judgment but on objective research, what are the strengths and weaknesses of your advertising and that of your competitors?

Media Strategy and Expenditures

- Where, when, and how do you and your competitors use the media?

- What is the media spending both overall and by medium for your company and your competitors? Do you dominate any one medium? Where are your competitors the strongest? How does this situation compare from market to market?

Merchandising

- What is the merchandising philosophy of your competitors? Is your merchandising similar or different to that of the competition? Why? Does your merchandising help to communicate your positioning? Which specific merchandising executions by your company and the competition appear to be most effective?

Publicity

■ Do you have an active publicity program? Does your competition? How much publicity did your product receive versus competitive products? What was effective?

Testing/Marketing Development

■ What tests did your company and the competition execute in the past year? Were they successful? What did you learn from the tests?

Summary of Strengths and Weaknesses

■ Based on the information above, what are the strengths and weaknesses of your company as compared to each major competitor?

STEP 3: TARGET MARKET EFFECTORS

This step moves our analysis to the next level of identifying customer and non-customer segments and their awareness, perceptions, and behavior toward your product(s). In the Product and Market review you were analyzing a first level of target market behavior, as measured by product performance—company and product sales, purchases by price points, and use of distribution channels. In this section, we look at the next critical level of consumer and customer understanding—segmentation, or the breaking of the aggregate consumer or customer of products identified in Section II of the business review into groups of consumers or customers with similar needs, wants, or purchase patterns. From this point on, we will look at these segments to learn everything we can about their awareness, attitude, and behavior towards your product and its product category. This information will be the bridge to developing marketing objectives and strategies later in the marketing plan.

The target market effectors are based upon the premise that the marketer must first define target segments. The marketer must then determine the segment's awareness to the products or company, the needs in terms of attributes, how the product or company is ranked on those needs, and finally, trial or behavior.

More specifically, the target market effectors help you analyze your business in the following manner.

Target Market

Determine for the industry and for your company the market segments which purchase the product. Provide the following:

—Description of segment

—Size of segment/number of potential purchasers

—What dollar volume sales segment accounts for

—Profit attributed to segment

Awareness

For each of the above segments, measure the awareness for your product and industry products (competitive products).

Attributes

For each of the defined segments, determine the most important purchase attributes (e.g., product quality, after-sale service, selection, security, price, etc.). Then rank your product's performance against that of the industry and/or specific competitors.

Trial

Determine the percent of the target market universe which has tried your product. Also, determine other key behavior variables relevant to your product category, such as average number of purchases a customer makes, the dollars spent per purchase, and the decision-making process.

Example: In the target market section you might have determined that one segment of purchasers was research and development staff positions at food companies. You determined how many there were in the industry and how many customers you had in this segment. You then determined the volume from the R&D food company sales. Now, be specific as to how many R&D staff people from food companies have ordered from you within the past year. Determine the average order amount and the average order dollars, among other behavior data.

Retrial

What percent of the customers initially try your product and then make a repeat purchase?

By breaking the target market effectors into the steps consumers take when purchasing (awareness of product, the formation of attitudes, trial, and retrial) we can identify areas of concentration later in the marketing plan.

Example: A product is competing in a large market segment, yet only a small percentage of the target market is aware of the product. Of those who are aware of the product, there are strong, positive attitudes, trial, and retrial.

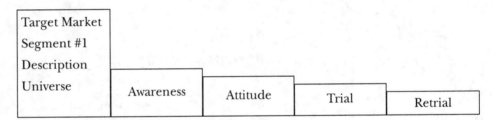

In this situation, there is an adequate target market universe, but the volume of actual customers is small. (See the small trial level relative to the potential target market box.) The problem is a low awareness level. One potential solution here would be to increase awareness, with the assumption that a percentage of those who are aware will try and retry the product.

Example: A product is competing in a large target market segment; a significant percentage of the target market is aware of the product, but their positive attitudes are small in comparison.

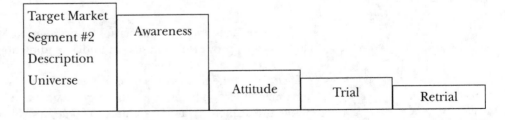

Here the problem is poor attitudes. In this situation, the target market is large enough and awareness is high, but there is a big drop in positive attitudes and relatively small trial and retrial percentages. The solution here would involve product changes and communication addressing the attitude problems.

Target Market Effectors—What's Needed and How To Use Them

Target Market	Awareness	Attitude	Behavior *(Trial and Retrial)*
	WORK TO DO IN BUSINESS REVIEW		
• Determine category and company product segments • Define number of potential consumers and customers in each segment • Determine sales volume accountable to each segment	• Determine awareness by segments—company product versus competition	• Determine attribute importance by segment • Determine company/product ranking	• Average purchase amount, frequency purchase for each industry consumer and company segment • Trial and retrial per industry and company segment • Decision-making process for each industry and company/product segment
	USE IN MARKETING PLAN		
• Defining target markets	• Communication Awareness Goals (Example: increase unaided awareness from 10% to 14%) • Communication strategies • Spending strategies	• Communication Attitude Goals (Example: shift attitude rating from 40% to 60%) • Communication strategies • Product strategies	• Establish marketing objectives (Example: increase purchase frequency from 1.5 times per year at $38 to 2.0 times per year at $45)

There are many additional scenarios that can unfold in your plan. The above examples should provide a good start in understanding how we use this section of the business review later in the plan.

Each step of the hierarchy is used in specific sections of the marketing plan. The target market section helps define the target market and its size later in the plan. The middle two sequences, awareness and attribute, provide information needed to establish communication objectives and strategies. The behavior sequence is used to develop marketing objectives, because marketing objectives affect target market behavior quantitatively, translating to sales. A chart is located in Appendix B that you can complete pertinent to your company for the target market, awareness, attitude, trial and retrial hierarchy of this review.

Task 1
Review of Consumer and Business-to-Business Target Market Segments

The business review provides a format that sorts current and potential customers into segments. Segmenting allows customers to be grouped according to common demographic, product usage, or purchasing characteristics. This allows for the analysis of which customer group is currently most profitable and which noncustomer group has the most potential for your company. The end result of segmenting is that a company is able to focus its marketing resources against an ultimate target market that has some common characteristics. Instead of trying to be all things to all people, the company can direct its energies (its resources, messages, product, and other marketing mix elements) toward satisfying essentially one person, as characterized by the target market segment or segments. Such directed efforts are considerably more effective and efficient.

The business review further provides a format which describes the profile of the current category consumer as compared to the company's current customer. This allows the marketer to determine if the company's customer is different from the general product category consumer. The similarities and differences will be important when determining future marketing strategies. A company may find that its product is consumed by a far older population than the general product category's consumer. This important information can be used in the marketing plan to further target this older age segment or to develop plans to attract more of the younger, mainstream consumers.

Volume and Concentration

Two measures by which target markets can be determined from data are volume and concentration. Simmons Market Research Bureau (SMRB) and Mediamark Research, Inc. (MRI) provide these data for most consumer categories. See Chapter 1, Sources of Information.

- *Volume:* The total number of purchases or percent of total purchases attributable to any given demographic target market segment. An example would be: Total sales in a category equal $1MM, and 18 to 24 year olds constitute 15 percent of the total purchases, or $150M. (Throughout this book M = thousands, and MM = millions.)

- *Concentration:* The percent within a given demographic target market segment that purchase the product. An example would be: Of all 18 to 24 year olds, 80 percent are purchasers of the product.

Volume is the most critical of the two measures from the standpoint that a company must have a large enough target market base and resulting sales base to sustain an ongoing business. At this point in the business review, your job is to analyze the potential target market by determining segments based upon similar demographic and purchasing characteristics. However, keep in mind that the segments must be large enough to assure adequate volume potential. (The method of determining demand using a demand analysis is covered in the target market chapter.)

Volume can be measured in terms of purchases (units or dollars) or in terms of actual numbers of consumers (purchasers or users). In the chart shown in Exhibit 2.14, for matters of consistency, we use the term purchases.

This chart demonstrates the demographic profile in terms of age for the product category nationally from a volume standpoint. If more than one brand exists or if there are segments within your business, a chart for each should be developed. If you

Exhibit 2.14 National Demographic Description of Product Category Consumers: Volume Measure

Demographic Descriptor	Percent of Total Population (210MM)*	Percent of Total Purchases ($900MM)†
Age		
Under 18	18%	36%
18 to 24		
25 to 34		
35 to 44		
45 to 54		
55+		

*This number provides a total population number. In this example, the total universe of teens through 55+ is 210MM. (Throughout this book, M = thousands and MM = millions.) With this total figure you can calculate the total population for each demographic category. For example, the total population for 18 to 24 year olds would be 18% × 210MM = 37.8MM.

†This number provides the total dollar volume or unit volume of the category depending upon which measure you use for percent of total purchases. In this example, the total dollar purchases for the product category are $900MM. This information allows you to calculate the dollar volume potential for each demographic category. For example, the total purchases for 18 to 24 year olds would be 36% × $900MM = $324MM.

Note: A similar chart would be developed for all products, product categories, or services your company sells.

sell shoes, a chart for total shoe purchases and separate charts for athletic, dress, casual, and children's shoe purchasers should be developed.

The easiest way to determine a volume measure is to look at the "percentage of total purchases" column to determine the percent of purchases for which each demographic category is responsible.

Exhibit 2.15 demonstrates the demographic profile of the product category nationally from a concentration standpoint. A chart for you to fill in with data pertinent to your own business appears in Appendix B.

Volume numbers are often a function of category size, while concentration numbers are a true measure of the propensity to purchase. There may be more 25- to 34-year-old purchasers of shoes than 18- to 24-year-old purchasers because of the large number of 25- to 34-year-olds in the population. Yet, for particular styles of shoes, while there are fewer total 18- to 24-year-old purchasers, the age category may demonstrate a greater concentration of purchases. For example, 25- to 34-year-olds may constitute 22 percent of total purchases for a particular style of shoe and 18- to 24-year-olds only 15 percent (volume measure), yet the data may show that only 20 percent of the 25- to 34-year-olds purchase the style of shoe, compared to 40 percent of the 18- to 24-year-olds (concentration measure).

Thus, the marketer may find it more profitable to concentrate on the 18- to 24-year-olds when selling specific styles of shoes. A high concentration of purchasers within a specific demographic category allows for a more efficient and effective marketing effort. The marketer can focus on addressing the similar needs and characteristics of the consumers in the category. There is not much wasted effort, since a vast majority of the people in the category demonstrate a propensity to purchase the product.

In summary, both volume and concentration must be taken into consideration when developing a target market database. Volume is a benchmark type of variable. There must be enough people interested in purchasing the product in order to justify any business. Once volume levels are deemed sufficient, concentration numbers

Exhibit 2.15 National Demographic Description of Product Category Consumers: Concentration Measure

Demographic Descriptor	Percent of Category That Purchases Product (75%*)	Concentration Index: Category/Total
Age		
Under 18	40%	53
18 to 24	50*	66*
25 to 34	75	100
35 to 44	90	120
45 to 54	100	133
55+	50	66

*Nationally, 50 percent of the 18- to 24-year-olds purchase the product; 75 percent of the total population purchase the product. The index of 66 is derived from dividing 50 by 75 and tells the marketer that 18- to 24-year-olds have a lower propensity to purchase the product category than does the whole population.

can further define demographic target market categories by showing strong propensities to purchase within given demographic categories.

Industry Category versus Company Target Market

It is important to develop target market databases for both the industry product category nationally and for your company's purchasers. This will allow you to compare the two profiles to see if your company's target market description matches that of the industry product category. If not, you can spend time determining why and how the differences might help or hurt your situation. One of our retail clients determined that their target market skewed younger (18 to 34) than purchasers nationally, even though the client's marketing was planned to correlate to the heavy user in the category, women ages 25 to 44 with children. While our client did well against the heavy user target market, the data showed that they could improve relative to the competition through new marketing and product strategies.

Exhibit 2.16 demonstrates the demographic profile of your company's purchaser as compared to the average purchaser profile nationally. A chart that you can complete with information specific to your own business is included in Appendix B.

Review of Consumer Segmentation Methods

The following six segmentation methods are common to many businesses. As just described, all depend on looking at profiles which have high volume or concentrations in terms of users/purchasers and/or purchases. Each of the methods should also compare the industry category with the company/product as discussed above.

Customer Tenure Segmentation

Many times there are purchasing differences based upon how long the customer has been doing business with your company. First-year customers may not buy as much, purchase as many times, utilize your entire product mix, or come back next

Exhibit 2.16 Demographic Description of Company Purchasers Compared to Category Purchasers

Demographic Descriptor	Percent of Purchasers of Product Nationally ($100MM)*	Percent of Purchasers of Company Product ($20MM)*	Index: Company to National Purchasers
Age			
Under 18	10%	10%	100
18 to 24	20[†]	10[†]	50[†]
25 to 34	40	30	75
35 to 44	10	20	200
45 to 54	10	20	200
55+	10	10	100
Total	100%	100%	

*This provides a total dollar volume figure to help calculate total dollars for each demographic category. For example, the total dollar volume for the category is $100MM. Total dollar volume for the company is $20MM. Company purchases among 18- to 24-year-olds is $2MM (10% × $20MM).

[†]20 percent of the purchasers of the product are 18 to 24 nationally, while 10 percent of your company's purchasers are 18 to 24. This results in an index of 50, meaning that your company sells to 18- to 24-year-olds at half the expected average (the average being an index of 100).

year (retrial) as often as longer-term customers. If so, a natural first segmentation is new versus old customers.

Demographic Segmentation (Description and Size)

The marketer's traditional method of defining purchaser and user groups and segmenting markets is by utilizing demographic factors. There are many examples of segments developed to demographic drivers where a specific demographic is responsible for the majority of the sales. One example would be the use of higher education or colleges. The vast majority of the users of higher education are 18–24, with family incomes above $40M. Another example would be travel. The majority of cruises are taken by older adults. This is a period in their lives when they are unencumbered by children and have the disposable income, time, and interest to travel.

Demographics can be determined for either individuals or households (the configuration of individuals making up a living unit). Following is a brief discussion of the demographics that should be analyzed to determine if current or potential consumers can be segmented or grouped according to common similarities and to determine your company's customer profile as compared to the category customer. The key to determining segments is identifying whether a specific demographic or combination of demographic variables predicts a significant volume or concentration of usage or purchases. For each of the pertinent demographic segments, list the number of consumers for the category and number of customers for your product based upon the most pertinent demographic descriptors.

Sex

There are often major differences between male and female purchasing and usage habits. Sex is often used in conjunction with another demographic descriptor to define the target market. For a regional HMO, The Hiebing Group research determined that women are the most influential decision makers in family health care decisions. Marketing, communication, product, and merchandising decisions reflect the particular needs and tastes of this segment.

Age

Target markets can be broken out by age. Many times age determines the needs and wants of a specific product brand or service. Most beer companies recognize the importance of young adults (from legal drinking age to age 34) in the consumption of beer. Studies have shown that males within this age group are above average and heavy users. More importantly, many beer drinkers form lifelong brand preferences during this time period. Thus, age is a very important demographic variable not only for beer companies, but for many marketers.

Whenever possible, try to gather demographic information by media age breaks (2 plus, 2 to 11, 6 to 11, 12 to 17, 18 plus, 18 to 24, 18 to 34, 18 to 49, 25 to 49, 25 to 54, 55 plus). This will allow for more accurate media planning and buying. It will also allow for a better direct link from target market definition to actual purchasing of media designed to reach the target market. Unfortunately, media breaks consistent with national rating services such as Nielsen and Arbitron don't always correspond to secondary sources of target market information such as SMRB and MRI, but for consistency purposes, try to use media demographic categories whenever possible.

Income

Income can predict in broad terms what a family's lifestyle will be like. There are many product categories, such as cars, appliances, and leisure goods, for which purchases rise with increase in income. Yet purchase rates for other more basic product categories, such as food, remain fairly stable regardless of income size. Income is often combined with geographic information to further determine the location of specific consumers. Marketers often pinpoint geographic census tracks that have households with approximately the same income range. Identification of these clusters can determine the locations of new outlets for retailers who do well against the identified income range. The clusters can also be used in media selection, such as targeted direct mail, or for the advertising or promotion of income-sensitive product offerings.

Education

In general, the higher the individual's education, the higher the income. Thus, education and income are often analyzed in tandem.

Occupation

Similar to education, income is also a function of occupation. While some of the major differences between white-collar and blue-collar purchasing habits have diminished due to double incomes, there are still major buying patterns affected by occupation. For example, the carpenters, craftspeople, and foremen professions spend less for clothing and purchase different clothing than service, professional, and clerical workers.

In working with a regional menswear store, it was determined that there were differences in purchasing rates of suits not only between white-collar and blue-collar professions, but also within white-collar professions. Salesmen, for example, purchased suits at greater rates than some other business professionals. In addition, occupation combined with age further delineated the purchasing segments. Young professionals spent at greater rates than average on suits, because they were establishing wardrobes far different from the clothes they wore in college. Conversely, the number of suits purchased drops slightly as the younger person ages and starts a family. Purchases increase again as that individual gets older, reaches the top of his profession, and can afford to purchase suits more often.

Family/Household Size

Family size often determines the quantity sold to the household, with larger households purchasing greater amounts. Family size may dictate that greater quantities of a product are used within a given household, but each person within a family may or may not use more of the product than an individual living alone. Thus, per capita rates of purchasing should also be taken into consideration when developing target markets.

Family size is often combined with the age of the family to identify the family's lifestyle as determined by its life cycle. At The Hiebing Group, we tend to break the family life cycle into five categories: single under 35, married under 35 with no children, married under 35 with children, married 35 or over with no children, and single 35 or over. Each category has different purchasing patterns and often purchases similar products in different quantities. For example, households with small children purchase products like quick, easy-to-prepare meal packages, appliances, diapers, hot dogs, and household cleaners at greater rates than other family groupings.

Region/Geography

Many products are not sold evenly across the country due to distribution capabilities of the manufacturing company or to the unique and differing tastes, lifestyles, and needs of consumers. You should determine the geographic location of your potential consumers as well as the varying levels of usage by geographic area. A situation may exist in which a region has very few actual consumers, but those consumers consume at higher than normal levels, making that region more important than the small number of customers would indicate. (Actual usage levels by geographic region are determined through Category Development and Brand Development indexes discussed under the Trial Behavior section of Target Market Effectors.)

There are many examples of targeting by geography. Small-town women have a much higher incidence of purchasing crafts through the mail. There are a host of weather-related products which have northern geographic targets, such as downhill skis. And there are regional fads and consumption patterns which skew consumption to one area or region of the county. An example would be bratwursts in Wisconsin (due to the German influence), the beignet in New Orleans, and grits in the South.

In preparing a business review for a real estate firm, we discovered that total population and total home sales outside the city, but still within the metro area, had experienced twice the growth than that of the city itself. We also found that the firm's share of home sales was high in the city but low outside the city in the metro area, which was the major growth area. Based on this comparative data, the marketing program was developed to target home buyers and sellers in suburban areas throughout the metro area as well as in the city. The marketing plan called for a targeted advertising strategy that resulted in the advertising theme, "East side, west side, all around the county, your home is our profession." In addition, the marketing plan recommended broad metro media coverage and the opening of branch offices on the periphery of the city. The results of this geographic targeting were dramatic increases in the realtor's sales and profits, with its market share of home sales going from fourth to first in two years. A chart for you to fill in specific to this information can be found in Appendix B.

Questions to Be Addressed

- Do the different user groups have differing demographics? What is their size in terms of volume of purchases and number of consumers?

- What is the industry category (consumer) demographic profile of the product category nationally? What is the profile of the individuals who consume or purchase the most from a volume standpoint? Do some demographic categories have a higher concentration of purchasers?

- Do new customers purchase at different rates than older established customers?

- Which consumer profile or segments are growing the fastest in terms of volume?

- What is your customer's demographic profile? How would you describe your customers in terms of age, sex, income, occupation, education, number of children, marital status, geographic residence, and ownership of home?

- Do your dominant customer segments differ from the dominant industry category segments?

- What company customer segments are growing the fastest in terms of volume?

- How many customers purchase your product? How many potential industry consumers exist in your product category? Has the number of consumers been growing or shrinking over the past five years?

- Are there geographic areas where the product category is purchased at greater rates? How many industry consumers and customers are there in each geographic area?

Product Usage Segmentation

For some products, demographics aren't as important as the reason the product is purchased or how it is used. Many times purchasers with similar demographics purchase the product for different reasons. This offers the opportunity to segment consumers based upon usage of the product. Baking soda is purchased by women who bake from scratch and need the product in the baking process. It is also purchased a refrigerator deodorizer. Many of the purchasers of baking soda as a deodorizer do not bake on a regular basis, so they do not purchase the product for baking. Thus, usage of this product helps define customer segments, and knowledge of the customers' usage is critical to determining how this product would be marketed to each of the two customer groups.

There is an opportunity in the banking business to develop target markets based upon how consumers use the bank services. For example, younger users of banks have a significantly higher propensity than older bank customers to utilize automatic teller machines. Younger customers also need credit cards and inexpensive checking. This is in comparison to middle-aged consumers, who need lines of credit, home equity loans, and serving instruments for college education.

We targeted users of Triptiks, a AAA map product for road travelers. These people were traveling and coming into AAA, yet they had a very poor rate of using AAA travel services (reservations, tickets, etc.) beyond the use of the maps.

Questions to Be Addressed

- How is the product used in terms of the overall product category? Is the industry product used in the same manner as your company's product?

- If there are multiple uses of your product, are there consumers who use the product for one type of use or benefit but not another? Are there multiple, independent user groups? How many consumers and customers are there for each of the uses?

■ Are there products purchased by a specific target market which might be used as a foundation to cross-sell the target to other company products?

Psychographic/Lifestyle Segmentation

Marketers effectively use lifestyle factors or psychographics to help identify target markets. Lifestyle descriptors attempt to define a customer segment in terms of the attitudes, interests, and activities of the consumer. This is an attempt to go further than demographic descriptors to really get inside the consumer's mind. A description of your consumers, taking into consideration some of the following, is helpful in further describing and defining the target market.

■ *Personality descriptors:* Do your customers tend to be affectionate, likable, dominating, authoritative, passive, independent, self-assured, sociable, stubborn, followers, leaders, conformists, experimenters, individualists, etc.?

■ *Activities:* Do your customers engage in outdoor or indoor sports, cultural events, environmental activities, political activism, volunteer groups, social clubs, home entertainment, travel, etc.?

■ *Purchase Attitudes:* Are your customers economy minded, impulsive, planners, price conscious, style conscious, value conscious, quality driven, self-service oriented, status conscious, purchasing with cash or credit, etc.?

Lifestyle segmentation is usually combined with demographics to form a more precise definition of the target market. For example, we worked with a financial advisor firm that specialized in environmentally sound investment options, targeting high income individuals who were environmentally aware and concerned.

Lifestyle characteristics can often be combined with demographics to form a more precise definition of a target market.

There are four lifestyle systems which are commonly used: PRIZM, ClusterPlus 2000, VALS 2, and MicroVision.

PRIZM

PRIZM is an acronym for Potential Rating Index for Zip Markets. Under this system, every neighborhood is assigned to one of 62 different clusters, each defined by a combination of demographic and lifestyle characteristics. These clusters have somewhat colorful names describing the type of people that live there. Examples include Blue Blood Estates, Towns and Gowns, and Shotguns and Pickups.

(PRIZM is a lifestyle segmentation analysis developed by Claritus, a division of VNU Information Services. VNU is a family of marketing information companies organized by three groups—consumer targeting, advertising expenditures, and multimedia measurement.)

For example, those living in Blue Blood Estates clusters tend to be the following:

■ 35–54 years old

■ College graduates

■ $94,500 household income

■ Professional

- Belong to a country club
- Own mutual funds
- Have a car phone
- Watch golf on TV
- Read business magazines

On the other hand, those living in the Shotguns and Pickups cluster tend to be the following:

- 35–64 year olds
- High school graduates
- $29,300 household income
- Blue collar, farmers
- Smoke pipe tobacco
- Have medical loss-income insurance
- Purchase Canadian whiskey
- Listen to country radio
- Read hunting and car and truck magazines

A PRIZM analysis of your customer database might show, for example, a very high concentration of people in a Shotgun and Pickup cluster. You now have a much better picture of your primary target consumer and are more able to tailor a message or promotion that would tie directly to the lifestyles of these consumers. In addition, efforts to expand the business into other geographic areas can be focused towards those areas that are also Shotgun and Pickup Clusters, since these areas would probably have the highest potential for success.

Therefore, these systems benefit you in two ways:

1. They provide a better and deeper definition of your primary target consumer.

2. They help you find more people just like the primary target consumer.

ClusterPlus 2000

Conceptually, this system is very similar to PRIZM. Though the descriptive names are somewhat different, they have a comparable number of clusters (60 versus 62) and each basically segments the population according to a combination of both demographic and psychographic factors.

Most media vehicles can be directionally measured against the various clusters, and many direct mail lists are PRIZM and ClusterPlus coded, which means that one can rent a list of people who fall within specific clusters.

VALS 2

Another system that helps define target markets beyond the standard demographic definitions is VALS 2 (Values and Lifestyles, a product of SRI). VALS 2 separates the population into eight segments, each defined in terms of attitudes, distinct behavior, and decision-making patterns. VALS 2 is built on a self-orientation concept (how one sees himself as an "achiever") coupled with a definition of the resources (income, education level, etc.) that people have at their disposal to accomplish their goals.

Exhibit 2.17 VALS 2 Segmentation System

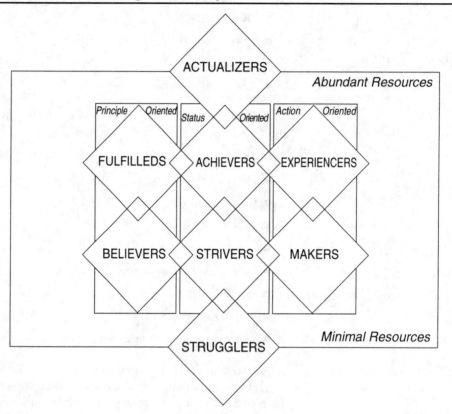

Self Concept   As defined by VALS 2, there are three self-orientations. Principle-oriented consumers are guided in their choices by abstract, idealized criteria, rather than by feelings, events, or desire for approval and opinions of others. Status-oriented consumers look for products and services that demonstrate the consumers' success to their peers. Action-oriented consumers are guided by a desire for social or physical activity, variety, and risk taking. (SRI International)

Resources   The area of resources refers to the full range of psychological, physical, demographic, and material means and capacities consumers have to draw upon. It encompasses education, income, self-confidence, health, eagerness to buy, intelligence, and energy level. (SRI International)

Exhibit 2.17 is a graphic description of the VALS 2 segmentation system.

One of the major differences between a system such as a PRIZM or ClusterPlus and VALS 2 is that, whereas the former provides insight into what people do, the latter provides insight as to why they do it. Put another way, whereas PRIZM will help you find the best consumers, VALS 2 will help you develop the best message. For that reason, a strong program might be one that makes use of both systems.

MicroVision

MicroVision classifies all U.S. consumer households into separate lifestyle segments on a zip code geographic level. Each segment represents a similar group of people in terms of lifestyle, media viewing, purchases, and spending levels.

The chart in Exhibit 2.18 provides an example of MicroVision.

Exhibit 2.18 MicroVision Example

Target market: MicroVision segments that represent prospects likely to become autoclub members for ACSC (Auto Club of Southern California).

MicroVision Segment and Description	Index ACSC/ Population	%HH Penetration	HH Non- Members
01 "Upper crust." 45–55. Very high income. Managers/professionals. Luxury homes. Eat out. Travel U.S. and overseas.	205*	75.7	23,034
09 "Building a homelife" parents. 25–44. With children in elementary school. Medium income/education. Technical/sales professionals. New home owners. Purchasing appliances. Value conscious. Family auto vacations.	179	65.8	6,195

*ACSC has more than twice the number of "upper crusts" in its membership compared to the overall population.

The point of the chart is that the two segments would be treated very differently in terms of appeals to join the autoclub. The value aspect of the club and road travel would be stressed for the "builders of home life" and the travel club aspect and privileges of ACSC would be stressed for "upper crust."

Questions to Be Addressed

- What are your customer's personality descriptors, activities, and interests?

- Do religious, political, or other social economic factors make a difference in the purchase of your product or service?

- Can you further break a demographic segment into subsegments based upon different lifestyle characteristics?

- How many industry consumers and company customers are there for each psychographic segment?

Attribute Segmentation

Some products are purchased because of specific product attributes. The segments can't be defined by age, but by a specific purchase attribute. In our work with Western Publishing, the primary segmentation variable for the game "Key To The Kingdom" was purchase or use of an adventure board game. Boys 8–16 bought all types of games. "The Key to the Kingdom" was purchased by boys in this age group that liked adventure games. In the roasted coffee business, the desire for quality coffee was the driver in defining segments who purchased whole bean and gourmet coffee. Thus, the whole bean coffee customer segment is defined primarily by attributes and not by age, income, or education demographics.

Exhibit 2.19 Example of How to Calculate Heavy User Segments From SMRB Data

Number of Home Plastic Files Purchased per Year*		Number of People Purchasing (M)		Total Product Purchased ($ or Units) (M)	
1	×	5,000	=	5,000	
2		4,000		8,000	
3		1,000		3,000	
4		1,000		4,000	
5		1,000	} 4,500	5,000	} 22,000
6		500		3,000	
7 Plus		1,000		7,000	
Total		13,500		35,000	

*Heavy user for home plastic files defined as three-plus purchases per year.

Heavy User Percentage: To compute add number of people purchasing three plus divided by total number of people (4,500/13,500 = 33%).

Heavy User Percentage of Purchases: To compute add total product purchased by people purchasing three plus divided by the total product purchased (22,000/35,000 = 63%).

Heavy users represent 33 percent of the total population of purchasers and account for 63 percent of the total dollar or unit purchases.

Questions to Be Addressed

- Is there a key attribute that defines how products in the industry category are purchased? Are there different purchasing segments based upon a desire for a different attribute?

- Is there a key attribute that determines purchases for your company products?

- How many industry consumers and company customers are there in each of the attribute segments?

Heavy User Segmentation

Most product categories have a group of heavy users—consumers who purchase or use the product at far greater rates than that of the average consumer. According to our definition, a category has a meaningful heavy-user segment if approximately one-third or less of the consumers account for approximately two-thirds or more of the purchases. A retail example of this can be found in the shoe business, where one-third of the purchasers buy more than 63 percent of the shoes. The demographic description of the heavy-user shoe purchaser is women 25 to 44 with children. A heavy-user shoe purchaser is further defined as someone who purchases seven or more pairs of shoes per year. (The average person purchases fewer than three pairs per year.)

Heavy users are important because they offer the potential of marketing to a smaller, more defined group of people who account for the majority of purchases. If you do not have primary research that determines the percent of purchasers attributable to the heavy user, you can make directional estimates by using Simmons Market Research Bureau (SMRB) or other secondary sources. Exhibit 2.19 presents an example of how to calculate a heavy user segment from the SMRB resource. Similar

Exhibit 2.20 Heavy User Demographic Descriptors Compared to All User Demographics Descriptors

	Heavy User Demographic Profile	Total Demographic Profile
Age	24 to 35	18 to 45
Sex	Female	Female
Household Income	$40M–$50M	$24M–$50M
Education	Graduated College +	Graduated High School +
Employment	White-Collar/Professional	White- and Blue-Collar
Family Size	4 plus	2 plus
Geography	Western United States	Midwest & Western United States
Home Ownership	Yes	Yes

Lifestyle Description of the Heavy User Compared to the Average User

The heavy user is far more social oriented than the average user. The heavy user is more style conscious and quality driven than the average user. Overall the heavy user is more upscale with attitudes and purchasing habits shaped by concern over family, neighborhood, and social expectations.

methods can be used with other secondary research information. If nothing is available to you, make the best estimate based upon your knowledge of the market.

In summary, it is important to determine if there is a heavy-user group in your product category. Then develop a demographic profile of the heavy-user group to determine if it is similar to your customer profile.

The chart in Exhibit 2.20 compares the heavy-user demographic profile to the total demographic profile (see Appendix B for a worksheet). This is essential information that will help you in making decisions such as whether to focus on a smaller, specialized segment of the market or cater to heavy users. Companies have done well using both approaches, but in either case you need to make sure that there are adequate numbers of potential customers in your defined target market and that you will be able to attract a sufficient number to purchase your product frequently enough to assure profitability. (See Step 10, Demand Analysis, for further detail.)

Questions to Be Addressed

- Is there a group of heavy purchasers of your product? What percent of the purchasers do they constitute and for what percent of the purchases are they responsible?

- What is the difference between the demographic and lifestyle profile of the heavy user and that of the overall user?

- How many heavy users are there in terms of the industry and in terms of your company customers?

Review of the Business-to-Business Segmentation Methods

Business-to-business firms typically have far fewer potential customers than consumer companies. In addition, each business-to-business customer usually generates larger sales than the typical consumer customer. As with consumer target markets, it is important to segment so that you can determine which type of business is most profitable and has the most potential for your company.

Target Market Segmentation and Standard Industrial Classification (SIC) Categories

One of the best ways to segment businesses is by utilizing Standard Industrial Classification (SIC) codes. Businesses are classified into ten different broad, two-digit SIC categories: Agriculture/Forestry/Fishing, Mining, Manufacturing, Construction, Transportation/Communication/Public Utilities, Wholesale Trade, Retail Trade, Finance/Insurance/Real Estate, Services, and Public Administration. Within each two-digit SIC category there are further breakouts into four- and eight-digit classifications. Within the Retail SIC there is category 56, Apparel and Accessory stores; and within category 56 there is 5611, Men's and Boy's Clothing.

Firms such as Dun's Marketing Services specialize in providing mailing lists and other market information for businesses according to any SIC classification. We have used Dun's to target specific types of businesses by industry type. We helped generate incremental sales for a statewide CPA firm by creating individual campaigns for small businesses within each SIC code. Different tailored messages were developed for retailers, the service industry, financial institutions, etc. Each industry received multiple marketing pieces explaining why specialized accounting practices were important for their specific business. The campaign was so successful that for every $1 the CPA firm invested, it had a return of $2—a 100 percent return on investment over a two-year period.

The first step in developing business-to-business target market segments is to break down your customer base by SIC. Next, determine how many different business segments you sell to. List the segments in which you have the most customers or clients first, and then continue listing the segments in sequential order from most customers to least. Finally, determine the penetration of each segment (percent of the total category that you can classify as a customer). Worksheets for completing these charts are found in Appendix B.

You may be surprised to find that you are doing business with multiple segments of businesses. You may also find that there are some segments where you do business with only a small percentage of the total, thus providing a large degree of growth potential. This information will help you define target markets and develop marketing strategies later in the plan.

Questions to Be Addressed

- To what SIC segments or other user segments do customers who purchase your product belong?

- What is the demand potential for your product? What is the penetration of your company in each SIC category? How many businesses that are in SIC categories that purchase product in your category are not purchasing from you? Why aren't they?

Other Methods of Segmenting

Once you have your target market broken into SIC categories, there are additional criteria you should evaluate to provide for a complete understanding of your target market.

Dollar Size   Determine the total company sales volume for each SIC, and then calculate the average dollar size of each client in the category(ies) by dividing the total company volume in each SIC by the number of clients you have in that SIC. When

Exhibit 2.21 Revenue Distribution of Clients by SIC Category

SIC	Number of Customers	Total Company Sales per SIC Category	Average $ per Client ($M)	Index to Average (Average $ per Client/Average All Categories)	Index to Average (Total Sales per SIC Category/Average $ per Client All Categories)
Agriculture/Forestry/Fisheries					
Mining					
Construction					
Manufacturing					
Transportation					
Public Utilities					
Wholesale Trade					
Retail Trade	100*	$100,000*	$1,000*	50*	100
Finance/Insurance/Real Estate Services					
Public Administration					
Total	500	$1,000,000			
Average All Categories	50	$100,000*	$2,000*		

*The company has 100 retail trade customers worth $100,000 in sales with the average dollar sales per retail client being $1,000. Based upon the norm for all categories, the retail trade indexes below the expected, or 50, for average dollars per client ($1,000/$2,000) and the expected, or 100, for total sales generated by SIC category ($100,000/$100,000). Thus total sales potential in this category is a function of the large number of businesses in the SIC, not the average sales per client.

combined with the penetration information developed earlier, this can tell you a lot about the current and future potential of the different categories. Exhibit 2.21 provides an overview of clients' revenues by SIC category. Compare this chart to previous charts breaking out customers and total businesses by SIC categories. (See Appendix B for a worksheet to complete with information specific to your company.) If an SIC classification averages substantially above other SIC classifications in terms of average dollar per client and your company has not fully penetrated that classification (your company's clients represent a small percentage of the total businesses in the SIC), then that classification should be targeted for further expansion.

Employee Size   Another way to segment business is by the number of employees, or employee size, of the firm. Employee size often is an indicator of the company's volume and how they do business. For example, large companies tend to be more centralized and have formalized organizational structures, while smaller companies tend to be less formalized. Pricing, product, and service requirements often differ between large and small companies. Thus, the marketing approach may differ due to a function of the size of the business customer.

Heavy Usage Rates   Are there categories of heavy or light users? Determine the reasons for this. Maybe a category of light users would become heavier users if you were to modify your product, service, or pricing. Or perhaps you should consider narrowing your firm's focus to concentrate on just the heavy-user categories, especially if the earlier analysis determined that there was potential growth in these categories.

The chart in Exhibit 2.22 provides the business-to-business firm with an alternative way to look at its business. This chart is for the firm with many types of customers across dealers and distributors or within one SIC. Worksheets for these analyses appear in Appendix B.

Product Application/Use   Essentially, this is how the organization uses your product. If you find that there are multiple different uses for your product, you can segment

Exhibit 2.22 Product Category Purchases by Outlet Type

Outlet Type	Where Crafts Are Purchased	Percent of Total Outlets	Company's Business
Craft store	86%*	21%*	15%
Needlecraft store	67	16	40
Discount store	64	15	30
Mail order	63	15	15
Department store	62	15	—
Craft supply chain store	41	10	—
Art material store	36	9	—
Total	419%	101%	100%

*86 percent of craft purchasers utilize craft stores to purchase crafts (most craft purchasers utilize more than one outlet, which is why the total equals 419 percent). However, craft stores account for only 21 percent of the total craft outlets, and only 15% of the company's business.

target markets by usage type and begin to provide more focused service and expertise to each segment.

Organizational Structure   Different companies have different organizational structures. Find out if your company sells better to one type of company than another. You might find you get more business from centralized organizations with formalized bidding procedures and thus want to target these types of businesses within the SICs you currently service. You might analyze why you don't do as well with decentralized entrepreneurial firms and then make changes to increase your success with them. Subsequently, you may do well targeting headquarters but perform poorly in generating sales from branches. In summary, you may need to develop independent marketing strategies and executions for different target groups as defined by their organization structure, purchasing habits, and purchasing requirements.

New versus Repeat Buyers   Some companies are good at getting new business and poor at developing long-term relationships. For others, it's just the opposite. Determine the percentage of your business that comes from new buyers versus repeat buyers. Analyze your ability to keep repeat customers. Correct your weaknesses if it becomes evident that you either aren't getting new business or can't develop long-term clients.

This area is a good client satisfaction check and should be analyzed yearly. It also allows you to develop alternative marketing strategies depending upon the type of customer (new versus repeat) you are targeting.

Geographic Location   In analyzing sales, you may determine that you are strong in one part of the country but weak in another. It could be the result of your distribution system, it might be caused by a competitive situation, or you may find that demand is higher in some geographical areas than others. In addition, you might discover that you do very well against a particular SIC category in one region of the country but that you haven't marketed to that SIC category elsewhere. By analyzing where your current business exists and where you have potential to expand, you can segment your target market by geographic location. Worksheets for these analyses appear in Appendix B.

Decision Makers and Influencers   Finally, you need to determine who actually decides to purchase your product and who influences the purchase of your product. Remember, *companies* don't buy products, *people* do. Analyze the purchase decision-making process. Describe who is the entry person at a company for your product. Also decide who makes the ultimate purchasing decision, how they arrive at the purchasing decision, what the purchasing criteria are, and to what degree people influence the purchaser. The purchaser may be a committee, which means you will need to target many individuals if all have an equal role in the decision process. Typically, the decision maker or purchaser becomes your primary target market, and those individuals influencing the decision become the secondary target market.

Questions to Be Addressed

- What is the revenue distribution for the industry category and your company by SIC or other applicable segments?

- How many industry category consumers and company customers are there for each SIC or other applicable segment?

- Based upon the above two questions, you can now calculate the average dollar revenue per industry category consumer and company customer. What are they?

- What is your company's penetration in each SIC segment? Do any of the segments with high average dollar per customer have low company penetration rates?

- What size are the companies that purchase from you? Do large companies respond differently from small ones? If so, why?

- Are there heavy users within SIC categories? Are some SIC categories heavier users than others?

- Do different SIC category businesses use your product for different purposes? Why do SIC categories use your product? Is your product used more by some industries than by others? Can you expand use to others?

- Are purchasers of your product original equipment manufacturers (OEMs) who utilize your product in the manufacturing of another product? Do they sell to another business or directly to the consumer? How exactly does your product fit into the OEM's manufacturing structure? Why is your product important? How is it used?

- What is the organizational structure of your customers' companies? Do you have more success with centralized companies than with decentralized? Why? Do purchasing procedures differ among customers? Do you get more business from companies with a single purchasing agent versus those with a purchasing committee that requires more formalized bidding?

- Are the majority of your customers new or repeat buyers? Why?

- Where are your customers located? Are there areas of the country that have businesses from SIC categories with which you are successful but which you currently are not covering? Are there potential customers that match your customer profile that you are not reaching? Do some parts of the country provide more business for you than others? If so, why? Is it due to servicing, distribution, sales efforts, or competitive factors? Or do some parts of the country use more product than other parts for other reasons?

- Who are the decision makers and influencers in the purchase of your product? What is the decision maker's function and role in the purchase decision? What is the decision sequence? What are the purchase criteria?

Task 2
Product Awareness
and Attributes

We have documented in case after case that an increase in awareness of a quality product leads to increases in purchase rates or, in the terminology of our firm, *increased share of mind leads to increased share of market.* Therefore, awareness of your product or service is an important barometer of its future success.

Product Awareness

Awareness is typically measured through primary research on two levels, unaided and aided. *Unaided* is generally considered a more accurate measure because it involves consumers recalling specific product names without any assistance. *Aided* awareness is the awareness generated by asking individuals which product they are familiar with after reading or reviewing with them a list of competing products. (See Appendix B for charts.)

When analyzing awareness, we typically review the following levels in order of importance.

Unaided Awareness

First mention, top of mind   This is the awareness level which will most closely parallel with market share. It is obtained through telephone research in which the interviewer asks the respondent which products or companies come to mind in a specific product category—shoes, propellers, spray-dried ingredients, banking services, etc. The respondent mentions the companies, firms, or products with which he or she is familiar, the *first* one mentioned being the first mention or top of mind. Typically, the first mentioned company or product is the first choice or one most recently purchased—a direct correlation to shopping intent.

Total Unaided   All companies or products mentioned without prompting are part of what is known as the evoked purchase set—considerations when the respondent purchases. In situations where more companies or products are mentioned than less, it is an indication that the category exhibits less loyalty from its purchasers and that there is more shopping around either before purchase or between purchase situations. This fact should be noted and used strategically later in the marketing plan. For example, in nonloyal categories, promotions are often heavily used to steal market share and customers with strong after-purchase retention programs.

Aided Awareness

Once the respondent has provided unaided responses, the interviewer can say "have you ever heard of _____." If the respondent says yes, it is considered aided awareness. We feel this is a very weak measure of association or familiarity with a company or product. However, it does serve as a disaster check. If, after prompting, the respondent has not heard of your product or company, there is little chance they will be a purchaser or customer.

Awareness by Segments

The awareness measures need to be broken out by the segments developed in the target market section. For example, let's say you determined there were three main segments for your high volume banking products as determined by age and product use.

Age	*Banking Product Use*
18–34	Checking, TYME machine, credit card
35–54	Credit (home loan, home equity, car loan)
55+	Savings (CD, money market, trust management)

You would need to determine awareness levels for all three age segments. You may find vastly different degrees of awareness from one segment to the next, signifying a need for different communication strategies and spending levels.

Awareness measures allow the marketing manager to fine-tune the advertising message and media strategies. Some examples of how awareness is used to help formulate subsequent marketing strategies are:

- Low awareness levels signal the need for a more aggressive or effective advertising and promotional plan. Often, the primary problem is that the product has low awareness among consumers, not that the product necessarily needs a repositioning. This is especially true if the product has positive attribute ratings from current users and it has a high trial/repeat usage ratio.

- Markets with high levels of awareness often don't need as much media weight to sustain existing sales levels as those markets that have low awareness. It often requires less media weight to generate successful promotions in established markets with high awareness than in newer markets, where a customer base is not yet established and only a minimal number of potential consumers have heard of your product or company. As an example, markets in which a product has low awareness often require larger print ads than markets with higher awareness levels. Our experience has shown that small newspaper ads are more likely to be seen by current users and that it takes larger ads to attract the attention of infrequent users or individuals who are not aware of your product.

- Markets with falling awareness levels often indicate isolated, market-specific problems such as increased competitive activity. These problems may require an individual market plan tailored to the specific market situation, along with investment spending over the short-term to stabilize and increase awareness levels.

If you cannot afford primary research, you can informally conduct an awareness study for your product. However, keep in mind, doing your own report could lead to misleading information that could hurt your product's success. Randomly call individuals in your geographic selling area. Ask them if they have used products and frequented stores in your category in the past year. If they have, ask them to name all the stores in the area where they can purchase the product category or to name all the brands (or companies) they are familiar with in the product category (unaided awareness measure). Try to get between 100 and 200 responses. Also keep track of first mentions (those products or stores mentioned first by each respondent without receiving assistance), as this is a good prediction of your company's market share relative to the competition.

With this information you can infer what percent of the potential customer base is aware of your product and where it ranks relative to the competition. This will provide a rough approximation of unaided awareness levels for your product and the competition. You can also determine the first mention level, a strong indication of market share, actual use of the product, or propensity to use.

Questions to Be Addressed

- What is the unaided and aided awareness of your product among the various target market segments in your industry and among customers of your company? How do those awareness levels compare to those of your competition? Have awareness levels been increasing or decreasing over the past five years?

- What is the first mention level of awareness (first product mentioned) within each target market segment.

Product Attributes

Product attributes or benefits are derived from consumers' perceptions of the product. This step of the business review allows the marketing manager to define the strengths and weaknesses of the company's products relative to the competition. It is necessary to identify which attributes are important to the purchasing segments and users of your product and then to determine how your company or product compares to the competition on these attributes. There may be attributes that you need to improve for certain segments, or you may find there are certain needs that no one in the marketplace is fulfilling, providing your company the opportunity to dominate an important niche or purchasing segment. The repositioning of a menswear chain we worked with was brought about because the research determined that the most important attributes to the heavy-user target market segment (businessmen) were quality and value, not low purchase price, which was being emphasized. The repositioning emphasized value (a good price on perceived quality brands). The theme line became "Pecks Businessmenswear," which denoted a special quality and expertise and labeled a specific group of people identified with quality men's clothing (heavy-user purchasing segment).

Attribute Importance by Segment

Rationale Attributes   The first step is to determine which attributes are most important for each target market segment you are analyzing. In the shoe retail category, quality, comfort, and value are of primary importance to women with children. Price is middle of the pack. In the highly technical computer diagnostic business, product reliability, service response time, software, and ease of use were the top required attributes for the research and development target segment, with price, state-of-the-art design, supplier reputation, upgradability, and application support being more important to the purchasing agents.

Emotional Attributes   In addition to ranking the rationale attributes, we also develop a list of the most important emotional reasons customer segments purchase. For example, the women customers of a large HMO desired partnership. When we explored what that meant, it translated into the willingness to accept the fact that the patient has to do his or her share to stay healthy in today's medical climate. But the doctor has to be willing to listen and should not treat the patient simply as a number or as a disease. In this case, partnership meant two-way communication.

Attribute Ranking by Segment

Next, your company is ranked against the most important attributes relative to the competition. This is again typically done through survey research. You are then able to say that quality is the number-one desired attribute and that our company either does or does not perform well on this variable. This type of analysis, based upon the realities of the marketplace, puts the consumer in the position of guiding the direction the company takes. (See Appendix B for chart.)

Questions to Be Addressed

The information needed to answer these questions is normally obtained through primary research. If your company cannot afford to undertake primary research to answer these questions, then you should use available secondary research and attempt to answer them yourself in as much detail as possible. Also, have other individuals in your organization answer them to see if your perceptions match those of your coworkers. You might even get individuals outside of your company to answer the questions in order to compare their answers with those from people within your organization.

- How is your product used? What is the product's primary benefit to the industry category consumer segments?

- What are the important product attributes of your product's industry category against each segment? What are the important attributes of your competitors' products? How do your company's products rank on those attributes versus the competition on a segment-by-segment basis?

- What does each purchaser and user segment like and dislike about your product?

- Are there differences between heavy users' likes and dislikes as compared to the other user segments of your product category?

- Are there substitutes that can be used in place of your company's product or the product category?

- Is there anything unusual about how your product is manufactured or designed that would be of interest or benefit to consumers? Is there anything about your product that can help differentiate it from the competition? For example, how is it manufactured? Does it have a unique color, shape, or texture? Does your product last longer than others like it? What about guarantees? Are there unique performance attributes that make it superior to the competition? Is there unique packaging? Is your product more convenient to use than the competitor's? Is your product of better quality? What about the competitors' products?

- Are there any inherent product qualities that have not been communicated but that are important to the buyer segments? (Same for your competition.)

- For each segment, what are the rational attributes and emotional attributes that are important predictors of purchasing in your product category and/or for your company's products?

- If you have many competitors, how does your product rank in terms of overall quality? How does your product rank in terms of value (the combination of quality and price)? Where does your product rank in terms of performance, durability, serviceability, and aesthetic appearance when compared to the competition? How does your product rank, relative to the competitive products, across other key purchasing attributes by each target market segment?

- What is the history of your product? When was it first marketed? What changes have been made to the product and why? (Same for your competition.)

- Is your product accepted by a broad consumer base or a narrow segment? Why?

- Does your product have any patents that are active? Does your unique advantage depend upon a specific design, formula, or manufacturing capability that could be readily copied? Or is your product unique due to patent protection or some manufacturing process that is difficult or costly to duplicate?

- What are the new developments in your product category? What will be the next big innovation? What product improvements do consumers desire?

Product Life Cycle

Most products go through a product life cycle. Understanding your product's stage in the product life cycle will help predict anticipated target markets, competition, pricing, distribution, and advertising strategies. The following is a brief outline of how we view the product life cycle and how each stage affects these five areas.

Introduction Phase

Target Market   Usually innovators try new products. The goal is to get opinion-leader types of people to try and use the product. It is usually more difficult to sell a new product or concept to a mass audience during the introduction period.

Competition   Typically, there are few competitors in the introduction stage, as the technology and start-up costs for a new product or product category are high.

Pricing   Usually the company that first introduces a product has the freedom to set prices as desired. Companies can "cream the price," setting it high for maximum profits on each unit, or set a low price in an attempt to obtain as many customers as possible. The pricing decision is often a function of the company's ability to produce the product, product availability, and the amount of anticipated competition.

Distribution   During the introduction stage, distribution is usually through specialized channels rather than mass distribution channels. This is because a good deal of attention needs to be paid to educating consumers about the product and how to use it.

Advertising   Advertising of a new product is usually educational in nature, convincing people to try the product and explaining how the product will provide benefits not currently found in the marketplace.

Growth Phase

Target Market   The market is still growing, with new users purchasing the product for the first time. The product is becoming accepted by a wider profile of consumers.

Competition   As product acceptance grows, the number of competitors increases.

Pricing   While competition is focused primarily on product attributes, pricing variations are introduced along with diversification and differentiation of the product. Price cutting occurs, and discounters try to steal market share and broaden the customer base by making the product or service more affordable. Higher priced, higher quality products are also introduced and marketed.

Distribution   Distribution expands from specialty stores to more mass distribution channels, such as chains.

Advertising   The communication focus moves away from selling the product category and educating consumers. As a result of product differentiation and increased competitive levels, advertising takes on the role of positioning particular products with specific attributes or benefits against the competition.

Maturity Phase

Target Market   The product is now accepted by all or most consumers. When bank automated teller machines were first introduced, only young innovators used them, with older adults preferring to go into a bank for transactions. Now, after a prolonged introduction period, people of all ages more readily use the machines.

Competition   The market is very competitive at this stage.

Pricing   In this stage, pricing becomes very important. Products are often standardized, with fewer product innovations and fewer discernible differences. Thus, the selling emphasis is not as much on product attributes as it is on price and customer service.

Distribution   All channels now have access to the product.

Advertising   The communication strategy shifts towards keeping and improving brand name awareness and differentiating your product from the competition's. By this time, share of mind equals share of market. The company needs to communicate its brand name and have it included in the "evoke set" of brands that comes to mind when a customer is thinking of purchasing.

Questions to Be Addressed

- Where is your product in the product life cycle? How will this affect your marketing decisions?

Task 3
Trial and Retrial
Behavior

Trial Behavior

The marketer should analyze purchase rates and buying habits of the consumer and customer segments to further determine where, how, and why consumers and customers are purchasing. Buying habit information can provide invaluable insight into the target market and provide impact for marketing objectives and strategies during the writing of the marketing plan. These decisions revolve around taking advantage of consumption patterns, changing current consumption patterns (which is most difficult), or recognizing the patterns and modifying the product and the way in which the product is sold to better meet the needs of the target market.

Buying Habits

Analysis of the following factors should yield a picture of the target segment's buying habits. Most of this information can be quantified and forms the basis of marketing objectives later in the plan.

The first task is to quantify the number purchases and the average dollar amount per purchase per industry category and company target segments. Now determine the average time between purchases. Knowing this, the marketer can decide how frequently to advertise the product or provide purchase incentives. The next task is to analyze the number of items purchased per customer. If there are multiple items purchased per customer, this would significantly add to the average value of each customer. It also provides insights into cross-selling strategies (moving customers to multiple product purchases) for later in the plan.

In addition, the marketer should determine if the purchase is made spontaneously or is a planned purchase.

Finally, in looking at buying habits, everything about the purchasing environment and buyer actions should be detailed. These include some of the following, and more:

- The buying decision process of the customer. Are there other key influences that need to be addressed (spouse/child influence, point of sale merchandising, ego gratification, etc.)?

- The average purchase ratio (the percentage of store visits that result in a purchase, or the percentage of sales calls resulting in a closed sale).

- The seasonality of purchases for each of the segments analyzed.

Questions to Be Addressed

- What factors are important to the purchase decision-making process? What is the purchase decision sequence each segment makes when purchasing your product? How can you positively affect this?

- What is the average purchase amount (number of times per year and dollar amount per year) for consumer segments in your product category and for your customer segments? Do these vary? Is there an opportunity to narrow the purchase amount between the industry average and your company if you are below the average? Specifically, what is the average number of purchases per year, dollar size, and quantity of each purchase for the industry consumer segments and for your customer segments? (One, two, three bars of soap per trip/large, medium, or small package sizes?) Do consumers and customer segments purchase in bulk, stock up, or purchase your product one at a time?

- How frequently are purchases made? What is the purchase cycle for your product or service in the industry compared to your company? What is the frequency of purchase for heavy users versus other segments?

- What is the purchase ratio among industry consumer and customer segments? What percent of consumers and customers purchase when they visit the store/office or receive a sales call?

- How important is customer service, personal selling, and salesperson advice/consultation to each of the segments?

- Is the buying decision spontaneous or planned? What percent of the buying decisions are made at the point of purchase versus at home or over a longer period of time?

- Do the heavy users have different buying habits than the overall users?

- Do different target segments display unique or strong seasonality purchases? How do seasonality purchases differ among target segments?

Purchase Rates of the Industry Product Category and Your Company's Product by Geographic Markets

Geographic markets should be analyzed for their importance in sales for the category (Category Development Index, or CDI) and sales for your company's product (Brand Development Index, or BDI).

The Category Development Index (CDI) determines the *product category's* strength on a market-by-market basis. It provides a quick index of whether the geographical area or any given market's purchases are at, above or below the average, given the size of its population in relation to the total country's population. CDI information allows the marketer to determine markets that have strong per capita sales potential. This information can be used in recommending expansion markets, predicting sales, or as rationale for investment-spending decisions.

The formula for calculating the CDI is:

$$CDI = \frac{\text{Percentage of product category's national dollar volume in a given market}}{\text{Percentage of U.S. population in a given market}}$$

Exhibit 2.23 presents a chart that can be used to develop this information. A blank worksheet is provided in Appendix B.

The Brand Development Index (BDI) provides an index that determines whether a geographical market purchases your *company's product* at, above or below average rates, given its population in relation to your company's national market population. For example, if your company only did business in three cities, those three cities and their surrounding trading area population would define your company's national market population. BDI information is used to help formulate geographic spending strategies. Strong company markets can be protected, and weak markets can be targeted for growth.

The formula for calculating the BDI is:

$$BDI = \frac{\text{Percentage company's dollar volume in any given market}}{\text{Percentage of company's national market population that lives in any given market}}$$

Exhibit 2.24 presents a chart that can be used to develop this information. See Appendix B for a blank worksheet.

CDI and BDI numbers are often used together. High CDI markets mean the potential exists for good sales, as the product category as a whole does well. If these same markets have low company BDI indexes with adequate product distribution and store penetration/market coverage, the markets are often targeted for aggressive marketing plans. Thus, strong category sales (high CDI) and low company sales (low BDI) can mean potential for your company's growth.

Questions to Be Answered

- Where exactly do your customers reside? Where does the research segment reside? Do they live nationwide or are they limited to certain regions? Are they living in large cities, suburbs, or rural areas (C and D counties)?

- Where are sales for product category strongest and weakest nationally (CDI)? Where are your company's sales strongest and weakest (BDI)?

Exhibit 2.23 National Category Development Index (CDI)

DMA*	Percent of U.S. Population	Percent of Product Dollar Volume	Category Development Index: CDI (Volume/Population)	Population Number (000)	Dollar Volume of Product Category Nationally (000)	Per Capita Consumption
Chicago	3.5%†	4.5%†	129†	8,493‡	$827,548‡	$97.4‡
Madison						
Philadelphia						
Minneapolis						
Atlanta						

*DMA = Designated marketing area defined by television viewing audience.

†3.5 percent of the U.S. population lives in Chicago; 4.5 percent of the category's national sales volume (for example, all shoes sold nationally) is from the Chicago DMA. The Chicago DMA does better in category business than the average DMA as is indicated by the CDI of 129 (4.5/3.5 = 129).

‡Further, 8,493,000 people live in the Chicago DMA. The Chicago population consumes $827,548,000 worth of the product for a per capita consumption of $97.4.

Exhibit 2.24 Company Brand Development Index (BDI)

DMA	Percent of Company's National Market Population	Percent of Dollar Volume	Brand Development Index: BDI (Volume/Population)	Population Number (000)	Dollar Volume Company (000)	Per Capita Consumption
Chicago	11.2%*	10.0*	89*	8,493†	$200,000†	$23.55†
Madison						
Philadelphia						
Minneapolis						
Atlanta						
Etc.						

*11.2 percent of the company's total market population lives in the Chicago DMA; 10 percent of the company's sales are from the Chicago DMA. The BDI for Chicago is 89 (10/11.2 = 89) which means the DMA has a below average BDI as compared to other DMAs in the system.

†Further, 8,493,000 people live in the Chicago DMA. Company sales in Chicago are $200,000 or $23.55 per person.

■ What markets have above or below average consumption per household or per person (CDI)? Does your company have different geographical distribution from that of the category in general?

■ What are the markets at above or below average purchase rates on a household or per person basis (BDI)?

■ Are national sales increasing at greater or lesser rates than the population growth? Are there specific markets where this is different?

Trading Areas

In addition to CDI and BDI information, the retail/service marketer should determine the trading area for the product. A trading area is the geographical territory where consumers and customers live. This is important from a media purchasing standpoint and also for determining future store locations, as discussed in Chapter 11, Distribution.

Exhibit 2.25 Trading Areas by Store

Zip Codes Surrounding Store	Percent of Customers Over 1 Week Period
53704	20%
53705	30
53703	20
53702	10
53711	10
53708	5
53709	1
Other	4

Through a simple in-store customer survey, as shown in Exhibit 2.25, you can determine where your customers come from. Or, if you keep accurate customer mailing lists, they can allow you to construct trading areas.

Questions to Be Addressed

- What is the trading area for your product category? How far do consumers in the category typically travel in miles and time to purchase the product?

- How far do consumers travel to purchase your product?

Retrial Behavior

After trial of the first purchase of your product, it is critical to generate a second purchase or repeat. If you don't generate a repeat purchase you will never get the purchaser to become an on-going customer. If you continually generate trial but poor repeat, chances are your product is inferior to the competition and it requires your attention for improvement.

Brand Loyalty

While repeat is more immediate, brand loyalty is a measure of how loyal your consumers and customers are over a period of time. If your customers primarily use only your company's product, they are brand loyal. If they use your product a majority of the time but occasionally use your competitors' products, they are moderately brand loyal. Low brand loyalty exists if brand or product switching occurs regularly in your category or with your products.

Brand loyalty is analyzed to provide insights into the following types of issues:

- How difficult it will be to keep your own customers

- How difficult it will be to steal market share from competitors

- The degree of promotional offers that will be needed to induce trial

- How much media weight will be necessary to increase trial, retrial, and sales

- Whether a true product difference or innovation is needed to compete

A product category with extremely high brand loyalty will require more media weight, larger promotional offers or inducements, and perhaps even a product in-

Exhibit 2.26 Brand Loyalty

Brand	All	Sole	Loyalty Index	Sole and Primary	Loyalty Index
Cooper	16.4%	2.7%	16	11.6%	71
Hiebing	12.9	2.6	20	9.5	74
Dorton	11.5	1.2	10	6.9	60
Michaels	9.9	1.9	19	6.0	60

novation in order to steal market share from existing competitors. With a low brand loyalty product category it is extremely difficult to keep your own customers, but it is also easier to steal market share.

The chart in Exhibit 2.26 provides a measure of the brand loyalty that exists within the product category. For example, 9.9 percent of all purchasers use Michaels brand, while 1.9 percent use only Michaels brand. The resulting loyalty measure of 19(1.9/9.9) compares favorably to the other brands in the category. However, the category as a whole does not exhibit strong loyalty.

Questions to Be Addressed

- Is buying by brand name important to consumers in your category? What percent of the consumers in the category are brand loyal most of the time, all of the time, and never?

- How brand loyal are your customers? Is brand switching common? Do heavy users have different loyalty than the overall users?

Trial to Retrial Ratio

Another important area of investigation is trial and retrial by consumer and customer segment. The Hiebing Group did work for a dominant national client that had a specialty line of consumer package good products. The product sold was basically the same, but each was packaged for specific uses—packages for the car, the teenager's bedroom, dad's work area, and the woman's purse. The initial thinking was that we would expand usage categories for the products; in other words, find other places besides the car for consumers to use the product geared to the car (kids taking it to school). However, after studying the buying habit findings in the situation analysis, we discovered two things:

1. Overall trial of the family of products was very low.

2. Of those people who tried the products, retrial was very high.

In summary, the challenge was not to find more uses for the family of products, but to promote trial. Once consumers tried one of the products, the chances were good they would continue to purchase them. However, if we had found that the retrial rate was in fact very poor, we would have had another set of product-related problems on which to focus, thus taking our marketing emphasis in the direction of finding out why customers weren't satisfied with the product. The chart in Exhibit 2.27 provides a summary of trial and retrial (consumer acceptance) percentages

Exhibit 2.27 Trial/Retrial

Brand	Percent Ever Used	Percent Used Last 6 Months	Loyalty Measure: Percent Used Past 6 Months/Percent Ever Used
Company X			
A	81%	48%	59
Competition			
C	58	22	38
D	43	17	40
E	30	15	50
F	25	17	68

Brand A has a much higher trial (ever used), retrial (used last 6 months) and thus loyalty rate higher than any other competitor with the exception of Brand F. However, while Brand F has strong loyalty measure (68) it has a low initial trial figure, a problem that should receive primary attention in the marketing plan.

(found in sources such as SMRB or your own primary research). Use the worksheet in Appendix B to develop information specific to your company.

Questions to Be Addressed

■ What is the trial and retrial ratio of industry consumer segments? What is the ratio for your customer segments?

■ What percent of the consumer segments have tried the product category?

■ What percent of your customer segment have tried your products?

■ How common is retrial? What percent repeat? What percent become regular or loyal users?

■ Do heavy users have different trial and retrial rates than the overall users?

BUSINESS REVIEW WRITING STYLE

Now that you have answered the questions in each section and completed the charts, it is best to summarize the important findings from each section. This is helpful for two reasons:

1. It is much easier to develop problems and opportunities (as you'll be doing in Chapter 3) if the business review has been condensed and summarized.

2. The summary statements provide a good management summary and support during presentations.

We've found there is no way to shortcut the length of a business review. Marketing is very broad, and the marketer needs to look at relationships between many, many numbers in order to come to sound conclusions regarding his or her company, the marketplace, the competition, and the needs and wants of the consumer.

We recommend developing summary statements for each section of the business review. They should precede each section, serving as a management summary when the final business review is ready for presentation. Your summary statements should be objective. This is no place for developing strategy. Keep the statements concise and focused on reporting the facts. Include summary rationale when needed. Examples summarizing major findings for a canning company would be as follows.

Target Market Effectors—Target Market Example

Canned vegetable consumption is dominated by medium and heavy users. Thirty-seven percent of canned good purchasers account for over 65 percent of the canned good vegetables used per month.

Target Market Effectors—Trial/ Retrial Example

Canned vegetables are used by a high percentage (80 percent) of households. Canned vegetables are a relatively high usage category. Fifty-nine percent of homemakers use four or more cans per month. Twenty-nine percent use ten or more cans per month. Thirteen percent use 16 or more cans per month.

Product or Market Review—Sales Example

While the canned tomato category has increased dramatically (140 percent) for the industry over the past five years, Company X has experienced only moderate growth (20 percent). This is far below the industry growth pattern.

Do's and Don'ts

Do

- Develop an outline and charts before you start digging for information. This will keep you focused on the important issues.

- Always report data with reference points for comparison—use your company compared to the industry or this year compared to last year.

- Keep your summary statements as objective as possible.

- Take as much time as possible to compile a database. It will make writing the remainder of the plan much easier and far more effective.

- Make sure each chart you prepare has a descriptive title that explains the purpose of the chart.

- Round whole numbers and percentages to the nearest tenth (200.5 thousand or 13.4 percent). Business review data should be used for directional purposes. Numbers carried out too far (beyond a tenth of a point) connote an exactness that should not be implied in the business review, where interpolation of numbers is sometimes needed to provide findings when using secondary data. Remember, it's the trends and the comparisons, not the absolute numbers, that are important. Whether your company sells 15.2 percent or 15 percent of its product in August is going to make little difference when determining seasonality and media spending strategies.

- As you work on your business review, keep a notebook nearby in which to jot down ideas for the marketing plan as detailed in the Introduction. Also keep a list of problems and opportunities that stem from working with the data. Doing this gives you a head start in writing the plan.

Don't

- Don't use the business review to develop objectives and strategies. Keep your findings objective and report facts. Don't develop solutions.

- Don't give up if you can't find some information you need. Call trade journals, the library, media reps, etc. The answers are out there.

- Don't develop a marketing plan without first understanding your target market, your product, and your marketing environment as thoroughly as possible.

Step Two   Problems/Opportunities

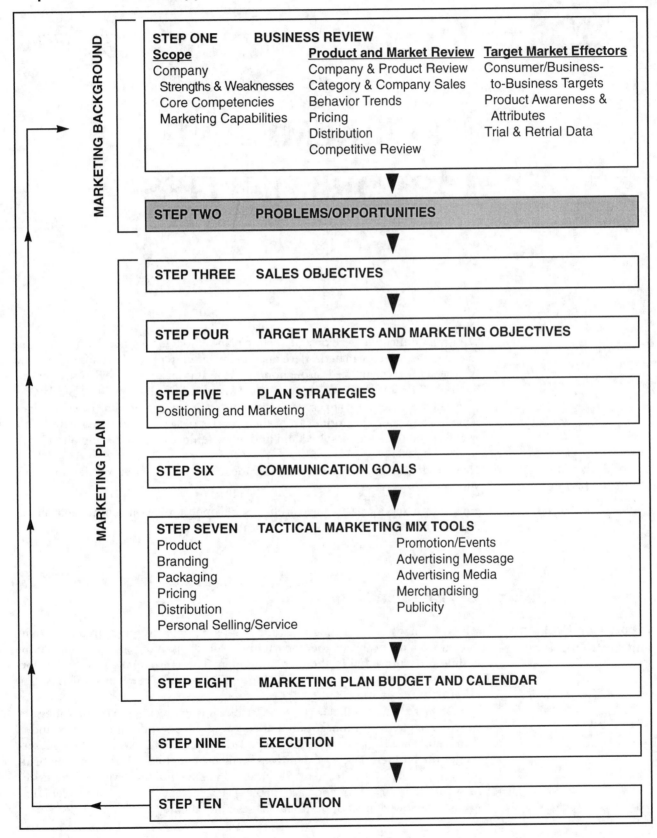

MARKETING BACKGROUND

STEP ONE   BUSINESS REVIEW

<u>Scope</u>	<u>Product and Market Review</u>	<u>Target Market Effectors</u>
Company	Company & Product Review	Consumer/Business-
Strengths & Weaknesses	Category & Company Sales	to-Business Targets
Core Competencies	Behavior Trends	Product Awareness &
Marketing Capabilities	Pricing	Attributes
	Distribution	Trial & Retrial Data
	Competitive Review	

STEP TWO   PROBLEMS/OPPORTUNITIES

MARKETING PLAN

STEP THREE   SALES OBJECTIVES

STEP FOUR   TARGET MARKETS AND MARKETING OBJECTIVES

STEP FIVE   PLAN STRATEGIES
Positioning and Marketing

STEP SIX   COMMUNICATION GOALS

STEP SEVEN   TACTICAL MARKETING MIX TOOLS

Product	Promotion/Events
Branding	Advertising Message
Packaging	Advertising Media
Pricing	Merchandising
Distribution	Publicity
Personal Selling/Service	

STEP EIGHT   MARKETING PLAN BUDGET AND CALENDAR

STEP NINE   EXECUTION

STEP TEN   EVALUATION

3

PROBLEMS AND OPPORTUNITIES

It is very difficult to develop a marketing plan without first consolidating and summarizing the objective material developed in the business review. The business review is a reference to be utilized throughout the year. It is meant to be exhaustive in the amount of data it presents and analyzes. However, in order to write a marketing plan, the marketer needs to crystallize specific company and product category challenges. The major conclusions from the business review should be polarized into problems that need to be solved and into opportunities that can be exploited.

**From This Chapter
You Will Learn**

How to identify problems and opportunities from the material you developed in your business review.

How to write succinct, actionable problems and opportunities in a format that allows an organized transition into writing your marketing plan.

OVERVIEW

**Identifying Problems
and Opportunities**

When writing your marketing plan, the marketing objectives and strategies come directly from the problems and opportunities. Ideally, each problem and opportunity should be addressed in the marketing plan. Therefore, make sure to develop problems and opportunities that are appropriate for each section of the business review.

First, make headings that correspond to the steps and sections in your business review. Leave plenty of room to summarize the problems and opportunities under each section heading. Worksheets are provided in Appendix B. Next, review each section of the business review to identify as many meaningful problems and opportunities as possible. Make sure to read each section in the business review at least twice. Ask yourself: Is this information actionable? Is it a current or potential problem that needs to be solved or an opportunity that can be exploited?

Problems

Problems are derived from situations of weakness. As with opportunities, a problem statement can be drawn from a single finding or set of findings that make for a potentially negative situation. Reviewing the target market section in the business review for a retail client, we discovered that there was a heavy-purchaser group, 30 percent of which purchased 65 percent of the product. The heaviest concentration was in the females 35 to 49 with children group. Our client was strongest in attracting younger purchasers, and while the heavy purchaser shopped at our client's store for some products, the majority of her purchases were made elsewhere. This information led to the following problems under the target market effectors section:

- The company's purchaser tends to be younger, with fewer 35 to 49 purchasers (the single strongest purchasing segment for heavy users) when compared to the profile of the heavy purchaser.

- The heavy purchaser is shopping our stores but is making a majority of her purchases elsewhere.

Thus, to target the heavy user, the retailer had to develop a program to more fully satisfy the heavy purchaser's needs through the merchandise selection and also do a better job of selling the customer on the full line of products.

In summary, problems focus on your firm's weaknesses. Problem statements also address market conditions that can result in a disadvantage for your company or the industry as a whole. The common denominator is that problems are defensive in nature; you will be correcting a negative.

Opportunities

Opportunities are developed from strengths or positive circumstances. Often a combination of circumstances makes for a potentially positive situation, creating an opportunity. When we reviewed the competitive situation for a statewide accounting firm, we determined that there were very few accounting firms with aggressive, disciplined marketing programs. Even fewer of these firms actually advertised through mass communication vehicles. Also, we found that, of the firms advertising, none were targeting small-to medium-sized businesses. An earlier demand analysis had shown that the greatest potential for our client was in providing a full range of accounting services to small- to medium-sized businesses in the retail, service, and financial SIC categories. This combination of information provided the following opportunities:

- While there is fairly heavy competition in the trading areas of the CPA firm, there is limited advertising of CPA services; no single CPA firm dominates either consumer or business awareness of accounting firms.

- No CPA firm is directly communicating to the small- to medium-sized business target market, yet this market represents the majority of potential business in terms of actual numbers of clients.

These opportunities meant two things:

1. Because of the limited advertising clutter pertaining to accounting firms, an aggressive, targeted campaign could dominate the accounting advertising and build high awareness levels.

2. If the messages were strategic and meaningful to the target audience, then the increased share of mind or awareness level should be translated into increases in share of business or share of market.

In summary, opportunities are statements that point out strengths of the firm. They also identify areas where your company can exploit a weakness of the competition. They address market conditions that can result in an advantage to your company if positive action is taken. Opportunities are offensive in nature; they will result in an action capitalizing on strengths.

Problem or Opportunity?

Many times, what appears to be a problem can also be an opportunity. An example is the following sales analysis problem:

■ While Heartland Men's Apparel sales are strong during the holiday period of November and December, sales are below that of the men's apparel category nationally. This situation occurs because Heartland Apparel stores are not located in malls that generate heavy traffic during these periods.

While this is a problem for the company, it is also an opportunity. If national sales are at a peak during the November and December periods, then the opportunity exists to capture a larger percentage of these sales. However, because of the stores' locations, it is difficult to do as well as the average store nationally during this period. Thus, this statement is both a problem and an opportunity.

As a rule of thumb, try to determine if the statement is more of a problem or an opportunity. In this example, it is very difficult to change locations in retail, so this overriding factor would make the above statement a problem. In either case, however, the marketer would probably choose to address the problem or the opportunity by attempting to increase sales in the months of November and December.

HOW TO WRITE ACTIONABLE PROBLEMS AND OPPORTUNITIES

Problems and opportunities should be concise, one-sentence statements that draw conclusions. If necessary, there can be a brief follow-up using supporting data or rationale.

The rationale should utilize key factual data or findings from the business review. This will enable you to quickly support your problem and opportunity statements during a presentation.

Writing Style Examples

The following are examples of problems and opportunities that demonstrate the writing style to use when formulating these statements. We picked five categories of problems and two categories of opportunities for examples. Remember that in your own problem and opportunity section there will be problems and opportunities for *each section* of the business review.

Product and Market Review—Sales Section

Example Problems

- *The men's suit and sport coat market constitutes a relatively limited market.* Total purchases of suits and sport coats by males in a given year are low in the absolute, and the category has lower purchase rates when compared to most other nondurable consumer goods. In addition, while small percentages of males purchase any suit or sport coat in a given year, the majority of those purchasers buy only one suit or sport coat per year.

- *The Reed Company has experienced a market share decline over the past five years.* This loss in market share has primarily been to the market leader, Birkenshire, which increased share during the last five years. The remainder of the market has remained fairly stable during this time period.

	Market Share	Percentage Change Last 5 Years
The Reed Company	10	−12%
Birkenshire	25	+15

Example Opportunity

- *Sales data show that a small number of distributors account for a majority of sales dollars.* Forty accounts provide nearly 70 percent of the distributor's sales, yet these 40 accounts make up only 12 percent of the distributors who purchase from Seth Cooper & Sons Office Supplies.

Product and Market Review—Competitive Review Section

Example Problems

- *The top three competitors outspend Sweetbriar Inc. by 20 percent.* Furthermore, Sweetbriar Inc. does not dominate any one medium, and its media spending has declined since last year in television, the medium in which the majority of its media dollars are spent.

- *The Sweetbriar advertising messages are inconsistent and present no unifying selling theme.* In contrast, the top four competitors each communicate one strong, identifiable positioning in all of their advertising.

Target Market Effectors—Target Market Section

Example Problems

- *Multiple target markets exist.* Each target market has different demographics, needs, and wants. No single dominating customer group can be targeted.

- *The facial tissue's customers skew very old, with a small to nonexistent percentage of users coming from teens and young adults.* The brand is developing virtually no new users from which to regenerate the consumer franchise.

■ *General Hospital does not have a religious orientation.* The city of Johnsonville has a high concentration of Catholics (40 percent of the population). Of the two hospitals, the Catholic-affiliated hospital dominates market share. Thus, religious factors influence the choice of hospital.

Target Market Effectors—Awareness and Attribute Sections

Example Problems

■ *Unaided awareness for the Philo company is fourth.* This continues its trend downward relative to the top three competitors over the past three years.

■ *Of the top ten competitors, the Cale Company ranks second in quality of product relative to the competition.* Quality is the single most important purchase attribute for the category.

Example Opportunity

■ *Very little clear differentiation of accounting firms exists, except on the basis of size.* Service offerings, expertise, etc., remain relative unknowns among clients, referrals, and prospects.

Target Market Effectors—Trial and Retrial Behavior Sections

Example Problems

■ *While the Southwest consumes more of the product on a per capita basis than any other part of the country, The Torger Company has relatively poor sales in this region.* This is because it has yet to fully expand distribution to this portion of the country.

■ *The average shopper is extremely brand loyal.* Brand choice is developed at a young age, with a majority of consumers continuing purchases for life.

Example Opportunity

■ *Although total trial of the company's brands is very low, retrial is above the category average.* Thus, greater rates of consumers become regular users than is normal for the category, meaning product acceptance is very high.

Keep Your Statements Factual

Finally, it is important that your problem and opportunity section stay factual by summarizing findings from the business review. Problems and opportunities do not show what is to be done, but point out areas that need attention. They describe the current market environment. Leave the solutions to the marketing plan.

The following is not an opportunity, but a marketing strategy:

■ Advertise during the strong seasonal times of the year that exist during August, September, December, and April.

It is a strategy because it is not reporting facts, but demonstrating what should be done. Leave that for the marketing plan, when you can review all the problems and opportunities together and then determine what should be done. The correct opportunity statement relating to the above would be:

- The industry is extremely seasonal, with strong purchasing months of August, September, December, and April.

Dos and Don'ts

Do

- Draw as many meaningful conclusions as possible from each section of the business review. Read and reread each section. Try to look at each set of facts in as many different ways as possible. Ask yourself, "What are the positive and negative aspects of the data?"

- Write concise, factual statements summarizing the business review.

- Organize your problems and opportunities so that they reflect each section of the business review.

- If it helps you to better see the big picture, summarize all the problems and opportunities into five to ten key problems and five to ten key opportunities, including them at the end of your problem and opportunity section.

Don't

- Don't try to write objectives and strategies in this section. Keep the statement factual.

- Don't make the statements too long. Keep them short, and focus each one on a single problem or opportunity.

- Don't shortchange the number of problems and opportunities—compile an inclusive list. Once you have your final list, make sure you go back and eliminate any that are redundant. This will allow you to concentrate on a more focused, manageable list of meaningful problems and opportunities.

- Don't include problems and opportunities that are not based on information included in your business review.

PART TWO

MARKETING PLAN

Step Three Sales Objectives

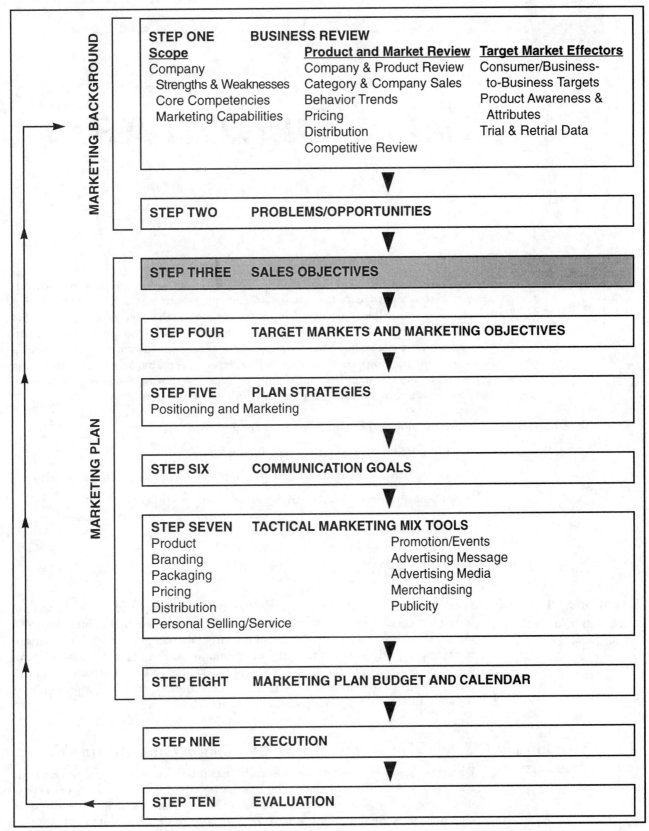

MARKETING BACKGROUND

STEP ONE **BUSINESS REVIEW**

Scope **Product and Market Review** **Target Market Effectors**

Company — Company & Product Review — Consumer/Business-
  Strengths & Weaknesses — Category & Company Sales — to-Business Targets
  Core Competencies — Behavior Trends — Product Awareness &
  Marketing Capabilities — Pricing — Attributes
               Distribution — Trial & Retrial Data
               Competitive Review

STEP TWO **PROBLEMS/OPPORTUNITIES**

STEP THREE **SALES OBJECTIVES**

STEP FOUR **TARGET MARKETS AND MARKETING OBJECTIVES**

STEP FIVE **PLAN STRATEGIES**
Positioning and Marketing

STEP SIX **COMMUNICATION GOALS**

STEP SEVEN **TACTICAL MARKETING MIX TOOLS**
Product — Promotion/Events
Branding — Advertising Message
Packaging — Advertising Media
Pricing — Merchandising
Distribution — Publicity
Personal Selling/Service

STEP EIGHT **MARKETING PLAN BUDGET AND CALENDAR**

STEP NINE **EXECUTION**

STEP TEN **EVALUATION**

MARKETING PLAN

SALES OBJECTIVES

Now that you have completed the background section of the planning process, you are ready to prepare the actual marketing plan. Your first task for the marketing plan is to set the sales objectives. Without the required sales, you will not generate the necessary profits. Remember, profits are "king." That is why you are in business. Further, because it sets the tone of the entire marketing plan, setting sales objectives is one of the most important but demanding steps in preparing an effective marketing plan. The more you understand about the process of arriving at a sales objective, the easier it is to write a marketing plan that will meet sales objectives.

From This Chapter You Will Learn

The definition and importance of sales objectives.

What to keep in mind when setting sales objectives.

The quantitative and qualitative factors that affect the setting of sales objectives.

How to set your own sales objectives using a three-step process.

OVERVIEW

Definition and Importance of Sales Objectives

Sales objectives are self-defining in that they represent projected levels of goods or services to be sold. Everything that follows in the plan is designed to meet the sales objectives—from confirming the size of the target market and establishing realistic marketing objectives, to determining the amount of advertising and promotion dollars to be budgeted, to the actual hiring of marketing and sales personnel, to the number and kinds of distribution channels/stores utilized, and, very importantly, to the amount of product produced or inventoried.

What to Keep in Mind When Setting Sales Objectives

Sales Objectives Must Be Challenging and Attainable

Because sales objectives have substantial impact on a business, they must be simultaneously challenging and attainable. If not, they could have a disastrous effect on short-term, bottom-line profits as well as on the long-term success of the business. If sales objectives are dramatically increased, the cost of doing business will also rise dramatically to accommodate the projected increase in sales. Accordingly, if your sales objectives are set too high and cannot be attained, your resulting expenses to sales ratio will be very high, causing profits to fall below expectations. If you dramatically underestimate your sales objectives and have inadequate production capacity or inventory, you will not be able to sufficiently fulfill demand, meaning opportunity is lost to the competition. Over the long term, this may translate to the loss of good distributors, loyal customers, and first-time customers.

In summary, sales objective should be based upon an accurate estimate of the market opportunity and the capacity of the organization to realize those opportunities.

Sales Objectives Must Be Time Specific

You must set time-specific sales objectives in order to provide a start and end date for your marketing program. It is also important to set both short- and long-term sales objectives. Short-term sales objectives are generally for one year or less, while long-term objectives usually include sales objectives for a minimum of three years. Long-term sales objectives are needed to plan the future direction of the company or product in such areas as equipment, real estate, personnel, and capital. Further, what you include in year one of your marketing plan will affect sales objectives set for years two and three. Testing new products and service programs in year one might be required in order to meet sales objectives in year three.

Sales Objectives Must Be Measurable

Setting measurable sales objectives provides the means for determining what must be included in your marketing plan and for evaluating its success. Accordingly, sales objectives are quantified in terms of dollars and units for manufacturing firms, dollars and transactions (and occasionally units) for retail firms, and dollars and persons served for service firms.

You must set sales objectives for *both* dollar and units/transactions/persons served. Dollar sales cover your expenses and provide a profit, and they reflect the impact of any increase or decrease in the price of your product. Units/transactions/persons served indicate the fundamental health of your business. If you are continually projecting increased dollar sales but decreased unit sales, you will eventually experience a decline in dollar sales, because price increases will no longer compensate for the loss of unit sales.

Sales Objectives Are More Than Dollars and Units/Persons Served

Projected profits, a direct result of sales, should also be included along with sales objectives. Accordingly, as the author of this plan, you must have an understanding of profit expectations in order to effectively prepare and evaluate the marketing plan.

Further, if you are not operating in a pure business environment, keep in mind that sales objectives can be defined in terms other than dollars or units. For a nonprofit organization, the goal might be the funds raised to support its programs. In a government agency such as an employment service, it may be number of job placements. Or for a political campaign manager, it may be percent of votes cast for your candidate by county or district. Whatever the organization, there must be sales objectives or a simulation thereof.

Quantitative and Qualitative Factors Affecting the Setting of Sales Objectives

Both quantitative and qualitative factors must be taken into consideration in the development of sales objectives. Quantitative factors, inputted first, are hard numbers based upon objective, historical data. Qualitative factors are more subjective due to nonavailability and difficulty in quantifying certain types of information. Therefore, interpretation of these additional subjective factors leads to an adjustment of the quantitatively-based sales objectives.

Quantitative Factors

Sales Trends

In preparing to set sales objectives, the past is a good place to start. The tending of the market and company sales will be major factors to consider when projecting sales.

Market Sales   Review the trending of the market over the past five years in terms of dollar and unit sales. Has the trending of the marketplace been upward, downward, flat, or erratic? Within the total market history of sales and units, what has the trending been of market segments that make up the total market? If you were tracking total market shoe sales, you might have found a flat to slowly upward-trending market, but athletic sales as a subset were trending upward at a percentage rate more than twice that of the total market. Accordingly, if you were selling athletic shoes in your store, you would take this trend into consideration when setting objectives.

Company versus Market Sales   Next, compare how your company's sales are trending year to year versus the total market's sales. In most instances, project your sales to equal or surpass the market rate of growth; otherwise you will be losing share of market.

Market Share Trends   Another factor to consider is the trending of your market share—for the company/division, for the product line and each product, or for the retail/service category and each major department. At what rate has your share of total sales been trending relative to the market? Has it been growing in a growing market? Has your share been going up in a market that is shrinking? Or has your share of market been decreasing in a declining market? If you find that your product is losing share in a market that is declining, it would be unrealistic to project sales increases unless your strategy is to reverse this trend through a major marketing commitment. When setting sales objectives keep in mind that not only is it difficult to reverse a product's sales decline in a one-year period, but it is also extremely difficult to reverse a product's decline within a declining market.

Size and Purchase Rates of Your Target Market

A good double-check of the above methods in the determination of accurate sales objective estimates is an independent appraisal of the size and purchase rates of the target market for your product or service. Many new business ventures and good new products fail because of an overly optimistic estimate of the size and trending of the market. It is very important to review census and industry data, as well as primary research if available, in your business review to determine how big the market really is and how it is trending.

Sales objectives often are set too high year after year because the company's management does not recognize a continual erosion of the target market, an erosion that could have been documented through published industry data, company sales data, and/or primary research. Through primary research , our agency was able to document for a fabric chain that the number of women who sew garments declined approximately 5 percent per year over a ten-year period.

Many times, particularly with new products and the development of entire new market categories, there is limited market data and no company sales data on which to project sales objectives. In these instances, you use a simulation approach and track sales growth of categories and/or companies in different, but somewhat related, product and market situations. You can use the target market and its purchase rates as the data base shown at the end of Task 1 in "The Process of Setting Sales Objectives."

Budget, Profit, and Pricing Considerations

In determining realistic sales objectives, it is helpful to have an understanding of your company's historical operating budgets and profit expectations. Ideally, sales cover expenses and provide for profits. The simple fact is that you need a minimum level of dollar sales to stay in business and grow. For this reason, the cost of doing business, or expenses incurred to operate your business, is an important quantitative factor to consider when setting your sales objectives. In setting sales objectives, you should also understand the overall profitability history and expectations of the company and the level of profitability within segments of your product line or retail/service offering.

Along with the above, planned product price increases or decreases must be factored into all sales objectives, because they dramatically affect sales volume and profitability. These product price changes, whether they are for the entire year or just portions of it, should be factored in after you have reviewed the historical sales trends but before you apply the qualitative factors which will be discussed next.

Qualitative Factors

Economic Considerations

One factor affecting sales objectives that is difficult to forecast is the economy. Adjust your sales objectives based on your estimation of the economic factors that will directly affect your business. Are you forecasting sales for a recessionary, inflationary, or relatively stable period? If you are projecting sales for an inflationary period, you will probably be estimating dollar sales to increase at a greater percentage than unit sales.

Interest rates are also an important factor in establishing sales objectives. Businesses that rely heavily on their customers purchasing on credit, such as auto dealers and real estate firms, usually see their sales slump as interest rates rise.

In addition, you must plan accordingly for any major changes in the tax laws. For example, elimination of an investment tax credit for heavy machinery would dramatically affect the sales of companies manufacturing heavy equipment.

Review national economic factors as well as those that might directly affect your product's market on a more local geographic basis. Pockets of unemployment can dramatically affect your sales objectives.

In summary, remember that, although you cannot control economic factors, you can thoroughly evaluate what impact they could have on your business and then adjust your short- and long-term sales objectives.

Competition

What you identified as a large and growing market can be diluted by strong and growing competition. Before finalizing sales objectives, review the competitive data in the Product and Market Review section of your business review. Has a major competitor noticeably expanded its sales force, increased the number of trade deals to retailers, added distribution channels/store locations, changed its product mix, or introduced a new product or service? Based on your competitive review of advertising media, is the competition increasing or decreasing its level of spending? Increased competitive advertising spending, particularly in a consumer marketplace dominated by a few major competitors, can negatively affect the chance of your marketing program meeting its sales objectives.

It is often difficult to determine the direct impact on sales of an increase in competitive advertising. At this point, telephone survey research of your potential market can quantify its impact on your sales. Through this type of research, we were able to measure a 50 percent increase in awareness for our client's direct competitor. We then translated this awareness into increased sales for the competition and an erosion of our client's market share. Accordingly, an anti-competitor plan, along with a revision of the short-term sales objectives, was recommended for our client.

Fad Volume

While it is difficult to forecast, many businesses must deal with "fad" or erratic sales volume. You must learn to recognize and deal with it realistically when setting your sales and profit objectives. Fad volume could be occasional, such as a convention or sports tournament that brings an incremental number of people to your town and your restaurant. Fad volume could also be much longer lasting, such as that created by a highly publicized health care study indicating that the use of fish oil and/or aspirin prolongs life. Likewise, when there is an event that has negative effects on your short and/or long term sales, you must factor in its effect when projecting sales. If your company markets products that are affected by positive or negative fad volume movement, you must estimate the impact of this phenomena in terms of volume over time. How many consumers will it affect and for how long?

Your Product's Life Cycle

Another consideration when setting sales objectives is to review where your product is in its life cycle. Do you have a new product with a large untapped target market, minimal competition, and substantial growth potential? If successfully introduced, are your product's sales still growing, have they plateaued, or are they in decline? Your short-term sales objectives should reflect the current life-cycle stage of your product, while your long-term objectives should concurrently reflect the stage of the life cycle into which your product is moving. Many times, to assure a clearer picture of where your product is in its life cycle, it is wise to stand back and review competitive products or draw comparisons to different products with similar characteristics in other industries. After these companies introduced their products, at what rate did they grow, when did they level off, and at what point in their existence did they decline? By determining if specific products they sell are in a growth, plateau, or declining stage, manufacturers and service firms, as well as retailers, can more accurately forecast expected sales growth for their companies.

The Mission and Personality of Your Organization

An important qualitative factor to consider is the mission and personality of your organization. What are your company's expectations? What is its reason for being? What is its philosophy of doing business?

Is your company conservative and careful or a moderate risk taker? Is it an old line, "don't rock the boat" company, or a young and charging, "we can do it" com-

Exhibit 4.1 The Process of Setting Sales Objectives

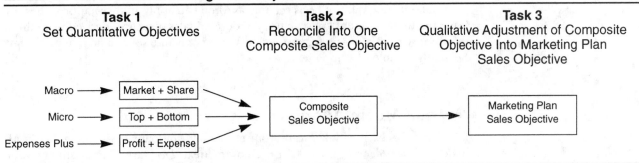

| **Task 1**
Set Quantitative Objectives | **Task 2**
Reconcile Into One
Composite Sales Objective | **Task 3**
Qualitative Adjustment of Composite
Objective Into Marketing Plan
Sales Objective |

pany? Also consider the aggressiveness of your organization in terms of growth and innovation—product improvements, new products, and the opening of new distribution channels and new markets. Take all of the above into consideration when estimating future sales.

Marketing Plan Expectation

Somewhat related to organization personality is another very important qualitative factor—your initial expectation of the overall marketing effort dictated by your marketing plan. The employment of a new, well-integrated, disciplined marketing plan will usually generate incremental sales, everything else being equal. Further, you would adjust your sales objectives upward if you intend to change the way you market your product, such as improving your product, investing incremental media dollars, adding promotional dollars, or lowering the price of the product.

HOW TO SET SALES OBJECTIVES

The methodology of setting sales objectives is both quantitative and qualitative, which means your sales objectives will be a composite of data-based estimates and educated guesses. If you use a disciplined process in setting sales objectives, these goals will be based more on realistic estimates and less on guessing.

The Process of Setting Sales Objectives

The recommended process to set your sales objective(s) is based on three tasks:

1. Set individual sales objectives using three different quantitative methods.

2. Reconcile these different quantitative goals into composite sales objectives.

3. Adjust the quantitatively-based composite sales objectives through the interpolation of the relevant subjective qualitative factors, such as the economy, competition, and the personality of your organization.

A graphic description of the process of setting sales objectives is shown in Exhibit 4.1. Worksheets for each task and a marketing plan format for writing the sales objectives are provided in Appendix C.

Task 1

Set Quantitative Sales Objectives

We suggest that, if the data are available, you use the following three different quantitative methods: outside macro, inside macro, and expense plus. Each method will develop a sales objective estimate, and each estimate will provide one of three parameters from which to make realistic judgments in arriving at a final sales objective(s). Each method can be used exclusively in arriving at a sales objective; however, the final outcome will not be as reliable as when you apply all three approaches. By using the three different approaches, you develop sales objectives derived from three different sets of data—a safeguard against using only one set of data that might not be totally reliable or complete.

Outside Macro Approach

In this approach, first look outside your immediate company environment and estimate *total market or category sales* for each of the next *three years*. Then, estimate your company's current and future share of the market for the next three years. Finally, multiply the total market or category projections by the market share estimate for each of the next three years to arrive at your sales objectives. You should end up with a three-year projection for both unit and dollar sales.

In order to arrive at these estimates, begin with a review of the past five-year trend of each marketplace in which your product, service, or retail store competes. (If five years of sales data are not available, use what data you have and supplement with available data from similar businesses to arrive at a trending of the marketplace.) If the market is trending up at a 5 percent rate, you could project the market to continue to grow at this rate for each of the next three years.

Market Trend Line Sales Projection

Rather than applying a straight percentage increase to arrive at market volume for future years, you can statistically develop a market trend line. If you were projecting sales in dollars for 1999 and you had a market change from $800,000 in 1991 to $900,000 in 1996, you would do the following:

Market change 1991 to 1996 = $100,000 ($800,000 to $900,000)
Market change period = five years (1991 to 1996)
Average $ change per year = $20,000 ($100,000 ÷ 5)
$ change for eight-year period (1991 to 1999) = $160,000 ($20,000 × 8)
Projected $ sales for 1999 = $960,000 ($800,000 from base year 1991 + $160,000
for change over eight-year period)

This method of projecting sales, referred to as *freehand*, is the simplest method of determining trend lines. You can use this trend line approach for both dollars and unit sales. If there is a substantial fluctuation in past sales year by year, you can arrive at a mathematically-generated trend line by using the least squares method. If this is necessary, we suggest you refer to a text on business statistics.

Company/Product Trend Line Share Projection

To arrive at a share of market estimate, review the change of your company's share over the past five years and project a similar share change for the future. You can estimate a percentage point change or use the same freehand approach shown in the above example. If you were estimating a share number for 1997 and your share changed from 10 percent in 1991 to 16.5 in 1996, you would do the following:

Share change 1991 to 1996 = 6.5 points (from 10 percent to 16.5 percent)
Share change period = five years (1991 to 1996)
Average change per year = 1.3 points (6.5 points ÷ 5 years)
Share change for six-year period (1991 to 1997) = 7.8 points (1.3 × 6)

Exhibit 4.2 Sales Objectives: Macro Method

Market and Share Data

	Market Sales Volume				Company Share Percent of the Market			
	$ (MM)	Percent Change Previous Year	Units (MM)	Percent Change Previous Year	$	Percent Point Change from Previous Year	Units	Percent Point Change from Previous Year
Previous 5 Years								
1992	$ 952.2	13.3%	449.1	5.1%	5.0%	0.1	4.0%	0.2
1993	1,067.0	12.1	484.0	7.8	5.1	0.1	4.7	0.7
1994	1,135.1	6.4	508.2	5.0	6.1	1.0	5.2	0.5
1995	1,202.9	6.0	527.9	3.9	6.5	0.4	5.7	0.5
1996	1,275.0	6.0	544.0	3.0	6.6	0.1	6.1	0.4
Projections Next 3 Years								
1997	1,355.7	6.3	567.7	4.4	7.0	0.4	6.6	0.5
1998	1,436.4	5.9	591.4	4.1	7.4	0.4	7.1	0.5
1999	1,517.1	5.6	615.1	4.0	7.8	0.4	7.6	0.5

Three Year Sales Projection for Company

	Dollars			Units		
Year	Market Sales Volume (MM)	× Company Share Percent of Market	= Company Sales (MM)	Market Sales Unit Volume (MM)	× Company Unit Share Percent of Market	= Company Unit Sales (MM)
1997	$1,355.7	7.0%	$ 94.9	567.7	6.6%	37.5
1998	1,436.4	7.4	106.3	591.4	7.1	42.0
1999	1,517.1	7.8	118.3	615.1	7.6	47.0

Projected share for 1997 = 17.8 percent (10 percent share from base year 1991 + 7.8 percentage point change over six-year period)

Again, once you have arrived at a projected number for market sales and units and a projected share of the market for each, multiply the total market estimates by the estimated market shares to arrive at a sales objective for dollars and units. You would apply this Macro method in each of the years for which you are developing sales objectives. Exhibit 4.2 provides an example of how this method can be used. A worksheet that you can use to apply this method is provided in Appendix C. Modify this worksheet to include transactions if you are in the retail business; modify it from units to persons/companies served if you are in the service business.

Inside Micro Approach

Having reviewed the outside market sales, next review your own organization's sales history. Start at the *top*, or with a review of your organization's total sales. Using the straight percentage increase or the trend line approach, arrive at projected three-year sales for your company. From the top go further, and using the straight percentage or trend line approach, estimate sales for each product or department, adding the projected sales of each product/department together for a three-year company total. Reconcile this total with your initial sales estimate for the entire organization to determine an ultimate top projection.

Next, review your sales by dollars and units from the *bottom up* to arrive at an estimated sales figure. Bottom up means estimating sales from where they are generated, such as sales by each channel, store unit, or service office/center. Based on history and changes in the marketplace, estimate sales for each bottom-up sales generator and add them together to determine each year's projection. You can use the straight percent change or trend line approach for each year's projection. However, if you have either a vast amount or very little data to process, you might have to estimate, rather than calculate, each sales projection.

Exhibit 4.3 provides an example of how to prepare a top-to-bottom sales forecast. Worksheets for the top and bottom sales forecasting needed to apply the Micro method are provided in Appendix C.

If you are in a manufacturing business, your bottom-up generator becomes the distribution channel (direct accounts, wholesaler/distributors, etc.). If you are in the retail business, build up to a total sales estimate by estimating by store, by market, and by district/region. Use this same approach if you are in the service business. It is often a good idea to have participation from the sales force or the retail/service people in the field, as they estimate sales in their area of responsibility.

To arrive at a final micro sales objective, you must then reconcile the organization's sales estimates derived from the top with those derived from the bottom.

Expenses Plus Approach

Once you have the outside, macro-based estimates and the inside, micro-based sales estimates, it makes good sense to estimate the sales level needed to cover planned expenses and make a profit. This budget-based sales objective approach is more short term in nature and is most useful in helping to arrive at your one-year sales objective. However, you can develop sales objectives for each year of a three-year sales period by employing this approach. A sales objective derived from expense and profit expectations can differ dramatically from a sales objective generated from a market or company sales trend projection. This difference in projections may signal the need for a more conservative or aggressive marketing plan. Although very simplistic, it is also very real, because it details the sales that have to be generated in order to stay in business and make a profit.

To arrive at a sales objective using this method, you will need budget data. If your company has been doing business for a number of years, it is relatively easy to estimate expenses and expected profits for the next year by reviewing your historical financial data. It is a good learning experience, particularly if you are new in the business, to review the cost of goods, operating margins, expenses, and profits within the industry and for other comparable businesses. Industry guidelines such as these are available from libraries, trade associations, and the Business Census.

A number of methods can be used to develop a budget-based sales objective. With "expense plus" a common approach that we apply in our business, you first estimate your operating expenses (marketing, administrative, etc.) in total dollars for the upcoming year. Next, subtract your expected profit (pretax) percentage from your expected gross margin percentage (Gross Sales – Cost of Goods Sold = Net Sales; Net Sales ÷ Gross Sales = Gross Margin) to determine an estimated expense percentage. The gross margin percentage is available from historical company records and/or from industry guideline data. The estimated expense percent is divided into the estimated expense dollars to determine the required sales necessary to meet expense and profit goals. Once you have developed your dollar "Expenses Plus" sales objectives, you can arrive at a corresponding unit objective by dividing the dollar objective by the average sales unit price. Exhibit 4.4 presents an example of a review of data and calculations for the expense plus approach. A worksheet for your computations is provided in Appendix C.

Exhibit 4.3 Sales Objectives: Micro Method

Projection from Top: Sales Forecast for Manufacturing, Service, or Retail Category*

	Company Sales Volume			
	$ (MM)	Percent Change Previous Year	Units (MM)	Percent Change Previous Year
Previous 5 Years				
1992	$ 47.7	10.3%	20.2	6.0%
1993	54.1	13.4	22.8	12.8
1994	68.8	27.1	28.8	26.3
1995	78.0	13.3	32.7	13.5
1996	84.2	7.9	34.0	4.0
Next 3 Years Projections				
1997	93.3	10.8	37.5	10.3
1998	102.4	9.8	41.0	9.3
1999	111.5	8.9	44.4	8.3

Projections from Bottom: Sales Forecast by Distribution Channel for Manufacturers*†

	Existing			New		
	Number	Dollars (MM)	Units (MM)	Number	Dollars (MM)	Units (MM)
Direct Accounts	25	$29.2	9.2	6	$5.6	2.4
Wholesalers/Brokers	74	62.4	26.5	6	2.1	0.9
Other	—	—	—	—	—	—
Total	99	$91.6	35.7	12	$7.7	3.3

Projections from Bottom: Sales Forecast by Store for Retailers*†

	Existing Stores	
Market	Dollars (000)	Transactions (000)
Green Bay/Store Number		
3	$ 773.7	73.6
4	276.8	25.2
5	449.8	41.8
7	285.6	23.2
8	343.5	30.5
Market Total	$2,129.4	194.3
Madison/Store Number		
1	644.1	59.5
2	396.6	35.0
6	534.7	46.0
9 (new, open 9 months)	400.0	36.0
Market Total	$1,975.4	176.5
Grand Total	$4,104.8	370.8

*Based on your type of business, include in your sales projections dollars and units/transactions/persons served, and take into consideration *new* products, distribution channels, stores or services, and price changes. Service organizations use service office/center in place of stores. Manufacturers use net dollar sales to trade/intermediate markets and retail/service firms use dollar sales to ultimate purchasers.

†For bottom-up projections, develop projections for each year for a three year period.

Alternative New Product/Category Approach

As mentioned in the discussion of quantitative factors, you can use a target market approach to setting sales objectives when you have limited or no sales history. This approach is particularly useful for new products or product categories, such as the

Exhibit 4.4 Sales Objectives: Expense Plus Method

Review of Historical Financial Data

Previous 5 Years	Gross Margin Percent of Sales	Profit Percent of Sales	Percent of Sales	Expenses Dollars (MM)
1992	33.4%	4.5%	29.1%	$13.9
1993	35.1	3.1	32.1	17.1
1994	37.2	3.1	34.1	23.5
1995	35.2	1.0	35.5	27.7
1996	31.3	1.0	30.1	28.0

Method Calculations

Planned Margin	33.5%
Planned Profit	−3.5%
Operating Expense	30.0%

Budgeted Expense Dollars of $28.5MM/Operating Expense of 30.0% = Sales Objective of $95.0MM

introduction of the first VCR or soft soap. Review the potential target market and work backwards to a sales objective number. An example for a package goods product follows:

Potential target market consumers	2,500M
(Defined by demography, geography, usage, etc.)	
Expected trial rate	4%
Initial trial units	100M
% making repeat purchases	40%
Repeat purchases	40M
Number of repeat purchases	5
Repeat units	200M
Initial trial units	100M
Units sold nationally	300M
Cases (12 units per case)	25M
Gross sales (@ $10.74/case)	$268.5M

The initial estimates of the target market potential, trial, and repeat projections are obviously critical to this type of sales objectives. Unless based on historical data closely related to your product, sales objectives generated in this manner are highly speculative and thus can be highly inaccurate. It is best to use the target market approach only when data for the other methods of sales forecasting do not exist or in conjunction with one or all of the other quantitative methods previously discussed.

Task 2
Reconciling Sales
Objectives

Now that you have arrived at outside macro sales objectives, inside micro sales objectives, and an expense plus sales objective, you must reconcile the differences to establish the sales objectives for your marketing plan. After reviewing your sales objective alternatives based on the macro, micro, and expenses plus methods, you may decide to go with a pure average of the three or a weighted average, placing more emphasis on one alternative than the other. You may use the (weighted) average of two, or just one. The important aspect of Task 2 is that you have reviewed the data from various quantitative perspectives. This will help you arrive at a sales objective with your eyes wide open and with an understanding of the dynamics that go into setting a sales objective. For the most meaningful sales projections, attempt to apply all three methods or, at the very minimum, two methods that you can use for

Exhibit 4.5 Reconciliation of Sales Objectives

	Macro		Micro		Expense Plus		Composite Sales Objectives	
	Dollars (MM)	Units (MM)	Dollars (MM)	Units (MM)	Dollars (MM)	Units (MM)	Dollars (MM)	Units (MM)
Short Term 1997	$ 94.9	37.5	$ 96.3	38.2	$ 95.0	37.7	$ 95.4	37.8
Long Term 1998	106.3	42.0	103.4	40.1	104.4	40.9	104.7	41.0
1999	118.3	47.0	112.2	45.1	111.0	43.5	113.8	45.2

comparison. Exhibit 4.5 shows how reconciliation of the three methods' goals into a composite sales objective(s) can be accomplished. A worksheet is provided in Appendix C.

Task 3
Qualitative Adjustment of Quantitative Sales

Now that you have arrived at quantitative sales objectives, you should review the qualitative factors that will have an impact on the future sales. You need to temper the numerically derived sales objectives with the more qualitative forecasting factors. Using the appropriate qualitative factors, you can increase or decrease the composite dollars and units/transactions/persons served sales objectives through an assignment of positive or negative percentage points, depending on the estimated degree of impact by each qualitative factor. If the economy is growing and the economic outlook is bright, you might increase the composite sales objective by two percentage points. Or, you may decrease the composite sales objective by four percentage points because an aggressive competitor moved into your trading area. If there is more than one major impacting factor, you can balance their effect through averaging. Exhibit 4.6 illustrates how to calculate these factors. A worksheet for you to use in adjusting the composite sales objectives by the qualitative impacting factors is provided in Appendix C.

Final Reminders

Include Rationale with Sales Objectives

Once the sales objectives are determined and agreed upon, also include a brief rationale. This rationale should summarize the processes used, assumptions made, and factors considered in finalizing the sales objectives. Although they are not included in the worksheets for sales objectives, you can also include specific profit objectives for each year. Any additional pertinent supporting data related to sales and profit objectives should be included in the marketing plan appendix.

Involve Upper Management in Setting Sales Objectives

If you report to upper management, make sure you have an understanding of the company sales and profit expectations and have reviewed the company business plan, if available. Many times, upper management dictates the sales objectives to the marketing department. When this occurs, it is even more important for you to have systematically arrived at your own sales objectives. Based on your input, management can adjust its sales objectives (if very different from your sales projections) or,

Exhibit 4.6 Qualitative Adjustment of Quantitatively Derived Sales Objectives

Qualitative Impacting Factors	Point Change	Percentage Adjustment	×	Composite Sales Objective (MM)	=	Adjusted Sales Objective (MM)
1. Economy	+2	1.02		$95.4		$ 97.3
2. Competition	−4	.96		95.4		91.6
Total						$188.9
Final Adjusted Average (Total of adjusted sales objectives divided by number of calculated factors)						$94.5

1. List qualitative factors and to what extend they will impact on the previous numerically arrived at sales objectives. Adjust composite sales objective(s) accordingly to arrive at final sales objective(s).
2. Use qualitative adjustments for units, transactions, or persons served, as well as for sales dollar objectives for each year of three year projection. However, percentage point adjustment may differ from dollars.

at the very least, gain additional perspective as it reviews the marketing plan designed to meet the dictated sales objectives. To ensure developing a plan that reaches the agreed-upon sales objectives, it is a good idea to involve upper management regarding the sales and profit objectives before the remainder of the marketing plan is written.

Plan to Revise the Sales Objectives

The sales objectives will most likely be revised more than once as you write the marketing plan. You may uncover greater than expected sales potential among a target market. Or you may determine that your company does not have the necessary capital, that there is greater competition than expected, or that there is not enough consumer demand, all of which could negatively affect the estimated sales objectives.

Once your marketing plan is written (ideally, two or three months before the start of your fiscal year), it is wise to keep your sales objectives current. Review your sales objectives at two months, five months, and eight months into the marketing plan year in order to adjust the sales objectives for the second, third, and fourth quarters of your fiscal year. This will help you maximize your sales and control your expenses in a timely and profitable manner. However, keep in mind that, once you have agreed to a sales objective for your company, you cannot change the budget throughout the fiscal year, but you can change the sales objective in your forecast. The budget is permanent and serves as your benchmark, while your forecast is flexible and reflects your adjustment to the changing status of your business and the marketplace.

DOS AND DON'TS

Do

- Set sales objectives in a disciplined, step-by-step manner.

- Set short- and long-term sales objectives that are time specific and measurable.

- Make your sales objectives challenging and attainable

- Review the sales history of the market and your product.

- Consider the size, growth, and decline of your specific target market and its purchase rates as a double check on those of your projections that are based on past sales history or are for new products and categories.

- Determine where your product/service/store concept is in its life cycle.

- Get upper management's agreement to sales objectives before finalizing the marketing plan.

- Review industry averages for cost of product/inventory, expenses, and profits.

- Use more than one method in developing your quantitative sales objectives to help guard against a "one-sided" sales projection.

- Realistically plan for pricing changes.

- Qualitatively adjust your numerically derived sales objectives.

- With today's unlimited personal computer potential, investigate the possibility of using computer-generated sales objectives based on the methodology provided in this chapter.

- Once you have arrived at your sales objectives, consider developing a range forecast of high and low to give perspective on up-side potential and down-side risk. This will provide for contingency options as the year progresses in order to realize unforeseen potential or cut your losses should the business not perform as expected.

- Depending on your type of business, break down your annual sales objectives into smaller segments such as quarters, months, and/or weeks—possibly even days for retail and service firms. This breakdown will be of major assistance when you formulate your annual marketing calendar.

- Revise your sales objectives as needed during plan preparation and revise your marketing plan budget accordingly.

- Remember the big picture when setting sales objectives. Sales for your product can come from three sources: 1) an all-new market in which you have not competed, 2) growth of the market, and/or 3) the competition.

Don't

- Do not guess.

- Do not set dollar sales objectives only.

- Do not accept upper management's sales objectives without independently arriving at your own.

- Do not always believe that your company alone can buck a marketwide decline; don't set sales objectives based on achieving unattainable sales increases.

- Do not overestimate the size of the market.

- Do not feel secure with your long-term sales objectives if your share of market is increasing in a declining market. Increasing share cannot continually supplement a declining market. Look for other avenues that will put your company in a market growth situation.

- Do not consider just the qualitative factors presented in this chapter, but consider other qualitative factors that pertain to your specific industry.

- Do not neglect to get input from upper management and those delegated to generate the sales (i.e., sales force, store managers, etc.) before setting sales objectives.

- Do not underestimate the impact of competition when setting sales objectives.

- Do not set sales objectives based on what you or the company wants and needs, but on what the market will bear.

- Do not set a sales objective and leave it. Update sales objectives for the fiscal year on an evolving forecast basis, but do not change the sales budget.

Step Four   Target Markets and Marketing Objectives

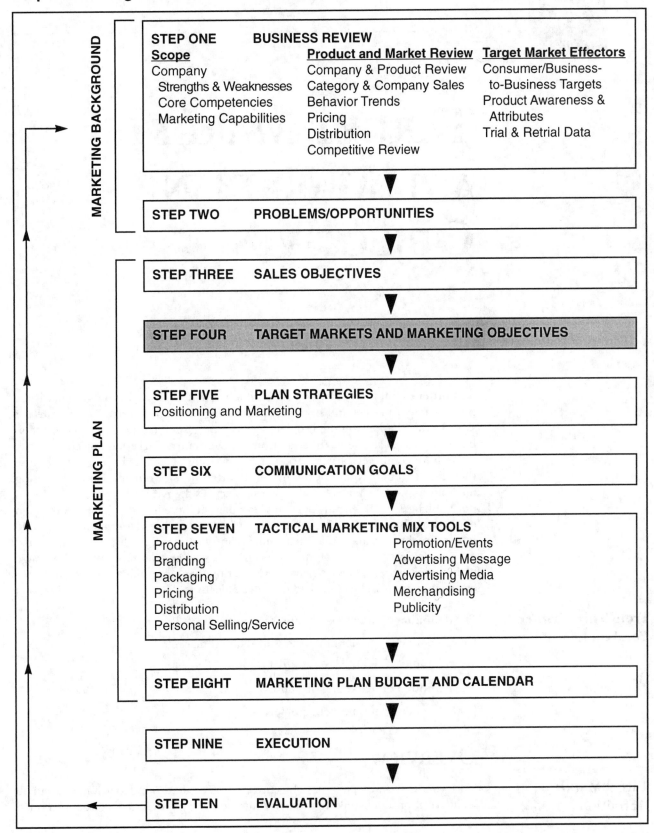

5

TARGET MARKETS AND MARKETING OBJECTIVES

In order to fulfill the sales objectives which you have just set, you must clearly define the target market and necessary purchasing behavior needed to generate the sales. In this chapter you will learn how to identify target market segments and then link those target segments to sales through quantitative marketing objectives.

We have combined target market and marketing objectives in one step because their link together is one of the defining differences of our marketing planning methodology. Many plans fail after sales objectives are established because there is not a link back to sales in any portion of the plan. If there is not a direct link through marketing objectives and target markets to sales, the marketing manager should have no real expectation that the strategies and tactics will really achieve the stated sales goals. In summary, *you can't manage what you can't measure.* You can manage plans which tie marketing objectives to quantifiable target market or segment behavior that, in turn, locks back to the sales objectives.

From This Chapter You Will Learn

The definition of target market and segmentation.

How to define consumer and/or business target markets.

How target markets and marketing objectives are locked to sales.

The definition of marketing objectives.

How to develop your marketing objectives.

OVERVIEW

Target Market Definition

Once you have developed sales objectives, you must determine to whom you will be selling your product. Making this determination is really defining a target market; a group of people or companies with a set of common characteristics. Target marketing allows for a concentration of effort against a portion of the universe with similar descriptors, product needs, or buying habits.

Companies don't *sell* products, customers *purchase* them. In effect, your company exists because of the customers or target markets you choose to serve. Since we define marketing as the process of identifying the target market(s), determining the needs and wants of the target market(s), and fulfilling those needs and wants better than the competition, the determination of the target market is the most critical step in the marketing planning process.

Your business review analyzed potential target markets by looking at many industry category and company target segments responsible for product sales volume. The biggest marketing mistake is to attempt to be all things to all people. It is in this section that the marketer must decide which target segment(s) will form the core of the business and receive the emphasis of effort and budget.

The targets are the key to all that follows in the marketing plan, because your target markets are the reason for your product's existence and the key to finding marketing answers. Let your target market drive your marketing plan.

Segmentation

Segmentation is a selection process that divides the broad consuming market into manageable customer or non-customer groups with common characteristics. Segmentation provides the marketer the opportunity to exploit these common characteristics of the consumer or customer group through the company's marketing efforts. Instead of marketing to the "average" consumer, you are able to pinpoint specific clusters of consumers who have unique, yet similar, demographics, lifestyles, attitudes, concerns, purchasing habits, or needs and wants. The most effective marketing communication is essentially the one-on-one sales call, where the skilled salesperson can address the needs of the individual prospect. Due to the similarities inherent in a given segment, marketers too can address groups as if they were communicating with individuals, and direct communications to groups of consumers with similar characteristics via more meaningful products, pricing, and messages. Thus, segmentation allows you to realize the greatest potential sales at the lowest cost.

There are two broad segments for most businesses within which you will develop additional subsegments for targeting:

1. *Current customers.* Customers and segments of the customer base with whom you are currently doing business.

2. *New customers.* Segments in which you are not currently doing business or in which you feel there is potential to do more business.

Before you start developing additional target market segments within the two broad segments listed above, think about what you are trying to achieve. More than simply looking for consumer or customer similarities, segment identification involves identifying similarities that are directly tied to sales and profits. When you develop target market segments, you do so by grouping like segments of customers or potential customers with the objective of finding those segments that are responsible for the most dollar volume, profit, or purchases and that also demonstrate future potential. If you completed your business review, this work has been done. You now just need the parameters which help you make the right target selections. The remainder of this chapter will do just that.

Short-term and Long-term Target Market Segments

Remember to develop short-term segments (those responsible for sales within the next year) and also distinct, long-term segments (those which you wish to develop over the next two to three years but which will not account for significant sales in the short term). Long-term target markets typically require significant changes in product, distribution, or operational requirements prior to effectively satisfying the customers in these groups.

Primary and Secondary Target Markets

When you develop your target market segments, remember that there are varying degrees of importance among the target segments. We group these segments into primary and secondary target markets. While the spending and focus emphasis is different for primary and secondary targets, both are responsible for generating and tying directly to sales.

Primary Target Market

A primary target market is your main consuming group. These consumers are the most important purchasers and users of your product and will be the mainstay of your business. In some cases, the primary target market is the heavy user (one-third or less of the purchasers who account for two-thirds or more of the purchases). For companies who are more niche oriented, the primary target will be a smaller, though viable, section of the market which requires selective or specialized goods and services. And in some situations, there will be a primary target market which is an intermediate channel, such as a distributor, and a primary target which is a consumer or end user. Both targets will have different ties to sales (for example, a wholesale price and a retail price, respectively), and both will require separate plans.

The following criteria should be fulfilled before you finalize a primary target market choice:

- Make sure the customer base is large enough in terms of actual numbers of consumers and dollar volume of purchasers. What percent of the product category's volume does your primary target market consume? Given your projected market share, is it enough to support your business? (See Demand Analysis at the end of the target segment methodology section in this chapter.) A common reason for a plan's failure is a target market that is too small and limiting. Ideally, try to get your primary target market profile to be accountable for approximately 30–50 percent of the category volume. For example, if 18 to 24 year olds accounted for only 10 percent of the consumption, the marketer would need to expand the age criteria beyond 18 to 24 year olds until the age group was broad enough to account for more volume. However, if the purchase behavior or the purchasing criteria were distinctly different among 18 to 24 year olds than among other age groups, the marketer would need to establish a number of smaller target markets—something that is much more difficult and expensive to execute.

  The 30–50 percent criteria can be lower if you are going to specialize against a more narrow purchaser/user base but obtain a larger market share against this segment. However, you must be certain that your company has some special tie to the narrow niche which will command loyalty.

- Make sure the target market is profitable. Determine that the target market purchases sufficient quantity to assure profitability.

- Try to estimate the trending of your primary target market. Is it a growing or shrinking segment? If it is shrinking, will the market be large enough to support your business at its current market share in five years? If not, this should be a danger signal.

- Make sure that your primary target market can be narrowly defined by one unified profile. The primary target market should be a group of individuals or companies with the same basic identifiers and purchasing behavior. This will allow your marketing effort to be focused against essentially one type of individual.

The primary target market becomes the company's reason for being. You are in business to determine the primary target market's wants and needs and to provide for those wants and needs better than your competition. This pertains to providing the product, service, shopping or sales environment, distribution channel, and price structure that is required by the customer for purchase. The better the definition and description of the consumers in your primary target market, the better you will be able to market to them.

Secondary Target Markets

Most plans will identify multiple target markets. The primary target markets receive priority and a majority of the marketing spending, because they will most directly influence the short-term financial success of the plan. The secondary target markets are important, because they provide additional sales and/or influence on the sales to the company beyond that of the primary target market as well as future sales to the company. A secondary target market can be one of the following:

- *A segment currently too small to be a primary market, but shown to have future potential.* In some cases, you may identify segments with great growth potential, but which currently are very small in absolute purchasing power. In other cases, there might be a large segment which would become a primary target as a result of fundamental marketing changes making your product or service more attractive to this market.

- *A demographic category with a low volume but a high concentration index.* Often there is a distinct demographic category that accounts for a small percentage of the volume but contains a high concentration of purchasers. For example, 18 to 24 year olds may account for only 10 percent of the total product category purchases, but 50 percent of the 18 to 24 year olds may purchase the product. This may be due to popularity of the product among this age group, but fewer total purchase occasions or purchase of more inexpensive product models. In any case, a great percentage of the target uses the product, providing the opportunity for efficient use of marketing dollars and little wasted coverage in targeting the segment.

- *Subsets of purchasers or users who make up the primary target markets.* As stated in the primary target market section, your primary target market should ideally be one unified profile of customers accounting for greater than 30 percent of the category volume. This allows for a focusing of resources and message in the marketing effort. However, there are situations in which the volume of any one target market is not substantial enough to qualify it as a primary target market. In addition, each smaller target market has different demographics, needs, wants, product usage, and purchasing behavior. An example of this is in the target market we developed for a regional menswear retailer. The retailer was selling primarily suits and sport coats. There were many purchasing profiles, but no single profile group provided enough volume to allow for targeting against that group. The primary target market became very broad and encompassed all white-collar males who were 18–54 years of age. However, the following secondary target markets were developed, with subsequent marketing emphasis and programs against each.

—Men, 18 to 24, college graduates, entering the working world and looking for affordable suits

—Men, 45 plus, higher income, at the top of their profession, interested in quality menswear and needing to update their wardrobes

—Women 18 to 34; women have a great influence over men's purchases of suits and sport coats. Spouses also purchase a substantial number of sport coats as gifts and accompany men in more than 50 percent of their shopping trips, serving as advisors.

—Blue-collar males who need an all-occasion suit; price is a concern.

—Target markets were also broken out by type of profession, as this helped dictate quantity and style of suit purchases.

■ *Influencers.* Influencers can be both a primary or secondary target market, though in most situations they are a secondary target market. These are individuals who influence the purchase or usage decision of the primary target market. A good example of this is the influence children have on their parents in the purchase of many consumer goods, from toys to fast food.

Influencers are of particular importance in public sector marketing, where outside forces can affect the success of an organization's marketing program. In a statewide bus transit marketing effort, we concentrated marketing efforts against current and potential riders as our primary target, but we also targeted opinion leaders, major employers, and education leaders, all of whom affect communities' public support of the bus system, as our secondary market.

In business-to-business situations, a secondary target can often be a customer who currently does not purchase heavily from your company but who has high purchasing potential. You can delineate the potential of this customer by estimating your competitors' sales to this customer and determining what additional needs your company can fulfill for this customer.

Further, manufacturers most often include an intermediate channel as a secondary target segment. This target might be a fabricator, distributor/wholesaler, or retailer that should receive special attention in order to make sure the product is available for the end user to purchase. This is particularly true in marketing consumer goods, with minimal retail shelf space available and multiple competitors selling the same type of product. Often, so much time and money is devoted to selling to the end user that the intermediate channel is taken for granted.

Conversely, many business-to-business manufacturers, because they are selling directly to an intermediate target market (which is their primary target), *push* these products through the primary distribution channel (often using low prices and promotions) and put less marketing emphasis on the end user to *pull* the product through the channels. It might be more efficient in the short term to push the product through intermediate markets. However, the end user should not be totally ignored, as this may mean a loss of demand and loyalty for your product or brand over the long term.

Purchaser and/or User Determination

Many times the purchaser of a product is different from the user. If this is true, you need to decide who has the most influence over the actual purchase. Does the one who drinks the beer request a special brand, or does the beer drinker drink what the shopper purchases? In most cases, the individual who does the purchasing becomes the primary target market. However, when the purchaser primarily buys what the user requests, then the user receives primary attention.

You must determine whether the primary target group will include purchasers, users, or both. However, keep in mind that it is very difficult (not to mention expensive) to effectively market against two primary markets. Because this is an encompassing step in the defining process, step back and attempt to determine which of these two targets is the driving force and what makes up their purchase and usage behavior. Consider these two factors in your determination:

1. The inherent benefits of your product to one target or the other

2. Who the competition chooses as its target market

If the user and the purchaser are different, who should be the primary target for your marketing efforts: the user or the purchaser? Or do you target both? The following examples show how to make this determination.

- In testing a hot water faucet for Elkay Manufacturing, one potential target market was small businesses, because the Hot Water Machine eliminated the mess of making office coffee. We knew that business managers and presidents were the primary decision makers and purchasers in small to mid-size businesses. For both of these titles we could purchase actual names for a direct mail test. However, every office had a "coffee maker" who was the user. While we couldn't purchase names for this function, we felt we could effectively use the title and each office would know who we were addressing. We tested different direct mail lists and found that the "Office Coffee Maker" label on the mailer was by far the most productive.

- For Kerry Foods, we focus primarily on the Research and Development target (the users who first determined to incorporate Kerry's spray dried ingredients into a new or existing food). Secondarily, however, we create different messages for the purchasing agents (purchasers), who often have a major influence on whether Kerry Foods products continue to get purchased after the initial trial generated by the R&D staff.

- To whom should powdered soft drinks that are consumed primarily by kids age 2 to 11 but are purchased by their mothers be marketed? Ideally, if you dominate the category and have adequate marketing dollars, both should be targeted. If you are a low-share competitor and have limited marketing dollars, as was the case for one particular client, concentrate on a single target market. In this case, the primary target market was redefined as kids 2 to 11, with marketing focus concentrated against the user rather than the purchaser. The result was a revival in sales and a share increase. Therefore, if you do not or cannot dominate the market in terms of sales and marketing dollars (which is most often the case), concentrate your marketing efforts against one target market rather than fragmenting your efforts over many. Also, evaluate the competitive environment, looking for targets which have not received emphasis but which provide volume potential.

- In the case of shoe purchasers and users, a mother who buys shoes for her children, herself, and her husband and is responsible for 80 percent of family purchases is the heavy purchaser. She becomes the primary target market and receives the major marketing emphasis.

■ McDonald's is the exception. As it is a dominant player in its category, it has substantial marketing dollar leverage. As a result, McDonald's puts major emphasis against two primary targets: kids, who as users and influencers are considered the cornerstone of their business; and adults, because they are also users and, more importantly, because they are purchasers who bring their kids to McDonald's.

Target Segmentation Methodology

The methodology for determining either current customer or new customer segments involves seven tasks. (Note: The following methodology is designed for a target which consumes a *group of products* within the scope of an industry (i.e., shoes for the family or a range of accounting services, etc.). If you have one product, the same methodology applies except you eliminate Task 1 and Task 6 and start with Task 2 listing the segments for your one product. Worksheets for developing your target markets strategies appear in Appendix C.

Task 1
Sales/Profits

The target market process starts with first identifying industry and company *products* which demonstrate strong demand and sales growth. Go back to the business review and list the products which had the most category and/or company sales, profits, or transactions and are demonstrating the most growth. (Product and Market Review—Sales section) See Exhibit 5.1.

Task 2
Segments

We define target markets by first focusing on the target market segments responsible for purchasing or using the products which:

1. Account for the greatest industry and company product sales volume, and/or profits, and/or transactions, and/or number of customers (see Product and Market Review—Sales section and Target Market Effectors—Target Market section in the business review).

2. Are industry or company growth products that are trending up in sales, and/or profits, and/or transactions, and/or customers and that are estimated to be major volume producers in the future.

The segmentation process we use starts by looking at the two broadest segments which account for sales of the products identified in Task 1 above.

■ Current customers and

■ New customers (potential customers)

Review the business review to determine the number of current customers and non-customers that consumed the products identified in Task 1. List the number of customers and potential customers in the target market, the average dollar per purchase occasion, the dollar purchased per customer, the number of purchase occasions/number of purchases per year, the penetration (customers as a percent of the potential total category consumers), the retrial rate, and the growth trends in terms of customers/consumers using or purchasing the product.

Now break the large segments (customers and non-customers) into smaller segments looking for characteristics which predict volume. Note the volume of each segment along with the specifics just identified (number in target market, number of

Exhibit 5.1 Product Sales Volume

Example

List the largest sales volume, profit, and fastest growth products from the category. Provide sales trends, profits trends, and percent of category sales. Provide company information (sales trends, profit trends, percent of category sales and market share) for the same leading products.

M = $000

Category 5-Year Trend

Cross-Country Ski Example

Category's Highest $ Volume Products	Sales Yr. 1	Yr. 2	Yr. 3	Yr. 4	Yr. 5	% of Category Sales* Yr. 1	Yr. 2	Yr. 3	Yr. 4	Yr. 5	Profit** Yr. 1	Yr. 2	Yr. 3	Yr. 4	Yr. 5	# Transactions/Purchases Yr. 1	Yr. 2	Yr. 3	Yr. 4	Yr. 5
1) Skating skis	$100MM	$120MM	$110MM	$150MM	$160MM	10%	14%	12%	15%	16%	45%	45%	44%	44%	44%					
2) Wax touring skis																				
3) No-wax touring skis																				
•																				
•																				
•																				

*In year 1, 10% of the category's sales came from product 1.
**Could be percent of profit or profit margin. In this case it is a gross margin.
Note: Dollars are not real industry figures.

Company 5-Year Trend

Company's Highest $ Volume Products	Sales Yr. 1	Yr. 2	Yr. 3	Yr. 4	Yr. 5	% of Company Sales*** Yr. 1	Yr. 2	Yr. 3	Yr. 4	Yr. 5	Profit Yr. 1	Yr. 2	Yr. 3	Yr. 4	Yr. 5	# Transactions/Purchases Yr. 1	Yr. 2	Yr. 3	Yr. 4	Yr. 5
1) Skating skis	$10MM	$20MM	$30MM	$30MM	$40MM	10%	22%	30%	30%	35%	45%	44%	44%	43%	42%					
2) No-wax touring skis																				
3) Telemark skis																				
•																				
•																				
•																				

***In this example, the company's number-one selling product matches the industry's number-one selling product (skating skis). However, the company's number two and three selling products (No-wax and Telemark) differ from the category's number two and three selling skis.

Products	Company Market Share**** Yr. 1	Yr. 2	Yr. 3	Yr. 4	Yr. 5
1) Skating skis	10%	17%	27%	20%	25%
2)					
3)					
•					
•					
•					

****Company ÷ Category (Example: $10MM ÷ $100MM)

Index Company to Category

$ Volume Products	Sales % Change Company (5-year trend) Yr. 1 to Yr. 5	Sales % Change Category (5-year trend) Yr. 1 to Yr. 5	Sales Index Company/Category Yr. 1 to Yr. 5	% of Sales***** Index Company/Category Yr. 1	Yr. 2	Yr. 3	Yr. 4	Yr. 5
1) Skating skis	300%	60%	500	100	157	250	200	218
2)								
3)								
•								
•								
•								

*****Company % of sales ÷ Category % of sales (Example: 10% ÷ 10% = 100, 22% ÷ 14% = 157, etc.)

purchase occasions, the dollar purchased per customer, etc.) for each of the segments. Finally, list the segment description which accounts for the most purchases, sales, profits, transactions, and/or customers; the second most for each of the top-performing products. See Exhibit 5.2.

If your current customer segments (based upon expected retention rates) and their respective dollar volume do not add up beyond your sales goal based upon historical purchasing averages, develop new customer segments to include in your marketing effort.

New customer segments may be identical to current customer segments if you find you still have plenty of customer market share or penetration potential. For example, a customer target market may be 18–24-year-old college students, yet your business review shows that you have only 20 percent of a particular state's college students as customers. Obviously, the target market can still be mined for new customers in that state. New trial segments may also be strong industry category segments in which you don't do well but where the segment's purchasing needs or criteria match your product's attributes. Therefore, it makes sense to target poorer performing customer segments that are relatively strong performing industry segments, especially if the competitive environment is not fiercely intense.

Based upon your findings, you may want to alter your initial target market profile description to more closely mirror the product category's target market in order to expand your current customer base. For example, through an analysis for a retail client experiencing low sales per store, we found that its customer target market was primarily blue-collar with an annual income of under $30,000, while the majority of purchases in the total category were white-collar with annual incomes over $40,000, skewing to $60,000 plus. The analysis involved in this exercise may also point out the major differences between the customer profiles of your company's product and those of the category and provide insight as to why your company is successfully capturing a specific segment of the product category and how to attract even more of the same consumers.

On the other hand, based upon your analysis, you may want to target a smaller, but growing, segment not targeted by the competition. Factors such as the size and growth of the market, above-average expenditures per customer, and the strong awareness and positive attribute ratings of your company might lead you to focus on a segment which does not mirror the category's heavy-user target segment.

A final word of caution: Before you go on to develop a new market or modify an existing target, make sure you have fully exploited the profit potential of your current customer base. This is particularly true in retail, service, and business-to-business marketing, where you have personal contact with your customers. In most cases, your own customers are your most important and potentially most profitable target market, because they are responsible for your firm's current existence and are a prime target for future sales. Target your current customers not only to retain their purchase loyalty but also to motivate them to make more and bigger purchases and to refer new customers. (Target Market Effectors—Target Market and Behavior sections). See Exhibit 5.2.

Segmentation Categories

The following segmentation categories were reviewed in the business review under the Target Market section of Target Market Effectors. Use these as you develop your target market segments against the high performing products in Task 1.

Consumer Tenure

Existing customers often display different purchasing habits (number of purchases, amount of purchases, different product mix) based upon the number of years they have been a customer. In addition, the retrial or renewal rate is often different by

Exhibit 5.2 Target Market Descriptions/Target Market Behavior

Example

List the target market description for the largest industry or company product category (based upon sales volume, sales growth and/or profitability), the second largest, third largest, etc. Use a separate form for each target market description.

List the target market behavior rates for the category and company.

Target Segment Descriptions

Consumer: (demographic, geographic, use attributes); Example—College students, 18–24.
Business-to-business: (SIC, end user, channel, size, organizational structure); Example—Service Standard Industrial Code (SIC), service
  businesses over $1MM

Segment #1: College Students

Segment accounts for 30% of Total Category Sales*			Segment accounts for 25% of Total Company Sales			Percent or Penetration	
	CATEGORY			**COMPANY**		**COMPANY/CATEGORY**	
	This Year	5 Year Growth Rate		This Year	5 Year Growth Rate		Penetration This Year
Number of users	300,000	7%	Number of users	100,000	10%	Number of users	33%
Number of purchases	850,000	5%	Number of purchases	300,000	10%	Number of purchases	35%
$ Customer	$15	15%	$ Customer	$10	5%		
Retrial rate	82%	3%	Retrial rate	70%	—		

*30% of the product category's sales is accounted for by this segment.
Note: The company has a higher purchase per user rate (300,000 ÷ 100,000 = 3) than the category average, but it has a lower retrial rate. Further exploration would probably demonstrate a segment of the users purchasing at very high rates and being very satisfied and another segment purchasing once and then not trying again. This information would be valuable when establishing subsequent target market and marketing objectives priorities.

tenure. As mentioned in the business review, AAA's renewal rate was significantly higher for members with five or more years of membership than for those with four or less. The new members used the organization significantly less (fewer services and usage amounts per service), which was a major factor in the smaller renewal rate. These findings resulted in establishing specific target market segments, objectives, and strategies against customers with 0–4 years of tenure.

Demographics

Demographics include descriptors such as age, income, education level, marital status, employment/job classification, race, and home ownership. Most of the purchasers of consumer products are predicted by demographics. The purchase of household products and kids' games are two examples.

Buying Habits/Product Use

Segmentation can be based upon how the product is purchased or used, the number of times purchased per year, the time of year the product is purchased, loyalty, or tenure of product use. For example, baking soda target markets are segmented based upon their use of the product either for cooking or as a refrigerator deodorizer.

We defined a target for the AAA Chicago Auto Club around the product users of Triptiks (routing maps) and maps. We discovered these customers were using a travel service (the Triptik or map provided by AAA for members) but were then booking the majority of their trips through alternative travel agencies. Therefore, we targeted users of Triptiks and maps (provided through the AAA Chicago club membership), with the objective of cross-selling this target into a package travel purchase. This idea was translated into the Triptik Plus program.

Many consumer goods firms target consumers based upon buying habits, specifically the consumer's propensity for multiple purchases. We worked with a game company in the puzzle business whose heavy users purchased 8–12 puzzles per year. Much of our target market segmentation work and many of the subsequent marketing objectives were developed around this purchasing behavior. We developed objectives to increase the number of company puzzles purchased per year, and strategies which called for series of puzzles and incentives to generate loyalty to this particular company's puzzles.

In addition, there are many product categories where the product is used/consumed differently by different target market groups. This is common in the business-to-business area, where spray-dried cheese is used very differently by Frito Lay in the processing of snacks than by Swanson in its TV dinners. Segmentation by different levels of consumption use is also common in consumer package goods marketing. For example, the snack industry segments users by individual, family, and party size, among others, when developing its package sizes.

Lifestyle Characteristics

Psychographics (values, lifestyles, interests, attitudes) are often used in conjunction with demographics to identify target market descriptors. One example would be a new five-blade propeller that we helped Mercury Marine introduce to the market place. We targeted against two lifestyle or interest psychographics—waterskiing and bass fishing. The five-blade prop provided significantly better "hole shot," or acceleration. Both of these segments had a need for this type of product, and they were predicted to account for a significant percentage of the sales volume for the five-blade propeller. They were targeted in terms of media, advertising (testimonials from expert waterskiers and bass fishermen), distribution of the product, and point-of-sale merchandising.

Geography

Purchasing rates often differ according to geography. Segmentation can be based upon climate, the consumption habits of certain regions, and other factors which cause differences in volume and usage by geography.

You should have determined regions, markets, and/or areas of markets that have the greatest consumption potential for your product by comparing the overall category sales to the sales of your product in comparable geographic areas. (See discussion of BDI and CDI in Target Market Effectors—Trial Behavior section.) Based on this analysis, you may want to expand, reduce, or merely refine the geographic focus of your target market.

Attribute Preference

Different consumer groups purchase different product categories due to product attributes and benefits.

With a retailer marketing fabric to sewers, product attributes or benefits became the primary means of defining the target market. As not all sewers consider both large selection and low prices of fabrics to be equally important when choosing one fabric store over the other, the retailer made "selection shoppers" its primary target, because it could not profitably deliver the price benefit as well as selection.

Heavy User or Purchaser Segment

Analyze the target market data in your business review to determine if there is a heavy user for your product. As a guideline, you have a heavy user in your product category if approximately two-thirds or more of total product is consumed by approximately one-third or less of the total users. A few percentage points below 67 percent of total usage and a few points above 33 percent of users is acceptable. For example, 35 percent of canned vegetable users consume 65 percent of canned vegetables.

With a *one-third user to two-thirds consumption* determination, this heavy user usually becomes your primary target. Define the heavy user segment based on descriptive data available to you. For the consumer market, the heavy user descriptor could include demography, geography, and/or possibly lifestyle and product benefit/usage information, if available. For business-to-business markets, the heavy user might be a specific industry type (SIC code), a relatively small number of distributors, or the customer group that has been ordering for more than 10 years.

Task 3
Awareness

Review the business review to determine if there is average to above-average awareness for your company and/or products among the segments you are considering for your target market(s). If not, you will need to spend considerable dollars increasing awareness. Remember, *share of mind leads to share of market* (Target Market Effectors—Awareness section). See Exhibit 5.3.

Task 4
Attitudes

Go back to the business review to determine if the segments in Task 2 have positive attitudes across the most important purchase criteria for each segment. If not, you will need to make a significant effort to change attitudes across the most important purchase attributes in order to convince the segment to purchase in meaningful numbers. Remember, it's always easier to build on strengths than to change a weakness (Target Market Effectors—Attitudes section). See Exhibit 5.3.

Task 5
Decision Criteria

Now, make a decision to target all or some of the segments which provide you the following:

- Strong industry and company sales or growing company or industry sales

- Strong awareness

- Positive attitudes toward your company or brand

- Large size or large potential size (smaller numbers of company customers but large industry category consumers or potential customers)

- Strong dollar-per-customer average, more profit per customer, or high number of transactions per customer

- Loyal segments with strong retrial rates

If the segments in Task 2 do not meet all of the criteria, look for those which have the greatest combination of them.

Exhibit 5.3 Awareness and Attribute Rankings

Example

List the awareness of the target markets for the company and the leading competitors. List the top purchase attributes for the target markets and the relative ranking of the company versus the leading competitors.

TARGET SEGMENT AWARENESS RATINGS

Target Segment: Women 18–34, Single, Income of $40M+

Yr.	1	2	3	4	5
Company	10%	12%	15%	17%	18%
Leading Competitor	28%	35%	36%	32%	30%
Leading Competitor	16%	15%	16%	15%	16%
Leading Competitor	15%	14%	13%	12%	10%

TARGET SEGMENT ATTRIBUTE RATINGS

Target Segment: Women 18–34, Single, Income of $40M+

Note: 1 = best; 5 = worst

Top 5 Attributes	Company Ranking					Leading Competitor A Ranking					Leading Competitor B Ranking					Leading Competitor C Ranking				
Yr.	1	2	3	4	5	1	2	3	4	5	1	2	3	4	5	1	2	3	4	5
1) Quality*	3	3	2	2	2	2	2	3	3	3	1	1	1	1	1	4	4	4	4	4
2) Selection	2	2	2	2	1	1	1	1	1	2	3	3	4	3	4	4	4	3	4	3
3) After Sale Service	2	2	2	2	2	4	3	3	3	4	3	4	4	4	3	1	1	1	1	1
4) Price	3	3	2	3	2	2	2	3	2	3	4	4	4	4	4	1	1	1	1	1
5) Location	4	4	4	4	4	3	3	3	3	3	1	1	1	1	1	2	2	2	2	2

*The data demonstrates that competitor B ranks best on quality over all five years and with the company dominating second place over the last three years, having moved past competitor A. Competitor C ranks worst on quality, the most important attribute to the segment.

Task 6
Product Mix of Segments

Look at the mix of products consumed by these segments. Not all of the products in the mix will be the highest volume, fastest growing, or most profitable products, but since that's where you started (originally defining the segment around the largest volume products in Tasks 1 and 2), you will be assured that the final product mix will be of significant volume.

Target Market versus Product Plans

This task forces you to develop target market plans and not simply product marketing plans. By looking at the natural mix of products the target market consumes within the scope of your business, you are forced to analyze your company's mix of product offerings to the target market later in the plan. Target market plans lead you to market a mix of product/service offerings to the consumer, while product plans are much more focused on selling only what you have—one product or service at a time. Ideally, you will pick final segments which perform positively on a majority of the above steps. This allows the marketer to essentially minimize the number of weaknesses which must be addressed and to market to segments that have the greatest potential to be profitable and are predisposed to purchase your product.

Task 6 is critical, for it moves you back to developing target market plans rather than product plans. If we looked only at the largest volume products (Task 1) and defined the target markets from those products (Task 2), we would essentially be developing plans on a product-by-product basis. But in Task 6, we review what *group or mix* of products these customers of the high volume purchase. Once we detail the mix of products, we are now in a position to write a target market plan that attempts to affect target market behavior towards the entire mix of products this segment consumes.

Task 7
Demand Analysis

The last step in determining target markets is to attempt to calculate the demand for your product in your chosen target market segments. The demand analysis is a check to make sure that the target segment is large enough to warrant your effort. The conclusions will be directional and are intended to provide you with a rough estimate of the size of your market and the potential business you might generate. It should give you a first check to make sure the sales goals you set in the plan are realistic and obtainable. The final check will be when you quantify your marketing objectives at the end of this chapter.

The following outlines the procedures to take in estimating demand for your product.

1. *Target Market:* How many consumers are there in your target market? Define the target market in terms of numbers of potential customers. For example, if your target market is women 25 to 49, provide the total number of women 25 to 49. This is the top-level figure of potential customers. It can be used for calculating future or potential demand.

2. *Geographic Territory:* How many consumers are in your defined trading area or geographic market territory? Define your geographic territory and determine the number of your target market customers in this area.

3. *Consumption Constraints:* What consumption habits exist that limit the potential customer base of your target market? Determine if there are consumption constraints that will reduce the target market for your product. For example, apartment dwellers have no real need for garden tools or lawn mowers. From this review, develop a final estimate of customers in your geographic territory.

4. *Average Purchase per Year per Customer:* Determine the average number of purchases of your product per year. From the business review and the purchase rates/buying habits section, you should have access to the average number of purchases per year for your product category.

5. *Total Purchases per Year in Category:* What is the total number of purchases made by the target market in your geographic territory per year? Multiply the number of customers in your territory by the average number of purchases per year to get total purchases.

6. *Average Price:* Determine the average price of your product. Utilize the pricing section of the business review to obtain this information.

7. *Total Dollar Purchases:* What are the total dollar purchases of your product category in your geographic target market? Multiply the total purchases (number 5) by the average price (number 6) to determine total dollar purchase.

8. *Your Company's Share of Purchase:* What is your company's market share? Is it trending up or down? Review market share data and trends from the sales analysis and competitive market shares, strengths, and weaknesses from the competitive analysis section of your business review. Also, consider loyalty measures from the target market effector/trial and retrial section of the business review. Multiply your market share by the total dollar purchases (number 7). Adjust this number up or down depending upon the increases or decreases of

Exhibit 5.4 Demand Potential

1.	**Target Market**	
	DMA population	2,000,000
	Target market male 18 to 65	720,000
2.	**Geographic Territory**	
	Target market male 18 to 65 in trading area of stores 1 and 3	400,000
3.	**Consumption Constraints**	
	None	
4.	**Average Purchases per Year per Customer**	
	Average customer purchases .40 suits/sport coats per year	.40 suits/year
5.	**Total Purchases per Year in Category**	
	.40 × 400,000	160,000 suits/year
6.	**Average Price**	
	Average price is $150	$150/suit
7.	**Total Dollar Purchases**	
	$150 × 160,000 suits per year	$24,000,000
8.	**Your Company's Share of Purchases**	
	Estimated market share is 15 percent	$3,600,000
9.	**Additional Factors**	
	None	
Final Demand Expectations for Your Company		$3,600,000

your company's market share versus the competition over the past five years (e.g., if your company has been losing five percent market share per year over five years, project this average loss into your market share projection).

9. *Additional Factors:* What additional factors are there that strongly affect demand for your product? What competitive factors will affect demand? How and why will recent or expected changes in these factors change demand for your product? Additional factors that correlate to the demand for your product, such as a new competitive set, the state of the economy, demographic fluctuations, changing consumer tastes and lifestyles, etc., should be analyzed for their effect on the demand for your company's product. For example, the influence of rising or falling interest rates on demand should be analyzed if your product is extremely interest-rate sensitive and there is good probability that interest rates are going to rise or fall within the next year. Likewise, if your product's sales are teen oriented, determine whether the number of teens is growing or shrinking and project the effect this will have on sales. Based upon this information, adjust the final share of purchase figure you derived (number 8). At this point you should have a fairly reasonable estimate of your company's potential share of total dollars and customers.

Exhibit 5.4 presents an example of how a demand analysis can be calculated for a men's clothing retailer (see Appendix B for a worksheet you can use to develop information specific to your company). The chart provides the retailer with a rough projection of demand for suits in stores 1 and 3. Using figures derived in the above calculations, the chart could easily be expanded to include demand information for the total market. Use a similar procedure for other types of businesses.

Further analysis should be done utilizing information developed in the business review, such as competitive factors, store location and analysis, competitive advertising expenditures, store loyalty, and the future economic factors affecting the purchase of suits, to provide input for the final adjustment up or down of the demand expectation generated in the above calculations.

BUSINESS-TO-BUSINESS TARGET MARKET SEGMENTATION

The previous target market methodology can be used for all types of businesses—consumer, service, retail, and/or business-to-business. The following is another methodology specifically designed for business-to-business firms. See the worksheets in Appendix C.

Task 1
Define Your Existing Core Customers

Through your target market analysis in the business review, you should have a clear understanding of your current customer companies in terms of Standard Industrial Classification (SIC) size, geography, application of your product, organizational structure, and new versus repeat usage. You must decide whether to focus your marketing efforts on selling more to your primary customers or selling more products to lesser-purchasing customers who have high purchase potential. Toward this end, list your customer segments in order of total sales, average dollar per customer, and number of customers. What segment is most efficient? What holds more short- and long-term potential?

Make sure you segment your current customer base into heavy and light users of your product to determine where you should concentrate your marketing energies and dollars.

Task 2
Target High Potential New Customers

After redefining your current customer target market to fully exploit its buying potential, compare your target customer to the marketplace (national and state SIC charts in the business review), selecting those customer SIC categories (or other applicable segments) with the greatest potential in terms of new customers, average dollar per customer, and total segment sales.

New Potential Customers In SIC Categories With Which Your Company Does Business

In each SIC category with which your company does business, target companies that best match your high-volume customers in terms of size (sales dollars, employees, number of outlets if retail) and geography, not neglecting application of product and organization structure (one location versus branches). You can select these market potential companies from the individual state industrial directories (available from state government), which provide a complete listing of in-state commercial and industrial firms.

Famous Fixtures, a company that manufactures and installs new store fixtures for retailers, segmented their current, high-potential retail SIC category by size and geography using their current customer profile as a guide. They targeted retail companies with five or more outlets in a contiguous three-state area, so they could market to larger, regionally concentrated store chains that would be most profitable and easy to service.

Potential Customers In SIC Categories With Which Your Company Does Not Do Business

Also, do not neglect the SIC categories in which your company has no or minimal market share if it sells a product or service that would fulfill the needs of companies in those categories. In working with a statewide CPA firm that was strong in serving the accounting needs of companies in the financial field, we found it was also very effective to market their services to retailers, even though this CPA firm originally had only a small share of this category.

Task 3

Define the Decision Maker(s) and the Decision-Making Process

Once you have segmented the customer and noncustomer companies, you must target the specific decision makers, as well as determine their function and influence in the decision process. Further, you must determine the decision sequence and the purchase criteria. Which decision maker does the initial screening of your product? Who makes the final decision? Is the decision maker looking for the very best quality product and then the best price, or vice versa? Is service most important?

Many times you cannot answer these questions unless you first define who the real decision maker is and determine if there is more than one. In working with a firm that manufactured computer paper, we found through quantitative research that it was not the manager of the computer department alone who made the purchasing decision; the purchasing agent manager was also part of this decision process, providing an important final approval role. The purchasing agent's decision was based primarily on price, while the computer department manager's decision was based primarily on the quality of paper and the service. Based on this determination, each decision maker was then targeted with a tailored direct mail and personal selling program.

HOW TO WRITE TARGET MARKET DESCRIPTORS

Once you have arrived at your final target market selection(s), you can use the worksheets provided in Appendix C to list your target market(s). Include a brief rationale under the final target market selection and reference additional supporting data in the business review. Exhibits 5.5, 5.6, and 5.7 illustrate the format for writing target market descriptors for a package good, retail, and business-to-business firm.

LOCKING THE SALES, TARGET MARKET AND MARKETING OBJECTIVES TOGETHER

Our marketing planning methodology quantitatively locks marketing objectives to target markets and then to the sales objectives. This is where most marketing plans begin to lose focus and become very soft and subjective. Think of each of the three components (sales objectives, target markets, and marketing objectives) in the following manner:

Sales are the reason you are in business.

Target markets provide sales. Satisfying the target markets is the way a company stays in business.

Marketing objectives define the target market behavior required to produce sales—behavior such as retention of current customers, increased purchases from existing customers, trial from new customers, or repeat purchase from new customers.

Exhibit 5.5 Target Market for a Packer of Canned Vegetables

Primary Market

Consumer: heavy users (35 percent of the users and 65 percent of the total consumption) who store large quantities of inexpensive food for their families
    Female homemakers
    Age 25 to 49
    Blue-collar occupation
    Household income $15M to $30M
    Reside in size B and C counties
    High school education
    Family size 3+, skewing to 5+
    Eastern and Midwest regions

Trade: buyers for chain supermarkets and independent grocers that cumulatively represent a minimum of 65 percent of total canned vegetable sales; current brokers/wholesalers

Note: In the above example, there would be two potential primary target markets—one leading to a consumer marketing plan and the other to a trade marketing plan. Emphasis would be dependent upon the importance of each target and the overall budget.

Exhibit 5.6 Target Market for a Retail Casual Apparel Chain

Primary Target Market: value-conscious purchasers of casual apparel for the family
    Married women
    Age 18 to 49
    Household size 3+
    Household income $25M+
    Employed
    Reside in size B and C counties
    High school education

Secondary Target Market: purchasers of durable, value oriented casual/work apparel for self
    Men 18 to 49
    Income $25M+
    Reside in B and C counties
    Better education than women's apparel purchasers

Understanding the target market is the key to marketing planning. All too often, however, the target market is not closely linked to each step of the marketing planning process. In our disciplined planning methodology, target markets are locked to sales through marketing objectives that define the behavior needed to achieve the sales. Thus, the marketing objectives quantify the target market behavior needed to deliver the required sales results. The end result is that the marketing objectives under each target market sum to a sales result, and combining the target market sales sum to the aggregate sales objective. Then, target markets and their corresponding marketing objectives are also locked directly to the remaining portions of the plan through the strategies developed to accomplish the marketing objectives. Finally, the marketing plan communication awareness and attitude goals are locked to delivering the behavior of the marketing objectives and are fulfilled by the cumulative communication generated by each marketing tactical tool. (This method will be explained in Chapter 8, Communication Goals.) Exhibit 5.8 visually demonstrates this link.

Marketing Objective Definition

A marketing objective defines what needs to be accomplished. Differentiating between marketing objectives and marketing strategies is not always easy and is a source of confusion even for marketing professionals who have been in the business many

---

Exhibit 5.7 Target Market for a Manufacturer of Computer Form Paper

Primary Target Market
Current Customers: firms that purchase customized stock form computer paper
  Companies
    SIC: 20 to 39 (Manufacturing), 60 to 70 (Finance, Insurance, and Real Estate)
    Size: 25,000 cases or more purchased per year per company
    Geography: East Central and West Central regions
  Decision Makers
    Data processing managers
    Purchasing agents
Prospects: firms that purchase customized stock form computer paper
  Companies
    SIC: 20 to 39 (Manufacturing), 60 to 67 (Finance, Insurance, and Real Estate)
    Size: Minimum 10,000 cases or more purchased per year
    Geography: East Central, West Central, and Atlantic Seaboard Regions
  Decision Makers
    Data processing managers
    Purchasing agents
Secondary Target Market
Prospects: firms that purchase customized stock form computer paper
  Companies
    SIC: 70 to 99 (Business Services)
    Size: Minimum 10,000 cases or more purchased per year
    Geography: West Central and Atlantic Seaboard regions
  Decision Makers
    Data processing managers
    Purchasing agents

---

years. To show the difference between the two, we have detailed those properties that we believe make up a marketing objective. A marketing objective must:

- *Be specific.* The objective should focus on a single goal.

- *Be measurable.* The results must be quantifiable in terms of a target market's behavior and the resulting sales.

- *Relate to a specific time period.* This can be one or more years, the next six months, or even specific months of the year.

- *Focus on affecting target market behavior* (retaining customers, trial of a product, repeat purchase of a product, larger purchases, more frequent purchases, etc.).

Current Users and New Users

Marketing objectives relate to target markets and focus on influencing their behavior. Marketing objectives will therefore fall into one of two target market categories: current users or new users. There are several possible objectives to be achieved within each category.

Current Users/Customers

Retention of Current Users

An important marketing objective is to retain the customer base at its current size from both a number and a dollar standpoint. This objective is defensive in nature. If your company has been losing customers over the past year or two, it becomes necessary to reverse this trend and maintain your customer base. You need to first direct

Exhibit 5.8 Disciplined Marketing Planning Interlocking Overview

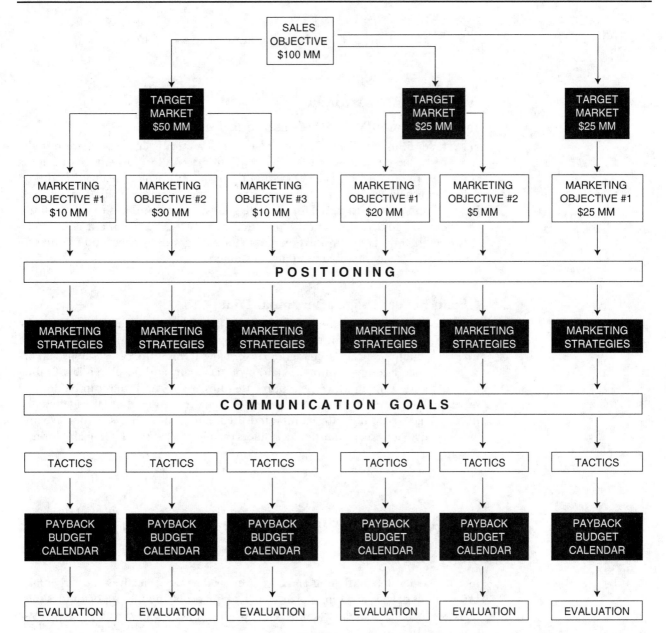

total focus towards determining why business has been lost and then towards stabilizing the customer base.

Increased Purchases from Current Users

If your customer base is very loyal, the objective can take a more offensive direction, with strategies designed to obtain additional business from existing customers. This can be accomplished in three different ways by getting your customers to purchase:

- More often or more times in a given month or year.
- A more expensive product or service.
- Greater volume or amounts of product during each purchase.

New Users/Customers
Increase Trial of Your Product or Service

For retailers, this equates to first getting traffic of a specific target segment into the store. Most retailers have a fairly consistent purchase ratio (percentage of times a consumer purchases versus leaves without purchasing), which means that the retailer can usually rely on a certain percentage of the increased traffic actually making a purchase. Increased trial for package goods, service, and business-to-business firms equates to actual use of the product from new target segment consumers. However, in both the retail situation and in package goods, service, and business-to-business, trial relates to obtaining new customers.

Obtain Repeat Usage after Initial Trial

If your company has obtained high degrees of initial trial, it is important to make sure that you establish continuity of purchase and loyalty. Often, large amounts of trial exist, but the repeat purchase ratio is very low. If this is the case, establish an objective to increase repeat purchase and product loyalty and develop a fact-finding program to determine why repeat purchase rates are low and what can be done to increase them. Even if repeat purchase rates are fairly strong, there is usually some need to make sure they are maintained. Remember, it is far less expensive and more profitable to keep your new customers than it is to prospect, yet again, for new ones.

How to Develop Your Marketing Objectives

In order to develop marketing objectives, review the sales objectives and target markets sections of your marketing plan, as well as the problems and opportunities summaries of your business review. Each provides guidance in developing realistic marketing objectives.

Task 1
Review of Sales Objectives

Sales objectives provide a guideline for determining marketing objectives, as marketing objectives are established specifically to achieve the sales goals. All marketing objectives are quantifiable and measurable. The numerical quantifier used in the marketing objectives must be large enough to assure success of the sales goals.

Assume the sales objective for a large package good firm is to increase sales 8.7 percent, or $26MM, from $300MM to $326MM. If the marketing objectives were to retain 70 percent of the current customer base and to increase current customer purchases from 3 to 3.2 times a year over the next 12 months, we would have to assure that this action will guarantee a sales increase of $26MM. In order to calculate this, we need to know the customer base size and the average purchase price of the target market. This leads us to the next step: a review of the target market.

**Task 2
Review of Target
Market**

The target market is the generator needed to achieve the sales goals. By reviewing the target market sections of the business review (Target Market Effectors—Target Market section and Exhibit 5.2 of this chapter), you will be able to define:

- *The potential size of your target markets.* This will allow you to determine the number of people in your primary and secondary target markets, or the actual potential universe of category customers.

- *The size of your current customer base.* This will allow you to determine the number of customers you have versus the number of potential customers across each target market segment.

- *The purchasing rates of your company target market, including average purchase price and number of purchases per year.* This will provide you with the behavior or transactional data needed to quantify the target market behavior back to sales numbers.

Let's examine a couple of the current customer objectives mentioned in Task 1:

- Retain 70 percent of the customer base.

- Increase purchase rates from 3 to 3.2 times per year.

Unless we know how many customers there are and the average purchase price, we can't translate these objectives to actual sales dollars. If, on the other hand, we know there are 5MM (M = 000) customers who purchase three times per year at $20 per purchase, both of these objectives can now be quantified.

By reviewing your sales goals and your target market size, you have the potential to calculate the total effect of your marketing objectives and determine whether they are realistic in terms of helping your company reach its sales goals.

**Task 3
Review of Problems
and Opportunities**

The problem and opportunity summaries of the business review provide insight into the content of the marketing objectives. Review each problem and opportunity that relates to the target market's behavior. Solving these problems or exploiting these opportunities will be the basis for your marketing objectives.

One of the opportunities we discovered while working for a national package goods firm was stated in the following manner: Though trial of the product is very low, repeat purchase is above average when compared to the industry standard.

The implication from this opportunity was that, although trial was low, consumers liked the product's benefits and there was a high degree of product acceptance and loyalty. Thus, the new customer marketing objectives from this opportunity become:

1. Increase new trial of the product by 3MM customers (86 percent increase over the estimated 3.5MM existing customers) among the target audience over the next 12 months or obtain another 3MM new customers, 6 percent of the total 50MM potential target market.

2. Achieve repeat purchase of 70 percent from new users over the next 12 months.

**Task 4
Quantify the
Marketing Objective
In Terms of Sales and
Target Market Behavior**

The last step is to quantify the objective. Assume the product is in the early stage or second year of its product life cycle; the sales objective is to increase sales 8.7 percent, or $26MM. Here, the work you did in reviewing your sales objectives and target market becomes important.

A major problem had been low trial of the product (10 percent of the target market). However, while trial was very low, repeat purchase among users was high (over 70 percent). Thus, consumer acceptance of the product was very positive, and the major problem to overcome was low overall trial of the product by consumers.

Exhibit 5.9 Quantifying Your Marketing Objectives

Sales Objectives	Increase dollar sales 8.7% over the previous year from $300MM to $326MM
Target Market	Women 25–49
—total potential target market size	50MM
—existing customers	5MM

Marketing Objective Current Customers

Retention of 70%
Increase purchase rate from 3 times per year to 3.2 times per year at current average price per purchase of $20.

Projected Sales Dollars
5MM × 70% = 3.5MM
3.5MM × $20 × 3.2 = $224MM

Marketing Objective New Customers

Obtain 3MM new customers at the current average purchase rate of $20.
Obtain a 70% repeat purchase of one time at the current purchase rate of $20.

Projected Sales Dollars

3MM customers × $20	$60MM
3MM × 70% × $20	$42MM
Total	$102MM

Current and New Customers

Total Sales Last Year	$300MM
Total Projected Sales	$326MM
Customer Retention	$224MM
New Customers	$102MM
	$326MM

The sales objectives will be fulfilled by the following marketing objectives:

- _Existing customer marketing objective:_ Retain 70 percent of existing customers and increase purchases among current customers from 3 to 3.2.

- _New customer marketing objective:_ An incremental 86 percent increase (3MM new customers over the 3.5MM base after retention is calculated) in new customers, with a repeat of one purchase at 70 percent.

Exhibit 5.9 illustrates an example for quantifying your marketing objectives.

Long- and Short-term Marketing Objectives

Typically, businesses develop one- to three-year plans while actually operating from the current one-year plan. It is a good practice to develop both long-term (two to three years) and short-term (one year) marketing objectives. Even if you don't have a long-term plan, the exercise of writing long-term marketing objectives forces you to focus on the future and consider the long-term implications of short-term marketing objectives, strategies, and executions. You might realize that, while your short-term marketing objectives can be realized through increased sales from the _existing_ product line, long-term marketing objectives will be realized only through the development of a _new_ product line. With this knowledge, you can plan for this inevitability sooner rather than later and perhaps develop a strategy of testing new products.

In another example, you may realize that you will eventually need to develop new markets in parts of the country where you do not currently market your product in order to meet long-term marketing objectives. With this in mind, a strategy or program can be initiated to study and recommend new geographic markets where you are most likely to succeed. Then, when the time comes, you will be ready to proceed in an orderly, disciplined fashion.

In summary, most plans have long-term objectives that provide overall direction for the next one to three years. Short-term objectives and strategies are specific to the current year. However, the short-term objectives and strategies should be focused towards helping the company achieve both short-term and, in two to three years, long-term objectives.

Differences Between Retail, Package Goods, and Business-to-Business Marketing Objectives

Marketing objectives reflect the major differences between types of businesses. Marketing objectives for *retailers* affect consumer behavior in a retail environment. This means that there is a concentration on increasing store traffic, transactions, items per transaction, dollar sales per transaction, multiple purchases, and greater repeat purchases among both current and new users. The following marketing objectives might help a retailer achieve its sales goals:

> Increase purchases per transaction of women 18 to 49 from 1.23 to 1.35 pairs of shoes during the heavy seasonal sales months of back-to-school in August and the holiday months of November and December.

> Increase dollar sales per transaction among the current users by 10 percent from $22.00 to $24.22, over the next 12 months.

> Increase traffic of women 18 to 49 by 1 percent from existing levels of 180 people per day over the next 12 months. Maintain the current purchase ratio of 45 percent.

> Generate a two-to-one purchase-to-walk ratio among all customers over the next 12 months.

Package goods marketers also focus on affecting the consumer behavior of existing and new customers, but the emphasis is really on two different target markets, with a separate plan for each: the consumer and the trade. Marketing objectives must be established to achieve sales goals by affecting purchase rates of the trade and the consumer in the store. The following marketing objectives might help a package goods marketer achieve sales goals:

- Trade marketing objectives:
  - —Retain 95 percent of current customers at existing spending levels.
  - —Maintain current purchase rates of existing trade customers over the next year, resulting in three purchase frequencies at an average of $880 per purchase.
  - —Increase trial of the target market by 10 percent over the previous year in the Western region of the country.
- Consumer marketing objectives:
  - —Retain 80 percent of current customers at existing spending levels.
  - —Increase repeat usage of the product from 20 percent to 25 percent among current users over the next 12 months.
  - —Increase new trial of the primary market, females 25 to 49, by 5 percent over existing levels during the next year.
  - —Increase trial of the product among the secondary target market of males 18 to 35 by 10 percent over the next year.

Business-to-business marketing objectives are focused on affecting the behavior of other businesses. In business-to-business marketing, remember that there are often multiple target markets as defined by SIC or other user categories. Each one should have specific marketing objectives which, when added together, will meet the sales objectives. The following marketing objectives might help a business-to-business marketer achieve the sales goals for two specific target markets, construction companies and manufacturing businesses:

- Construction companies (Construction SIC): Retain all 10 construction company customers. Maintain current reorder rates of existing customers over the next 12 months—four reorders, at an average of $1,500 per reorder.

- Manufacturing businesses (Manufacturing SIC): Develop 10 new accounts over the next 12 months with average sales of $100M.

Worksheets for writing your marketing objectives and strategies appear in Appendix C.

In summary, this process allows you to very quickly see where you should allocate your marketing dollars, as certain targets and objectives will result in far more sales dollars than others. Or it will become obvious through the target market and objectives development that a specific sales objective will be more difficult to realize and that a revision of the sales goal might be necessary.

DOS AND DON'TS

Do

- Use a step-by-step, disciplined process when reviewing target market alternatives to ensure that you consider all viable targets.

- Make sure you identify the target market segments which have the greatest current and future sales potential.

- Make sure the target market you select is big enough to meet your sales objectives.

- Compare your customer profile to that of the competition and the market to isolate additional target markets with potential.

- To really understand your target market in terms of demographics, usage, purchasing characteristics, and needs/wants, look to the extreme: look to and thoroughly understand the heavy purchasers/users of your product.

- Remember the test used in the determination of the heavy purchaser as the target market: one-third or less of purchasers/users purchase/use two-thirds or more of the target.

- With multiple potential target markets and limited marketing funds, focus your marketing efforts against one target market whenever possible, giving secondary emphasis to other markets with minimal support and only when needed.

- In business-to-business marketing, remember that *companies* don't buy your products/services, *people* do. Market to the specific needs of the individual decision maker(s).

- Consumer goods manufacturers that have both consumer and trade target markets with different sales objectives should consider preparing a separate marketing plan for each target. In this way, the necessary focus will be placed against each critical target and each plan will more clearly communicate the specific marketing approach.

- Quantify your target in terms of numbers, usage rates, and retrial.

- Remember that all objectives must
     be specific in focus.
     be measurable.
     relate to a specific time period.
     relate to a target market.
     focus on affecting target market behavior.

- Remember that marketing objectives must be responsible for affecting target market behavior so that you will achieve the sales objectives. Hold marketing objectives accountable and provide quantifiable rationale that they will provide the required results to achieve the sales objectives.

- Keep your marketing objectives to one sentence and the rationale to one brief paragraph.

- Take considerable time in developing your marketing objectives. They form the basis of your whole marketing plan. You should give them a considerable amount of thought and review prior to finalizing this portion of the marketing plan.

Don't

- Don't try to sell your product to everybody—segment!

- Don't guess who your target market is; quantify by the numbers whenever possible.

- Don't expand into markets that have low target market product usage and a high level of competition.

- Don't assume that the purchaser of your product is also the user and the only target market affecting the purchase.

- Don't expect all individuals within the same target market to buy a product for the same reasons.

- Don't overlook the potential of your current customers when considering new target markets.

- Don't expect the most obvious target to be the target with the most potential for your product; the competition and limited marketing resources might dictate otherwise.

- Don't overlook the importance of the intermediate market or the end user, whether you sell directly to them or not.

- Don't necessarily limit the number of marketing objectives to one. It's fine to have only one marketing objective, but make sure it will meet your sales objective. If not, you may need multiple marketing objectives, each focusing on a more narrow target market or a specific area of consumer behavior.

- Don't write slogans and think they are objectives. "To be the best," or "to provide the best customer service" are slogans. They are not measurable, time specific, or behavior defining. They don't tie directly to sales results that can be measured.

■ Don't include communication goals with marketing objectives. Increasing awareness or changing attitudes are communication-based goals and should be included in the communication segments of this plan. Concentrate on marketing objectives that change target market behavior. Remember, marketing objectives alter actual behavior while communication objectives alter a thought process.

Step Five Plan Strategies

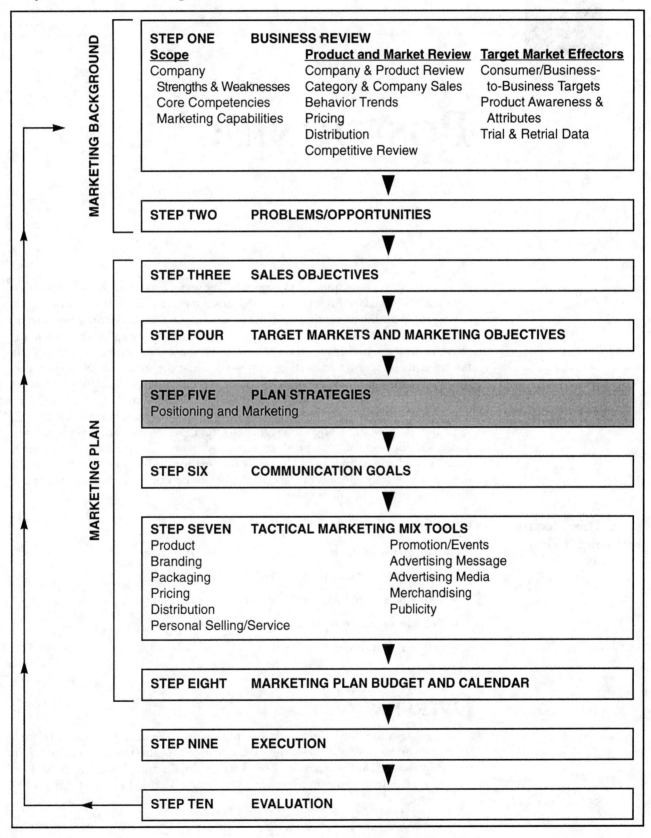

6

POSITIONING

Now that you have quantified target market segment(s) and corresponding behavior through marketing objectives, the next step is to develop the overall plan strategies. While the marketing objective(s) is *what* you want to accomplish in terms of marketing behavior, the next step in the development of strategies is the *how* in the planning process. In this step you will develop an umbrella positioning strategy and the subsequent specific marketing strategies. While the marketing strategies provide direction as it relates to specific tactics, such as pricing, distribution, and advertising, the positioning strategy guides the marketing strategies and is the glue that provides for a unified image execution of the tactical marketing mix tools.

In this chapter you will gain insight into the development and execution of a market positioning for your product, service, or store. The positioning process is both fun and frustrating, because it calls for creative thinking on one hand and a sorting out of multiple sets of data on the other. Be open-minded and visionary; think as a buyer rather than a seller.

From This Chapter You Will Learn

What positioning is and why it is important.

Positioning considerations.

How to develop your own positioning.

- Position by matching, mapping, and emotional relationship methods.
- Prepare a positioning strategy.
- Select a positioning execution.

OVERVIEW

Before going into a formal definition of positioning, the authors want to relate a short story and give you a brief quiz to demonstrate how this thing we call positioning really works. The story comes from Lisa Fortini-Campbell and her book *Consumer Insight.*[1] In a game between the Oakland A's and the Texas Rangers, a

[1]Lisa Fortini-Campbell, *Consumer Insight* (Chicago, IL: The Copy Workshop, 1991).

promising rookie named Jose Canseco stepped up to the plate. The pitcher, Nolan Ryan, wound up and let his famous fastball go. Canseco swung, connected with a loud crack, and blasted the ball right over the center field wall. As Canseco rounded the bases, one of the bat boys picked up the bat he'd dropped and carried it over to Bert Caulfield, the A's equipment manager. The two of them sat together, heads down, pointing to and talking about a place on the bat.

What were they talking about? The sweet spot. They were talking about one of the things that made Canseco's hit go so far. They were referring to a special place on the baseball bat, golf club, or tennis racket that drives the ball farther, faster, and with less effort than when it's hit anywhere else.

Consumers also have sweet spots. When your marketing or communications idea hits that sweet spot, your sales will go flying. The sweet spot is the place in the target person's mind where you make the connection between a consumer's insight and the product or brand insight. You might think of it this way:

Consumer Insight + Branding Insight = Sweet Spot

What we are saying here is that you must define your customers or potential consumers by the way they think of themselves and how they look at life. You must look at your product not for what you believe it offers but for what they expect and receive from your type of product. Another way you can look at the sweet spot concept is by combining a *rational benefit* via product insight and an *emotional need* via consumer insight—a strong combination for a strong positioning.

While the sweet spot concept is one way of describing positioning, another way is for you to take the following quiz and answer each question.

1. Who was the first person to fly solo across the North Atlantic Ocean? Who was the second?

2. Who was the first person to walk on the moon? Who was the second?

3. What is the highest mountain in the world? What is the second highest?

4. Who is first in copiers? Who is second?

If you are like most people, you could answer the "first" questions correctly for one through three, but have a difficult time answering who was second. And, as for question number four, most answer "who is first in copiers" with Xerox, which is wrong. The correct answer is Canon Copiers, which has been number one for more than a decade. However, Xerox is still usually perceived as first in copiers. And that's the point. Securing a meaningful place in the minds of the target market, such as first, sets the product apart from all the others and causes it to be remembered. Although the author's can't recall the name of the originator of this positioning concept, they truly believe it is a strong positioning building block for you to remember. The principal to remember is that, like a memory bank, people's minds have slots or positions, with one position or slot for each piece of information they have chosen to keep. You want your product to own that position. The question is how to develop this positioning equity in the minds of people within our target market. Let's begin with a formal definition of positioning.

Definition of Positioning

By positioning, we mean creating an image for your product in the minds of the people to whom you are attempting to sell your product. Positioning establishes the desired perception of your product within the target market relative to the competition. If there is no real or direct competition (such as for some nonprofit organizations), the organization still needs a point of reference in order for the target market to understand and remember what is being communicated. In the case of the competitive marketplace, a positioning positively differentiates the product from the competition. Remember, positioning is used to differentiate your product to a specific target market, not to the whole world.

Importance of Positioning

No matter what you are marketing, salient positioning is necessary. Positioning is the basis for all of your communications—branding, advertising, promotions, packaging, sales force, merchandising, and publicity. By having one meaningful, targeted positioning as a guide for all communications, you will convey a consistent image. By conveying a common positioning, each vehicle of communication will reinforce the others for a cumulative effect, maximizing the return of your marketing investment. Accordingly, everything you do from a marketing perspective must reinforce one positioning. Otherwise, you will undermine your marketing efforts and confuse the target group as well.

Further, because everything you do should reflect one positioning, the positioning must be correct, or your marketing activities will be ineffective. Worse yet, incorrect positioning could even destroy a successful product. You must look for a positioning that is not only right for your product now but that will also be adaptable years into the future for both the marketplace and the product. The *macho* positioning of "Marlboro Country" and *a friend as you travel* positioning of "Fly the Friendly Skies of United" are examples of positioning for the long term.

As a side note, if you must develop a new brand name for a product, it must reflect the product positioning. For those of you who need to create a new product name, there is a discussion in Chapter 9, Product/Branding/Packaging, on how to develop a branding program that will be a guide for new name generation.

Positioning Considerations

In order to arrive at a successful long-term positioning, you must take into consideration these factors:

- The inherent drama of the product you are selling

- The needs and wants of the target markets

- The competition

The business review and the problems and opportunities you have completed, along with the target market determination and marketing objectives you developed, are key to arriving at the right positioning. You must understand the strengths and weaknesses of your product versus that of the competition. Where is your product comparable to the competition and where is it different? Where is it unique? Most importantly, what do these competitive differences, if any, mean to the target market? If the positioning reflects a difference that your product cannot deliver or that is not important to the target group, your positioning will not be successful. Even if your product possesses a meaningful difference, your positioning will not be effective if the target group does not perceive it as meaningfully different. The key point is that, as you develop your product positioning, you must deal with the target group's *perception* of the competing products, even if it is not altogether accurate, because they are the buyers, and consequently, *their perception is truth.*

Further, the odds of arriving at a successful positioning increase dramatically when you have done market research of the potential target market. Primary research will help identify key users/purchasers and meaningful product attributes. Also, quantitative research will show how the primary market perceives these important attributes relative to the competition. Even without primary market research, if you have diligently employed the disciplined marketing plan process, you should have a good start in developing a positioning that communicates effectively to the target market.

To repeat, everything in a marketing plan evolves from the target market and how you strategically meet the needs of the target market with your product. Therefore, no matter how you position your product, the target market must be central to the positioning. As you consider various positioning alternatives, let the problems and opportunities of the business review be the basis, the target market be the focal point, and the marketing objectives provide direction.

HOW TO DEVELOP YOUR OWN POSITIONING

We recommend the following steps to help you position your product:

1. Use the three positioning methods of matching, mapping, and emotional relationship to thoroughly understand how your product relates to the target market and the competition. In order to fully utilize these three approaches, you must have a thorough understanding of the business review and, particularly, of the problems and opportunities summary of your marketing background section.

2. Prepare a positioning strategy.

3. Review potential positioning executions and decide which is best for implementing the positioning strategy for your product.

POSITION BY MATCHING

Simply stated, this positioning method matches your product's inherent and unique benefits or competitive advantage to the characteristics and needs/wants of the target market.

Task 1
Analyze Your Product versus the Competition

A good place to start the matching method is with an analysis of your product and your competition. Based on your business review, list your competition on the top left side of the worksheet provided in Appendix C (see Exhibit 6.1). The competition could be one major competitor, a number of key competitors, a specific business category, or a number of key business categories. In the positioning of an off-price menswear retailer, it was determined that specific competition varied by geographic market, but the competitive business categories remained the same in all markets—department stores, specialty men's clothing stores, and off-price/discount stores.

Task 2
Identify Product Differences versus Competition

Next, write down the key positive and negative differences of your product versus those of the competition relative to your primary target market. These differences should be listed as they relate to key elements of the marketing mix that are appropriate to what you are selling.

Sometimes a difference, although seemingly negative, can become a positive. A small retailer with limited square footage and, thereby, limited variety of product offering can create a positioning of specialty selection and personal attention.

For Coors, a meaningful difference was the quality of beer, because it is unpasteurized and fresh, with the beer shipped from the brewery refrigerated. For Cheer, it was the one laundry detergent ("All Tempercheer") that washes all types of clothes

Exhibit 6.1 Positioning: Matching Product Differences to the Target Market's Needs/Wants

Retail Fabrics Chain Example

Competition
1. Specialty chains
2. Mass merchants

Differences from Competitor
Product/Store/Service Attributes
Larger selection of fabrics and notions
Slightly better quality
Favorite store of sewers
Always new merchandise
Carries variety of goods for sewing, home decorating, and
   crafting

New Products/Improvements
Greater expansion into craft and home decorating
   merchandise

Packaging/Store Appearance
Best store layout
Larger stores
Does not have promotional appearance

Branding/Name/Reputation
Established reputation

Distribution/Penetration
Greater number of outlets in most markets

Price
Perception of higher prices and less value

Advertising
Have more advertising

Key Target Market
Practical and creation sewers
Women 25–54
Average household income
3+ household size

Characteristics—Needs/Wants
What
Wide selection of merchandise from which to choose
Be able to purchase everything at one store
Lowest prices/good values
Quality fabrics

Where
Sews at home

When
After work and weekends (seen as recreation)
Throughout the day (considered part of family responsibilities by
   practical sewers)

Why (Benefit)
For fun and as a hobby
To express creativity
For herself and children
To save money
For better fit of garments
For feeling of accomplishment

How Purchased/Used
Usually sew alone
Visit a fabric store on average every two weeks
Like to shop for deals
Shop for enjoyment

How the Target and Its Needs/Wants Are Changing
Less sewing to save money
More sewing for fun and recreation
Not enough time to sew
More sewers working out of the home
Using fabrics not just for sewing garments but for crafting and
   decorating the home
Buying more fabric-related merchandise for special occasions/
   holidays

in hot, warm, or cold water. For Funny Face powdered soft drink, the children-oriented name was the key, which led back to a pure kids' positioning. For a retail ski client, being new to a market and offering innovative customer service led to its positioning as the "new age of ski shops." This was a very appropriate positioning, because the skiing target market was young adult, contemporary, and into "change." For a business-to-business firm selling to office supply stores, its established reputation and many office product innovations led to a leadership positioning, "Organizing the American office since 1949."

For each area, ask yourself, "How is my product different and how is it better?" Is your product different through product superiority, innovation, or size—number of customers, volume of goods sold, number of outlets? Whenever possible, use quantitative research for objectivity.

Task 3
List Your Key Target Market

Insert your key target market on the top right side of the same worksheet (see Exhibit 6.1).

Task 4
List Key Target Market Characteristics

Now, list the characteristics of your target market in terms of wants and needs on the right side of the worksheet. With or without research, ask yourself the following questions, listing brief answers below each question:

- What is the target market really purchasing? Is the product to be used by itself or in conjunction with a number of products (i.e., Are women purchasing dress shoes separately or as part of a fashion ensemble?)? For what purpose is the target using the product (i.e., Is the baking soda for baking a cake, deodorizing the refrigerator, or brushing teeth?)?

- Where is the target market purchasing/using it—by geography (i.e., in sunny, very warm climates) and/or by place (i.e., in the home, car, etc.)?

- When is the target market using it—time of the year, month, week, day, during or after work?

- Why is the target market purchasing and/or using the product or why are they purchasing from one store over another? Is it because of a particular feature? Is it a convenient location or greater selection? Does the product save time or money?

- How is it purchased/used? Is it purchased/used alone or with other people? Is it a frequent or infrequent purchase? How is it used (i.e., Is the tissue used to wipe one's nose or clean the windows? Is the beer used to relax after work or celebrate and party?)?

- How is the target changing? Is the market changing by demographics, lifestyle, size, or SIC classification? How are purchasing/usage habits of the product changing (i.e., Is fashion becoming more important than durability, value more than price, service more than just product quality?)?

Task 5
Match Your Product's Characteristics to the Target Market's Needs/Wants

Having listed the differences of your product and the key needs/wants of the target market, try to match what is unique about your product to the meaningful needs and wants of the target market.

In Exhibit 6.1, using a retail fabric chain as an example, we have listed the specific competition and retailer's competitive differences on the left and the target market and its characteristics on the right. A worksheet is provided in Appendix C.

Based on the listing of the competitive differences, it would appear that this fabric retailer has a competitive advantage by offering an abundance of fabric-related merchandise in larger, better-designed stores. The merchandise selection appears superior not only in the amount but also in the variety of merchandise offered to complete a sewing project, as well as related crafting and home decorating projects. This retailer could be viewed as a leader with an established reputation offering a variety of quality merchandise, though not at the lowest prices or greatest values.

The target market, on the other hand, is a mix of both practically and recreationally motivated sewers who want a large selection of all types of fabric-related merchandise that is very competitively priced and is a real value. This retailer definitely has the desired selection and quality but not necessarily the lower prices and value. The target also wants all of the required merchandise under one roof in order to enjoy a fun and rewarding shopping experience, as well as to fulfill the needs for both practically and recreationally motivated projects.

Further, the listing indicates changes occurring within the target market. It appears that sewers have less time or need to sew regularly, are creating fewer garments, and are becoming more recreationally oriented, with interest growing in craft and home decorating projects.

In the retail fabric chain example shown in Exhibit 6.1, there appears to be a number of competitive advantages coming together under "superior selection offering" (wide variety, quality, fashionable, growing selection, and larger stores). These advantages would appear to match the target's growing desire for a fabric store with a large and complete offering of sewing, craft, and home decorating merchandise.

By matching the key differences to the key target market needs/wants of the positioning listings, you could arrive at the following positioning statement for this fabric retail chain: "Each store provides *everything* a woman needs to fulfill fabric-related sewing, crafting, and home decorating expectations."

After you have prepared your positioning worksheet, draw lines from the major competitive positive differences to the paralleling want/need characteristics of the target market. Ask yourself again what really is important to the target market in terms of how your product is different and better. Based on this, eliminate lines until you have the two or three most meaningful potential positioning connections between product and target market.

In some cases you might combine two product differences or advantages to fill an important want. If you were a retailer, you might combine the attributes of brand name products and very competitive prices to arrive at a *value* positioning, which ties to an important consumer desire.

In some situations you will draw lines between product and target market characteristics and find that a most important consumer need/want is not being fulfilled by your product or the competition. For example, Virginia Slims, a cigarette for women, was created to fill a consumer void or gap. Going to the other extreme, you might find that all of the competing products fulfill the target's need/want, but no one competitor, including your product, has claimed it as their reason for being. Or, it might be that there are changing needs that are not being met and evolving needs that will provide positioning opportunities. This type of situation is illustrated in our next matching example.

Another matching example, as shown in Exhibit 6.2, is a food ingredients manufacturer that sells its products to food processors who in turn sell their finished products to the retail market for eventual consumer use. This is an example of positioning to meet an evolving target market need worldwide. This client produces spray-dried ingredients that are purchased for use in producing products such as snacks, sauces, and baked goods. This ingredients manufacturer wanted to break out of being viewed as a commodity producer, which was how the target market of food processors, such as Kraft and Land-O-Lakes, viewed the ingredient industry. As with most commodity-driven industries, competitive price (which usually means low margin) was a major need/want of the target market, along with consistent and acceptable quality and continuous supply. Further, particularly among the R&D staff of the processing companies, there was a need for a wide variety of ingredients that could be used in a number of different new products or be incorporated into one product. In fact, with the accelerated growth in consumer convenience food products, there was a need for each ingredient to perform more than one function. For example, an ingredient might be created that provided flavor, had great "mouth feel," and would be microwaveable.

In reviewing the left side of Exhibit 6.2 under "Differences From Competition," you will see that the food ingredients manufacturer was well known, had multiple plant capability, and could make available many different ingredients. Also, as this

Exhibit 6.2 Positioning: Matching Product Differences to the Target Market's Needs/Wants

Business-to-Business Food Ingredients Manufacturer Example	
Key Competition 1. Mid Am 2. Kraft 3. Land-O-Lakes	**Key Target Market** (Food Processors) 1. R&D Staff 2. Marketing Department Staff
Difference from Competitor **Product/Store/Service Attributes** 　Capability to customize 　Largest dedicated R&D Staff 　Greatest availability—1,000 ingredients 　Major food engineering capability	**Characteristics—Needs/Wants** **What** 　Product 　Quality 　Consistency 　Continuous supply 　Competitive price
New Products/Improvements 　Capability, but not important	**Where** 　National
Packaging/Store Appearance	
Branding/Name/Reputation 　Strong brand—respected	**When** 　Samples delivered to customers within 24 hours of request
Distribution/Penetration 　Four different plants	**Why (Benefit)** 　Like variety in number of ingredients and their capabilities (more than just flavor)
Price 　Low price/low margin	**Future** 　Multifunctionality (one ingredient can fulfill more than one requirement)

manufacturer had the largest R&D staff, it could better custom-make ingredients for customers, and it had the ability to engineer ingredients to have multiple functions in products.

While the target market wants of product quality, consistency, continuous supply, and competitive price were important, other manufacturers could also deliver on these needs. However, with the goal to break out of being a commodity product, the food ingredients manufacturer decided to match up its food engineering capability and R&D strength with the target market's changing need for ingredients with multifunctionality. The ability of this large, well-known ingredients manufacturer to add value for its customers by providing multidimensional products allowed it to be seen as different and more valuable than competing ingredient suppliers.

Based on this match, the food manufacturer positioned itself as the leading provider of value-added, spray-dried ingredients to the food processing industry, which led to the theme line in its communication, "The Engineered Ingredients Leader." The new positioning caused this ingredients manufacturer to be named one of the top food manufacturers in the country and allowed them to raise their prices and experience increased margins and profits.

POSITION BY MAPPING

This approach is a practical application of mapping methodology based on multidimensional models. Although theoretical in origin, we actively use the mapping approach in the positioning of our clients' products and services. Using this approach, you map out visually what is important to your target market in terms of key product attributes. The competition's products, including your own, are then ranked on these attributes. This type of mapping is extremely useful in positioning a product and, again, is most effective when based on quantitative research that is representative of the marketplace. Your preconceived notions about what the target market thinks can differ dramatically from what quantifiable research reports.

However, if you do not have market research, it is still helpful to use this method when positioning to help sort out what you believe is important to the target market. Further, this positioning approach will help you to more clearly evaluate how your product and your key competition are perceived on each attribute. Because this mapping method is somewhat involved and you will most likely not have research to assist you, read through the three steps before beginning the actual mapping process.

Task 1
List Product Attributes by Importance

Acknowledging your built-in bias while being as objective as possible, the first step is to list in order of importance the product category attributes on the right side of the mapping worksheet provided in Appendix C (see Exhibit 6.3), moving top to bottom, from most important (10 value) to least important (1 value).

In the retail category, the most important attribute to the consumer might be quality, followed by selection, price, service, and fashion, with location listed at the bottom. In business-to-business, reliable delivery might be ranked most important, followed by product consistency, quality, price, and favorable reputation, with knowledgeable sales force being least important.

Task 2
Rate Your Product and Competitors' Products for Each Attribute

Once you have listed the key target market attributes, rate each competitor from best to worst for each attribute. For each rating, place the initial of each key competitor, including your product, on the line of each attribute ranking. Make a master listing of these keys under company/product/store code.

If quantitative research is not available before you begin mapping, it's a good idea to gather a number of people knowledgeable about your product category and have each one of them list the most important attributes. Next, as objectively as possible, have them independently assign a number from 1 to 10 (10 being most important and 1 least important) for each attribute. Take an average of these estimates for each ranking. Based on each composite estimate, rank order the attributes.

After ranking attribute importance, ask the participants to agree on the top three to five market competitors, including your product. Then have each of them independently assign a rating of 1 to 10 for each competitor on each attribute, with 10 being best. Average the ratings for each competitor and insert a rating for each competitor, by initial, in line with each attribute ranking.

In your plotting of the competitive market, you might have great disparity between competitors on one attribute and no differences on another. Ideally, you want your product ranked the best versus the competition on all attributes, but particularly on those that are most important to the consumer. The more you see your product's initial on the right, especially on those attributes at the top of the chart, the stronger the position of your product in the marketplace.

A note of caution: Using a knowledgeable group of people to assist in arriving at key attributes and competitive ratings is not very accurate compared to using survey research that will quantify the perceptions of the users and/or purchasers. However, with no research available, this approach will at least give you more perspective than if you just positioned by matching.

Exhibit 6.3 Original Price Positioning

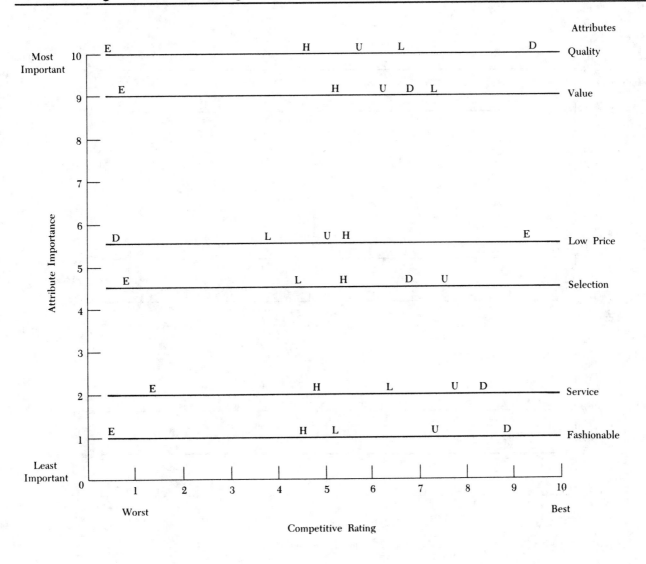

Task 3
Visualize Desired Position on Map for Your Product

Once your positioning map is complete, review how your product ranks on the more important attributes relative to the competition. Next, visualize where you want your product positioned on the map based on what the consumer wants and what your product can provide relative to strengths and weaknesses of the competition. Finally, from the various types of positionings previously discussed, select the positioning approach that will positively affect the target market's perceptions and attain your visualized positioning.

To illustrate, we will use a classic case example of Famous Footwear from a number of years ago when we had just become their agency. As shown in Exhibit 6.3, our then-new client, a very price-oriented shoe retailer (code letter H), rated second to last competitively on the two most important attributes for the retail category: quality and value. Declining sales had prompted this 20-store chain to do market

Exhibit 6.4 Original Price versus New Value Positioning

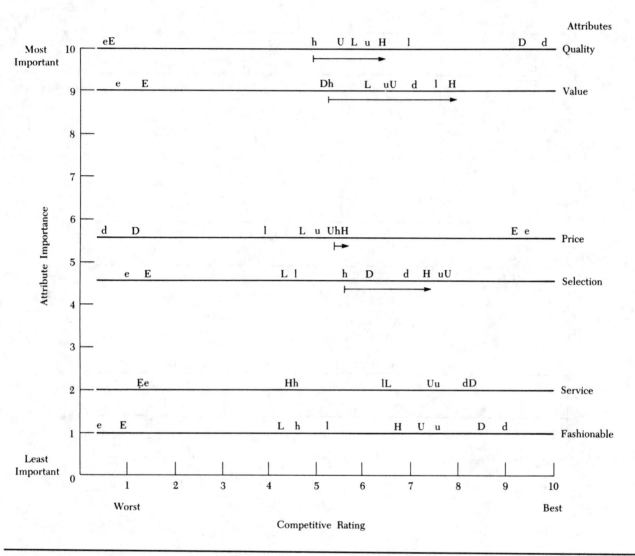

*Lowercase letters represent original positioning; uppercase letters represent new positioning.

research among consumers. This research indicated, among other things, that, although price was important, quality and value were most important. Based on this data, the company changed its position from a "store with low prices" to "the value shoe store"—a store with quality merchandise at competitive prices. Translating this goal to the map visually would mean it would be the first store from the right for the value attribute. Accordingly, this retailer upgraded its merchandise mix and the appearance of its stores. The advertising was also changed to convey a value image.

The results of this value positioning versus the former low price/discount price positioning were dramatic. Comparable store sales for the year increased more than 30 percent. Market research conducted 18 months after the benchmark research study revealed dramatic positive shifts in how the consumer perceived this retailer versus the competition on the key attributes. As you can see in Exhibit 6.4, the retailer's competitive rating (H) on *quality* moved from second to last to second. Further, its competitive *value* rating moved from second to last to first, while the

Exhibit 6.5 Positioning by Customers versus Noncustomers

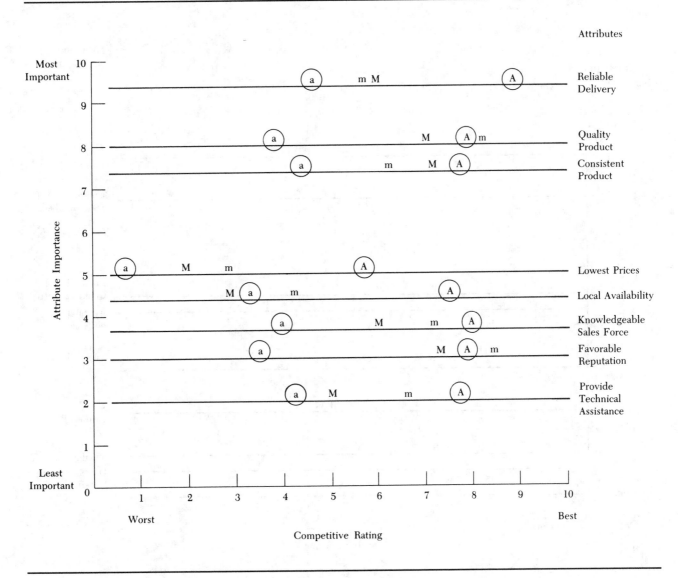

*Uppercase letters represent customers; lowercase letters represent noncustomers.

price rating remained virtually the same. Even the retailer's competitive rating on *selection* showed considerable positive movement from third to second place. This change in positioning resulted in a 30+percent store-for-store sales increase in each of the two years following the value positioning. Today this once-floundering chain of 20 stores is now nationwide and growing, approaching 1,000 stores.

Mapping Customer versus Noncustomer Perceptions

When putting together your maps, you must consider the makeup of your target market. Accordingly, you can put together one map for customers and another for target market noncustomers. Many times, what is important to your current customers might not be as important to noncustomers. Noncustomers will usually rate your product more negatively than will your customers.

Exhibit 6.6 Positioning to Fill a Gap

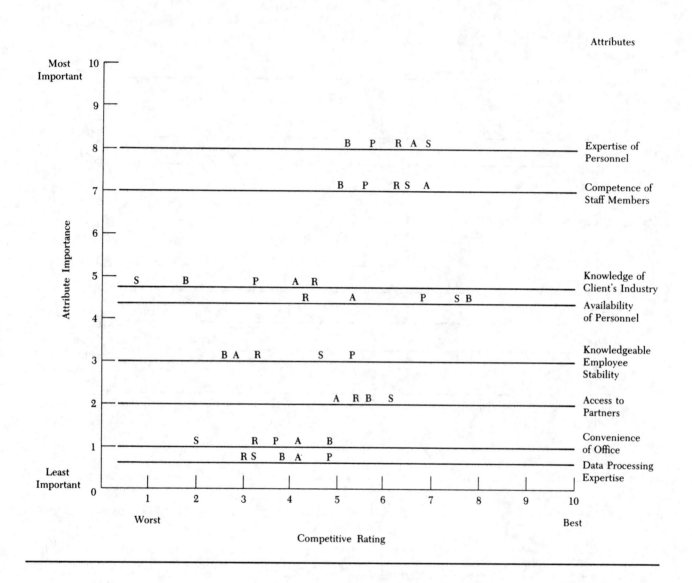

To illustrate through a business-to-business case, you can see in Exhibit 6.5 how highly *customers* rated Company A (uppercase) versus its key competitor, Competitor M, and how poorly its *noncustomers* rated the same Company a (lowercase). This firm, which originally emphasized price to attract new customers, changed its positioning to one of "best performance" in terms of reliable delivery, product, consistency, and quality—all of which the company said it could or did provide. This new positioning was supported with an aggressive advertising and personal selling program built around the new performance positioning. The result was a substantial increase in new customers.

Look for Positioning Gaps

Using the mapping approach, you can isolate differences for your product versus the competition that will lead to effective positioning. Often, however, there are no meaningful differences but only attribute opportunity areas that no one has taken advantage of. To find this type of opportunity gap, review your map for an important attribute vacuum that your product can fill. In Exhibit 6.6, for a business-to-business company B selling its professional accounting services to small and mid-size firms, we see no one fully satisfying the target market on the third most important attribute, "knowledge of client's industry." Because competitors appeared strong in the two most important attributes, "expertise of personnel" and "competence of staff members," we positioned our client as the accounting firm that understands and tailors its services to the clients' specific business. Accordingly, the target market was segmented by SIC and size. Each industry target segmented by size received tailored-frequency direct mail advertising. The result was a substantial increase in new clients and a 90 percent return on the marketing investment.

Look For Strengths and/or Groupings

Our last mapping example, shown in Exhibit 6.7, demonstrates how you can position by isolating strengths that are meaningful and grouping them under a common umbrella attribute. In Exhibit 6.7 you see a map for analytical equipment manufacturers selling their products to quality control technicians in a wide variety of industries. In this case example, the manufacturer M was the fourth player in the market by size, selling primarily through attractive pricing against the larger competing companies. In order for manufacturer M to improve the perceived value of its products and thus increase its share of market and its margins, it grouped together three out of the top four attributes where it was rated most favorably (product reliability, software, and ease of use). All of these attributes were driven by equipment that required state-of-the-art technology. Accordingly, manufacturer M then made superior technology its meaningful difference, avoiding the service attributes, where it was weaker, and making price secondary to technology. Being a fourth tier competitor in a highly competitive field, manufacturer M could combine technology strengths to become a major player in a "high tech" category against the large competitors who had larger sales and service staffs.

POSITIONING BY EMOTIONAL RELATIONSHIP

All positioning efforts seek to establish a connection between product and target market. But the emphasis can differ dramatically. Attribute positioning, which is the basis for the mapping method, focuses on the target's rating of the product relative to the competition; it focuses more on attributes like value, quality, or convenience. Emotional relationship positioning emphasizes the *feelings* of the target market: their feelings about the product, about themselves or about others, towards the company's personality, and about the meaning of the product in their lives.

This more "emotional" approach offers a number of advantages:

- Once a relationship is established, it is harder for competitors to attack than specific product attributes.

- You can maintain the relationship despite radical changes in technology or product features.

Exhibit 6.7 Positioning by Strength/Group of Strengths*

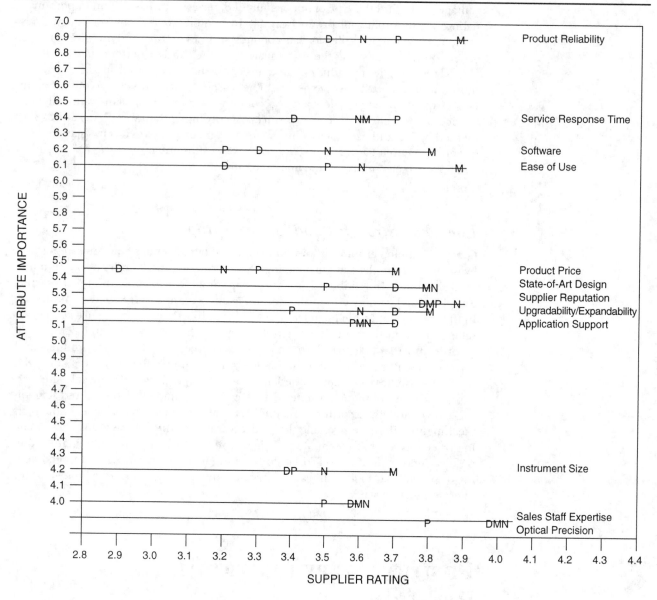

*On this map the attribute rating is on a one to ten scale and the individual competitive ratings were on a one to five scale.

There are also some disadvantages to this approach:

- If your product has a unique advantage (for example, a patented process), this approach may not focus enough on the product.

- If you cannot afford the media dollars to establish and defend this position, a larger, better-funded competitor can steal it from you.

- You must be able to deliver on the emotional promise. If you promise "friendly" and deliver "indifferent," you will make matters worse.

In many business categories, the marketing battleground has already seen some movement from rational benefits to emotional relationships. The reason? The consumer now faces a bewildering array of product choices. Unique product features or technical breakthroughs are quickly duplicated. The result is that the consumer does not have the time or energy to know everything necessary to make the right choice. He or she needs a simple relationship with a company that can be counted on over time to be a good choice.

The value of an emotional relationship with the company is even great when

—there is high emotional involvement in product selection.
 (perfume)

—the competitive frame is saturated and complex.
 (soft drinks)

—the degree of personal, financial, or emotional risk is great.
 (cars)

—the business category is perceived as a commodity.
 (sugar)

Having an emotional relationship with a company or product is like having a relationship with another person:

—How does this relationship make me feel about myself?
 (If I wear Air Jordans I feel like a winner.)

—What will other people think of me?
 (OshKoshBGosh Overalls vs. Guess Jeans)

—What key emotional needs does this relationship meet?
 (Michelin tires make me feel like I'm protecting my family.)

—What personality characteristics can I count on over time and across product experiences?
 (Apple vs. IBM)

—What values does this company stand for?
 (Ben & Jerry's Ice Cream vs. Häagen Dazs)

Many of these emotional questions are subconscious and irrational. They may even sound silly when stated out loud. You will probably never hear someone say "I feel like a rich man when people see me in my Cadillac." But that is how they feel. Such feelings can be powerful motivators to buy your product.

Building an emotional relationship starts with the consumer rather than with your company or product. The goal is to build on their feelings, perceptions, and emotional needs. You will have to live in the consumer's hidden emotional world. Get ready to be surprised.

Emotional relationship marketing requires the use of fairly sophisticated qualitative research techniques, the ability to listen "behind" or "below" what consumers are saying, and the ability to create a wide range of positioning hypotheses to test. Before you undertake emotional relationship positioning, you may want to seek the assistance of a marketing communications firm, an advertising agency, or a marketing research firm with proven experience in this area.

Before you explore how to do relationship positioning, you may find it helpful to look at the experience of one of our clients.

Case study: A regional health care clinic

DeanCare is a large multi-specialty clinic serving 11 counties in southern Wisconsin. The clinic's primary competitor had established a clear brand image based on the quality of their physicians. Focus group research revealed that Dean had no clear brand image in the marketplace other than being perceived as "big." Consumers sometimes referred to it as an impersonal "Dean Machine." DeanCare wanted to improve their image to keep the patients they had and to attract more patients.

The first step was to identify their highest-opportunity customer. National research available in trade publications revealed that women made 80 percent of all health care decisions for their family, including themselves, their children, their spouses, and their parents. Industry norms and local patient counts showed that the heaviest users of primary care were women with children. Qualitative and quantitative studies confirmed that the choice of clinic was based primarily on the choice of pediatrician. Therefore, the target market was defined as women aged 25 to 49 with children. The lowest-opportunity customer was young single men.

By combining national and local demographic information with hospital experience, the following profile of the clinic's heavy user was developed.

"Mary" is a thirty-five-year-old white mother of two young children (preschool and elementary school age). She works part-time. Her husband is the primary breadwinner and she is the primary caregiver. Their combined annual family income is around $50,000. She has made considerable personal and professional sacrifice to be a mother. She is consumed by the demands of home and family (cooking, cleaning, shopping, chauffeuring, homework, bill-paying, raising children) and has very little discretionary time. She has traditional midwestern values: her home and family are the most important things in her life. Yet she does not want to be a traditional, '50s stay-at-home mom and longs for some time for herself. She is responsible for the day-to-day care of the family's health. She takes care of her children when they are sick. She (more than her husband) chooses the pediatrician.

Once the consumer had been identified, DeanCare needed to find a key emotional benefit. Based on good logic, DeanCare physicians believed that board certification, credentials, knowledge, experience, facilities, technology, and expertise were the most critical attributes in the patient decision. The doctors believed that a successful interaction was one in which they did a good medical job.

Six focus groups were conducted with DeanCare and non-DeanCare patients to identify the difference between a good doctor experience and a bad doctor experience. They were asked:

1. To describe their best and worse experience with a doctor.

2. To supply adjectives describing a good doctor and a bad doctor.

3. To describe competing clinics as if the clinics were a person.

4. To rank the different competing clinics based on different medical specialties, including pediatrics.

The women in the focus groups said that they really wanted a doctor who would listen to them and treat them like human beings with feelings. Listening, eye contact, personal treatment, and taking the time to explain things were consistently ranked first. Physician experience and knowledge were consistently ranked last, because these attributes were taken for granted.

Based on this new insight, a positioning opportunity for DeanCare was developed. In the mind of the customer, DeanCare could own "patients" instead of "doctors" and "human feelings" instead of "physician expertise." DeanCare's new positioning: the clinic that treats people like human beings with feelings.

A radio, print, and billboard campaign was created to communicate this new positioning. Within the first three quarters of advertising, patient visits increased by 20 percent. In the critical pediatric category, patient visits increased 29 percent. DeanCare was also able to extend the positioning to other medical services and markets, including cardiac care.

Now that you've seen an example of emotional relationship positioning, you can better understand the tasks you will need to undertake for your business.

How to Build an Emotional Relationship with the Consumer

Task 1
Develop an individual profile of your highest-opportunity consumer

This individual profile contains things like demographics, lifestyle, values, emotional needs, life experiences, philosophies, hobbies, and interests of the heavy purchaser. This profile is then contrasted with that of the person who is the lowest-opportunity consumer or the light purchaser. This contrast will often point to the key underlying motivator. DeanCare used many different sources of information to develop their profile: national studies, trade magazines, local demographic information, focus groups, quantitative studies, and even direct experience.

Task 2
Brainstorm for motivators

Brainstorm with your staff or people knowledgeable about the product to develop a wide range of underlying, feeling-generated motivators to test with consumers. It is even valuable to include motivators that you know are wrong in order to get clearer feedback that points you in the right direction. For example, when DeanCare extended the positioning to cardiac care, they tested several emotional motivators (fear of dying, joy of living) against several attribute motivators (experience, physician expertise, mortality rates).

Task 3
Rank the motivator choices with target consumers

For example, DeanCare focus group members were shown positionings both in the form of written boards and as tape-recorded patient statements. Participants then ranked their most favorite and least favorite statements. You should plan to do a minimum of two different focus groups.

Task 4
Identify the consumer's primary emotional motivator(s)

Motivations can differ significantly depending on the purchasing occasion, the stage of your life, or the role the product plays in your life. For DeanCare's pediatric customers, contrasting their good and bad doctor experiences helped reveal the key motivator—the need to be treated like a human being with feelings.

Task 5
Validate qualitative analysis with quantitative survey results

If at all possible, use survey research to test several different positionings (both emotional and attribute) to verify the results of the focus groups regarding the appeal of the key motivator relative to the size of the market. This will prevent you from selecting a key motivator that is very strong but that is significant only for a very small group of people.

Task 6
Use strongest motivator for positioning strategy

This will establish a relationship with your target person and also establish a core brand personality for your company or product.

PREPARE A POSITIONING STRATEGY

Having gone through the matching, mapping, and emotional relationship methods with your product, you should now have some direction or thoughts on how you want your product to be perceived as meaningfully different from the competition by the target market. With this, you are ready to write alternative positioning strategies. It is wise to write more than one positioning strategy in order to make a comparison of strategies and evaluate which positioning best reflects your product relative to the competition and fulfills the needs/wants of the target market. Your alternative positioning statements should vary by the degree of emphasis placed on the product advantage, the competition's weaknesses, and the target market benefit.

The key word is *focus* when writing a positioning statement. Rather than keeping it simple and straightforward, the tendency is to write a positioning statement that reads like a litany. The shorter and more to the point, the better the positioning strategy. A succinct positioning will provide clear and specific direction for the employment of the tactical marketing mix tools. For this reason, choose each word that you use in your positioning statement thoughtfully. Once you have prepared the alternative positionings, select the one that will best suit the target market and fulfill the marketing strategies using the format provided in Appendix C.

The following is a three-step process that you might want to follow to prepare your positioning strategy.

1. Look for meaningful differences.

2. Prepare alternative positioning strategies that vary by degree of emphasis:

   ■ Product advantages

   ■ Target market benefits

   ■ Competitor weaknesses

3. Decide on a final strategy that has focus.

To demonstrate this three-step process in the development of writing a positioning strategy, we will relate back to the Famous Footwear example in Exhibit 6.3, in which the key attributes the target market sought in a shoe store were quality, value, price, and selection. With the concept of Famous Footwear being a brand name, discount shoe store, it was believed they could never be perceived as the shoe store with the highest quality shoes, an attribute which is usually owned by the local department store. Further, by just using price as their primary benefit, Famous Footwear would continue to be perceived as a discount store, something it was clearly not with its branded shoes. Also, the singular lowest price emphasis was eroding their sales and margins. Accordingly, the mapping method led them to identify two meaningful differences: value and selection in Task 1. Value was identified because Famous Footwear had many quality, branded shoes at very competitive prices; selection was identified because Famous Footwear had some 10,000 square feet of space filled with all types of branded shoes, from dress and casual to athletics and boots, for men, women, and children.

For Task 2, they prepared the following three alternative positioning strategies, all with a value orientation. One alternative featured a product difference of value only. Another alternative put greater emphasis on the target market, emphasizing greater selection for a family. The third alternative incorporated a competitive advantage as it related to department store shoes. The three positioning alternatives were:

1. Position Famous Footwear as the *value* shoe store.

2. Position Famous Footwear as the store with the *greatest selection* of value shoes for men, women, and children.

3. Position Famous Footwear as the value alternative to purchasing shoes at *department stores*.

   ■ Same quality

   ■ Better selection

   ■ Lower prices

In Task 3, a final revised positioning strategy was developed which emphasized the strong value attribute and also incorporated a family target market orientation, because they were the only branded discount store that had men's, women's, children's and athletic shoes. The positioning strategy and corresponding theme line became:

Position Strategy

Position Famous Footwear as the *value* shoe store for *families*.

Theme line for communication

"Good Prices on Great Shoes (That's Why We're Famous)."

Below are examples of positioning strategies for consumer and business-to-business products, a service company, and a nonprofit organization.

Consumer Package Goods

Position Funny Face as the *kids'* powdered soft drink for summertime fun.

Position Miller Lite as the only beer with superior taste and low caloric content.

Business-to-Business

Position W.T. Rogers as the *established office supply leader,* improving the look and efficiency of the office environment.

Service

Position Stark Realtors as the *most professional realtor* for home buyers and sellers *throughout Dane County.*

Nonprofit Organization

Political campaign: Position the Democratic candidate for governor as the *only wise choice* to handle the unprecedented challenges facing the state.

SELECT A POSITIONING EXECUTION

Having decided on a positioning strategy, the final step is to develop an execution for that strategy. This step is particularly important to the communication of that strategy across all of the tactical marketing mix tools. Below is a discussion of eight different types of executions for your consideration.[2]

Position by Product Difference

Ask yourself: What is meaningfully different about what my company is selling? Do I have a unique product feature? Pillsbury took a commodity product—flour—and put

---

[2]Rothschild, Michael L. *Advertising: From Fundamentals to Strategies* (Lexington, MA: D.C. Heath and Co., 1987); Al Ries and Jack Trout, *Positioning: The Battle for Your Mind,* rev. ed. (New York: McGraw-Hill, 1986); and David Aaker and J. Gary Shansby, *Positioning Your Product in Business Horizons 25.* (May/June 1982).

a recipe inside the sack to make it different from the competition, calling it "the Idea Flour." Another example of using a product difference as a feature is Famous Fixtures, a manufacturer and installer of store fixtures that sells to retail store chains. It positioned itself as having actual retail experience, because its own parent company is a retailer—"Famous Fixtures: retailer owned, retailer built, retailer tested." Thus, their product difference is not just their product but their service as well. Also, the more inherent the product difference, the better. For example, Ready Crisp Bacon is already cooked, and all you have to do is pop it in the microwave oven for five seconds a slice. "Tasty bacon without the mess."

Many times a product difference can be easily duplicated. In the first example, Gold Medal Flour matched Pillsbury and put a recipe in its packages. However, as the second example illustrates, if the product feature is truly part of the inherent drama of your product, it is not as easy to duplicate. Unlike Famous Fixtures, most fixture companies were not created by a retailer, and they really don't have a retailer's perspective in building and installing retail store fixtures. Patented products position against product differences that cannot be easily duplicated. This was the case for Mercury Marine's Quicksilver Power^2 propeller, which shifts automatically like an automatic car transmission. Unlike other fixed propellers, this variable pitch propeller shifts down for maximum lift to propel the boat out of the water and shifts up once planing on top of the water for maximum high-end speed. Built around a patented product difference, this position execution was very preemptive.

Further, in all of these positioning examples, the product positioning began with a recognizable difference that was meaningful to the target market. To homemakers, the product difference was the inclusion of a recipe, which meant new or better baked goods for a family. To bacon lovers, it was bacon that was precooked, which meant convenience. To retailers, Famous Fixtures, being retail-oriented, knew best how to fixture their stores for increased sales and understood the importance of quick installation in order for the store to open on time. To boaters, they can see and actually feel the acceleration of the Power^2 propeller as it shifts from low to high pitch.

Position by Key Attribute/Benefit

Ask yourself: What benefit does my product offer that the target market will consider meaningful? In the changing health care environment, which calls for more preventive health care and controlling health costs to patients, we have helped a medical group client position itself as the catalyst for two-way sharing in the maintenance of the patient's long-term health and control of patient health costs. Research said patients did not want to be dictated to by physicians; they wanted to work together with their physicians to be healthy, to get healthy if ill, and to stay healthy after illness—all in an affordable, cost-effective manner. This led to a partnership attribute and positioning built around "Together, partners in your good health." As a side note, many times the image you position outside your organization can have a major positive effect on those employed within the organization to deliver on that positioning.

The meaningful attributes to the purchaser and user vary by product and service. In the retail area, the key consumer attributes are usually quality, selection, price, service, and location. Depending on the concept you are retailing, the order of the attributes will change according to their importance to your target market. For example, quality and price are important not just for retailers but to the positioning of many other products and services as well. A key point to remember is that the two attributes of quality and price very often translate into a third important attribute: value. However, value can be driven by the combination of many other different attributes as well, including selection, service, and durability. Value is a good competitive image to own if you can first establish it and then hold it.

Position by the Users of Your Product

By going right to the users/purchasers of your product, your positioning will become more salient to the target market, creating an image among this group that the place, products, or service is especially for them. The classic example of this positioning execution was the presentation of Virginia Slims as the cigarette for women through "You've come a long way, baby." In another example, we helped a regional hospital position its new OB center and its single delivery room concept as a very special place created just for mom and her baby for the time before birth, during birth, and after delivery. Originally named the "Baby Place," the television execution featured a baby extolling all of the amenities of the Birthing Center suites that provided the luxury of the finest hotels.

We employed a user positioning for a business-to-business client that marketed a hot water machine to offices for making instant coffee, replacing the need to brew coffee. In this case, we directly positioned the product to the target: "Office coffee maker, say 'Goodbye' to the office coffee mess." Not having a mailing list of individuals (or title) responsible for making the coffee in the office, the direct mail piece carried the title "Office Coffee Maker" on the mailing label. Thus, the user was directly targeted in both the positioning and the actual delivery of the piece within the office.

Position by Usage

Many times you can position by how and when the product is used. For the Coors young adult summer urban program, we positioned Coors as the summertime, fun time beer for parties. We translated this positioning to "Coors Celebrates Summer in the City," purchasing the music rights to the song "Summer in the City" by singer John Sebastian. A number of years ago, another beer, Michelob, positioned itself on the basis of usage occasion and then expanded the time of the usage occasion. Michelob moved from a weekend to every night position—"Weekends were made for Michelob" to "The night belongs to Michelob." The switch was made to broaden the usage time period and appeal directly to the younger beer drinker who is both a weekend consumer and weekday beer drinker.

Another example of a positioning execution by usage, not of time but of place, was for Canon copiers. For Canon's major independent marketer of copiers, we worked against a positioning usage execution of "America's workplace."

Positioning Against a Category

In this very common positioning, you establish your product not at the expense of a specific competitor but at the expense of a specific category within which you are attempting to steal business. This approach is particularly effective when your product is new to the market—when you are building a new market or subset of an existing category. A classic example was the positioning of light beer against regular, higher-calorie beer. This positioning was so successful that it built a whole new light beer category. Over the years however, the "light beer" category expanded to include major competitors. Now, Bud Light and Coors Light have become major problems for Miller Lite, because it could no longer be preemptive with "Great taste, less filling." At the time of this writing, Miller Lite had slipped to third by volume in the light beer category because of an older and shrinking customer base. Why? Because, as a result of competition, Miller Lite has lost a meaningful difference in terms of consumer perception. Although making numerous executional shifts in its advertising, it appears Miller Lite still has not found a meaningful positioning slot.

We used this anticategory approach in the service sector with the positioning execution of the "No necktie banker" for a financial client who was going against the entire category to increase its share of the loan market. While most financial institutions are very proper and the bank staff wear business attire and have all the formalities, we positioned this bank group and its service people as open, down-to-earth, and very approachable. This was particularly important to the blue-collar and non-college-educated consumers, many of whom are uncomfortable when asking for a loan. The "No necktie banker" positioning execution was not just in advertising; it carried into the bank, right down to the loan officers not wearing ties and the chairman cutting off his tie in front of the TV cameras, an event which generated major publicity coverage in the media. The result of this antibank category position execution was that so many loans were made beyond projection that the bank group had to execute a "CD" savings program to attract money to cover the required loan reserves.

In the business-to-business environment, we, as an advertising and marketing communications agency, have positioned our firm directly against other agencies, particularly those that are not truly full-service agencies:

"If your agency thinks all you need is ads, you need a new agency."

"If your agency believes advertising and marketing are the same, you need a new agency."

"If your agency thinks promotion is a dirty word, maybe you should clean house."

Positioning Against a Specific Competitor(s)

In this type of positioning, you go directly at a specific competitor(s) rather than at a product category. The classic example was Avis against Hertz—"Because we're number 2, we have to try harder." In the retail fast food category, we have seen Burger King, Wendy's, and Hardee's at various times positioning directly against McDonald's in terms of hamburger taste, size, and variety. Taken to new heights is AT&T and MCI positioning against each other.

We feel that, although positioning against a specific competitor can be successful, particularly over the short term, in the long run it has its limitations. This is particularly true when positioning against a strong leader in the category. The leader didn't get there by blowing smoke and using mirrors. Usually, the leader is very entrenched in its position. Hertz is still number one, while Avis is being pushed for number two, and McDonald's is just getting stronger. When going against the leader, ask yourself these questions: Does your company have the necessary resources and management's real commitment to challenge the leader? Will your company spend the necessary dollars to change the target market's perception of your product versus that of the leader? Will your organization be capable of delivering a better product that will make a meaningful difference in the mind of the user? Remember, it's difficult to go head-to-head with the king when you are only a serf.

Now, having said all this, we recently executed an anticompetitor approach for one of our clients, a large savings and loan organization, against a bank group owned by an organization outside the market that acquired a third bank group, making it the largest financial organization in the market. Our execution was built around an image of the big shark coming into the local pond and eating up all the smaller fish, the analogy being the big outside bank group acquiring the local, smaller financial organization, charging new higher fees for existing services, eliminating services, and in some cases, even eliminating bank service personnel. We know from research that, although it is difficult to change the primary banking relationships, it is possible to break that relationship when customers change residence or when a bank changes ownership. Accordingly, we developed a short, three-month, anticompetitor campaign at a time when the competition's name change occurred, along with changes in its fees, services, and personnel. This anticompetitor execution was very successful, with over a 30 percent increase in new checking accounts, of which the majority were estimated to have come from the newly merged bank organization.

Positioning by Association

With this type of positioning execution, you associate your product with a specific person, place, thing, situation, or perceived image. This type of positioning can be very effective if you don't have a distinct product difference or if the competition owns the inherent positioning relative to your product. The use of image and emotional advertising can successfully implement this kind of product positioning.

The classic example of this association with an image and use of emotional transfer is the association of Marlboro cigarettes with the macho cowboy of the West. Although minimal taste difference actually exists between full-flavor cigarettes, such as Winston and Marlboro, Marlboro surpassed Winston as the top-selling cigarette not only in the United States, but internationally as well. Much of this success has to do with the foreign markets' fascination with the American West.

Positioning by association is often seen in political campaigns, such as when a popular elected official endorses a relatively unknown candidate. This type of positioning can be implemented with limited resources and a limited amount of time to directly challenge the key competition.

An example of association with a place was executed for one of our previous clients, First National Bank of Rockford. It was in the mid-1980s, when the city of Rockford's local economy was on the decline and unemployment was in the 20 percent range. The major recession had rocked both the morale and the economy of this manufacturing city. Also during this period, the number one and number three financial institutions in the market came under the owner of an outside, big, Chicago bank conglomerate. First National Bank of Rockford, now number two in size, became as much of an underdog as Rockford was.

Accordingly, it associated itself with Rockford, becoming the city's cheerleader for its proud past and for how, together, they will make it happen again in the future. Truly they were fulfilling the theme line "The Spirit of Rockford Since 1876." The association positioning was an ongoing success, with the bank group doubling in size in less than 10 years, becoming a prized acquisition candidate, and eventually being purchased by the national Bank One organization.

Positioning by Problem

With this type of positioning, the product's difference is not as important, because there is minimal, if any, real competition, a situation which occurs quite often with nonprofit organizations, public sector programs, and utilities. In this situation there is a need to position against a specific problem in order to involve the target market, or in some instances, particularly in the private sector, you must build a market for a new product.

To illustrate we helped launch a new product that literally opened up a new product category. The product is known as the Diaper Genie, and it was positioned as the solution to the problem of dirty diaper odor. This disposable diaper disposal system guaranteed and delivered on elimination of diaper odor—something no other diaper pail could do. The result: the Diaper Genie alone doubled the entire diaper pail category one year after introduction.

Another example of positioning by problem deals with a nonprofit alcohol and drug abuse treatment program that was originally positioned as the program that can help in the treatment of the disease. This positioning was not attracting in incremental numbers those who were addicted or those indirectly affected, such as the spouse, children, or employers of the alcohol/drug user. The positioning needed to be changed, because approximately 40 percent of the adult population is affected directly or indirectly by alcohol and drug addiction, with most not aware of or not acknowledging their own problem. There was a need to position first against the problem and second against the solution. The positioning was thus changed from "the program's professionals are prepared to help" to "understanding and empathizing with the affected others' problems." The results were quickly evident. Within three months of the implementation of this new positioning program, admissions and revenues nearly doubled over the previous year.

Dos and Don'ts

Do

- Position with a meaningful difference.

- Position to take advantage of normal usage, not to try to change it.

- Position from your product's strengths and competitors' weaknesses to fill a target's need. Keep in mind that you could possibly group those strengths that have a common focus to create a stronger positioning of your product.

- Remember, a key to the development of a successful positioning is the trial consideration of the product, the target market, and the competition.

- Use qualitative research to gain personal insight into the target's mind, particularly on the emotional level. Whenever possible, use quantifiable market research to quantify the attribute importance and your product's rating relative to the competition, as well as the emotional relationship uncovered through qualitative research.

- When confused on how to position your product, let your target market and their purchasing and usage behavior in terms of needs/wants be your guide.

- Remember that there are limited slots in the target's mind and that no two products can own the same slot. Furthermore, the *first* product to own the slot usually wins.

- If you have a parity product, look hard and long for a meaningful need or want that is important to your target person but that has not been taken by a competitor.

- Look for the sweet spot position where the inherent drama of the product fulfills an important need of the target market.

- Use the product's name whenever appropriate for successful positioning.

- Make sure all elements of the marketing mix reinforce your positioning.

- Give your positioning a chance to reap success by supporting it with a substantial investment in time and marketing resources.

- Make your positioning statement as simple and succinct as possible.

- Ideally, thoroughly search not just for a short-term positioning but for one that can live long into the future.

Don't

- Don't try to position everything about your product/service to everybody. *To position means to sacrifice.*

- Don't position against a follower if you are a leader.

- Don't position only on price unless you can deliver a lower price profitably and consistently, because a price positioning can easily be preempted.

- Don't change your positioning if it has proven successful and there have been no major changes (or you anticipate no major changes) to your product, that of the competition's product, or the target market. However, attempt to sharpen the focus of your established positioning to present a clearer perception of your product in the minds of the target market.

- Don't position directly against another competitor unless absolutely necessary, and then only for a short term.

- Don't position directly against a leader unless you plan to settle for less than first or you have product superiority and sufficient marketing resources to outlast the leader.

- Don't use two different positionings for the same product to the same target market.

- Don't overdo price promotion or line extensions, as both can destroy a brand's positioning and, in the end, the product itself.

- Don't position your product based on a promise or attribute that it cannot deliver.

- Don't, if at all possible, change your positioning in one large leap if you anticipate losing a substantial portion of the current customer base. Position one step at a time, but still think long term.

- Don't take the first positioning that comes to mind; review a number of alternative positions.

- Don't expect to arrive at your product positioning immediately. Positioning might seem to be a simple concept to understand, but it is extremely difficult to apply. Arriving at the right positioning takes time and concentration. Don't settle for an "almost on" positioning. Persevere for the best positioning and, almost magically, the right positioning for your product will come to you.

MARKETING STRATEGIES

In this chapter we present marketing strategies and discuss how to develop them. While the marketing objectives (described in chapter 5) detail *what* needs to be achieved in order to meet sales objectives, marketing strategies describe *how* the objectives will be accomplished and provide direction for the tactical tools that follow.

From This Chapter You Will Learn

The definition and role of marketing strategies.

The eighteen different marketing strategy alternatives.

How to develop and write your marketing strategies.

OVERVIEW

A marketing strategy is a broad directional statement indicating how the marketing objective will be achieved. It provides the method for accomplishing the objectives. While marketing objectives are specific, quantifiable, and measurable, marketing strategies are *descriptive*.

Within your plan, the marketing strategies represent a first overview of various marketing elements and how they will be utilized to achieve the marketing objectives. The most commonly addressed strategy issues are as follows, though you should consider what is most appropriate for your particular situation:

1. Build the market or steal market share

2. National, regional, or local markets

3. Seasonality

4. Spending

5. Competition

6. Target market

7. Product

8. Branding

9. Packaging

10. Pricing

11. Distribution/penetration or coverage

12. Personal selling/service/operations

13. Promotion/events

14. Advertising message

15. Advertising media

16. Merchandising

17. Publicity

18. Marketing research and testing (R&T)

In some cases, the Marketing Strategies section of your plan may be the only place where some of these issues are discussed directly, such as building a market or spending. In such cases, the strategies you develop here will provide guideposts for a variety of tactical decisions later in the plan. For example, you may establish a market building strategy with the introduction of a new product. Such a strategy provides the context for advertising and promotion plans, among others, as you will need to build a high level of awareness and generate trial through a high level of activity for your new product.

You will notice that many of the marketing elements addressed in the marketing strategies are reconsidered from a specific tactical perspective later in the plan. The marketing strategies developed here serve as a reference for the tactical tools that follow. They provide the general strategic direction to accomplish the marketing objectives, but they do not include such specifics as "use television," for example, which belongs in the tactical media segment of the marketing plan.

The following provides a review of alternative strategy approaches around which to develop marketing strategies, as well as marketing strategy examples to get you started. You should consider all the strategy alternatives and then prepare marketing strategies that fulfill the marketing objectives of your plan.

ALTERNATIVE STRATEGIES FOR CONSIDERATION

Build the Market or Steal Market Share?

A critical strategic decision facing all marketers writing a plan is whether to build the market or steal share from competitors in order to achieve sales goals. The information regarding product awareness and attributes in your business review, and the product life cycle specifically, will help provide answers to this fundamental question.

A situation with a relatively new product where the current user base is small, the potential user base is quite large, and there is little competition, often requires a "build the market" strategy. Many times, the company that creates the market maintains the largest market share long into the future. An example of this would be

Miller Lite, which created demand for low-calorie beer. Miller established the light beer category and had been the market share leader for two decades. However, remember that it is usually easier to steal market share than to build the market, as Miller Lite can attest. Accordingly, Bud Light and Coors have passed Miller Lite in sales by stealing share of the light beer market Miller built. Because it is a two-step process, building a market takes additional time and money. You have to develop a need for the product and then convince a target market to purchase your particular brand. Many companies intentionally take a "second to market" product development strategy. They allow someone else to invest in building the market, and then introduce their brand.

In a situation where the product is a mature one with minimal growth (i.e., few new customers entering the marketplace), stealing market share from competitors is often called for. In this situation you have to convince product category users that your product is superior to that of your competition. In some cases, the market may be growing, which allows your firm to grow along with it. In this case, the question becomes, "Is the market growing at the same rate I want to grow?" If the answer is no, then you will still need to steal share from your competition. All of these scenarios would be described in the market share strategy.

The decision of whether to build the market or steal share must be made upfront in your marketing strategy section, as this is a very fundamental strategic decision that will affect all other areas of the marketing plan. A stealing share strategy, such as "steal market share from the leading competitor," requires that your company's target market definitions closely approximate those of the current market leader's customer profile. Also, the advertising will most likely communicate benefits or an image of your product that the market leader doesn't possess. To the contrary, a "build the market" strategy often requires first, educating new customers about the benefits of product usage and second, convincing them to use your company's products.

Build Market Strategy Example: Build the market for the new Quicksilver variable-pitch propeller as a replacement for a damaged propeller, as an upgrade to a current propeller, and as a propeller bought with new engines.

Rationale: The new variable-pitch technology in propellers is unknown to the consumer marine market, and Quicksilver must develop a market for this new type of prop. Their marketing objectives called for gaining trial of new customers in years one and two of the launch.

Steal Share Examples: Steal share from the premium segment of the green and ripe olive category.

Rationale: Introduce a new ripe olive product at premium price and, at the same time, increase the price of the existing green olive product to the same premium price in order to steal share from the premium priced olive competitors.

National, Regional, and Local Market Strategies

This marketing strategy category is often overlooked by the national and regional marketer. This strategy helps the marketer determine whether there will be a core national marketing plan or a combination of national, regional, and local marketing plans. Having a combination of plans requires a lot of work, but it is usually worth the effort. This strategy recognizes regional DMA (designed market area or television viewing area) and even local trading area differences by allowing for the application of specific territorial marketing programs.

If you are a retailer, for example, you may have a national marketing program as an overlay with special DMA plans and specific local marketing programs for each store.

If you are a national package goods company, it may be that, to accomplish your marketing objective of increasing new trial by 10 percent, you need to develop a national marketing program. However, to help guarantee your success, you will place special marketing and spending emphasis on specific markets which have demonstrated the potential to grow at far greater rates when given local, tailored types of marketing programs. These local marketing programs often have their own plans with specific marketing objectives and strategies. For instance, the Madison, Wisconsin market may receive special promotions that are proven sales generators in Midwest college towns, while Chicago may receive extra media spending because of its size, sales potential, and the amount of advertising clutter in the marketplace. Such an approach allows the marketer to tailor the media, message, and spending levels to specific markets. It is important to allocate your marketing resources geographically, particularly when geography is a key variable of purchase rates among your target market. Review the CDI and BDI calculations in the Purchase Rates/Buying Habits section of the business review.

Strategy Example: Concentrate marketing efforts (for a printing company located in Wisconsin) to customers that purchase directly versus those that purchase through advertising/design agencies in Wisconsin first, then in the immediate Midwest (Michigan, Minnesota, and Illinois), followed by the remainder of the United States.

Rationale: All objectives have a local (WI), regional (MI, MN, and IL), and national component, and marketing efforts will mirror that. This "pyramid" essentially allows the marketer—a high-end commercial printer—to focus on areas of high potential nearby, where their sales force can most effectively reach, and follow up with farther-reaching efforts by targeting key industries and corporations in locations beyond the Midwest.

Additional Examples:

- Develop a unified national marketing program with all efforts leveraged against one common advertising campaign and dealer sell-in program.

- In addition to the national marketing program, develop a local dealer marketing program with "turn key" marketing programs (from "how tos" to creative material for implementation) designed to meet specific objectives (increase trial, increase retrial, increase dollars per transaction, etc.).

Seasonality Strategies

Strategic decisions must be made about when to advertise or promote your product or store. Here, the seasonality portion of the sales section in your business review becomes useful. Several issues are important. The first is whether there are times of the year when your product category as a whole does significantly better than your company does. If so, why? Can you do something to increase sales during that period when customers of your product category are naturally purchasing at increased rates?

The second issue is whether you are going to advertise and promote all year, during stronger selling periods, or during weaker selling periods. If you have a limited budget, it is recommended that you concentrate only on those times of the year when sales are highest and attempt to capture as many purchases during that period as possible. Often, retail companies utilize in-store promotion strategies, such as bounce-back coupons, during stronger selling periods to entice customers back during down periods, thus using high volume months to help promote lower volume months.

Third, you need to decide if you are going to advertise and promote prior to, during, or between peak selling periods. In retail, for example, the holiday seasons are heavy purchasing periods. A strategic decision must be made on whether you are going to advertise earlier than your competitors, throughout the whole selling season, or just during the peak selling weeks. It is often recommended to lead the selling season, because there will be less competitive advertising clutter, and you can build awareness just prior to the heavy shopping period. An alternative strategy that is also successful is to concentrate advertising during the heaviest weeks of the holiday shopping period. Thus, the advertiser can dominate a critical selling period and be visible when it counts most.

Finally, you must consider your resource and production capacity. If your current seasonal sales peaks already have you operating near capacity, you're not going to be able to increase sales much in this period. This is true regardless of your product or service. For a restaurant, it may mean space, tables, and waitstaff availability. For a package goods producer, it may be the availability of ingredients. Your marketing expenditures and activities may be used effectively to stimulate demand to accommodate your production or resource limitations.

Strategy Example: Promote heavily during major back-to-school periods of late summer, as well as Christmas vacation and spring vacation periods.

Rationale: A national paper-products marketer targeted mothers of school-aged children with its travel-sized tissue product. Positioned as the tissue to keep in your desk at school, the school season influenced the purchase timing.

Additional Examples:

- Place the greatest marketing efforts and execute mass media marketing programs during the strongest selling months. Maximize the months with the most opportunity before trying to develop the poorer selling months.

- Build the month of December—a month that performs relatively poorly for the company but is one of the strongest months for the product category nationally.

Spending Strategies

Spending strategies outline how the marketing dollars will be spent. To achieve your marketing objectives, you need to decide on spending strategies regarding issues such as investment spending for a new product; whether to increase sales of weaker-selling brands, stores, or regions of the country; or whether to attract more customers to your stronger brands or stores. In order to make these decisions, you need to determine spending levels by brand, store, or regions of the country. In most situations you can't increase sales of a weaker-selling brand without making an incremental budget commitment to the brand. We know that one way to increase short-term sales is to place emphasis on a company's strengths. However, there comes a point when strong brands, stores, or markets can't be expected to provide additional growth. Long-term success requires building weaker brands, stores, and sales territories, and this requires some investment spending. (Note that this strategy category will affect later media spending decisions.)

Overall spending should also be addressed. Does your company plan to spend at a percent of sales for marketing and advertising consistent with past years? Or, because of new aggressive sales projections and marketing objectives, do you need to increase marketing spending from, for example, 5 percent of gross sales to 8 percent? The actual spending detail will be highlighted in the budget section of the marketing plan.

Strategy Example: Allocate marketing expenditures among two different tiers geographically. In tier 1, increase spending by 25 percent; in tier 2, maintain spending levels comparable to the previous year.

Rationale: This national retailer recognized that certain markets were particularly competitive and that additional spending would be necessary to maintain share growth.

Additional Examples:

- Increase advertising spending as a percent of sales to be competitive with the market leader.

■ Spend at significantly higher levels against the top three selling products, maximizing their growth potential.

Competitive Strategies

There is often need for a competitive strategy. The business review may reveal that a single competitor is almost totally responsible for your company's decline in market share, a new competitor is entering the market, or a single company or group of competitors may have preempted your unique positioning in the marketplace. If this is the case, you will need to develop a competitive marketing strategy in your marketing plan.

Competitive strategies vary depending upon the situation. Competitive strategies sometimes use an anticategory strategy, establishing your company as better than all competitors in the category. To achieve this, a company often takes a common, consumer-perceived problem in the industry (such as lack of customer service attention in retail or delayed flights in the airline business), establishes the problem as inherent to the industry, and then tries to set itself apart as better than the competition in this area of concern.

Sometimes competitive strategies focus on one competitor or a group of specific competitors. You may need to reestablish your product attribute dominance relative to a specific competitor, or a competitor may have done a better job of creating a lifestyle image in tune with the heavy user consumer in your category. In both of these situations, you might consider developing competitive strategies which require comparison advertising or advertising which counters specific competitive claims. You might also consider a competitive media tactic of advertising within the same time frames and media as your competition. Or you might try to dominate a medium which is heavily used, or perhaps not used at all, by the heavy user of your industry category.

Another common competitive situation occurs when a strong competitor starts doing business in your trading area or in a market you previously dominated. We developed a competitive strategy for a retail client when an aggressive, nationally known competitor announced it was moving into one of our client's important markets. The competitive strategy centered around taking advantage of the fact that our client was already in business and the new competitor wasn't. To implement the strategy, our client ran a half-price sale for two months prior to the opening of the competitor's stores. This was intended to get customers to purchase prior to the anticipated grand opening of the competing stores. The week of the competitor's grand opening, we mailed a promotional piece to consumers in the five-mile trading area surrounding the competitor's store. We continued heavy promotion during the competitor's grand opening by having a grand opening of our own to celebrate the opening of the 240th store in our client's chain of stores. This competitive plan resulted in our client's stores being up 40 percent during the promotional period and maintaining market share over the long run.

Finally, competitive strategies also include the development of new or improved product, packaging, selling, or merchandising techniques to counter competitive strengths.

Strategy Example: Target the second- through tenth-ranked competitors by aligning with Pioneer, the market leader, as the second hybrid of choice.

Rationale: This hybrid seed producer recognized Pioneer's dominance (40 percent market share) by aiming at the next level of competitors. To do this, the company capitalized on the fact that most farmers use two or more brands on their farm and positioned itself as the second seed with Pioneer.

Additional Examples:

■ Preempt the domination competitor X has on the value attribute by stressing the superior price/quality relationship in all integrated marketing communications activities.

■ Minimize competitor Z's entry into the market by heavily promoting during the three months prior to Z's grand opening—specifically targeting competitor Z's trading area.

Target Market Strategies

Your target market section detailed primary and secondary target markets. You must now discuss the emphasis you will place against the various target markets and how you will market to them based on your marketing objectives, which defined the purchase behavior you intend to gain from the target. For example, you may decide to target the heavy user through the use of a specific product in your product line that has proven appeal to heavy users or through in-store changes that appeal to heavy users. You may target a secondary target market only through in-store incentives or point-of-purchase promotional techniques, saving all mass media expenditures for the primary target market. Your company may have recently revised your primary target market to include the heavy user who may have shopped your product only as a second choice in the past. A target market strategy must reflect this change in target market description. This strategy to primarily target the heavy user in all marketing mix decisions affects all subsequent marketing strategies and individual marketing mix tool plans.

Strategy Example: Target women 25–54 with children through emphasis on pediatrics expertise and leadership.

Rationale: Women make 75–80 percent of all health care decisions in a family. Mothers tend to align their health care decisions around a pediatrician's choice. This medical center, associated with a regional HMO, was rated highly on its pediatric care and aimed to take advantage of this agent this target.

Additional Examples:

■ Target only the heavy-purchasing dealers—those that account for over 70 percent of the company's business—with incremental marketing efforts.

■ Target the primary target market through the entire spectrum of marketing mix tactical tools. Target the secondary target market only through in-store marketing activities.

Product Strategies

You must make strategic decisions regarding new products, product line extensions, product improvement, product elimination, and/or whether to build or improve weaker product lines or continue to maximize stronger selling product lines. Also, if applicable, overall branding strategy(ies) should be included in this section.

If repeat purchase rates are low and your company's product ranks poorly across product attributes, you must decide how to improve the product in order to meet your marketing objectives. Another area to consider is expanding alternate uses of the product. This is a viable strategy when you have a mature product with a static or limited customer base. An example is the expansion of the use of baking soda as a refrigerator deodorizer. This was a successful marketing strategy designed to meet the marketing objectives of increasing the purchase and usage rates by current customers and providing a reason for new customers to try the product.

The development of new products or new extensions of your existing product line should be addressed if they are necessary to meet marketing objectives. If you are developing new products, you need to establish a new product strategy. Describe in general terms the type of product you will be developing, including the new product's features and attributes. You will also have to address a program to develop a brand or name for the product. (see Chapter 9, Product/Branding/Packaging). Again, remember that these should be general strategies that provide overall marketing direction. You should develop a strategy addressing whether you are going to emphasize stronger or weaker product categories/brands in your marketing plan. Selling and emphasizing the products/brands with the greatest potential is particularly viable when growth potential still exists. This strategy can also be used to attract users with product or store strengths and then cross-sell to weaker-selling categories via promotions or discounts.

Many times a specific target market can also be attracted through the use of loss leaders or a specific strong selling brand in the product mix. You may have a marketing objective of building new trial among heavy shoe purchasers, women 35 to 44 with children. The problems and opportunities section may point out that women 35 to 44 shop your shoe store not for themselves but for their children. Therefore, your strategy may be to initiate trial by promoting children's shoes to heavy-user women and then cross-sell to the women's shoe department. Other incentives and merchandising techniques could also be created to encourage the purchase of women's shoes once trial is established.

Alternatively, building weaker product categories/brands is often attempted when it is felt that the company's strengths have been fully exploited. This strategic decision requires more initial money, as it is always more difficult to improve a weakness than to build upon a strength. However, this approach is worthwhile if it provides a company with more products that contribute more equally to profits. This also protects a company from major fluctuations resulting from having only one or two strong-selling products.

Finally, finding more efficient ways to produce the product might also be a viable strategy to help insure success of a marketing objective if the improved efficiency can permit you to achieve a price advantage. In addition, the improved efficiency might also provide greater gross margins, which can help achieve greater profitability or can be invested in stronger marketing programs.

Strategy Example: Combine product offerings as packages based on bundles of benefits consistent with consumer purchasing needs.

Rationale: High turnover plagued this national auto club due to low awareness of its full product line, including a travel agency, auto insurance, financial services, and more. Known merely for its road service, the best method to gain renewal of a club member was to use cross-selling of products.

Additional Examples:

- Develop new products or modify existing products in order to attract the newly defined target market of adults 55 plus.

- Continue to build and emphasize the stronger performing products and place the vast majority of spending and advertising emphasis behind these products. In addition, use the popularity of the top 10 products to cross-sell from stronger-selling products to weaker-selling products.

Branding Strategies

If you are going to introduce a new product or line extension, you will want to provide direction for the branding or naming of these products. Should the new product stand by itself or be under the umbrella of the family name? Should the brand name exclusively target current customers or current and new customers? If you are going to enter a new channel, you might want to change the name of your product line to appeal to different targets, or you might need a new name for stores carrying your products in discount outlet malls versus regional malls.

Strategy Example: Develop a new product name appealing to existing customers first and potential customers second.

Rationale: The largest segment of potential purchasers are existing customers.

Additional Examples:

- The new name for the stores located in the mall should use the brand name equity of the manufacturer.

■ The brand name should take into consideration the introduction of additional new products to different target markets.

Packaging Strategies

If you are going to develop a packaging plan later in the marketing plan, establish a general direction for your packaging strategy. Here you will need to consider and address the following issues regarding your product's packaging, referring to your problems and opportunities for direction.

1. Function—Is your product's packaging serving its primary function of holding or protecting the product?

2. Value-Added—Does your packaging add value to the product purchase and enhance its use experience for the consumer?

3. Communication—Does your packaging stand out in the retail environment compared to competitors? Does it communicate the inherent drama of the product?

A problem identified in the problems and opportunities summaries may point out that the company's packaging makes usage difficult. Therefore, a change in packaging might help achieve the marketing objective of increasing repeat usage and consumption among current customers.

Strategy Example: Develop packaging to reflect value positioning, distinct from the current product line offerings, while drawing attention on dealership shelves.

Rationale: A new line of accessories from this manufacturer was positioned differently from its traditional quality-oriented product line. In order to avoid confusion or the possibility of eroding the equity of the original brand, packaging for the new line needs to provide differentiation both from the competition and from the company's original line.

Additional Examples:

■ Change the packaging to make it more noticeable at the point of purchase.

■ Utilize the packaging to help increase repeat purchase among current customers.

Pricing Strategies

Pricing strategies should also be discussed. One area to address is whether you will use high or low prices relative to your competition or whether you will simply match the competition's price and depend upon service or superior product attributes for a competitive edge. Will you maintain margins with high-price strategies, or will you allow for lower margins and lower prices to develop trial? Also include whether your pricing will be uniform nationally or whether it will vary market by market, store by store, or customer by customer. Finally, if you are going to use price to help communicate a positioning, state this intent in this section. Some companies, for example, follow a premium-price strategy to help establish a premium positioning relative to the competition.

Strategy Example: Maintain a parity pricing approach (based on appropriately fitting printing jobs to capabilities) to existing customers, where service and quality are more important than price. Use competitive pricing to gain trial and entry into the new customers' printing "pool."

Rationale: Research indicated that price was an important element of a customer's decision as to whether or not to try a printer. Further, the research also revealed that the decision to continue a relationship with a printer was based primarily on print quality and service and less on price. However, a high-price strategy may allow a competitor to "buy" a customer's business. Therefore, a strategy of parity pricing seems most appropriate for this commercial printer.

Additional Examples:

- Utilize a premium-price strategy for the new line extension of ripe olives, while at the same time increasing the existing green olive product to premium prices.

- Because of production cost, upscale target market, and uniqueness of product, introduce the new product at a premium price.

Distribution of Product/Penetration or Coverage Strategies

The strategic decisions that must be made in this area are different for consumer goods and business-to-business firms than for retailers and service firms. Consumer goods and business-to-business firms must decide in what areas of the country to target their distribution efforts. They also must decide on the type of channels/outlets that will carry their product and on the desired market coverage among the targeted outlet category.

Retailers and service firms must strategically decide if marketing objectives can be achieved through existing outlets, whether new stores need to be added in existing markets without cannibalizing existing stores, or whether new stores need to be added through entering new markets. If sales per store have not been maximized in low penetrated markets, one way to build sales is to add new stores in existing markets. This allows for greater leverage of store operation and advertising dollars. However, if sales have been maximized in current markets and the markets have been fully penetrated to the point where additional stores/products could cannibalize existing sales, then a realistic strategy is to expand to new markets.

It is helpful to estimate market strengths (BDIs and CDIs) by reviewing the Distribution section of the business review prior to completing this section.

Strategy Example: Focus distribution through large retailers nationally.

Rationale: This distributor and publisher of alternative comic books recognizes that the vast majority of comics are sold through the larger comic retailers, who tend to carry alternative comics more than smaller retailers. National distribution is necessary to achieve sales goals.

Additional Examples:

- Do not expand to any new markets until existing markets have been fully penetrated.

- Concentrate on gaining incremental distribution in the Northeast.

Personal Selling/ Service/Operation Strategies

You need to determine whether you want to address a structured personal selling program through this marketing plan. You may want to address basic elements of that sales program, including whether you will use sales incentives; establish sales goals relative to pure dollar objectives, a particular product, or target market emphasis in terms of calls made, etc.; and define a sales methodology (e.g., soft sell versus hard sell). If you are a retailer, note whether your subsequent selling plan should include specific sales ratios (e.g., develop sales ratio of purchasers versus walkers based upon past history and future expectations).

Like retailers, manufacturers also need to decide whether they are going to establish specific sales ratios. If they choose to do so, a statement such as "establish specific sales ratios (number of prospects that become customers) to monitor the results of the sales force," should be included as a strategy in this section.

Additionally, you should consider whether you are going to establish service standards such as the number of days it takes to fill back orders or, for a retailer, the percentage of customers who are greeted as they walk in the door.

Finally, if necessary, this section should include a strategy for implementing your marketing department's performance. An example would be to create a marketing liaison between purchasing and marketing to assure that the product is purchased and available for marketing promotions.

Strategy Example: Develop detailed target volume objectives with the field sales organization to establish a forecast and performance criteria.

Rationale: This strategy for a national manufacturer of recycled paper products, which holds the market share lead in certain market segments, addresses the lack of quantifiable sales goals among the sales force in spite of aggressive overall sales objectives.

Additional Examples:

- Develop specific sales ratio goals, quantifying the number of specific prospects and those that become customers.

- Provide a strong and innovative incentive program during peak selling periods to improve sales performance.

Promotion/Event Strategies

Promotions should be channeled to meet specific needs and must be incorporated into the overall marketing plan in a disciplined fashion. These promotion strategies will set the areas of emphasis for the specific promotion plan later in the marketing plan, providing direction for the promotional efforts aimed at addressing specific marketing objectives. A retailer may have the marketing objective of increasing the number of units per transaction from the target market by 10 percent over the next 12 months. A marketing strategy to achieve this would be to encourage multiple purchases through promotional incentives. This strategy would then be expanded upon in the promotion section of the marketing plan, but the fact that transaction increases are going to come from multiple purchase promotional incentives would have been established upfront.

Strategy Example: Develop a promotional program to encourage existing advertiser customers to purchase more ad space. A tactic later in the plan, directed by this strategy, could be: Introduce a 13th edition in the year with special page rates.

Rationale: The problems and opportunities section for this monthly magazine indicated that the publication was a secondary buy among advertisers, that the advertisers typically purchase more in a special issue, and that the current customer advertiser had a relatively low purchase level. This strategy addresses all of these issues.

Additional Examples:

- Achieve multiple purchases through in-store promotions.

- Utilize promotion to encourage purchase during the weaker, seasonal months.

Advertising Message Strategies

The marketer needs to provide an overall focus for the advertising and communication. It is important to state upfront in your marketing strategy section how you are going to use advertising to fulfill your marketing objectives. Are you going to develop image advertising and build long-term sales, or will your advertising promote short-term sales through a harder-sell, promotional emphasis? Do you plan to vary your advertiser's message by region? Perhaps you will have both a national advertising program and a localized, market-by-market program.

Strategy Example: Develop an aggressive and comprehensive consumer advertising program to build awareness for the new product and educate the consumer about its unique features.

Rationale: The strategy for a new variable-pitch propeller responds to the need to build a market through consumer education and to generate maximum support from the trade to carry and merchandise the product.

Additional Examples:

- Develop image advertising to build long-term sales and brand loyalty.

- Develop both a national image campaign and a local, market-by-market advertising campaign that is more promotional in focus.

Advertising Media Strategies

The strategies developed in this section should be consistent with the direction established in the product, competitive, and spending marketing strategies. The primary goal in establishing an overall media strategy is to provide direction for the upcoming media plan and to establish geographic and product spending emphasis. You may decide upon a strategy that varies media spending by market or that spends more in markets with greater potential. You may invest in new markets to establish awareness and generate trial. You may consider developing a national media plan or developing both national and local media plans in order to support a dual marketing strategy. You may also address target market reach strategies by identifying how media will be utilized to reach the primary and/or secondary target market, influencers, etc.

Strategy Example: Advertise throughout the year to maintain awareness among all key targets.

Rationale: Multiple decisionmakers represent the target for this producer of anesthesia machines: anesthesiologists, biomedical engineers, materials management directors, hospital administrators, and financial managers, among others. Because the purchase of such equipment is not seasonal, awareness must be maintained among these segments on an ongoing basis.

Additional Examples:

- Invest media dollars in new markets to establish awareness and generate trial.

- While media should target key consumers, its primary purpose is to motivate the real estate sales associates.

Merchandising Strategies

A strategy is needed to set the tone for what will be done from a merchandising standpoint. This applies to all non-media communication; for example, in-store signage for retailers, point-of-purchase displays for package goods firms, and personal presentation sales aids such as brochures and sell sheets for business-to-business firms. An opportunity identified under problems and opportunities might tell you that 80 percent of purchase decisions are made in-store. Thus, the marketing strategy in this situation might be to utilize extensive point-of-purchase merchandising to affect in-store decision making.

Strategy Example: All in-store communication materials should be developed to reinforce the positioning themeline. This may include collateral materials, signage, and continuing service reference materials for buyers.

Rationale: A themeline based on the positioning had been developed for this large auto dealership. Considering the propensity for car purchase decisions to be made at the dealership, point-of-sale materials communicating this theme are extremely important.

Additional Examples:

- Utilize extensive point-of-purchase merchandising to affect in-store decision making.

- Provide the sales force with communication support materials to help close the sale.

Publicity Strategies

At this point in your plan development, you should determine if you are going to make publicity part of your marketing plan, as you will need to consider publicity opportunities when you develop the other specific tactical tool segments of your plan. For example, you might consider supplementing your overall advertising and promotion communication program with publicity, or you might use media cosponsors of planned promotional events or a charity "tie-in" to generate publicity. You may decide to develop an extensive publicity program to take advantage of new product development or ongoing trade show opportunities for your company. You may consider creating additional events, such as speaking engagements, to generate publicity in a manner consistent with your overall objectives and positioning.

Strategy Example: Utilize editorial programs to help build awareness and provide legitimacy to building a leadership peer position in the high-end commercial printing category.

Rationale: Primary competitors for the high-end commercial printing segment have established reputations among the target. This firm must build awareness and a reputation as a major player in the high-end segment through targeted publications and other "newslike" formats.

Additional Examples:

- Use media co-sponsors and planned events to generate publicity.

- Develop a publicity program to obtain articles in the leading trade publications.

Marketing R&T (Research and Testing) Strategies

Change is often important in generating trial and retrial of a company's product. A disciplined program to initiate this change is critical. In most businesses there is a need to continually expand and/or refine the company's product offering and marketing in order to continually build incremental sales. This can be accomplished through a planned and disciplined researching and testing program.

Marketing R&T is the lifeblood for perpetuating the success of your business. It takes time, money, work, planning, and perseverance to research, test, and produce readable results. But it is always worth it!

Research can help define your product's problem(s) and help determine the potential and needs of the target market, optimum pricing, effective advertising messages, and much more. If you plan to conduct primary research, now is the time to establish a research strategy. You may develop a research strategy to solve a specific problem that will help you to build sales and accomplish a marketing objective. Or you may decide to conduct an ongoing awareness, attitude, and behavior tracking study to assist with next year's plan and to provide a benchmark to evaluate the results of current and future marketing plans.

Testing keeps you ahead of the competition and helps you avoid costly mistakes. It can help you develop a new product or marketing activity, make it better, provide evidence of your program's effectiveness, and eliminate those ideas that aren't going to work before a costly investment has been made. You can test any part of a marketing program, from a product change and price increase to a new promotion, television commercial, or store format.

Once you have committed to some form of marketing R&T, this section should be used to define what you will be researching and testing—new products, services, merchandising programs, store layouts, packaging, media strategies, advertising messages, pricing, promotions, etc. Incorporate what you will research and test in the appropriate plan segments later in the marketing plan. To help you develop these strategies, refer to Chapter 21, Marketing R&T.

Strategy Example: Test among dealers the pricing elasticity and promotion programs for the variable-pitch propeller.

Rationale: As the variable pitch propeller is a new product with a premium price, there is little knowledge of how consumers will respond to this price and how dealers would respond to the promotional efforts by the manufacturer. Testing would help provide answers prior to rolling the product introduction out nationally.

Additional Examples:

- Institute a marketing testing program to develop new product alternatives.

■ Develop an on-going research tracking study among the target market to monitor consumer awareness, attitudes, and behavior.

HOW TO DEVELOP YOUR MARKETING STRATEGIES

To develop marketing strategies, review the problems and opportunities, target market, and marketing objectives as well as your positioning strategy. Then use your problems and opportunities as a guide in writing strategies for the marketing strategy considerations.

1. Review your problems and opportunities.

   Read through your problems and opportunities and make notes regarding ideas you have on how to solve the problems and take advantage of the opportunities. Be creative in this exercise and identify multiple solutions for each problem or opportunity.

2. Review your target market and marketing objectives.

   Review your target market and marketing objectives, then reread the problems and opportunities, along with your notes on how to solve the problems and take advantage of the opportunities. Determine which of the ideas will form strategies capable of achieving the marketing objectives.

3. Review your positioning strategy.

   What is the product image you want to instill in the minds of the target market relative to the competition? It is this meaningful image that must be reinforced individually and cumulatively by your marketing strategies.

4. Develop your strategies.

   Review the 18 alternative strategy considerations and determine which issues you need to address. As stated before, use the strategy approaches that fit your product's or company's particular situation—not all strategy alternatives will apply in every situation. Then, based on what you know from the problems and opportunities, develop clear and concise directional statements about how you intend to address each issue.

Remember that the strategies developed here should provide the direction for use of the marketing mix tools throughout the marketing plan. For example, your spending and seasonality strategies established here will be reflected in the detailed media plan later in your marketing plan.

In summary, after reviewing the marketing strategies, upper management should have a good understanding as to how you are going to achieve your marketing objectives from a strategic standpoint. However, the details of these strategies will be fully developed in the subsequent tactical marketing mix tool segments of the marketing plan.

Writing Your Marketing Strategies

Make sure to focus on one single idea at a time when writing your strategies. The strategies should be very descriptive and focus on how you are going to utilize a particular tool, such as promotions or packaging, to achieve the marketing objectives. Following each strategy should be a brief rational drawing information from the

Business Review, Problems and Opportunities, Target Market and Marketing Objectives, and Market Positioning sections to support the strategy.

DOS AND DON'TS

Do

- Make your strategies descriptive statements of how you will achieve your marketing objectives.

- Include all the meaningful strategies from your problems and opportunities. Make sure they meet your marketing objective requirements and that you address each of the strategic categories outlined in the strategy definition and overview section.

- Take considerable time in developing your marketing strategies: they form the basis of your whole marketing plan. You should give them a considerable amount of thought and review prior to finalizing this portion of the marketing plan.

- Whenever possible, steal market share; it's easier and less expensive than building the market. Also, it's easier to build upon marketing strengths than to improve weaknesses.

Don't

- Don't let the strategies become too executional. Keep the strategies broad and directional.

- Don't limit the focus to one or two specific marketing areas. Remember that marketing strategies should include direction across all areas of importance to your marketing plan.

- Don't write long, elaborate strategies; they should be simple and focus on a single idea. These aren't meant to be strategic plans, simply strategic statements to provide direction for the plans developed later.

- Don't be stagnant in your strategic thinking and get left behind in the increasingly changing and competitive business environment. Initiate a marketing R&T program so that you are continually developing new and proven marketing programs to replace those programs that aren't working or to help make an existing program even better.

- Don't expect the majority of your marketing R&T program to be successful. Remember, most new ideas fail. However, only a few successes (and sometimes only one) are needed to keep you ahead of the competition year after year; one success can often pay for multiple failures in a very short time.

Step Six   Communication Goals

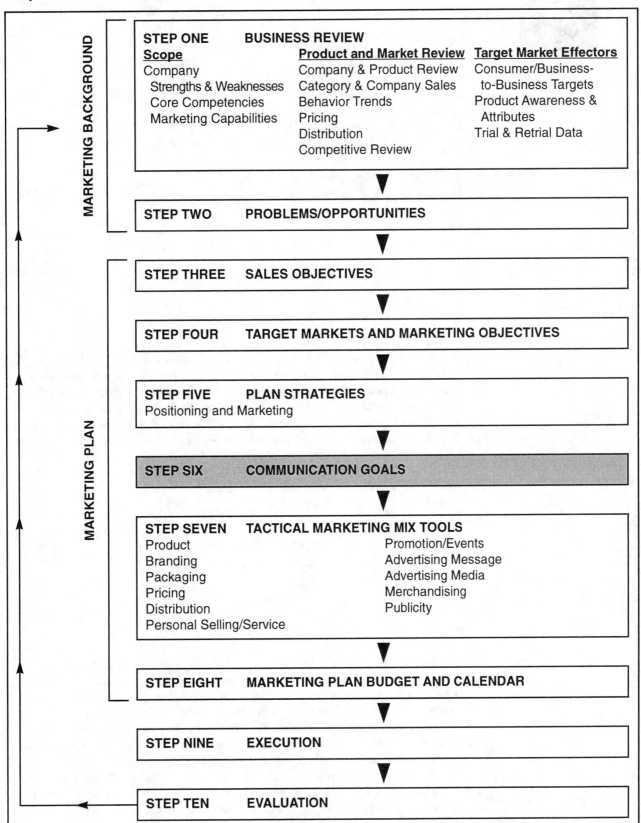

8

COMMUNICATION
GOALS

Now that you have arrived at your quantitative marketing objectives and know how your plan strategies will fulfill the marketing objectives, you must build a bridge that will lock these overall plan elements to the tactical tools that will provide the execution. The bridge is Step 6, the communication goals, in the disciplined planning method shown graphically on the opposite page. While the plan strategies fulfill the marketing objectives and guide the direction of the tactical tools, the communication goals of awareness and attitude *quantitatively lock* the required communication message to delivery of the marketing objectives that come before. These communication goals also lock to the tactical tools that follow by providing the allocation of the required communication among each of the tactical tools. You can visualize the process as follows:

Marketing Objectives

Communication Goals

Tactical Marketing Mix Tools

In this step, you are attempting to answer the question: How do I use communication to affect target market behavior? Prior to jumping into the tactical plans, it is necessary to develop a set of marketing communication goals overall and to allocate a share of the overall goals to each of the tactical tools that will cumulatively deliver the total plan communication. This will then help you determine what level of awareness and positive attitude is to be contributed from each of the tactical tools as you begin working on these segments of the plan.

It's essential that you understand: 1) how you will arrive at the marketing communication goals that must be met to deliver the positioning or image to the target market to generate behavior, and 2) how to allocate what each tactical tool must deliver in terms of target market awareness and attitudinal value to achieve the overall marketing communication goals. Arriving at the marketing communication goals and allocating the tactical values are some of the most difficult planning steps to accomplish, even for the most experienced marketers. Although we have attempted to make the task more manageable with our methods, it takes real thought and perseverance on the part of the marketing planner to make it happen.

From This Chapter You Will Learn

How awareness and attitude affect target market action or behavior (and vice versa) to fulfill the marketing objectives.

The process of locking sales to communication.

How to arrive at the overall marketing communication goals that will deliver the positioning.

How to allocate the necessary awareness and attitude values for each tactical tool that fulfills the overall communication goals.

The challenges and problems you will face in arriving at the necessary communication to achieve the intended effect on behavior.

OVERVIEW

Thus far we have shown you how to quantitatively lock the marketing objectives to a defined market segment that will deliver the sales objectives or a share of the sales objectives. Now the challenge is to lock each tactical tool to fulfill the overall communication goals which will deliver the positioning strategy and fulfill the marketing objectives. This challenge is extremely difficult and can become quite complex because of the many uncontrollable factors in the marketplace, such as competition and the ever-changing and unpredictable nature of the target market. It seems just when you understand what the target market wants and you fulfill their wants, their needs and wants change, as well as their behavior.

Nevertheless, we will attempt to explain how the communication process works and how it can positively affect target market behavior. The key point to remember is that everything begins with *fulfilling target market needs and wants* and *not* just with "how do we sell our product." Therefore, we must begin with the communications process and positively affecting the target market behavior which you have previously quantified in your marketing objectives. This statement begs the question, "How do we use communication to affect target market behavior?"

The Four A's of Communication Behavior

The "Four A's," representing Awareness, Attitude, Action, and Action^2, shown in Exhibit 8.1, describe the interfacing of target market communication and behavior. In order to have continual target market purchase, it is necessary to have communication down and up the Four A's axis, with attitude affecting behavior and behavior affecting attitude.

We begin our explanation of this process where the action is, at the purchase behavior level, and work backwards. Beginning at the bottom of the axis with A^2 (Action Again), you have either a purchaser who made one repeat purchase in the past year or a loyal customer who is a multiple purchaser of your product.

Moving up the axis, you must have the initial *action* or purchase or have trial of the product once in the past year before you can have repeat purchase. If this initial action is not a purchase, it must be an action that could lead to a potential purchase, such as sampling of the product.

Exhibit 8.1 The Four A's of Communication and Behavior

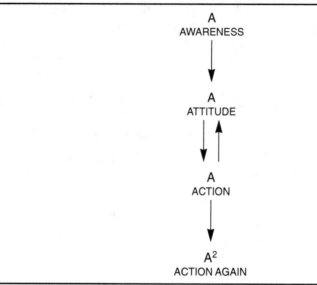

In most situations, a person must have a positive *attitude* toward the product before the initial action can take place. This could involve a long-term attitude development process, such as in the buying process of a new automobile, or low attitude involvement, such as that leading to an impulse purchase of a pack of gum at the check-out register. For example, even if the name of the gum is unfamiliar to you, you form an attitude towards the gum, however fleeting, from what is communicated via the brand name, how the gum is packaged/displayed, and perhaps the price. Your attitude towards a product could also be formed by some previous action or experience, such as sampling, but not buying, a product or calling for a brochure. Or, it may be that you had a positive attitude towards a product and purchased it, but after a bad experience with it, you subsequently formed a negative attitude and never purchased that product again. Accordingly, *attitude affects action and action affects attitude.* Hence, the two-way arrow in the Four A's model. If the targeted person has not acted on your product in the past year, there still may be attitude that has to be dealt with because of a relationship with your product, such as having been a previous purchaser of your product or user of a competing brand.[1]

We now move to the top of the Four A's axis. In nearly all cases, you must first be *aware* of the product in order to form a superficial or in-depth attitude towards a product. As discussed in the business review, there are different types of awareness. From the most to the least effective, they are:

- *Top-of-mind* is the first product name given by an individual when asked what product comes to mind in a particular category.

- *Unaided awareness* includes all the brands in a category one can think of on his own without assistance.

- *Aided awareness* is an individual's recognition of branded products when their names are given or products are shown to him.

[1]Don E. Schultz, Stanley I. Tannenbaum, Robert F. Lauterborn. *Integrated Marketing Communications: Putting It All Together and Making It Work.* (Lincolnwood (Chicago), Illinois: NTC Publishing Group, 1993.)

Exhibit 8.2 Effects of the Marketing Communication Process on Sales

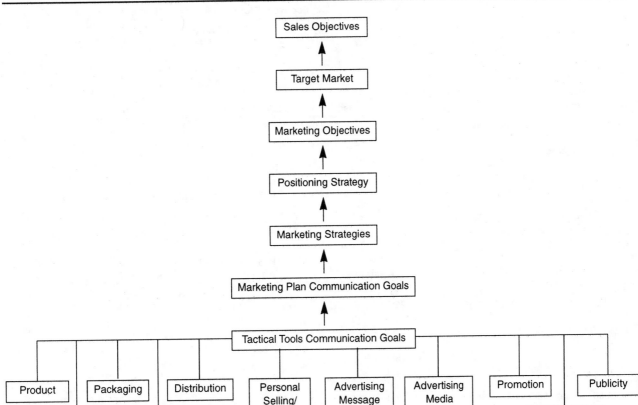

While it may seem basic, it is difficult to purchase a product unless you are aware of it. Many very good new products fail not only because they're not readily available to purchase but also because the target market does not even consider them—it is simply not aware of them.

The Process of Locking Sales to Communication

Effects of the Marketing Communication Process on Sales

Now that you have an understanding of the Four A's communication and target market behavior process, we will explain how this process interfaces with other plan elements and the ultimate goal of generating sales This approach is graphically depicted in Exhibit 8.2. In this process, the cumulative effect of the specific awareness and attitude generated from each tactical tool fulfills the overall marketing plan communication goals. The overall marketing plan communication delivers the positioning via the marketing strategies that fulfill the marketing objectives of target market behavior that will, in turn, fulfill the sales objectives.

Locking Sales to Marketing Objectives and Communication

While Exhibit 8.2 shows graphically the effects of the marketing communication process on sales, Exhibit 8.3 provides an example of how you can *numerically lock*

Exhibit 8.3 Locking Sales From Target Market to Marketing Objectives and Communication

Footwear Store Target Market Example

Total Sales
$5.5 MM

Total Target Market
664.1M

	Previous Purchasers (206.0 M)			Non-Purchasers (458.1 M)			
Segmented Target Sales Objectives	$4.9 MM			$0.6 MM			
Marketing Objectives	%	#		%	#		
Purchasers (via retention and trial)	41.3	85.1		3.1	14.2		
# of Annual Purchases	(Retention)	1.8		(Trial)	1.3		
Average $ Purchase		$32.15			$33.00		
Purchase Intent	%	#		%	#		
Believe They Will Definitely Purchase	55.0	113.3		7.0	32.1		

	Unaided Awareness		Positive Attitude		Unaided Awareness		Positive Attitude	
	%	#	%	#	%	#	%	#
Marketing Plan Communication Goals	95.0	195.7	69.0	142.1	29.0	132.8	12.0	55.0
Tactical Tool Communication Goals								
Product	10.0		16.0		2.0		3.5	
Branding	5.0		3.0		0.5		0.5	
Packaging	5.0		3.0		0.5		1.0	
Pricing	1.0		5.5		1.0		1.0	
Distribution/Penetration	7.0		3.0		2.0		0.5	
Personal Selling/Service	9.0		5.0		2.1		1.0	
Promotion/Events	14.0		8.0		2.5		0.8	
Advertising Message	12.0		8.0		3.1		1.6	
Advertising Media	17.0		6.0		3.8		0.5	
Merchandising	15.0		11.5		10.0		1.6	
Publicity	—		—		1.5		—	

the projected sales from the target market to the marketing objectives and to the required plan and tactical tool communication goals. We are exposing you to this overview of the complete method in order for you to understand how the completed plan elements will lock together. However, both the process and locking mechanics will be explained in detail later in this chapter. After you apply this methodology, you should be able to construct a top-down, sales-to-tactical-tool communication grid, as shown in Exhibit 8.3, quantitatively delineating how the ultimate sales objective will be delivered from the specific target market segments. A worksheet similar to this exhibit is included in Appendix C.

In Exhibit 8.3, the total sales objective of $5.5MM will be generated from the defined total target market, quantified at 664.1M. This total market is then segmented into 206.M previous purchasers and 458.1M nonpurchasers, with each segment receiving its own sales objective. The marketing objectives, which have been previously delineated in the marketing plan, call for retention of 41.3 percent of previous purchasers and trial by 3.1 percent of nonpurchasers. The estimated average number of annual purchases and average purchase dollar amount (1.8 × $32.15 for previous purchasers and 1.3 × $33.00 for nonpurchasers) multiplied by the total number of retention purchasers and trial purchasers equals the $4.9MM and $.6MM segmented target sales, respectively. In order to fulfill these specific sales objectives, 55 percent and 7 percent of each respective target market must have a definite intent to purchase. As you can see, there is fall off from the percent that intends to definitely purchase versus those who are projected to purchase. Using previous purchasers as an example, in order to have 55 percent purchase intent, a positive attitude is projected at 69 percent of the target, which falls off from the total unaided awareness projection of 95 percent. In order to deliver the projected 95 percent unaided awareness and 69 percent positive attitude goals, these totals are then allocated among each tactical tool. Each tool is then planned and executed to generate its share of the required marketing plan awareness and attitude communication goals.

By now you should have arrived at a sales objective and quantified the target market segment(s) that will deliver the sales. Also, you should have quantified the behavior required by the target market in your marketing objectives. What we will explain next is how to arrive at the purchase intent and required marketing plan awareness and attitude communication needed to generate the required behavior. We will then detail a methodology to arrive at the individual tactical tool awareness and attitude communication needed to fulfill the marketing plan communication goals.

Four Tasks to Development of Purchase Intent and Communication Goals

The four tasks to follow for developing and fulfilling the purchase intent and the marketing communication goals via tactical tool communication are:

1. In the business review, review awareness, attitude, and behavior experiences for your product, the competition, the category, and related categories.

2. Review the previously established target market behavior that has been quantified in your marketing objectives for both purchasers and nonpurchasers, as well as the marketing position and strategies.

3. Determine the overall marketing plan communication goals.

   A. Determine the attitude required by your target market to deliver the purchase intent needed to fulfill the marketing objectives.

   B. Determine the awareness levels necessary to positively affect target market attitude as required to achieve the predetermined purchase intent.

4. Set specific awareness and attitude value goals for each tactical tool that will fulfill the overall marketing communication goals.

COMMUNICATION GOALS APPLICATION

Now that you have a basic understanding of the relationship between communication and behavior and have been exposed to the four steps involved in locking the tactical tools to the marketing communication goals, we will describe the application of each task. Once you have reviewed these tasks, we will review the limitations and complexity of this process as it relates to the unique communication control challenges and inherent problems of your product and category. In addition, we will point out the difficulties in the measurement of the communication contribution of each of the tactical tools in the marketing mix.

Task 1

Review Awareness, Attributes, and Action/ Behavior Experiences for Your Product, the Competition, the Category, and Related Categories

Literally, all small, medium, and even large businesses lack much of the described information needed to apply the ideal communication goals strategy method. In fact, even the authors, with their academic experience and operation of a marketing communications firm that does consulting with companies from 10 million to billion plus dollars in sales, do not have all the data desired when applying the goals method. Hopefully, there is much data you have gathered in your business review that you can use as a basis in the application of this method. Specifically, look for information that will provide insight as to the effectiveness of each tactical tool's ability to deliver awareness and positive attitude to generate behavior and/or make the sale. You would like to have some indication as to what percentage of the target market is aware of your product and holds key attitudes toward your product, such as a "best quality," leadership, etc., and how these communication factors relate to the percentage of your target market that purchases the product.

If possible, you would like to know the awareness, attitude, and behavior of both customers and noncustomers in your target market, because you will find that the relationship between communication and behavior will vary dramatically between purchasers and nonpurchasers. For example, remember how the customers' attitudes toward the product were significantly more positive than those of noncustomers in the positioning by customer versus noncustomer mapping example in Chapter 6.

Understand Your Own Product History

Begin your review of awareness, attitude, and behavior data with your own product, store, or service. You should have uncovered some of this communication and behavioral data in the preparation of your business review. Next, review your business data for cause-and-effect relationships. For example, when a manufacturer secures display placements in 25 percent or more of the retail outlets in his service area, he sees an increase in sales from 30–50 percent. Or, for example, when a business-to-business manufacturer receives a feature article placed in a major industry trade publication, he generally sees an increase of 60–70 percent in inquiries. With this same manufacturer, over half of the inquiries each year can be tracked back to those trade shows at which there was a booth. When a retailer runs a test in which only the execution of one tool was changed (promotion tool changed from couponing to sampling), the retailer might record a 15 percent sales increase in test markets as compared to the control markets where no change was made.

If you have not been measuring and recording the effectiveness of the various tools or testing their effectiveness, it is something you will want to include in next year's plan. While the above observations measure cause and effect and do not answer the awareness and attitude questions, you can use this basic information to help estimate what percentage of the target market's unaided awareness and attitude caused the behavior. For example, if running twice the number of ads in a given period increased calls by 50 percent, the inference would be that there was a minimum of 50 percent increase in awareness created by doubling the number of ads. These types of inferences are far from empirical research, but they do provide some direction.

Implement Primary Research

While being able to relate cause and effect is a start to learning, it is necessary to do primary research to more accurately determine the awareness, attitude, and behavior levels of purchasers and nonpurchasers for your product and that of the competition. In most cases, the awareness, attitude, and behavior data derived by the survey research will be cumulative in nature and will not provide specific information for each tool. However, by applying the cause-and-effect information you have collected by each tool, you might be able to learn directionally about each tool's effect on awareness and attitude. For example, let's say that your primary research indicated a 40 percent unaided awareness for your product among the target market and that, by applying only three tactical marketing mix tools—personal selling, merchandising (product brochure for follow-up), and publicity—it was shown that 70 percent of your noncustomer inquiries came from editorial messages in trade publications—the direct result of your publicity programs. If this were the case, you could surmise that 70 percent of the total awareness came from the publicity tool and, therefore, that one could allocate 28 points ($.70 \times .40 = 28$ points) of current awareness to this tool. This is a very rough approach to allocation, but again, it demonstrates how you can use the interpolation of cause-and-effect data with research-derived awareness, attitude, and behavior data to arrive at an individual communication value for a tactical tool.

Many times companies use primary research to measure the effectiveness of specific vehicles for tactical tools. For example, for our client Famous Footwear we found that, for a specific promotion, 24 percent of the customers came to the stores because of an FSI (free-standing insert), while only 4 percent of customers came because of a newspaper ad. While primary research will provide much information in terms of awareness, attitude, and behavior information for your product and the competition, you can also learn more about cause and effect by reviewing the tactical activity of your competition and their expenditures relative to specific tools and total marketing budget. This is usually difficult information to uncover, but hopefully in your competitive review in the business review you have arrived at some cause-and-effect information that you can relate to specific tactical tools.

Review Secondary Sources

In addition to doing primary research to help you determine value data for your marketing plan communication goals and individual tactical tools, you should review industry and trade association(s) publications for research studies that might have been implemented. You should also review studies done within specific disciplines, such as *Advertising Age* for the advertising message, *Inside Media* for the advertising media, and *Promo* for the promotion tool. You can review some of the publications oriented to the academic world, such as the *Journal of Consumer Research* and *Journal of Advertising Research*, for insight into the impact of tactical tools, both individually and cumulatively, on various types and levels of awareness, attitude, and behavior.

From this type of review you will arrive at specific quantitative information that you can apply when determining your marketing plan communications goals and values for each tool. However, in most situations, your review of this type of information will lead only to broad, directional inferences that you can apply in the "value method." This review will also clearly point out what you know, what you don't know, and what you need to know about the relationship between communication and behavior relative to your product. Also, you will learn that most of the information you will apply will be more subjective than objective. In fact, the authors, before developing the goals method, went through a mental allocation process to determine what awareness and attitude thresholds were required for the marketing communication goals and each tactical tool. This method, while far from perfect, merely improves the chance for success in locking the marketing plan elements together most efficiently and effectively by providing a framework.

Exhibit 8.4 Communication Values Review Examples

Tactical Tool	Activity	Results	Directional Implications
Product			
Branding			
Packaging			
Pricing			
Distribution/Penetration			
Personal Selling/Service			
Promotion/Events	Trade show sampling of product	Received 180 responses from this trade show handout requesting sales presentations. This is double the rate from same show last year with no sampling.	Sample products at all trade shows.
Advertising Message			
Advertising Media			
Merchandising			
Publicity	Feature product stories Product news releases	—Generated 50 to 150 phone calls per story. —Generated minimal, if any, phone inquiries	—Place greater emphasis on product feature stories even if it means less news releases —Don't expand product news release program

To help organize, catalog, and summarize this diverse information from many sources as it pertains particularly to the tactical tools, use a structured format like that shown in Exhibit 8.4 and refer to the appropriate worksheet in Appendix C.

Task 2
Review Marketing Objectives, Positioning, and Strategies

In order to set the tactical tool values and then lock them to the marketing plan communication goals, you must understand the requirements of the marketing behavior objectives, and the direction provided by the position and marketing strategies.

Marketing Objectives

First review the specific behavior required in terms of retention of current purchasers, trial by new purchasers, and the amount of annual product purchase by both current and new purchasers. Ask yourself this question: Where is the greatest emphasis in terms of required behavior versus the previous years? Is the greatest emphasis on retention or trial? For example, if the emphasis is on trial and new customers, you will need greater awareness among nonpurchasers for your marketing plan communication goal, and accordingly, you will potentially require more support from specific tactical tools designed to generate greater exposure for your product, such as advertising media and publicity.

What is the total amount of product to be purchased by the current and new customers as called for in the marketing objectives? If the objectives call for substantial increases in the amount of purchases by small numbers of target companies or persons, you might consider greater support from tactical tools that are close to the point-of-purchase, such as personal selling or merchandising through store displays that encourage impulse purchase, and "loading" types of promotions (i.e., buy two, get one free).

What are the expectation levels for repeat buying and building loyalty among new customers that have tried the product? In this case, product performance and personal service could be tools used for more support.

Market Positioning

What are the specific drivers of the positioning of your product? What are key attributes around which your product is built? What is the attitude you want within your target market regarding these attributes relative to the competition? In the positioning chapter, we gave the example of Famous Footwear concentrating on the "value" attribute, with emphasis on creating the attitude among the target person that Famous Footwear has the *best* value on *branded* shoes for the *whole* family. Accordingly, these are the types of positive attitudes that Famous Footwear instills through all of its communication to generate a high purchase interest in the relatively broad target market of women 25–49 with families of household incomes of $40,000+.

Based on this position, *value* becomes the major driver affecting the attitudes of your target market. Accordingly, in setting your overall communications attitude goal, you will call for a higher percentage of the target market to believe that Famous Footwear has the best value. This will then translate to a higher percentage of the target market that intends to purchase and eventually will try Famous Footwear.

Famous Footwear's positioning provides not only the driving attitude(s) for the communication attitude goals; it also directs the use of tools that can deliver broad exposure, such as advertising and the presentation of a "value" attitude via branded product, good pricing, and aggressive promotion. It is these types of key positive attitudes that must be reinforced by each of the tactical tools. With each tool providing communication that instills the same intended attitude, a truly integrated communication program is created that delivers a unified image to help affect the intended behavior called for in the marketing objectives.

Marketing Strategies

Remember, each of the marketing strategies will provide direction indicating which tactical tools will be used and how they should be used to help communicate the position in terms of building awareness, presenting a positive attitude, and, in turn, fulfilling the marketing objectives.

First, review how the marketing strategies might have changed from the previous years. For example, does the distribution strategy call for a greater ACV (All Commodity Volume) distribution or store penetration in existing markets, which will lead to greater awareness? Was there a change in the pricing strategy from premium to commodity pricing? While the actual pricing of the product will have minimal, if any, effect on awareness, it will affect the target market's attitude towards this product.

Further, review each strategy in terms of awareness and attitude delivery and attempt to determine if there was any change from the previous year in importance relative to the use of other strategies in delivering the overall marketing plan communication goals. For example, was there a shift in importance from personal selling to advertising media in building awareness and positive attitude toward the product? Note these changes when identifying what communication value you expect from each tactical tool.

Task 3
Determine the Overall Marketing Plan Communication Goals

Purchase Intent

Now that you have a greater (but never complete) understanding of the relationship between communication and behavior for your product and category and you have reviewed the marketing objectives, positioning, and marketing strategies, you must next make some product purchase estimates. You should first attempt to estimate what percent of the target market purchasers believe they will *definitely* continue as purchasing customers and what percent of the target nonpurchasers believe they will *definitely* become new purchasers.

Hopefully, your research database will indicate what percent of target purchasers and target nonpurchasers believe they will definitely purchase your product. If you do not have this type of information—which will be the case for most products—you should make this estimate based on the information reviewed in Task 1. To help you make this estimate, you can break down each target segment from "definitely will not purchase" to "possibly will not purchase," "possibly will purchase," and finally, "definitely will purchase." A starting point for goal estimation is provided just after the forthcoming discussion of attitude and awareness.

Attitude and Awareness

Next, based on your review of the data in Task 1, review what percent of the target purchasers and nonpurchasers will have to hold a specific attitude toward the product in order to arrive at the specific percentage of each base that definitely will purchase.

Then, determine what percent of the target customers and target noncustomers must have unaided awareness of the product in order to affect the intended attitude and the predetermined purchase intent. "First mention" or "top-of-mind" awareness can also be used as a goal in place of total unaided awareness; *aided* awareness should *not* be used as a goal because it is not a reliable awareness measurement to use in the projection of attitude and purchase intent goals.

In setting attitude and awareness goals and projecting purchase intent, review the level of change in the target market behavior from the previous years and compare it to the marketing objectives of the plan you are preparing. For example, in previous years you have been averaging 3 percent trial of new purchasers, and your plan now requires that you generate 10 percent trial. The more aggressive the marketing objectives in terms of a change in behavior, the greater the increase in awareness and attitude goals and purchase intent. The more dramatic the increase in awareness and positive attitude for the competition's product as compared to the previous year, the greater the need for an increase in awareness and attitude goals for your product.

It is very difficult to recommend what the awareness, attitude, and purchase goals should be for a new product or a product for which you have no quantitative awareness and attitude data. However, some basic awareness principles to keep in mind are:

■ Target market unaided awareness exceeds target market purchase.

■ The higher the percent of the target market required to purchase, the higher the awareness required.

■ The greater the number of major competitors in a category, the greater the difference between the percent of a target market that has unaided awareness and the percent that purchase.

■ Purchaser unaided awareness is dramatically higher than the nonpurchaser unaided awareness—it can vary from up to two to five times or more in amount.

■ The greater the one-product dominance of a target market and the fewer major competitors, the closer the percentage of purchasers to the percentage with unaided awareness of the product.

Relationship of Actual Purchase to Intent, Attitude, and Awareness

General principles are very difficult to provide when describing the relationship between awareness, attitude, purchase intent, and actual purchase. However, a starting point—and only a starting point—for defining the total target market goals (purchaser and nonpurchaser) for percent to purchase, purchase intent, attitude, and unaided awareness is the "50% Happening" premise. As shown in the example below, this very subjective premise suggests you take the percent of the total target market that you project to purchase (including purchaser and previous nonpurchaser) and add 50 percent of each level to the next level of the sequence.

Total Target Market = 200,000

	<u>Target Market Effected</u>	
	<u>#</u>	<u>%</u>
To purchase	10,000	5.0
"Definite" purchase intent	15,000	7.5
Specific positive attitude	22,500	11.3
Unaided awareness	33,800	16.9

There are more exceptions than rules to this "50% Happening" premise, but it is a beginning sequence to follow if you have no data. Keep in mind that if there is a large number purchasing, if the product is very established, and if there is a great deal of positive trending in the marketplace, you will need to add less than 50 percent for each increment. Likewise, you will need to add more than 50 percent if you discover findings opposite the above in the marketplace.

Remember, the "50% Happening" approach is for the total target market. When you break out the target market purchaser and nonpurchaser separately, you will find the actual percentages in terms of intent to purchase, attitude, and awareness for *purchasers* to be substantially higher, with a "less than 50% Happening" for each level, as shown in the next exhibit. On the other hand, there can be closer to 100 percent difference between the percent purchasing and those that say they "definitely will purchase" for noncustomers and the total target market, as shown in Exhibit 8.5. Remember, this "50% Happening" is only a starting point, and you will modify the percentage levels at each increment based on your review of Task 1. Also, keep in

Exhibit 8.5 Method to Set Marketing Communication Goals to Fulfill the Marketing Objectives

| | Footwear Store Target Market Example | | |
| | Target Market | | |
	% Current Purchasers	% Nonpurchasers	% Total
Marketing Objectives Purchasers (via retention and trial)	41.3	3.1	4.5
Purchase Intent Believe they will definitely purchase	55.0	7.0	10.0
Marketing Communication Goals *Attitude* Rate store as having high-value shoes	69.0	12.0	14.5
Awareness Unaided awareness of footwear store	95.0	29.0	31.0

mind that applying a percent to a percent is not mathematically correct and is directional only. To be totally accurate, apply your 50 percent factor to actual target market whole numbers, as shown in the previous example.

An example of determining quantitative goals by beginning with the required target market behavior in the marketing objectives and then working back to purchase intent, attitude, and awareness is shown in Exhibit 8.5. To simplify the demonstration of setting marketing communication goals to meet marketing objectives, this example shows total target market purchasers by purchaser retention and trial by nonpurchasers. A worksheet to help you estimate the purchase intent, attitude, and awareness levels needed to fulfill the marketing objectives is included in Appendix C.

Although Exhibit 8.5 has precise numbers for calculation, marketing communication goals are directional. Remember that marketing is not a science, so you should use these calculations as estimates and temper them with common sense. The point to keep in mind in your evaluation is that, once the plan has been implemented and you review the target market purchaser and nonpurchaser intent to purchase, attitude, and awareness levels (via survey research), it is not important whether each goal was perfectly met. However, it *is* important to recognize the significance of reaching only half of the levels of your goals. If you missed your communication goals by 50 percent, it is safe to say that you most likely did not fulfill your marketing objectives and, consequently, did not deliver the required sales.

Task 4

Set Awareness and Attitude Value Goals for Each Tactical Tool

Now that you have set your attitude and awareness marketing communications goals, the final task is to set specific awareness and attitude goals for target customers and noncustomers for each tactical tool. The value goals you assign each tool are very important, because each tactical segment of the marketing plan will be developed to fulfill its respective value goals. The values assigned to each tool will be dependent on what you are marketing and where your product is in the product life cycle. Most importantly, you will set value goals for each tool based on your specific product situation and its competitive sets in the marketplace. Accordingly, you want to review Task 1 again before you begin setting tactical tool value goals in Task 4.

Rank Tactical Tools by Importance

Having reviewed Task 1 again and knowing that the value goals you set are very subjective and only a starting point, attempt to rank the tactical tools based on their

Exhibit 8.6 Tactical Tool Importance Ranking Example

Tactical Tool	Awareness		Attitude	
	Purchaser	Nonpurchaser	Purchaser	Nonpurchaser
Product	VI	MI	I	MI
Branding	I	VI	I	VI
Packaging	I	VI	I	VI
Price	I		I	
Distribution/Penetration	I	VI	I	VI
Personal Selling/Service	MI	MI	I	MI
Promotion/Events	MI	MI	VI	VI
Advertising Message	VI	MI	VI	VI
Advertising Media	MI	MI	VI	MI
Merchandising	MI	VI	VI	MI
Publicity	—	I	—	I

VI = Very Important   MI = Moderately Important   I = Important

importance in fulfilling the marketing communication goals. In order to do this: 1) review your tactical experience via the worksheet shown in Exhibit 8.4; and 2) review each tactical tool against the overall marketing strategies and against the respective strategy for each tool, such as personal selling/service, promotion, and advertising. This will help you determine the degree of emphasis to place on each tool. For example, if the personal selling strategy states "maintain sales force effectiveness comparable to that of the previous year," and the promotion strategy states "increase promotion activity to stimulate trial from new purchasers," the promotion tool would be given greater importance than in the past relative to the personal selling strategy. The key point to remember is that, if your strategic direction does not call for a change in marketing approach for a particular tool, that tool should not be given more or less importance in this year's plan versus the previous marketing plan.

Having compared one tool to the other, list "important" (I), "moderately important" (MI), or "very important" (VI) next to each tool to indicate its awareness and attitude value. As shown in the example in Exhibit 8.6, you would rank these values by importance as they relate to target purchasers and nonpurchasers. An Importance Ranking worksheet is provided in Appendix C.

Usually, every tool has some importance, but if you believe a particular tool has no importance relative to awareness and attitude, do not give it an importance ranking. For example, you might decide that, while the "price" tool is "very important" in affecting attitude, it really has no importance in building the overall awareness for the product.

Assign Values by Importance

Based on the importance rankings, assign awareness and attitude percentage point values to each tool for purchaser and nonpurchaser so that they total to the awareness and attitude marketing communication goals. An example of this assignment of value point goals is shown in Exhibit 8.7, and a comparable worksheet is included in Appendix C. In this example the totals of the awareness and attitude generated by the tactical totals equate to the total unaided awareness and attitude required in Exhibit 8.3 estimated to fulfill the ultimate sales objective.

The value point goals in this example total to the marketing communication awareness and attitude goals shown in Exhibit 8.5. If you have thoroughly gone through Tasks 1, 2, and 3, as well as the importance ranking process in your assignment of

Exhibit 8.7 Individual Tactical Tool Value Goals for Your Product by Awareness and Attitude

	Awareness		Attitude	
	Purchaser % Point	NonPurchaser % Point	Purchaser % Point	NonPurchaser % Point
Product Design	10.0	2.0	16.0	3.5
Branding	5.0	0.5	3.0	0.5
Packaging	5.0	0.5	3.0	1.0
Pricing	1.0	1.0	5.5	1.0
Distribution/Penetration	7.0	2.0	3.0	0.5
Personal Selling/Service	9.0	2.1	5.0	1.0
Promotion/Events	14.0	2.5	8.0	0.8
Advertising Message	12.0	3.1	8.0	1.6
Advertising Media	17.0	3.8	6.0	0.5
Merchandising	15.0	10.0	11.5	1.6
Publicity	—	1.5	—	—
Total	95.0	29.0	69.0	12.0

values, you will find some of your tactical tool goals virtually the same, while others will have major disparity between each other. These results are dependent upon what contributions you expect each tool to make in fulfilling the marketing communication goals.

Another point to remember is that if a tactical tool or a group of tactical tools has been given a relatively low goal value (which means minimum expectation for contribution), put a minimum of marketing resources against it when preparing this segment of the tactical implementation plan. Unless you can get this tool above the threshold level to make it effective, don't use it. For example, if the advertising communication tools received very low value goals, it might be best to concentrate your resources in personal selling and merchandising (the nonmedia tools), which are concentrated closer to the purchaser and do not have the higher associated costs. Put your major investment or increased investment against the few tools that will drive your plan.

Expect to revise these value goals as you prepare and interface the tactical tool segments of the plan. For example, you might assign more weight to the advertising media tool after determining that effectively communicating a specific promotion will require not only the merchandising tool via store displays, but also more media via newspaper ads. Further, as you finalize the marketing budget and reconcile it with the sales objectives and bottom-line goals, there most likely will be an adjustment in tactical tool values.

A major question we originally raised and have not addressed is: What is the multiple progression effect of integrated communication among all the tools that truly reinforces the market positioning and drives behavior? The authors acknowledge that, because this multiplier effect is virtually impossible to measure, it serves as your communication bonus for the plan, providing the safety margins to compensate for any shortfalls in those tactical tools that do not deliver the expected awareness and attitude communication. Think of it as your "goals" insurance policy in your overall plan delivery of the marketing communications.

Finally, even if you have no data (which is unlikely) or minimal data from which to develop your overall marketing communication goals and tactical value communication goals, it will be a good learning exercise for you and others in your company to arrive at estimates of awareness, attitude, and intent to purchase to fulfill your marketing objectives. Going through this process, even without numbers, will point out the challenges you will face as you proceed to Step 7, the development of your tactical tools. Working through this process will also point out the importance of beginning now to develop a database to help you make many of the forthcoming decisions.

Communication Control Challenges and Inherent Problems Regarding the Communication Value Method

Now that you have been exposed to the communication goal method, we will review some communication control challenges and inherent problems that make this method only a start to the process of arriving at overall marketing communication goals and allocating awareness and attitude requirements for the specific tactical tools.

Controlled to Somewhat Controlled to Uncontrolled Communication

There is much you can control in the communication of your product and/or service, such as your advertising message, publicity releases, brand name development, packaging, type of promotion and events, company direct service to customers, point-of-purchase message, etc. However, there is much communication that you cannot control. The sheer noise level in your particular marketplace can exceed your control. This noise level includes the communication of your message and that of your competition, as well as all of the messages your target market is receiving, both within a particular category and on a geographic basis, in their everyday lives. For example, it is estimated that the average adult is exposed to 200 to 300 ad messages every day.

There are also many other forms of communication that you cannot, or believe you cannot, control, such as your competitors' sales forces, promotion, and advertising; the retailer's/distributor's service level; and independent, third party communications. For example, a magazine reporter might use your product incorrectly because he did not read the instructions, have a bad usage experience, and then write a negative feature on your product.

Many times you have partial control over what may appear to be uncontrollable communication. For example, the magazine reporter who writes a negative story can be influenced. Perhaps the "facts" sheet sent along with the product and instructions was not enough to properly "prep" the reporter. But a phone call highlighting the instructions could have preceded and followed the sending of the instructions with the product. Further, some believe that the manufacturer has no control over the retailer's displays. However, having the company person call the retail contact with examples of how to build a retail display with corresponding manufacturer's incentive may provide some control over the retailer's communication of the manufacturer's product. The point is that a well-planned and well-executed marketing plan with detailed follow-through can provide some control over what might be originally considered uncontrollable communication and give your product a better chance to succeed.

Addressing the communication control challenges is critical to determining what overall marketing communication is required to move the target person to action and what is required by each tactical tool to deliver the overall communication for the plan. Yes, there is only so much communication you can control, and yes, because of the control challenge, your communication goals and values are only directional. However, the key is to be aware of what you truly cannot control and to make every effort to control as much as you can.

Application Shortcomings

In addition to the communication control challenges one faces when relating behavior to communication, you should also be aware of the many shortcomings in the application of the communication goals' approach.

1. Not all products are alike.

   Every product, category, and industry is unique, and what applies to one does not apply to all.

2. Communication is a fluid process.

   As shown in Exhibit 8.1, the effect of communication on building awareness, attitude, and usage is very fluid, with much overlap and no real beginning or end. Also, you should remember that the communication and behavior relationship can be very time sensitive. The time period needed for the process to take effect could be seconds, such as an impulse purchase, or years, such as purchasing a new auto or home.

3. Subjectiveness is involved in the method application.

   While we try to quantify throughout the application of this method, you will still need to apply intuitive judgment. Accordingly, another major problem regarding this method arises from the subjectiveness involved in arriving at the overall marketing communication goals and individual awareness and attitude value goals for each tool.

4. Marketing activities have a cumulative effect.

   Also, there is the problem of attempting to determine what the overall effect will be on target market awareness and attitude when you combine the communication power of the different tools. Is the whole greater than the sum of the parts? For example, let's say we give the advertising media tactical tool a value goal of achieving 10 percent awareness among the target market, in conjunction with a 10 percent awareness goal for merchandising and a 5 percent awareness goal for publicity. When you combine advertising media with merchandising and publicity, the awareness contributions of each tool combined together are not just additive but many times multiple in effect. What is the multiple progression effect on awareness and attitude from the combination of media advertising, merchandising, and publicity? We believe it is more than just the 25 percent awareness additive sum of the three tools just discussed. No one can really determine the specific multiplier effect. We do believe there is a cumulative effect on awareness, attitude, and thus usage.

5. Communication effects are difficult to measure.

   Another problem in the attempt to plan the effects of communication and behavior on each other relates to measurement. How much does a store display affect awareness and attitude in-store? How much effect does a personal sales presentation have in the awareness and attitude towards the product? What effect does sampling a product have on attitude? Accordingly, it's difficult to measure the effect of communication and behavior on each other. When it is possible to measure effectiveness, it is difficult to project these findings when planning in different product and market environments.

Keep in mind that, while the interactive communication behavior process is very complex, the proposed planning method is, by design, relatively simplistic in order to help you cope with the complexities. This approach does not take into consideration all elements of this very involved process. However, no method will ever be totally comprehensive or flawless when you are dealing with human behavior and communication. Nevertheless, this basic approach will give you an opportunity to at least circle the challenges in terms of basic understanding and deal with the very subjective nature of this planning task by providing a manageable framework that is disciplined and step-by-step in method. The net result is a process that will literally force you to allocate your marketing resources on a priority basis.

The authors arrived at this "goals" method after reviewing many application cases and primary and secondary research data and after much trial and error. This method has many assumptions and estimates for specific areas where hard data is not available. It is at this point that the authors have applied their experiences and intuitive judgment to arrive at what we believe is a workable method. Accordingly, the authors remind you that, while much of this method is directional and represents only a starting point in your communication planning, it does help order the many diverse elements into a meaningful framework which you can then adapt to your individual product and specific market situation.

DOS AND DON'TS

Do

- Understand that the relationship between communications and behavior is very complex and that, while awareness and attitude affect behavior, behavior also affects attitude and awareness.

- Remember, the Four A's principle is the key not to only introducing and sustaining a product, but also to identifying problem(s) such as why your product is not growing or why it is declining in sales.

- Understand the communication control challenges and shortcomings of the "goals" method to most realistically and effectively apply this method for your product.

- Start now (if you haven't already) to gather cause-and-effect information regarding your product, competition, and category.

- Review secondary sources for data on the impact of various communication tools on awareness and attitudes.

- To best apply the communication goals approach, use the findings from survey research whenever possible.

- After detailing the sales objectives and target market segments, go through the exercise of locking marketing objectives numerically to purchase intent, attitude, and awareness to best determine what will be required from each of your tactical tools in order to develop a marketing plan that will fulfill the sales objectives.

- Review the tactical tool value goals before you develop each tactical segment of the marketing plan in the next step in order to most accurately develop each tactical segment and effectively interface the tactical tools with one another.

Don't

- Don't expect predetermined action without adequate awareness and positive attitude levels among your target market.

- If you do not follow the four steps to arrive at and fulfill the communication goals via the tactical tool communication, don't expect to effectively lock the tactical tools via the marketing and positioning strategies to the marketing objectives, target market, and sales objectives.

- Don't expect to fully reap the benefits of the "values" approach unless you first thoroughly immerse yourself in the experiences for your product, the direct competition, the category, and related categories.

- Don't apply the "50% Happening" approach as gospel. It is only a starting point to use if you do not have the directional data from your own product experience to determine the purchase intent, attitude, and awareness percentage levels for your target market.

- Don't expect your value goals to remain constant once you have set them. Expect to change them as you prepare the tactical tools portion of your marketing plan.

Step Seven   Tactical Marketing Mix Tools

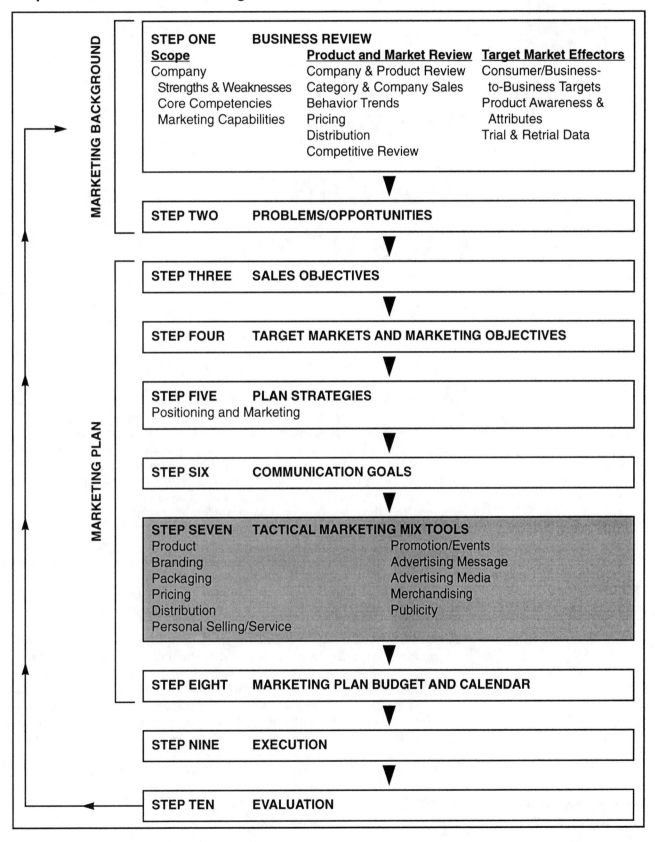

PRODUCT/ BRANDING/ PACKAGING

While your product, its brand identity, and its packaging have major impact on the contribution of awareness and attitude in fulfilling the positioning to deliver on the marketing objectives, you must also make very sure the product lives up to your planned positioning. Effective communication of a positioning may induce trial of a product, but beware—nothing will ruin a company faster than selling a poor product or a product which is not consistent with its positioning. Customers may be convinced to purchase once, but they won't be fooled again.

The product, the product's brand name and graphic identity, and the product's packaging are the most fundamental elements of the entire marketing mix. They make up the reality of the positioning. The attributes and the attitudes consumers have about your product are what define your brand relative to the competition. The packaging for your product is a component of the product's attribute composition, and helps communicate the brand identity. Because of the interrelationships between the product, brand identity, and packaging, we have included all three in one chapter.

Before you write the product/branding/packaging segment of the marketing plan, you must review the direction provided by the problems and opportunities, positioning, and the marketing strategies affecting each of the three areas. If you are not modifying or developing a new product, brand name, or package, there is no need to address these marketing mix tools in your plan. However, it is recommended that you read through this chapter to help determine your needs for product, branding or packaging modifications, their tactical tool value contributions to the plan's awareness and attitude goals, and for additional background in writing the remainder of the marketing plan.

From This Chapter You Will Learn

Product

The definition of a product and a service.

The definition and different types of *new* products.

What type of new product activity is indicated by business situation.

Issues affecting your new product plan.

How to establish product objectives and strategies.

Branding

Definitions of a brand and branding.

The importance of branding.

How to develop a branding plan.

Packaging

Functions of packaging.

Reasons for changing your packaging.

How to develop your packaging plan.

OVERVIEW

Definition of Product

In the case of consumer package goods, retail, and business-to-business companies, the *product is a tangible object* that is marketed to customers. However, for service businesses, the product takes the form of some *intangible offering*, such as a future benefit or future promise. Thus, while all products are offerings to the customer, there is an inherent difference between what is sold by a service firm and what is sold by a retailer or manufacturer.

Definition of New Products

A new product is one which has not been previously marketed by your firm. We use this definition because, even if a product is not new to the market, if it is new to your firm, it presents new marketing challenges for your company.

New products may come in any one of a number of forms:

- *A new positioning for an existing product.* This entails changing consumer perceptions of the personality and/or usage of your product.

- *Line extensions.* Line extensions add to the breadth of your product line with the addition of new flavors, scents, colors, or sizes. Line extensions can provide an effective way to reach new customers by leveraging the existing equity in your product's brand name, both at the consumer level and at the trade level, to assist in selling the product at retail.

- *Flankers.* Flankers are complementary products marketed under an existing brand umbrella. As with line extensions, flankers can be an effective way to increase sales by leveraging existing strengths. An example would be Gillette's capitalizing on the strength of its brand in the shaving products market to offer other health and beauty aids products, such as deodorant, under the Gillette name. Another example would be for our client Mercury Marine. Mercury, well known for its motors and engines, has become very active in marketing a line of inflatable water craft—small rubber boats that, as we say in the advertising, "get you from here to there." Finally, in our work in the shoe industry, we see daily the impact of Nike with its development of flankers in the apparel area. You don't have to work in the industry to notice the number of Nike t-shirts, hats, jackets, and other apparel being worn today.

- *Entirely new products:* These are products which simply did not previously exist. The VCR is a good example. Before the introduction of the VCR, people simply watched what was on TV, generally one show at a time. The VCR was a new product with an entirely new functionality, providing consumers with a new way to use television. The Internet would be another example of an entirely new service. Our agency has developed home pages for many of our clients hoping to attract business from the ever-expanding audience delivered through the Internet.

Any of the above changes to your firm's product constitute a new product introduction, and the impact/opportunities in the other elements of the marketing mix must be reviewed and considered.

Why New Products Are Important

Change is a fact of life for the marketer. It provides the opportunities that allow the firm to grow and prosper, but it also presents the forces that may render the firm's product(s) obsolete and leave the firm without sufficient sales and profits to survive. You must continually review your product's position in the competitive environment and in the context of the constantly changing consumer. This is the best method to ensure that your firm's product offering(s) are still relevant to the target market and remain competitive.

Issues Affecting the Product

Product Attributes

A major focus should be placed on determining if there is a need or an opportunity for product modifications, new products, or extended product lines. In order to accomplish this, it is important to first identify what attributes consumers find most important in the purchase decision for your product category and determine how your product ranks along these attributes compared to your competitors' products. (Review your business review—target market effectors awareness and attribute section— problems and opportunities, positioning and marketing strategies sections.) If there are critical areas where your product is less competitive and/or where there is a product void in the market, then you must develop product objectives and strategies to address the situation.

Product Segmentation

The desirability of segmenting your product to meet specific demographic and lifestyle needs should be addressed. For the manufacturer, one method of segmentation is to develop different product sizes based on product usage. Smaller sizes are often requirements of singles or light users and larger sizes are often needed by families or heavy users of the product category.

Another way of segmenting products is by utilizing different product features to attract different target markets. Many times new products are developed with a basic appeal to a broad, homogeneous market. As competition increases and the product reaches the growth stage in the product life cycle, differentiation occurs and marketing must more closely target the needs and tasks of specific target markets. Cross-country skis are a good example. Back in 1970, the sport of cross-country skiing was relatively new. There was basically one style: all-purpose, wooden cross-country skis. However, by the next decade, there were touring skis, racing skis (skating and traditional), deep-snow skis, and telemarking skis, not to mention multiple options on bindings, poles, boots, and ski construction. As the sport of cross-country skiing grew, manufacturers targeted specific needs.

Product Innovation

An important area of your business review is the analysis of change and innovation in the product category. Product innovations allow you to map out changes in your company's product. They compel you to determine how your product should evolve to meet customers' needs and the competitive pressures of the future.

There are essentially eight types of new product innovations:[1]

1. *A product with an entirely new function.* Generally, such new products grow out of a technical innovation against an existing consumer need. For example, the first TV was a product with an entirely new functionality (broadcast of picture and sound), but it served an existing consumer need for information and entertainment.

2. *A product offering improved performance against an existing function/need.* These products perform an existing function in a better way. Our client Mondial Industries is marketing the Diaper Genie, a new odor-free system to dispose of disposable diapers—a vast improvement over the old diaper pail.

3. *A new application for an existing product.* The classic example of a firm developing a new application for an existing product is Arm & Hammer's positioning of its baking soda product as a refrigerator deodorizer as well as a baking ingredient.

4. *New products with additional functions or features.* This is essentially an upgrade of an existing product that improves or expands its performance against consumer needs. An example is Mercury Marine's introduction of the High Five Propeller, a new 5-blade stainless steel prop which gets skiers out of the water faster than conventional three- or four-blade props.

5. *An existing product aimed at a new target market.* The attributes of the product may be unchanged, but the communications are oriented toward a different target. Marlboro was initially positioned as a cigarette for women. It was later marketed against the male segment, and the rest, as they say, is history.

6. *A product with a new price/value mix.* This type of new product entry addresses an existing consumer need with a new price and value combination. An example from the retail field would be the repositioning of Famous Footwear in the late 1970s from a low-priced shoe store to a value-driven shoe store featuring brand name shoes at discounted prices.

7. *Packaging improvements.* Packaging improvements may essentially constitute a new product when they alter the usage or purchase experience. Procter and Gamble's launch of liquid laundry detergent bottles with a unique no-drop spout designed for neater pouring is an example of this type of product innovation. In

[1]Adopted from Crawford, C. Merle. *New Products Management* (Homewood, IL: Richard D. Irwin, Inc., 1983), p. 35.

the retail and service areas, packaging improvements include the store or office. We spent over a year helping Famous Footwear redesign its in-store packaging to be consistent with its new positioning. The research phase included analyzing everything from traffic flow to which color impacted the target market most favorably to the most effective use of point-of-sale materials in-store. We will address this issue again in the packaging section of this chapter.

8. *Changes in appearance or form.* These new products represent incremental changes in the product that result (when successful) in improved performance against consumer needs. A packaged goods example would be the introduction of gel toothpastes.

HOW TO DEVELOP A NEW PRODUCT PLAN

A worksheet for developing your product plan is provided in Appendix C.

Task 1

Establish Your Product Objectives

Product objectives will center around one or more of the five following areas:

1. Developing new products

2. Developing line extensions for existing brands

3. Developing new uses for existing products

4. Product improvement

5. Finding more efficient ways to produce the product, in the case of manufacturers, or purchase the product, in the case of retailers

In addition to addressing one or more of the above, the product objectives should incorporate specifics on when the product will be available for distribution or inventory.

An example of a product objective for a manufacturer would be:

In the upcoming fiscal year, modify the product to reflect the current purchasing habits of consumers interested in low-salt foods.

Task 2

Establish Your Product Strategies

Your new product strategies should help your firm focus its product development activities against one of five approaches (the first four of which have been previously discussed in this chapter):

1. Developing a new positioning for an existing product

2. Developing line extensions

3. Developing flanker products

4. Developing entirely new products

5. Acquiring another firm or the rights to another firm's products that address your company's product strategies

An example of a product strategy would be:

Expand product line offering to include three new flavors based on product attribute research indicating flavor preferences.

WHY SO MANY NEW PRODUCTS FAIL[2]

Before we leave the topic of product development, we must briefly address why we believe most new products fail. Various studies have reported new product failure rates up to 90 percent.[3] Why do so many new products fail? Here are some of the key reasons:

- *Poor Planning*—Establishing objectives and strategies for your new product and all elements of the marketing mix is crucial to a successful launch. In light of the enormous obstacles facing a new product, it is not surprising that failure to sufficiently plan the introduction is a common cause of new product failures. Part of planning includes determining whether there is sufficient demand potential for a product. Very often, thorough research will show that the current size of the target market, with its current competitive set, is just too small to support another offering that does not have superior attributes.

- *Poor Management of the Process*—Without proper management attention, the new product development process can produce a final output that does not match the original, promising product concept. Even well-meaning input of many functional groups within your organization, all seeking to maximize the performance of their area, can derail the development process and lead to a less than successful product.

- *Poor Product Concept*—Sometimes the idea is just not good or does not provide any benefits or advantages over existing competitive products.

- *Poor Execution*—It's true that the genius is in the details. Even the best new product concept, with a thorough and disciplined plan, can fail miserably if the production process, distribution, or any aspect of the marketing plan is not followed through successfully.

- *Poor Research*—Good research is key to new product development. Testing should ideally be conducted at the concept stage and the prototype stage and should include actual test marketing of the product and the marketing mix supporting its introduction.

- *Poor Technology/Quality*—If the product does not live up to the target market's expectations, it is destined for failure.

DOS AND DON'TS

Do

- Review your business review, problems and opportunities, positioning and marketing strategies, and sales goals prior to preparing this section of the marketing plan.

- Keep an ongoing surveillance of competitive product innovations in your industry.

- Talk with consumers on an ongoing basis. Find out what they think about your product. Discover which of their needs are not being fulfilled by current products available in the category.

---

[2]Adapted from Gruenwald, George. *New Product Development* (Chicago, IL: Crain Books, 1985), pp. 11–22.
[3]Boyd, Harper W. *Marketing Management* (Homewood, IL: Richard D. Irwin, Inc., 1990), pp. 388–89.

- Be willing to make product changes, especially if market research discovers a product void or shows that your product is not competitive against attributes most important to consumers.

- Research and test product innovations and changes prior to making them standard.

- Expect that the vast majority of new product concepts will fail. However, remember that new product successes are the lifeblood of most successful organizations.

Don't

- Don't copy every competitive product innovation. Use research to determine consumer likes and dislikes with your product before modifying an existing product or developing a new one.

- Don't change one aspect of your product without considering what the change will do to the other attributes. Remember that consumers purchase for multiple reasons. A cheaper product from a price standpoint may receive less demand if the quality has also diminished. Consumers may like the lower price but may not be willing to sacrifice quality.

- Don't make changes in your product for purely financial reasons. Consumers purchase your product because of its product attributes, not because the product provides a bigger or smaller margin to your company.

- Remember, just as new product development is important to a company, so is the divestment or elimination of historically weak products.

- Don't just concentrate on the short-term bottom line while short-changing product development and long-term growth and profits.

- Don't overestimate the size of the market for your product. Many products fail because the market is not large enough in terms of sheer numbers of consumers.

Branding Overview

Some product categories, such as automobiles, are defined by a relatively high level of differentiation between competing product offerings, while others, such as paperclips, are relative commodities. It is the points of differentiation between your product and the competition, whether real or perceived, extensive or relatively few, and how you, the marketer of your product, communicate those differences that comprise your *brand*.

As a marketer, it is your task to develop your brand in terms of the name, graphic identity, and maintenance of marketing mix elements consistent with that identity and your positioning. If successful, the brand will be considerably more valuable to you than the sum of physical attributes that comprise your product.

In the branding section of your marketing plan you will focus on developing a brand name and graphic identity. The marketing mix elements will be addressed in subsequent sections. However, for the sake of providing a complete picture of the branding process, we will discuss the characteristics of a brand and the importance of branding, as well as how to develop a branding plan and develop a brand name.

Definition of Brand

In simplest terms, a brand is merely the identification of a product's or service's source, whether it is the manufacturer, a wholesaler, or some other entity. In slightly broader terms, the brand is composed of the title or name by which the product is commonly known and graphic forms of identification, including symbols, logotypes or signatures, tag lines, or characters. For example, we know through our work with the American Automobile Association (AAA) that the AAA brand is one of the most known and respected brands in America today. The AAA brand covers a vast number of products and services—from towing to maps to insurance to travel. All these services fall under the well-recognized AAA logo. In another example, Betty Crocker is a brand name applied to a number of products. Betty Crocker products can also be identified by the white type treatment in the red spoon symbol or by the Betty Crocker female character.

Betty Crocker, which is owned by General Mills, is an example of a *manufacturer's brand*—a name other than the producer's provided specifically for a product or collection of products. Use of a manufacturer's brand is typical in consumer packaged goods. Manufacturer branding does not just happen on the consumer side. We are currently working on restaging the entire line of Fort Howard industrial wipers—a project which will include repositioning and branding the entire wiper/industrial towel line. By contrast, many products bear the name of the manufacturer, such as Xerox copiers, Black and Decker tools, or American Family Insurance. These *trade names* are common among consumers durables, service industries, and business-to-business products.

In some cases, the manufacturer of the product is not identified either with their own name or with a brand name they own. Rather, a manufacturer might sell the product to wholesalers or retailers who provide their own brand names, known as *private labels*. For years, Sears was founded on private label Kenmore appliances and Craftsman tools. *Generic* products bear no brand at all. Generic products were popular among consumers in the late 1970s as a means of saving during an inflationary period.

Definition of Branding

Branding is a process of establishing and managing the images, perceptions, and associations that the consumer applies to your product, based on the values and beliefs associated with your product. These are managed through application of the brand elements (name and graphic components) and consistency with the product's positioning in all consumer communications relating to the product. The more effective you are in your branding efforts, the greater value your brand holds for you. The value of the brand, above and beyond the cumulative physical attributes of the product itself, represents *brand equity*.

Developing a brand and building equity in that brand are the broad components of the branding process. In this process, you have one goal for the brand: to generate consistent purchase behavior amongst a consumer base (thus providing you with a consistent return on the investment of capital in that asset). In other words, you seek to build and maintain *brand loyalty*. In our work with McDonald's and Coors beer we know that both the fast food retailer and beer manufacturer have strong, loyal consumer bases, but this loyalty is constantly tested by competitive efforts. It is only through careful management—to avoid erosion of the brand equity by their competitors or by their own actions—that McDonald's and Coors are able to reap the rewards of the successful brands they market.

The Importance of Branding

By its very definition, branding products provides a means of identifying your product from that of your competition, in much the same way branding cattle aids in their identification. Consumers must be able to recognize your brand in the name, the logo, the packaging, and in some cases, the slogan. But simple recognition is only the beginning of the branding process.

Branding can be thought of in the same terms as a high school dance, a college reunion, or a neighborhood party. Are you the type of person who goes to a party or reunion and then spends time with the people you don't know or do you talk with old familiar friends? Most of us stick with people (and products) we know. This is the essence of branding—letting the target market get to know and recognize your product is the first important step to achieving the eventual purchase.

Brands also aid the consumer's ability to make quick, safe product choices. What you seek from your brand is for the consumer target to make associations, as we described above. In this way, the consumer is able to recognize products and what the products represent for them more quickly in the retail environment. This is particularly important today, as the number of available products has increased dramatically in the last few years, while consumers' available time to research products and make purchase decisions has decreased.

The brand provides information on quality, reliability, and other attributes through the associations the consumer makes as a result of the marketer's branding effort and their own experience with the product. This function of branding is most important in categories where products otherwise lack differentiation or when rational, fact-based decisions are difficult.

DEVELOPING YOUR BRANDING PLAN

As we have stated above, the process of branding is complex and ongoing, involving all elements of the marketing mix. In the Branding section of your marketing plan, focus on your branding needs in terms of a brand name and graphic identity. Keep the other aspects of branding in mind, however, as you approach each of the subsequent tactical plan elements.

Task 1
Establish Branding Objectives

The first task in developing a branding plan is to arrive at objectives for your brand name, graphics, and legal protection of the brand. It is important to state the objectives of the brand in terms of the product strategies defined in the previous section. What are your objectives for how the new name and graphic will be used? Is this a new product, a repositioned product, an existing product, etc.? State your objectives and include a final decision date for selection of the final name, completion of a legal search, and adoption of graphics.

Examples of branding objectives are:

Develop a name by March 1 and logo graphic by June 1, for the new value-oriented line of accessories.

- Develop a final list of name options by November 1.

- Complete legal name search based on this list by December 1.

- Complete consumer research of names by February 1.

- Make final name selection by March 1.

- Develop a logo graphic for the new name by June 1.

Develop a new name to replace Big Jake's for the new family apparel store by the end of the fiscal year.

Task 2
Establish Branding Strategies

Before proceeding to develop a new name and/or graphic, it is important to develop strategies for the brand. Development of a branding strategy increases the likelihood that you will arrive at a name that is consistent with the product and its positioning and takes into consideration all of the users of the name over the long and short term. The branding strategy should highlight those components that will communicate the key perceptions to the key targets.

Your strategy should flow directly from the positioning statement and the product strategies. For example, if you are developing a new product and see long-term potential for line extensions, your branding strategy should address this so that the new name you develop accommodates it. For instance, it is reasonable to imagine the Alpo brand of dog food products extended into cat food products, but Milk-Bone brand cat food products probably wouldn't work. (There really is an Alpo cat food.) Further, the name and graphic treatment should be developed on the basis of the breadth of products to which they will apply. In our earlier example, we saw that the Betty Crocker brand applies to a wide variety of cooking and baking packaged goods. The name is not specific to one product, and the red spoon graphic acts as a unifying element across the product line.

Example branding strategies include:

Name the new line of marine accessories to reflect the value-oriented positioning—quality products at lower prices relative to the competition.

Develop a logo for the marine accessories line that can be used across the wide variety of marine products in the line (with the potential of additional products to be added in the future).

Task 3
Establish Branding
Property Parameters

The branding strategies should be followed by a list of parameters for the new name and graphic application. These parameters are an extension of the branding strategy and provide specific guideposts for name and graphic development.

Name parameters for consideration:

Reflects positioning of the product, and product attributes or benefits

Provides generic identification and clearly identifies with its functional category

Is preemptive

Contributes to awareness and knowledge of its purpose

Is simple

Is memorable

Elicits a mental image and emotion

Provides potential for growth under its umbrella (new entities, products, etc.)

Possesses a positive connotation in meaning, pronunciation, and visualization

Reflects the personality of the product

Has intrinsic meaning of its own (i.e., is not an acronym or a set of letters that signifies nothing)

Not limited geographically or topically as the organization grows

Lends itself to and allows for creative development both visually and in copy

Must work with current signage and packaging sizes

Is legally acceptable and protectable

Graphic parameters for consideration:

Must reproduce in large or small form

Must reproduce in black and white and in color

Should incorporate colors that reflect the positioning and are attention getting

Must have visual impact in print and broadcast media

Allows for umbrella look applied to a variety of products and packages

Task 4
Name Generation and Selection

Using the branding strategy and name property parameters as a guide, begin the name development process by generating a multitude of name alternatives. One first step would be to outline all of the qualities, characteristics, or descriptors that you would like to have associated with your product. Such an outline for a toothpaste might include words like "protective" or "refreshing." It might also include characters, animals, or objects that maintain similar qualities, such as "honey bee." This outline acts to translate the product positioning into simple, everyday words and associations and will help to stimulate ideas for names and graphics.

If you are not in a position to develop the names on your own, seek help. You can share the task with others in your organization, an agency, or with a professional brand identity development organization. For example, NameLab, of California, specializes in name development and has produced names for Compaq computers, Nissan automobiles, and others.

From here, it is conceivable that your name alternatives could number into the hundreds. Next, using the branding strategy and name parameters as the decision criteria in the screening process, pare back the names in a disciplined manner to approximately five to ten names. Follow this with a legal name search for trademark availability among your choices. Finally, you would be wise to research the remaining screened name alternatives, as well as graphic representations you ultimately develop, with the target market(s) before making final brand decisions.

Task 5
Legal Protection of Your Brand

Because brands hold value and do represent assets for the companies that own them, they are subject to extensive legal protection. Walt Disney is extremely sensitive about the use of its characters and has been known to file lawsuits to protect the value and equity of its brand and the characters that represent it. It is critical that marketers developing a new name or logo for their product register their final selections. Registration of a trademark takes place with the Patent and Trademark Office (PTO) of the U.S. Department of Commerce. Registration with the PTO lasts ten years and is renewable on the basis of intent to use the trademark and active protection thereof.

Dos and Don'ts

Do

- Reflect on the entire branding process, including your overall needs and goals for the brand.

- Review your positioning and product strategies before developing your branding plan. Use these as the basis of your branding objectives and strategies.

- Highlight the key image(s) you wish to communicate to your target market in your branding strategy.

- Develop an outline of qualities, descriptors, and related items that reflect your product and positioning.

- Use a disciplined process when developing a name for your product, firm, or store—from what you want the name to accomplish through a thorough name-generating process.

- If possible, use research to test alternative names and graphics among the target market.

- Choose the name which best communicates the branding strategy, keeping in mind that the name should be descriptive and have no negatives.

- Consider including your employees in the naming process. Have them generate name alternatives and communicate to them the reasons for the final selection before it becomes public.

- Make sure you have an established plan to communicate your new name to the audience. Acceptance of a new name is often determined by how well the new name is communicated.

- Have the final list of names go through a legal search to make certain you are not infringing upon someone's trademark. Also, once the name is selected, apply for a registered trademark for legal protection.

Don't

- Don't take the first name that comes to you, particularly if you think it's creative, cool, or cute.

- Don't complicate your product name. Keep it simple and memorable.

- If it is a name change, don't expect the new name to be readily accepted. Many people don't like change. However, familiarity breeds acceptability, so build high awareness for the new name quickly.

- Don't go it alone with a name change if your company and agency do not have the time and specific abilities to develop a new name. Consider hiring a consulting firm that specializes in developing new names and brand identity programs.

- Don't necessarily adopt acronyms or the initials of your firm's name as a new name in trade name situations. Don't assume your customers are as familiar with your firm's initials or a short version of your firm's name as you are. Large, well-know companies like IBM or AT&T are the exception, not the norm.

PACKAGING OVERVIEW

Earlier in this chapter we defined the product as the physical object the consumer purchases and uses, and we defined the brand as the collection of associations the consumer holds about your particular product. An important element of every product, which serves as a vehicle for the brand, is the packaging. The package bears the responsibility of holding or maintaining your product and communicating the essence of your brand. In this section of the chapter we will consider the functions of packaging, why you should consider developing new packaging for your product, and how to develop a packaging plan. If you are a retailer or service firm, the issue of packaging really refers to your store or business environment, and we will address that briefly.

Functions of Packaging

Protection

At its most utilitarian level, a package serves to protect. Packages serve the product to prevent damage (eggs), exposure to light (film), air (wine), contaminants (drugs), and spoilage (crackers) and, at the very least, hold or contain the product for presentation in-store. Today products can safely remain unopened on shelves for months, even years—the result of technology in preservatives and packaging. But the protective function of packaging goes beyond the product. Packaging plays an important role in protecting the consumer as well. For example, special caps minimize the misuse of products, particularly by small children (i.e., childproof caps), and packaging has been developed to minimize the potential for product tampering, particularly in pharmaceuticals.

Facilitating Product Usage

Packaging serves an important facilitative role in the use of the product. A bottle's shape, the type of pour spout it contains, its ability to be resealed, and other similar packaging attributes all contribute to the consumer's ease in using a product. The package essentially becomes an important component of the products itself. Microwave food products, for example, would not be nearly as effective if not for the packages that accommodate microwave cooking.

Different package sizes also accommodate differences in use of a product between various target market segments. Soft drinks are available in cases, twelve-packs, and six-packs of cans and in resealable bottles in 2-liter and quart sizes. In fact, the package size can address differences in the benefits sought between segments. Juices can be found in large, family-sized bottles, in individual-sized, 12-ounce cans for adults, or in smaller, lunchbox-sized boxes with straws for kids.

The package is, in many respects, part of the product. It contributes to the use experience of the product in a way that exceeds a mere supporting role. In many cases it is the package that provides the point of differentiation between one product and another. Your package's ability to aid the consumer in his or her use of a product better than that of the competing brand represents a competitive advantage for your brand. Toothpastes in special squeeze containers, salad dressing with shaker tops, squeezable butter, and resealable luncheon meats are examples of packages contributing to a brand's competitive edge. In fact, a packaging innovation occasionally spawns a new product or line extension for an existing product, as it allows entry into a new target segment and/or facilitates a different use for a product than the original packaging. Oscar Mayer Lunchables resulted from the technology in packaging that allowed physical separation of component products.

In addition to adding value to a brand through the normal use of the product, a package can also add value for the consumer beyond the product's common use or even after the product is consumed. Wines or juices are often sold in decanter-style bottles, which act as a premium item for the consumer; the bottle obviously serves to hold the wine and accommodate normal pouring, but it can be kept and used by the consumer after the wine is gone.

Communication

Your package represents an important, perhaps the most important, communications tool for you. Labels are used to provide useful information to consumers to aid both in the product and brand purchase decision and in usage following purchase.

Some of the relatively utilitarian, but nonetheless important, information often conveyed on packaging includes the brand name and product category definition. The box reads, in large type: Kraft (brand) Macaroni and Cheese (product). In extended brand lines the particular flavor or style is indicated on the package, including grades of oil, flavors of ice cream, applications of shampoo, etc. The Kraft Macaroni and Cheese example might include a designation indicating regular and bacon flavored. Finally, the package is utilized to provide warnings, directions for use, weight or volume measurements, contents and ingredients, date codes, nutritional information, and more.

Packaging also serves an important role in the marketing communications function. This communication effort is provided both explicitly and implicitly. Promotions and offers are often displayed, presented, and explained on packages. Flags, bursts, banners, and other graphic elements on package fronts direct the consumer's attention to specials, premiums, or other promotional offerings from the manufacturer. Cereal boxes are notorious for providing special offers and free gifts. The package can be further used to actually carry the promotional element, rather than simply communicating its existence. Label backs carry coupons or recipes, on-pack or in-pack premiums may be accommodated with the packaging, or contest pieces may be carried in the package, such as letters under soda bottle caps.

The primary way that packaging serves as a marketing communications vehicle is often less obvious than the use of banners and bursts. The package as a whole must communicate the brand's image and positioning. This happens in a variety of ways.

First, the package should appeal to the target market. Industrial products, for example, tend to be much more utilitarian than consumer products distributed through retail channels. Packaging for a brand aiming at the teen market will bear considerably different graphics, language, and size offerings than a brand positioned against mothers with young children.

Secondly, the package aids in product visibility and awareness, particularly in the retail setting. An important element of branding is product awareness and recognition among consumers. In today's cluttered retail environment some 30,000 brands fight for the shopper's attention, retailers are providing less sales assistance, and consumers are making more and more buying decisions at the point of purchase. In this context, your package serves an important role in getting your brand noticed, essentially taking the salesperson's place and encouraging impulse purchases. The package does this through graphics that are attractive or appealing to the consumer, by communicating product attributes and benefits, and by standing out from the crowd.

Finally, the packaging inherently contributes to the brand's image and equity and has a major impact on the target person's attitude towards the product. This role is partially fulfilled through the items mentioned above, in the combination of the package's graphics and structure. For example, the fact that a certain brand of paper towels is always packaged using simple graphics on the label, with bursts promoting special low pricing and a coupon for the next purchase, would help communicate the brand's image as a value-based paper towel. By contrast, the higher quality orange juice is expected to have a better resealable pour spout, perhaps a stronger container, and more attractive graphics. But a package's contribution to a brand's equity is established over time and transcends the functional roles it plays. Eventually, the successful package is clearly identified and associated with the brand. It is, in essence, the physical representation of the brand in the consumer's mind. Coke is the classic example. Coke's bottle shape is as much a part of the brand identity as the name, swoosh graphic, and colors, and it elicits the variety of images and perceptions associated with the Coke brand among consumers.

Functions of the Store or Business Environment

The retail or service environment serves functions similar to product packaging. It first serves a utilitarian function by housing the products and services you sell. Further, it facilitates the purchase and/or use of the products and services. Grocery stores must provide parking and signage externally to draw customers into the store effectively and efficiently. Internally, shelving is provided to display and hold the products, aisles are maintained for customers to walk along and view the products, signage is available to help them find what they're looking for, and lighting is designed to allow them to clearly see the products and labels. Moreover, the store layout is developed to draw consumers through the store past high margin items, and displays are used to encourage impulse purchases.

The retail and service environments, both internally and externally, also serve an important communications function. In particular, these settings promote an image to shoppers and reflect the positioning of the firm. Externally, theme decorations, lighting schemes, signage, and landscaping speak volumes to the consumer about the type of establishment he or she is entering. Inside, the interior design, including the color scheme, fixture design, sign style, and even the sound and smell, tell the consumer whether they are in Sak's or K-mart. All of these elements need to be designed to reflect an image consistent with the positioning for the firm and all of the other communications aimed at the target.

REASONS FOR CHANGING YOUR PACKAGING[4]

As you get set to begin developing the packaging section of your marketing plan, you need to determine whether or not you need a new package for your product. Clearly, if your plan is for a completely new product, a new package is a must. But if your plan is being developed for an existing product, there are a variety of situations that may indicate it's time to consider new packaging. They are as follows:

New product positioning: If you are repositioning your product, you may need to create a new package that reflects the new positioning. As we have stated above, the graphics, color, and package shape all must work together in a way that relates and even enhances the positioning of the brand.

Poor graphics: Take a look at your current package. How does it look and feel to you? How does it compare with competitive brands' packages? Refer back to your business review and research—did you get any feedback from the consumer about your package? What do they think about your package? If your package looks cluttered, indistinct, or outdated, it may be time to change.

New target segment for product: The target market is the group against which you position the product. If your company is changing target markets, and perhaps the product's positioning as well, you will need to consider changes in your packaging. This is necessary to more closely reflect the new target's needs and to develop packaging (form and function) which more effectively helps persuade the new target market to purchase. Even if the basic positioning does not change against a different segment, the package needs to be reviewed. Its styling and graphics must be relevant to its target audience. Further, a different target group may require different attributes of the package in order to facilitate their particular usage of the product.

Line extensions: In the previous section, we discussed how a brand name and graphic identity needs to accommodate future product plans, such as line extensions. Packaging must be adjusted or redesigned to accommodate these changes as they occur. Packages in these situations should reflect an image and general look consistent with the brand, yet communicate the differences between

[4]Alport, Howard. "Does Your Packaging Need a Face Lift?" *Marketing Communications.* March, 1989, pp. 38–41.

individual product types, whether they are new styles or flavors of the same product or are different products.

Wider distribution (new channels): To gain entry into a particular channel, a package may need to be adjusted in look, style, size, and/or shape to accommodate the display structure and method and the purchase environment. For example, a video tape sold in packs of six in consumer electronics stores may need to provide single packs in brighter packaging to be carried at checkout displays in grocery stores. The smaller and brighter unit may be more conducive to impulse purchases in an environment that is visually busy and competitive.

DEVELOPING A PACKAGING PLAN

As you prepare to develop a plan for your product's packaging, review your positioning, appropriate marketing strategies, and product and branding plans. Your packaging plan should reflect your positioning and flow from the objectives and strategies for the product and brand.

**Task 1
Develop Packaging
Objectives**

Establish objectives for your packaging that focus on the following issues:

- Communication of brand positioning and image to contribute to building equity in your brand

- Generating awareness and drawing attention to the product at the point of purchase

- Encouraging trial

- Providing protection for and enhancement of the product by making usage easier or adding value to the purchase

- Communicating promotional offerings

Provide a time frame for the development and production of your new packaging. An example packaging objective might be:

Have new packaging ready for introduction by March 1 of next year that demonstrates the following:

—Communicates the family-oriented positioning and extra servings per container

—Protects the product while displaying the product fully prepared

—Emphasizes the new brand name and graphic scheme

—Addresses the three flavors clearly, yet maintains a consistent look for the brand

**Task 2
Develop Packaging
Strategies**

Your packaging strategies suggest direction for achieving your objectives. They should address specifics about the packaging, such as:

- Physical attributes of the package—What size is the container going to be, or how many sizes will be provided? What is the type and strength of the package material? What color and design scheme will be utilized? What shape should it be? What copy elements should it contain?

- Whether an outside packaging firm, design firm, or agency will be called upon to assist in your new packaging efforts, and if so, when and to what extent they will be involved.

Example packaging strategies include:

Develop a uniquely shaped plastic package in a 12- and 16-ounce size that will accommodate extensive home and office use.

Use bright, bold graphics and provide product attribute statements to communicate a value orientation.

Assign an agency to the packaging project by October 1 to assist in design and research.

DOS AND DON'TS

Do

- Review your problems and opportunities, sales objectives, positioning, marketing strategies, and your product and branding plans prior to developing your packaging plans.

- Since packaging can be used to execute promotional plans, consider the package as a promotion carrier. If your package is to be used in this manner, address this in your packaging plan.

- Make sure the packaging clearly communicates the name and benefits of your product.

- Be as creative as possible with your packaging. Make it unique and make it stand out, but keep it simple and functional.

- Keep it simple. Put less rather than more on the package. Think of your package as a billboard—try to quickly communicate and catch people's attention while portraying the intended image.

- Packaging must provide a message, both explicit and implicit, consistent with the product positioning and brand image. Be sure all packaging conforms to a simple, unified set of graphic standards and guidelines.

- Test packaging options. It is important to know how consumers respond to new packaging or modifications in terms of visual impact, use, and competitive performance.

- If you're a retailer, your packaging includes the total store, from the parking lot and the exterior of the store to the interior of the store. Utilize the store environment in the same ways that manufacturers utilize the package for their products. It should quickly command attention to your product, make a statement about your image, and functionally dispense product or provide convenient shopping for your consumers.

- Compare your current package and new prototype to that of the competition in a real store environment prior to and during package development.

- Make sure your packaging meets legal requirements in terms of communication regarding content.

Don't

- Don't view packaging as just a means of product protection or as a way to dispense the product. Use it as a way to create a product difference and as a communication vehicle to build awareness and to positively affect attitudes.

- Don't change your packaging for change's sake but to increase sales. Like advertising and positioning, you can use familiarity of message to your advantage.

- Don't develop packaging inconsistent with the overall positioning of your firm and your product.

- Don't miss the chance for your packaging to improve your product. The outside of the package usually should enhance the inherent drama of what is inside.

- Don't hesitate to hire outside help for packaging development. Look for firms with knowledge of package manufacturing, design, and research.

PRICING

Pricing represents one of the basic elements of the marketing mix, and it is one of the most difficult elements for which to develop a plan. The importance of pricing is evident in its effect on the target market, as price represents the consumer's primary cost for obtaining your product. Unfortunately, the nature of pricing is very complex, with implications for your firm, your product, the competition, the target market, and the individual consumer. As a result of this complexity, setting prices is as much an art (and perhaps more so) as it is a science.

Our task in this chapter is to present you with an overview of pricing implications and a methodology for developing a pricing plan, utilizing as much hard data as possible. As you begin outlining your pricing plan, review your problems and opportunities, plan strategies, and communication goals for pricing direction. Our recommended methodology will give you a solid framework for your pricing decisions, but it will not guarantee results. You will also need some good, old-fashioned common sense.

From This Chapter You Will Learn

The definition of price.

Important pricing considerations.

How to develop pricing objectives and strategies.

Additional pricing tactics.

OVERVIEW

Definition of Price

For the purposes of this book, we will define price as the monetary value of your product(s) or service(s) to your target market. For retailers, pricing involves an overall pricing approach for your establishment or chain, as well as setting prices for each individual item. For service firms, there are fees and rates and the application of each in a given transaction. For most business types, there also exist instances of competitive bidding and negotiation, which are components of pricing. We will attempt to touch on all of these elements. Our emphasis, however, will be on arriving at an appropriate pricing approach—lower, higher, or parity pricing relative to the competition.

<table>
<tr><td>

Considerations in Pricing

</td><td>

Breakeven

Barring the use of loss-leader pricing to drive sales, there is a point below which it would be unreasonable to price your product, known as the breakeven. Obviously, the revenue you bring in for a product must be at least equal what you expend for that product or you are losing money, at least in the long term.

Two types of costs must be considered when establishing prices—variable and fixed.

Variable costs are costs that vary with the volume of production or sales—for example, costs associated with incremental payroll, new material purchases, etc.

Fixed costs are costs that do not change with fluctuating sales or production. Fixed costs are usually spread evenly over the company's brands or products, and in this manner are calculated for each individual product along with the variable costs of selling that product. Fixed costs are associated with depreciation on machinery, rent, insurance, real estate taxes, etc.

Also there are two pricing scenarios that the marketer should understand when making pricing decisions.

Short-Run/Excess Capacity Pricing: If there is excess capacity, management needs to set price so that variable costs are covered and there is adequate margin for some contribution to fixed costs or overhead. In the short run, if there is excess capacity, it is far better to take an order with less margin, because total year-end company profit will be greater or the total loss will be less than if the order was not taken and the sale not made.

Long-Run Pricing: In the long run, prices have to be established so that *all* costs (fixed *and* variable) are covered and there is a profit.

</td></tr>
</table>

The following formula allows you to determine break-even points to help ensure expenditures do not exceed sales. The break-even analysis allows the marketer to gain insight into the effect of pricing decisions on income and costs. The analysis enables you to establish a price that will cover all costs.

$$PX = FC + VC(X)$$

Where: P = Price

VC = Variable costs

FC = Fixed costs

X = Volume of units produced at break-even point (the number of units which must be sold)

Assume you are a shoe retailer and the average shoe will be sold at $25, and fixed costs are $10,000 per month, and variable costs are $15 per shoe.

$$\$25X = \$10,000 + 15X$$
$$\$10X = \$10,000$$
$$X = 1,000$$

1,000 shoes must be sold at $25 to cover monthly costs

Exhibit 10.1 Break-Even Chart

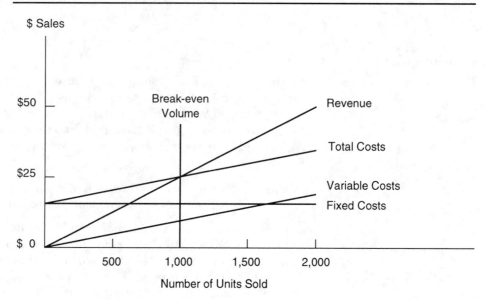

The break-even chart is shown graphically in Exhibit 10.1. The marketer can also use the break-even chart concept to plot fixed costs, variable costs, and revenues. In this manner, the marketer can usually determine the effect of a drop in price and a resulting increase in sales and potential profits.

Let's assume that the shoe company in the previous example was operating at above breakeven, selling 1,500 pairs of shoes per month at $25. As you will recall, fixed costs are $10,000 per month and variable costs are $15 per shoe.

Example A

Number of Shoes Sold	1,500	
Revenue	1,500 × $25 =	$37,500
Costs	$10,000 + ($15 × 1,500) =	$32,500
Profits per Month		$ 5,000

Now let's assume that the marketer, through past experience, can estimate that a drop in average price per shoe to $23 will result in a 30 percent increase in business.

Example B

Number of shoes sold at 30 percent increase (1.3 × 1,500)	1,950	
Revenue	$ 1,950 × $23 =	$44,850
Costs	$10,000 + ($15 × 1,500) =	$39,250
Profits per month		$ 5,600
Profit difference between Examples A and B		$ 600

The shoe marketer would make another $600 by lowering the price $2 with an anticipated increase of business of 30 percent. If the increase in volume were only 10 percent, the marketer would make less profit (try the formula to prove this to yourself). Thus, if you can predict your product's elasticity reasonably accurately, you can use the above formula to estimate changes in profitability due to price changes.

Price Sensitivity

The effect of a price on sales volume is the result of change in consumer demand determined by the market's willingness or capacity to pay that price for the product. This concept is known as *price sensitivity,* and it is influenced by two major factors: consumer attitudes and attribute preferences, and the status of alternatives.

The first factor affecting price sensitivity for your product involves the nature of that product offering—its attribute composition—and the attitudes the target has with regard to those attributes. Such consumer attitudes about your product are developed on the basis of their preferences for certain attributes—what they consider important in a product—and their perceptions of the performance of your product offering on those attributes. The better your product performs on important attributes, the more consumers are willing to pay for it. We have discussed this at length in earlier chapters, and your business review should provide information about how your product rates in this regard.

The second factor that influences consumer price sensitivity relates to the alternatives to your product, in the form of your competition or suitable product substitutes. Price sensitivity for your product is affected by the availability, attractiveness, and price of the alternatives. For example, if there are many alternatives available, either in the form of direct competitive offerings or substitutes, if those offerings are "suitable" alternatives with regard to the consumer's attribute preferences, and if the alternatives are "reasonably" priced, then the price sensitivity for your product is likely to be quite high.

The degree to which consumer demand is sensitive to price changes is referred to as *price elasticity.* After reviewing your pricing problems and opportunities from the business review you may find that demand for your product is elastic—by lowering the price dramatically you lower your gross margin (selling price less cost of goods sold), but you actually make more profits because of the increased volume. Or you may find that demand for your product is inelastic—higher prices only marginally affect volume, but margins and profits increase substantially. This is useful information in developing your pricing objectives and strategies.

Positioning

The positioning of your product plays an important role in the final price decision. A high, or premium, price suggests product quality. Consumers have come to associate high price with quality. Moreover, higher prices are indeed necessary for premium products to finance the product development and improvements, production technology, and quality components integral to a high quality final product. By contrast, a product can establish a low-price positioning, generating high sales volume to maintain low unit costs and necessary profit levels.

Appropriate distribution channels are an important component of each positioning and pricing strategy. For example, Rolex watches maintain high prices consistent with their quality image and are distributed through higher-priced jewelry stores, while Timex watches, available through mass merchants, are priced much lower. We see this same conflict where some shoe vendors hesitate to provide Famous Footwear, an off-price shoe retailer, the newest shoe models. They worry that an off-price retailer will dilute the quality and prestige image of their flagship brands which are positioned around performance, fashion, and style—not price.

As opposed to a strictly low-price positioning, many products, services, or retailers pursue a value positioning, which has many interpretations. Value can mean low price, but it is also evident in a high price. Value is broadly defined as substantial benefits gained relative to the cost incurred from the consumer's perspective, which can translate into a price/quality relationship. Consumers are willing to pay more for a product if it is considered a "better value," that is, if they get what they pay for. Famous Footwear began as a budget-priced shoe store chain and then changed to a value positioning. In this particular case, the value results from providing brand-name shoes for less.

One of our clients, a business-to-business manufacturer, established a positioning based on product quality, focusing on particular attributes considered important by the target. They then adopted a parity pricing approach, based on the fact that the target was very price sensitive and that the firm's performance was rated favorably on delivering a low price. In this way, the firm could differentiate itself from the competition in terms of attributes *and* remain competitive in pricing. The firm could not support a low-price strategy, which would have run counter to the positioning of quality, and the market would not bear a high-price strategy.

Target Market

Pricing helps to define your target market. Higher prices, for example, are generally appropriate for higher-income segments. For introductory products, higher prices allow marketers to reach innovators, who tend to be among the least price-sensitive segments. Lower prices are appropriate for mass-market distribution.

Marketers can segment the market through the pricing of their product. They can also segment multiple product offerings accordingly. For example, Toyota offers a range of automobiles at various price points for various segments, from the low-priced Tercel to the high-end Avalon. Above that, Toyota's Lexus line of luxury cars, selling for about $30,000, are available for the higher-income segment. Taking this concept one step further, marketers can also offer the exact same product at various prices for different segments. Movie theaters, for example, charge a lower price for children and senior citizens. This method of pricing is known as *discriminatory pricing*.

Promotions

Price is an important promotional tool for the marketer, and it is used extensively as a customer incentive for a variety of short-term objectives.

Limited price reductions can be used to increase sales quickly in specific markets, to reduce excess capacity or product overstocks, to induce pantry stocking by consumers prior to a competitive introduction, or to increase traffic at the retail level. Occasionally certain products will be priced at or near cost to generate traffic and lead to sales of higher-margin items. Such low-priced products are referred to as *loss leaders*.

Price increases can also be used to address reductions or shortcomings in capacity or to induce trial of a new or other alternative product from the same manufacturer.

Product Life Cycle

The stage of your product in the product life cycle has an important influence on the pricing structure in the industry and presents various implications for your pricing decisions. In each stage, a high- or low-price strategy may be appropriate for different objectives. Determine where your product is in the life cycle by reviewing the business review. The following provides an overview of the ramifications and alternative pricing strategy implications for each stage.

Introductory Stage

Products in the introductory stage see little competition and can be priced relatively freely. Such products sometimes utilize a low price—called *penetration pricing*—to build a customer base quickly. Lower prices encourage trial and mass consumption by a broad base of consumers. Thus, lower prices provide an opportunity to quickly establish a lower consumer franchise before other competitors enter the marketplace. Also, keep in mind that competitive pricing may serve as a barrier to entry to future competitors. Alternatively, a high price is very often set—called *premium pricing*—to generate profits to cover investment costs for the new product and maximize profits while there still is limited competition. If the product is unique and has little competition, the pricing choice can be one of maximizing profit per unit sold. The strategy involves selling to a narrow group of consumers who are willing to purchase because of unique product attributes. This premium price strategy helps keep the purchaser base smaller than a low price strategy, thus making allowances for limited production capabilities and/or distribution channels. Premium pricing also allows for maximum margins and potentially quicker payback on the research and development of a new product, as well as heavy levels of introductory advertising.

Growth Stage

In this stage, the market is growing, as a larger portion of the mass market becomes a user or purchaser. As the market expands, competition increases. Competitive offerings are typically differentiated on the basis of attributes, but price becomes a competitive tool, establishing low-priced and premium-priced offerings, among others. Setting or maintaining a high price at this stage, an option for products already in the category, can be used to build profits, known as *skimming*. Skimming often takes place in the growth stage and in the latter part of the introductory stage. By contrast, a low price can be used to build market share and deter competitive entries.

Maturity Stage

In this stage, market growth has slowed or stopped. Price becomes important, as well as service, as products become standardized and offer fewer innovations. It is best for a marketer to avoid this stage, or at least minimize its effects, by continually improving the product or service attributes. Pricing alternatives include maintaining high prices to finance new products or using low pricing to simply compete and maintain market share.

Decline Stage

Once a market begins declining, the remaining competitors should seek simple survival for their product offerings, or leave the market altogether. The appropriate pricing strategy involves recovering variable costs and providing some contribution to overhead.

Product Differentiation

In industries where products are not highly differentiated in terms of attributes, pricing and service become the only real points of differentiation. In some cases, particularly in growth markets, pricing can contribute to maintaining differentiation of a brand. This effort usually requires a higher-price strategy to generate revenues to finance product improvements and R&D, and as discussed earlier, the higher price connotates a quality image consistent with a differentiated product.

Competitive Bidding

For certain industries, a bidding process is common or even required. Construction-related industries rely on this method of determining pricing on a project-by-project basis. For such an approach, prices are calculated on the basis of estimated materials requirements (often at a cost plus a standard mark-up), plus labor hours at appropriate labor rates, and additional services (shipping, for example). Part of the process of setting the price includes determining the appropriate, or best, method of completing the work.

The competitive bidding practice combines a competitive orientation with an internal orientation. The estimator must calculate the firm's costs for a job and apply appropriate rates for specific services to be completed in the process of the project. Further, rates are often based on what the firm wants to earn for each hour of an employee's services. At the same time, rates are also based on going rates, and final project estimates are often adjusted based on the competitive status of the project bidding process, reflecting the involvement of a particular known competitor or an intuition of what the job is likely to "go for."

Business Goals

Your final pricing decision should take into consideration what you need to accomplish in other areas of your business. Such goals, including sales and profitability objectives, can be aided by the appropriate pricing approach or derailed by an inappropriate one. Following are some examples of business goals and the implications of lower, higher, or parity pricing on these goals.

Increase Short-Run Profits

Occasionally, additional profits are needed from a product offering, perhaps to finance a line extension or to offset a particular cost increase. A higher-price strategy overall attracts the less-price-sensitive segment of the market, and thus, a short-term increase will likely not lead to a drastic loss of sales volume. Short-run profits are typically a goal for new products, which cater to the less-price-sensitive early adapters, in an effort to recoup expenditures from the product development process. A mature market product may also maintain a high-price strategy for the sake of short-term profits—an approach known as *harvesting*. In such a case, other costs associated with the product will be cut to increase overall margins on the product, often to finance other investments by the firm. Obviously, an analysis of the price elasticity of demand for your product, along with a break-even analysis, are important prior to implementing any price strategy to affect short-term profits.

Increase Sales Growth

Often a large spurt of sales activity is needed, particularly with new products attempting to build a market. Typically, this business objective implies a low-price strategy, as the marketer attempts to influence trial to build a base of customers. Such an approach also discourages competitive entry into a market. Finally, a consistent low-price approach can be used to increase sales to a high level; it can then be maintained to create a discount positioning by reducing manufacturing costs due to economies of scale. The Rolex vs. Timex example discussed earlier illustrates this situation. By contrast to Rolex, Timex produces and sells a much higher volume of products, allowing for lower overall costs and a lower-price positioning.

Survival

At times the best a product can hope for is sheer survival, as alternative product innovations or consumer preferences and lifestyles make a category obsolete. In such cases, the product should aim to simply recover variable costs and provide a contribution to fixed costs.

Determine Your Pricing Needs

The last thing you must do prior to deciding the appropriate pricing approach is to review your problems and opportunities, marketing objectives, positioning marketing strategies, and communication goals for overall focus and pricing implications. Then, reflect on the considerations discussed above and what they mean for your product. From the problems and opportunities, marketing objectives and strategies, develop a list that details all of the areas that your pricing approach needs to impact and in what way. Include the implications of all of the issues discussed above, such as the product life cycle stage, the product's cost, etc. A worksheet designed to assist you in developing this list is shown in Exhibit 10.2 and is available in Appendix C. This list, which essentially details what you need from your pricing plan, will direct you towards an appropriate pricing approach.

HOW TO DEVELOP A PRICING PLAN

Task 1
Establish Pricing Objectives

The first major step in the development of a pricing plan is to establish your pricing objective—whether you intend to implement a lower, higher, or parity pricing approach relative to the competition. All other objectives, such as increased sales, higher margins, etc., are overall goals of your business or marketing plan to which pricing contributes.

Higher, Lower, or Parity Pricing

How you price your product or service has a significant impact on many aspect of your overall marketing efforts. Used in conjunction with the other elements of your plan, a given price approach supports your product's positioning, while contributing directly to consumer demand (thus sales volume) for your product and providing income to cover costs and contribute to the profitability of your firm. Following is an overview of each of the three approaches to pricing.

Parity Pricing

Often referred to as a "going rate" strategy, this approach maintains pricing levels at or near those of the competition. This is appropriate where other means of differentiation are common or are considered more important by the target. These other forms of differentiation often include specific product features and attributes, non-product advantages such as service, guarantees, location for retailers, or additional

Exhibit 10.2 Pricing Considerations

Consideration	Specific Situation	Pricing Implication	Potential Price Approach
Problems/Opportunities	The company's "standard" line is continually underpriced by the competition.	This line is losing share and losing distribution.	Match price of top three competitors.
Marketing Objectives	Increase new customer trial by 15% over previous year.	Price is an important attribute sought by first-time customers.	Provide price incentives around new customer promotions.
Positioning	Position as the most affordable competitive option.	Looking to position based on a price relative to competition.	Maintain price just below top three competitors.
Marketing Strategies	Build sales volume in off-season months of May and September.	Price incentives could be used to pump sales during off-season.	Use price promotions to tie off-season sales to seasonal purchases.
Price Communication Goals			
Break-even			
Price Elasticity			
Product Life Cycle Stage			
Product Differentiation			
Business Goals			
Competition Pricing			
Other			

distribution channels. Interestingly, it is also utilized when product differentiation is low and price is the basis of competition.

In mature categories with few competitors and little differentiation, such as the airline industry, parity pricing is the norm. If one carrier were to raise prices, demand would shift to the competition with lower prices. If one airline lowers prices, the others would be forced to lower theirs in response, which would lower profits for all in the industry and create a *price war*. Often, in such industries, one major player, typically the market leader, is considered the *price leader*. Others in the industry watch this leader for price activity.

Lower Pricing

This objective involves maintaining a price lower than the competition. One specific execution of this approach includes discount pricing, a direct result of a low-price positioning. This approach aims for a high volume of sales to offset typically low margins to achieve desired profit levels (low margin dollars but high volume). It also requires appropriate capacity and distribution channels to support the volume requirements. The reasons for a low price objective are usually:

- To expand the market, allowing new consumers who couldn't purchase at higher prices to become purchasers.

- To increase trial and/or sales due to price incentives.

- A situation exists with a strong price elastic product where a low price results in increased demand. The result is lower margins but increased profits because of the increased volume.

- To preempt competitive strategies, helping to steal market share. This is often necessary in a mature market.

- To remain competitive with your competition. If a majority of the competitors have reduced their prices, oftentimes you will need to do so, especially if you are in a price sensitive product category. If a strong competitor is also offering an attribute such as service with which you cannot compete, you may need to lower your price to counter the service offering.

- To keep competitors from entering the marketplace by having a price that is difficult for a new company with high initial investment costs to match. This policy of expanded market pricing allows a company to develop a large, loyal consumer base while keeping competition to a minimum.

Higher Pricing

As we have discussed many times, a premium price—a higher price relative to the competition—supports a quality positioning and provides high margins to support higher product and promotional expenditures. The reasons for a high price objective are usually:

- A need for a fast recovery of the firm's investment.

- A need for faster accumulation of profits to cover research and development costs. The profits can then be used to improve the product and to sustain competitive marketing tactics once competitors enter the market.

- To substantiate a quality image positioning.

- The product is price inelastic where the demand or sales decrease only marginally with higher pricing.

- The product or service is in the introductory phase of its product life cycle and represents a substantial innovation within the product category. Also, the company may wish to cream profits while there are no substitute products to force competitive pricing.

- The company is stressing profits rather than sales, thus, margins must remain high.

- The product has a short life span. An example would be fad products which last for a relatively short time. This necessitates a high price policy which will help recover the firm's research and development costs in a short time period.

- The product is difficult to copy and reproduce or has patent protection.

Determine Your Price Approach

Based on your list of pricing considerations, you should be able to establish a price objective that is either one of parity, lower, or higher pricing for your product or company. Your product, its positioning and other marketing communications goals, the target market's perceptions and behavior, the competition, and the industry, will all suggest the most appropriate course of action. Once you have determined which approach you wish to take, it becomes the basis of your pricing objectives.

Address Geography and Timing

Many times a company's or industry's pricing structure is not consistent across the entire country. One market may have greater competition, greater price sensitivity, or higher distribution costs, for example, than others. Thus, your objectives should state any differences that exist from market to market. Finally, timing should be addressed in your price objectives. Are the sales increases to be addressed by a particular price approach needed constantly or just up to a certain point in time? Will price changes for promotional purposes take place during certain seasonal periods or for another, very specific, period? While timing relates to the changing of your price on a seasonal basis, it also relates to the changing of prices in a timely fashion to address competitive price changes, cost changes, market changes, etc.

Writing the Price Objectives

The following examples present the appropriate style of pricing objective statements, including geography and timing considerations:

- Utilize higher pricing relative to the direct competition (minimum +10 percent) within the first year of the plan in all markets, consistent with a quality positioning.

- Increase prices during the strong tourist months of May to September, then lower prices during the off-season, while maintaining a relative parity-price approach.

Task 2
....
Establish Price Strategies

Pricing strategies state how you will achieve your pricing objectives. They provide the specifics you need to finalize your pricing plan. In developing your pricing strategies, the following steps should be taken:

- *Review your pricing objectives.* As the strategies are intended to provide direction for achieving price objectives, it is important to truly understand what price approach you need to achieve, when, and where.

- *Review your marketing strategies.* Again, relate your pricing decisions not only to the direction provided in the pricing portion of your marketing strategies, but also to the affect your pricing will have on the implementation of other strategies.

- *Review the product category and the competition.* What is the competitive price structure of the industry? At what stage is the category in terms of the product life cycle, and what is the competitive structure? What are the costs and pricing strategies of your competition?

- *Review your product.* Determine whether your firm has the capacity and/or capability to maintain a low-price strategy. Determine if your product has unique and defensible product attributes which could support a high price objective. What are your costs associated with the product, and what is the breakeven at various price points? Calculate at what price you are most likely to break even.

- *Review the marketplace.* Consider the target market make-up and segmentation, and determine the price sensitivity among the segments. What attitudes does the target hold with regard to the product category and the importance of price?

Finally, develop strategies that address how price levels, geography, and timing objectives will be accomplished. Using the information acquired in the three tasks above, detail specifics as to your pricing strategy. Consider the following two marketing strategies.

Marketing Seasonality Strategy: Increase sales among current customers during the off-season.

Marketing Pricing Strategy: Maintain a 45 percent margin for the year.

The *pricing objective* might be to utilize a parity pricing structure relative to the competition during the strong selling season nationally and a low price relative to the competition during the off-season nationally. Price then would be one of the tools used to execute the seasonality marketing strategy along with promotion and advertising. And pricing certainly would be used to execute the pricing marketing strategy.

The subsequent pricing strategies might be:

Utilize a price consistent with the top three market leaders in the northern markets and the top market leader in the southern markets during the months of August through December.

Utilize a price at 5 percent below the top three market leaders in the northern markets and 7 percent below the market leader in the southern markets during the off-season of January through July.

DOS AND DON'TS

Do

- Review your problems and opportunities, your marketing strategies, and communications goals related to pricing before developing your pricing plan.

■ Closely monitor the competition and keep consistent records of your competition's pricing.

■ Be flexible. Be prepared to adjust to competitive pressures and the marketing environment. Be willing to change your price and use it as a tool for achieving marketing strategies.

■ Review the product category life cycle and pricing structure as you develop your pricing strategies.

■ Use the pricing tool to help communicate the positioning of your product.

■ Consider the logistic implications of your pricing decisions for your firm in terms of capacity and resources. You must be able to support whatever price strategy you implement.

■ Test your price often. Test higher and lower prices and monitor the response in test markets. Apply what you learn to your total system. Make sure you test your pricing strategies for a long enough period to obtain realistic results.

■ Determine your pricing approach on the basis of the target market, not just on your firm's costs and needs. Calculate the market's price sensitivity. Analyze the importance of price relative to other attributes and how your firm or product is currently perceived by the target on these issues prior to initiating a price strategy or change.

■ Remember, the more intangible (service firms) or unique your product, the more flexibility you will have in setting higher prices.

■ Price your product to provide ultimate value to consumers. Remember, you can still give real value through high price (e.g., the product is higher priced than the competition, but the customer receives a special or better service).

■ Be aware of both the obvious and the hidden costs when determining your selling price (e.g., shrinkage through employee theft).

■ Make sure your pricing policy follows the legal guidelines.

Don't

■ Don't look at pricing as static. Your cost of doing business and the competitive activity in your marketplace is not fixed, so your pricing shouldn't be either.

■ Don't set pricing without first determining how it will affect sales, margins, and the ability of the company to cover variable and fixed costs.

■ Don't be afraid to use price to achieve other marketing goals, such as trial. Successful companies often plan for a period of lower prices in an effort to increase trial and build the customer base. Though profitability is reduced temporarily, it is often offset by a sustained period of repeat purchase at full price by the expanded customer base. However, it is a good idea to test this premise to make sure you are receiving adequate repurchase from the new customers to justify a rollout of the program.

■ While being flexible, make sure you don't confuse potential purchasers by constantly changing prices.

■ Don't overreact to the competition. Before you change your long-run pricing strategy, wait to see if the competitive price changes are temporary or permanent. At the same time, learn to anticipate and react to short-run competitive price changes.

- If you are attempting to build a value image don't lower an already competitive price—put greater emphasis on the quality of your product.

- Don't forget that the competition is probably watching you as much as you are watching them. Consider their reactions to your pricing strategies prior to implementation.

11

DISTRIBUTION

Y ou now need to consider the marketing mix tool of distribution. Up to this point, your efforts have been focused on developing plans to persuade the target person to purchase your product. Distribution focuses on making sure there is accessible product for the target market to purchase once you have initiated demand.

Begin this chapter by reviewing the distribution issues summarized through your problems and opportunities, the overall distribution direction provided in your marketing strategies, and the communication goals for the distribution tactical tool. Then utilize the specific information provided in this chapter to develop a comprehensive plan that will allow for effective distribution of your product.

From This Chapter You Will Learn

The definition of distribution.

Issues affecting your distribution plan.

How to develop your distribution objectives and strategies.

OVERVIEW

Definition of Distribution

We define distribution as the transmission of goods and services from the producer or seller to the user. By this definition we mean the method through which the target market user receives the product from the producer. It could be direct or through one or more intermediaries or channels that make available the right product at the right place and at the optimum price, time, and quantity.

Issues Affecting Distribution

In developing your distribution plan, five main areas should be addressed:

1. Penetration (retailers and service firms) or market coverage/shelf space (manufacturers)

2. Type of outlet or channels

3. Competition

4. Geography

5. Timing

Penetration or Market Coverage

Penetration Levels for Retailers and Service Firms

Charts completed in the business review will reveal whether your firm has enough penetration to maximize sales, fully utilize the media, and pay out the marketing investment in any given market.

If you do not have enough stores or office locations to take advantage of the market's sales potential, this market is *underpenetrated*. In this situation, you probably cannot afford broad scale advertising in the market, because the expense is too burdensome for a few stores/offices. It is important to realize that each store has a natural trading area that can usually be defined in terms of geographical size and number of people. Thus, each market, depending upon its population and the competition, can support a certain number of stores. If, for example, you are underpenetrated, with one store in a market of 300,000 households, and the business review determines that there should be one store for every 100,000 households, you will:

- *Not maximize your sales in the given market.* There are major areas in the market where customers will not be exposed to the store and will not drive out of their way to purchase an item that can be purchased at alternative outlets offering similar merchandise.

- *Not be able to maximize your marketing investment.* Instead of leveraging, for example, media and operation costs across three stores, all expenses are shouldered by the one store. Expenses will run above average because personnel and shipping costs cannot be amortized over the total sales of a multiple number of stores. Further, in order to keep advertising expenses within budget, the store will have limited media support, given the size of the market and the cost of the media. When mass media is purchased, there will be much waste, as the communication will be received by consumers outside the store's trading area. Given this scenario, effective, broad, marketable media such as television probably cannot be utilized.

Being *overpenetrated*, with too many stores or offices in a trading area, also has negatives associated with it. Too many outlets result in inefficiency, with duplication of coverage. Often the effect is cannibalization of one store's customers by another store. Accordingly, consideration should be given not just to opening new outlets but also to the need to eliminate one or more outlet locations within a market or to dramatically increase sales from the current locations in order to deliver the required profits.

Market Coverage for Consumer Goods Firms and Business-to-Business Firms

Coverage for consumer goods firms includes three areas:

- The number of potential outlets or distribution centers which carry your product

- The ACV (All Commodity Volume) of the stores which carry your product

- The amount of shelf space allocated your product

The most important distribution measure for manufacturers is not necessarily the number of stores carrying the product but the all commodity volume (ACV) of those stores. ACV is the percent of total category volume in the market done by the stores carrying a specific manufacturer's product. This is the critical measure of a manufacturer's distribution.

Review Distribution in the Product and Market Review section of your business review to determine how many outlets there are in each market with which you do business and the percentage of total business in your product category for which the outlets that carry your product account. If you are in only three out of ten grocery stores in a given market but those three account for 80 percent of the category's sales (ACV), then you don't have to spend a great deal of time trying to expand your market distribution. But if the three grocery stores have an ACV of only 30 percent of the business, an objective should be to increase market coverage.

In addition, review the distribution data in your business review to determine the percent of shelf space your product has relative to the competition. If it is substantially less than the competition, either nationally, in specific markets, or in specific grocery chains, then a distribution objective should address this problem.

Further, with an increasing number of consumer products available and with limited amount of shelf space, more retailers are requiring up-front slotting fees from the manufacturer to carry a product. You must either devise a means to avoid these allowances (sell-in your product to departments of the store which do not require slotting allowances—often the produce and meat departments) or build them into your cost of distribution.

For business-to-business firms the same process should be undertaken, except the focus of consideration should be intermediate channel targets. And instead of shelf space, the business-to-business marketer should consider the percent of his or her product purchased by each company, distributor, wholesaler, broker, or outlet within a particular channel.

Type of Outlet(s) or Channel(s)

Under Distribution in the business review you should have developed a chart which traces sales by distribution outlet for your product category. Analyze this data for any trends your firm should take advantage of during the next year. We did a business review for a manufacturer of sinks and disposals that had built its business through traditional plumbing channels via wholesalers. However, data showed that, due to the advent of the do-it-yourself movement, more sinks and disposals were being sold to do-it-yourselfers through lumberyards and home building centers than to contractors through traditional channels. Thus, the company developed a dual-channel strategy, using both the wholesale plumbing channels and the consumer home building center channels.

In addition, as with price, the type of product and the product life cycle greatly affect the channel decision. If your product is new and is still being tested, production levels will most likely be relatively small, requiring very specific and limited distribution. In addition, the product may require more in-depth, personal selling to the target market because of its complexity and newness. If this situation applies to your firms, determine what type of outlet can provide this service level before establishing distribution objectives.

If your product is already established, production levels will be higher and the product may be more standardized. This would require less demand for a specialized selling effort. Or it may be appropriate to sell your product in a self-service, self-help type of environment.

There are many different types of distribution vehicles or outlet types. Study the distribution data in your business review to determine the different distribution channels for your product category. Note which channels have the most volume and which are a growing influence in your industry. Then, list the different attributes of each distribution choice in terms of customer segmentation, customer service provided, and price orientation (discount, full price, etc.) to help you make the correct choice for your product.

Competition

Review competitive distribution patterns when making decisions regarding penetration/market coverage, type of outlet, geography, and timing. Consult your business review to determine competitive distribution patterns. This knowledge is helpful when deciding what markets to further penetrate. If there are two equal markets in terms of potential, the obvious choice for further penetration would be the one with the weakest competitive situation. In another example, if a competitor has shown dramatic sales increases utilizing a new channel of distribution which you do not use, this might provide the rationale to at least test the alternative channel structure for your products.

Further, what channels does the competition dominate? Are these channels/outlets so important to the way the target market purchases in the category that you cannot afford to not be in these channels? Or can you seek distribution in alternate channels in which your product could have a dominant position?

Geography

The marketer should also consider the BDI (Brand Development Index) and CDI (Category Development Index) data developed in the business review. A BDI demonstrates the sales-to-population ratio relative to other markets in the company's system. Distribution plans often take BDIs into consideration after they have completed the penetration or coverage analysis detailed earlier. A low BDI in any given market coupled with a penetration or coverage analysis which shows that a firm is underpenetrated points towards potential geographic expansion in those markets.

Also, geographic expansion should be considered for those markets that are underpenetrated and have high CDIs. A high CDI means that consumers in a given market purchase a product at higher rates than the country on a whole. Of course the competitive situation would also have to be taken into consideration, but the CDI provides a good benchmark for the success rate potential for different expansion markets. Below is a simplified BDI/CDI matrix that you might want to review before you set your distribution objectives:

	High CDI	**Low CDI**
High BDI	—Strong market with good market potential and product sales worthy of continual development —May require strong support to limit competitive entry	—Cash cow (don't spend marketing dollars to level of sales, use these dollars to fund development of other markets) —Will need to look to other markets for growth
Low BDI	—May be a market right for development or a competitor's stronghold to be avoided	—Not promising; generally markets to be avoided unless your firm can develop a dominant (and profitable) share of this limited market

In summary, distribution objectives should detail penetration/coverage goals and/or use of specific types of outlets and channels on a national, regional, or local basis, depending on the potential of the market and the situation of your product.

Timing

Finally, timing must be addressed in the distribution objectives. State whether the objectives are to be completed in a matter of months or years. Because distribution involves a commitment to actual construction or long-term leases in the case of retailers and requires the development of working relationships with wholesalers, brokers, and the retail trade by manufacturers, the distribution timing is often longer term than some of the other tactical tool considerations of the marketing plan. A retail store expansion program is usually a multiyear, ongoing development. What may be started this year may not be finished until next year and beyond.

HOW TO DEVELOP A DISTRIBUTION PLAN

A worksheet for developing your distribution plan is provided in Appendix C.

Task 1
Establish Distribution Objectives

Establish quantifiable distribution objectives for the following four categories:

1. Penetration (retailers and service firms) or market coverage/shelf space (manufacturers)

2. Type of outlet(s) or channel(s)

3. Geography

4. Timing

Distribution objective examples for a retail firm would be as follows:

Fully penetrate the firm's two largest BDI markets (Chicago and Detroit, which account for 25 percent of the firm's business) to attain the ratio of one store for every 100,000 households within the next two years (8 stores in this plan year and 10 stores the following year).

Continue to utilize strip centers in existing markets, testing outlet centers in new markets.

Task 2
Establish Distribution Strategies

Your distribution strategies should describe how you will accomplish your distribution objectives. The following points should be considered by each business category.

Retail and Service Firms

- Describe the criteria or methodology for penetrating markets or adding new locations. Where will you locate new stores? What demographic, location, cost per square foot, competition, or other criteria will you use to make these decisions?

- If you are expanding geographic penetration, detail if this will be done on a systematic, market-by-market basis or will occur wherever the opportunity develops within the total system.

- If a change is warranted, describe how you will make the change from one type of outlet to another.

- Describe your purchase or lease strategies.

Manufacturers

- Describe how you will attain market coverage goals and/or shelf space goals. Some of your strategies to achieve these goals will be incorporated into your promotional plan. If your business review details that your product does not differ from your competition's, your product is not established with the trade, and your product does not make a large impact on the trade in terms of profits, then you will have to rely more heavily on promotions and trade deals to meet aggressive market coverage and shelf space goals.

- If your objective is to increase market coverage, describe how you will choose the type(s) of channel to target for increased coverage and detail specifically what stores you plan to target.

- Outline whether you are going to use a *push* or *pull* strategy. A push strategy focuses on marketing to the intermediate targets, such as distributors and the outlets, to obtain distribution and shelf space. A pull strategy involves marketing to the ultimate purchaser or directly to consumers to build demand, forcing the outlets to stock the product.

- Describe how you will enter new distribution channels if this is an objective. Will you try to place your entire line or one top-selling product in the stores? What kind of merchandising and advertising support will you provide? Will you offer return privileges or lower your minimum order requirements? If storage, display, dispensing, price marking, or accounting specifics are important to the new channel, describe how you will make allowances to gain distribution trial. Will you provide special introductory pricing?

Assume a distribution objective for a package goods firm is to increase ACV market coverage 20 points among grocery stores in all top 100 markets over the next year. The strategies to achieve this objective might be:

Place additional sales emphasis against large independents with multiple store outlets.

Concentrate on first establishing the top-selling line of frozen foods before attempting to gain distribution of the entire line of frozen and canned foods.

Utilize special promotions developed in the promotion plan to help sell-in product, such as special display allowances designed to encourage initial trial and special introductory pricing incentives.

DOS AND DON'TS

Do

- Review your problems and opportunities and your marketing strategies as guidelines for developing distribution objectives and strategies, and consider the effect of distribution strategies on awareness and attitudes in contributing to the marketing communication goals. The number of stores in a market and their exposure alone has a major impact on the level of unaided store awareness by the target market.

- Study your competitors' distribution patterns. Learn from their mistakes and their successes. Look for opportunities to exploit channels that the competition is not in and/or channels which you can dominate.

- Make sure your distribution structure is consistent with your positioning and your target market's purchasing patterns.

- Be willing to change distribution methods if the marketing environment changes.

- Location of the store and proximity to the consumer must still be considered king in retail.

- Continually test new methods of distribution.

Don't

- Don't make quick decisions. Distribution of your product requires the development of long-term relationships and usually requires a fixed investment of capital. Don't change retail distribution patterns without thoroughly testing alternatives first. If you are going to expand distribution, do it on a market-by-market basis or on a regional basis in a disciplined, roll-out fashion.

- Don't remain static in your distribution patterns. Customers change their behavior and so must you.

- Don't just use intuition in making distribution decisions. Use hard data and the BDI/CDI method.

- Don't be inflexible with your distribution policy. There may be regional differences that you should consider.

- Don't expand distribution if you can't fully penetrate markets or consistently deliver product. Retail and consumer goods firms need minimum distribution levels within any given market to leverage advertising and other marketing resources.

- Don't expand your distribution at a rate that you cannot effectively support (adequate levels of product, quality service, media weight and support, etc.).

12

Personal Selling/ Service

Personal selling and service involve the personal, one-on-one contact your company has with the specific target person and the day-to-day administration of the selling program, the retail outlet, or the office. Whether it's business-to-business or consumer marketing, personal selling is a very important tool that incorporates the critical human factor into the marketing mix. *It is the one personal and direct link between the target market and your company.* Further, the degree of personal contact with the target person will affect the level of impact the personal selling and service functions will have on the awareness and attitude towards your product.

From This Chapter You Will Learn

The definition of personal selling/service.

The issues affecting your personal selling plan.

How to develop a personal selling plan.

Overview

Definition of Personal Selling

In this book, personal selling for retail and service firms, which is often referred to as operations, involves all functions related to selling, operations, and service in the store, office, or other environments, such as door-to-door solicitation, in-home selling, and telemarketing. This includes hiring and managing sales personnel, stocking inventory, and preparing the product for sale, as well as the presentation and maintenance of the facility. For business-to-business and consumer goods firms, personal selling relates to the manufacturers' selling and servicing of its products to the trade and/or intermediate markets (various buyers of the product within the distribution channel from the original producer to the ultimate user).

Issues Affecting Personal Selling and Service

Retail and Service Firms

The overriding issue facing retailers and service organizations is to determine a realistic and achievable sales ratio. You must determine a goal for the percentage of individuals walking into the retail outlet who will be persuaded to purchase versus those who will leave without purchasing. Or, if you are a service organization, a goal must be developed regarding the number of prospects versus the number of converted clients when making sales calls. If you have primary research, you will be able to track your sales ratio and that of your competitors from year to year. This should provide direction when establishing your sales ratio in the marketing plan. If you do not have primary research, we suggest that you initiate an information survey among your prospects/customers similar to the one discussed under Buying Habits in the Target Market Effectors section of the business review to help guide you.

Whether you have primary research or not, you should analyze the amount of traffic (retailers) or number of sales calls made (service) in daily and weekly increments. Next, estimate your current sales ratio and project what an increase of even 3 to 5 points would do for your sales. Finally, ask yourself if it is realistic to expect a 3 to 5 point increase. In some businesses where there is a lot of competition and consumers shop two or three stores before purchasing, the answer may be no. But in other businesses it may be very realistic to expect a higher sales ratio given the proper selling focus.

In addition, retailers and service organizations must address other *customer behavior goals* when developing personal selling and service plans. If you determine that customers are more likely to purchase if they have been given a demonstration or tried the merchandise, develop plans that encourage this type of behavior.

When developing a personal selling and operations plan, retailers must also consider the in-store selling presentation, and service firms must consider their basic selling environment. The retailer must determine to what degree the store is going to employ a self-service or full-service selling environment. Are you going to employ minimal sales pressure or utilize a harder and/or commission-based selling structure? In deciding the type of selling environment, you must analyze the needs of the target person, the merchandise being sold, the competition, and the positioning of your firm.

Providing service during and after the sale is critical for many products. Many retailers believe in the philosophy that *to service is to sell.* For example, in a shoe store environment, whenever a salesperson can provide the service of personally fitting the shoe for the customer, the chances of selling that customer can increase up to 50 percent. Likewise, good service after the sale can dramatically increase the chance of a repeat sale. A good example of this is how superior service by auto dealers dramatically impacts the chance of getting continued new car purchases from the same customer.

If the product is extremely technical and/or requires a major dollar outlay, the customer will probably require a great deal of information and a more professional selling technique. If the product is a standardized, utilitarian type of product, there probably is less need for an information and/or hard-sell approach. For example, many self-help or self-service store environments carry less-technical and less-expensive products with which the consumer has had previous experience. This type of selling environment addresses consumers' familiarity with the product(s). The customer can shop and make decisions independently and comfortably without the services of a salesperson.

Consideration of the consumer's need for information and the technicality of the product is only one part of this decision-making process. After you have considered these factors, also review the capabilities of your sales staff. It takes a great deal of product knowledge and selling skill to effectively sell potential buyers and not turn them off. If you decide upon an aggressive selling philosophy, your company must make the commitment to sales training and ongoing refresher courses.

Finally, the cost of selling is another key factor you must consider. A sales or in-store staff may be very necessary, but it is very expensive to maintain. You must determine the optimum number of salespeople and the dollar investment required to support the selling effort. The cost of selling as a percent of sales will vary depending upon your company, what you are selling, and the needs of the target market. You might want to review industry sources to help you determine what your company's selling/payroll cost should be.

Manufacturers

When addressing personal selling issues, package goods manufacturers consider brokers, wholesalers, and outlets while many other business-to-business companies think in terms of intermediate markets. Like retailers and service organizations, a key selling issue for manufacturers is a ratio of selling effectiveness. A sales ratio for manufacturers is determined by the number of prospects contacted versus the number that actually become customers. In order to arrive at a sales ratio objective, other quantifiable objectives need to be established, such as the number of sales calls and demonstrations made and the number of products sold to wholesalers, outlets, and intermediate markets. Many times the key to meeting a sales ratio objective is not only selling effectiveness but also arriving at a specific and qualified prospect list. These types of parameters provide direction to the sales force and also serve as a measurement tool when analyzing sales personnel results at the end of the year.

Manufacturers must decide how to sell the product to the outlets, distributors, and other businesses. Manufacturers use three basic methods to sell their product:

- *Direct:* to purchasers through an in-house sales force

- *Indirect:* to purchasers through agents (independent sales reps/brokers) or wholesalers/distributors

- *Mixed:* a combined selling system that uses both direct and indirect methods

The decision of which of the above selling methods to use is made after consideration of the following factors.[1]

Is the Market Horizontal or Vertical?

A vertical market is one that is made up of only one or two industries. It is very specialized. For example, craft manufacturers sell to craft wholesalers or directly to craft retail outlets. The number of wholesalers and retailers in the total industry is very small. Direct distribution is often used because selling is very personal and individual relationships become very important. However, if the market is horizontal, with the product being sold to buyers in many industries (for example, plastics manufacturers sell to multiple industry types), then the opportunity to reach large numbers of potential purchasers might be better with an indirect sales approach.

Quality of Product

With a direct sales staff you can control the selling effort, since the sales force is made up of your company's employees. For this reason, businesses with rigid product quality standards often use a direct sales force to ensure integrity of the quality associated with the product.

---

[1]The following discussion is based in part on lecture material presented by Dr. Michael Hutt at Miami University.

What Is the Market Potential?

Many times a company's only choice is to go through indirect channels. If the firm has only one product with limited sales potential, it is very difficult to generate enough demand to justify the cost of an individual sales force.

Geographic Concentration

If the market is geographically concentrated, it is easier to go direct. If clients are dispersed, indirect channels tend to be more favorable, as it becomes very costly to make time-consuming sales visits.

Technical Aspects of the Product

The more technical the product, the more a direct sales force is favored. The firm needs to supervise the training of the sales force and have a high degree of control over the selling and servicing process.

Standardized or Specialized Product

If the product is standardized, you can move the product through many different types of channels and selling methods. If it is specialized and requires a high degree of maintenance, specialized care, or instruction, then a direct sales force is often required.

Financial Strength of the Company

The manufacturer must consider the cost of each selling method and weigh this against specific market conditions and options for selling the product. A direct sales force is far more expensive than utilizing independent representatives. However, there are certain advantages of a direct sales force, as outlined above, that may justify the extra cost.

HOW TO DEVELOP A PERSONAL SELLING/SERVICE PLAN

A worksheet for developing your personal selling/service plan is provided in Appendix C.

Task 1
Establish Selling/ Service Objectives

Your sales, operations, and/or service objectives should be as specific as possible and should include the following types of goals:

For Retail/Service

- Customer contact—the percent of store visitors having contact and the number of contacts with store staff during visit

- Customer behavior goals such as percentage of customers who are persuaded to try a product or experience a demonstration of merchandise

- The specific sales ratio

An example of personal selling objectives for a retailer would be:

Establish a minimum of one contact with 90 percent of store visitors and a minimum of two contacts with 60 percent of visitors.

Achieve a 50 percent trial ratio of customers—customers who actually try the merchandise during a hands-on demonstration in-store.

Achieve a 40 percent sales ratio (40 percent of the people who visit the store make a purchase) over the next year during the holiday selling season and a 30 percent sales ratio during the remainder of the year.

For Manufacturers

- The number and type of companies that must be contacted by the sales force
- The number of sales calls that must be made to each prospect and/or current customer by company type (industry, dollar volume, etc.)
- The sales ratio (number of contacts versus the number of sales)
- The average sales dollar volume and the number of orders per salesperson per year
- The number of actual product presentations/demonstrations or percentage of product sampling or trial that must be achieved during sales presentations
- Additional customer behavior goals, such as the percentage of customers who are persuaded to sign up for future sales/product information

Personal selling objective examples for a manufacturer would be:

Contact each current customer twice and make a sales presentation to the top 50 percent of prospect companies in the newly developed construction and manufacturing SIC target markets.

Make full product demonstrations to 75 percent of the prospects.

Obtain a sales ratio of 85 percent among existing customers and 30 percent among new prospects.

Obtain an average dollar sale of $2,500 and generate an average of two hundred sales per salesperson per year.

**Task 2
Establish Selling/
Service Strategies**

It will be helpful first to review the questions pertaining to selling under Distribution in the business review. Answering these questions will help you to form specific selling strategies for your company. The areas to address when you establish specific selling/service/operations strategies to meet your selling/service objectives include the following:

- *The type of selling environment/method.* A retailer must decide whether the selling environment will be self-service or whether there will be a full-service sales staff. If there is a full-service sales staff, a decision must be made regarding the selling orientation—hard sell or soft sell. A manufacturer must determine whether to use a direct, indirect, or mixed sales staff.

- *The administration parameters of the sales force.* The selling strategies should outline hiring qualifications, training, and evaluation procedures.

- *Seasonal and geographic requirements.* If staffing is a function of seasonal sales or if there are different staffing requirements by store or by market, there should be a selling strategy developed to address these issues.

- *Demonstration requirements.* This personal selling/service strategy section should also direct service and/or demonstration technique. For retailers, is there a certain technique that should be followed to increase the chance of closing a sale? A shoe retailer may require that its sales force initiate as many trial fittings as possible. This might result from data that shows fitting customers and allowing them to try walking in the shoe leads to a 50 percent higher sales ratio. Similar selling technique decisions should be considered for manufacturers.

- *Timing and priority of the sales presentation.* Manufacturers and brokers/distributors must determine when and in what priority accounts will be given sales presentations. For example, if you were a manufacturer selling to retailers, you might make sales presentations to some retailers before others because you want some retailers to have your product before others.

- *Sales staff selection by presentation.* Depending on the customer or potential customer, the manufacturer or broker/distributor must determine who should make the sales presentation. Should it be the salesperson alone or should a sales management person, technical person, or corporate executive also be involved?

- *Sales force compensation.* Other things equal, people will tend to perform in ways that will get them the maximum compensation. In a highly measurable area such as sales (number of contacts, individual sales ratios, and the like are generally easily tracked), employees will tend to act in ways in which they are motivated to behave. Therefore, it is critical that the sales compensation approach be in sync with the desired type of selling environment. For example, a retailer that wishes to position itself as a low pressure, self-service-oriented store would be unwise to structure a large sales commission component into its sales force compensation, as this tends to encourage aggressive closing efforts.

- *Special sales incentives.* If they are going to be used, special sales incentive programs should be developed in this section of the plan. When special incentives are provided for a special event or promotion, for example, make sure the sales staff is made totally aware of the specifics of the special incentive program before, during, and after the event.

- *Store operation guidelines.* Selling and operation strategies should cover

    —retail staffing requirements in terms of when, where, and what.

    —stocking/merchandising procedures.

    —store maintenance considerations.

    —organization/appearance of the store, office, and shelf display for retailers, service companies, and manufacturers, respectively.

    —in-store product presentation (plan-o-grams), office presentation, and displays of product for retailers, service companies, and manufacturers, respectively.

Examples of Retail Selling Strategies

The following are examples of selling strategies for a ski retailer whose selling objectives were to increase the sale ratio from 30 percent to 45 percent during the next year and to obtain a 35 percent ski equipment demonstration ratio among customers in the store.

Develop an aggressive selling environment designed to sell customers during an in-store, one-on-one sales presentation.

Develop a program that assures that all customers are greeted upon entry to the store.

Utilize the training hill outside the store as a means to get customers to actually try the equipment and achieve the demonstration goals established in the selling objectives.

Utilize 2 percent commission plus salary to encourage salespeople to sell.

Establish a bonus system to reward the top producers for each week and each month of the year.

Utilize mystery shoppers to rate service and selling effectiveness. Rate each salesperson at least once every six months.

Utilize annual and semiannual reviews of the sales staff to improve performance. Send each salesperson to one selling seminar per year.

Develop quarterly seminars to keep salespeople aware of the latest technology and products in the industry.

Examples of Manufacturers' Selling Strategies

The following are examples of selling strategies for a manufacturer of a new plastic patented toy boomerang that has a distribution objective of 50 percent ACV of toy stores and 30 percent ACV of college stores in year one. The selling objectives for this manufacturer are 90+ percent contact rates for both targets, sales ratio of 60 percent toy and 40 percent college, and an annual average dollar volume of $500 for toy stores and $200 for college stores. The strategies are:

Employ sales representatives and brokers to call on toy stores.

Employ a national rep organization that calls on college book stores.

Compensate reps and brokers with 10 percent commission on initial orders and 7 percent on all follow-up orders.

Make Toys 'R Us the number one priority, and follow up with sales calls immediately thereafter to the top tier of toy stores.

Train sales representative groups with a demonstration tape.

DOS AND DON'TS

Do

- Review your problems and opportunities, marketing strategies, and personal selling communication value goals before developing your selling/operations/service plan.

- Review your customers' shopping habits and product information requirements before deciding on a selling method.

- If you are a retailer, make sure you plan to train your sales staff properly before you decide to utilize a hard-sell approach.

- If you are a manufacturer, review the seven considerations outlined in this chapter before deciding whether to use a direct, indirect, or mixed selling method.

- Make sure your sales force compensation plan matches your desired selling approach.

- Have your sales staff reinforce the positioning of your product and your advertising and promotion efforts. Your individual marketing mix tools are far more effective if each one complements and reinforces the other.

- Support your sales staff. They will be more effective salespeople if given the support of brochures, samples, and special offers when interacting with the customer.

- Manufacturers, make sure you are selling to the real decision maker(s) when calling on new prospects.

- Make sure there is diligent, detailed monitoring of each selling program in terms of personal sales calls made and follow-up of sales leads received.

Don't

- Don't expect your company to change selling methods overnight. It takes a lot of training and the right type of personnel to perfect different selling styles.

- Don't overlook the importance of making sure you have a sound operations system in place to execute your sales plans. This is particularly true in the service industries in which there has not been a strong selling orientation, such as health care and legal professions. Operations is also important in retail, where you have many variables to control, including people, product preparation/inventory, presentation, and maintenance of the facility. It is our experience that many marketing plans fail, not because they are strategically wrong, but primarily because of poor execution in the field.

- Don't forget that the selling function needs ongoing attention from management in order to be effective and to show improvement.

- Don't forget, although money motivates, a formalized program to recognize an individual's accomplishment also increases selling effectiveness.

- Don't expect to sell everyone at one time. Set priorities in terms of when prospects should be sold based on short- and long-term potential.

- Retailers, your salespeople can't sell from an empty wagon. You can't sell the product if it is not available for the shopper to purchase. The operations plan must ensure that there is adequate communication between marketing and the merchandisers so that adequate inventory is stocked in the stores prior to heavy, seasonal selling periods and promotions.

- Don't just provide service, use service as a method to *sell* your customers and generate repeat sales!

- Don't let your sales force forget that, while selling new customers is important, the reason for your company's existence is to service and satisfy existing customers.

13

PROMOTION/EVENTS

Promotion is a powerful short-term marketing tool. Developing a promotional plan requires strategic thinking and creativity. In many instances, marketers begin at the execution stage and randomly consider idea after idea without any thought as to the ends they are trying to achieve. The result is usually costly, with time and effort spent on developing promotion ideas that are inappropriate to the target market and the competitive situation and, consequently, do not pay out. The key is to establish promotion objectives and strategies first and then develop innovative, yet *targeted*, executions. Also, keep in mind as you write this promotion segment of the marketing plan that, once executed, it must fulfill the awareness and attitude tactical communication value goals.

From This Chapter You Will Learn

The definition of promotion; promotion differences by industry, incentives, and categories; and the five keys to successful promotions.

How to develop your promotion objectives.

How to develop promotion strategies.

How to develop alternative promotion executions utilizing a promotion format.

How to determine the costs of promotions and analyze promotion payback.

How to select the most appropriate promotion execution alternatives and integrate different executions into a total promotion plan.

What event marketing is and how to select and plan an event.

The available promotion tools and how they can be delivered.

OVERVIEW

Definition of Promotion

Promotion provides added incentive, encouraging the target market to perform some incremental behavior. The incremental behavior results in either increased short-term sales and/or an association with the product (e.g., product usage or an event-oriented experience). For the purposes of this book, we will define promotion as an activity offering incentive above and beyond the product's inherent attributes and benefits to stimulate incremental purchase or association with the product over the short run. While this promotion segment of the planning process focuses primarily on direct product movement, we do address how to approach event marketing from a planning perspective in terms of product association or experience in the latter portion of this chapter.

Consumer and Trade (Business-to-Business) Promotion

There are two broad categories of promotion—consumer and business-to-business, or trade. The goal of *consumer promotion* is to influence the end consumer or the ultimate purchaser/user to "pull" the product through the channels or, for example, off the shelf. *Trade, or business-to-business, promotion* influences the trade or intermediate markets that purchase and resell the product to "push" the product through the channels or onto the shelf. In most cases, some combination of "push" or "pull" will be most effective. This chapter discusses both types of promotions.

One major difference between consumer and trade promotion, other than different target markets, is delivery. With consumer promotions, the incentives are delivered either by mass media or through in-store devices such as on-pack/in-pack offers. However, because of the relatively narrow customer base for trade promotion, mass communication media are usually not cost efficient—there is too much wasted coverage. Therefore, with trade promotion, added incentives are usually delivered through such targeted media vehicles as direct mail or trade publications or through the sales force.

Promotion Incentives

Promotion incentives fall into one of four major areas:

1. *Price incentives*—some form of savings off of the original price of the product

2. *Product*—providing a sample of the product

3. *Merchandise or gifts*—giving customers the opportunity to obtain merchandise or premiums with the purchase of the product

4. *An experience*—participation of an individual or a group of individuals in such special events as contests, sweepstakes, parties, or some unique experience. Participation is rewarded either by the chance to win a prize, money, trip, etc., or through the pure enjoyment of the event.

Types of Promotion Categories

There are many different types of promotions. Each has unique advantages and disadvantages that are listed in the Appendix to this chapter. The ten promotion categories most commonly used by marketers to communicate or deliver the incentives are:

1. Price Off/Sale

2. Couponing

3. Sampling

4. Bonus packs/multi-packs

5. Refunds

6. Premiums

7. Sweepstakes/Games

8. Packaging

9. Trade Allowances

10. Events

Timing of the Incentive Payback to the Target Market

The target market receives the incentive for purchase in one of three time periods:

- *Immediate*—the consumer receives the incentive instantly with or without the purchase of, or association with, the product.

- *Delayed*—the consumer receives the incentive at the next purchase or within a specified period after the purchase of, or association with, the product.

- *Chance*—the consumer has the chance of receiving the incentive within a specified period of time (immediate or delayed) after the purchase of, or association with, the product.

In summary, promotions are a short-term, behavior-oriented, multifaceted marketing tool that provides flexibility to the marketer in terms of the incentive offered, the promotional vehicle used, and the time period in which the incentive is awarded.

Five Keys to Developing Successful Promotions

As you proceed with this chapter in the preparation of the promotion segment of your marketing plan, keep in mind the five keys to successful promotion development:

1. *Promote what the target market wants.* Don't promote what you can't sell or what is out of fashion. Develop promotions around what will be most appealing to the largest segment of your target market.

2. *Provide the necessary incentive to stimulate behavior.* If you want to get maximum promotion participation, make sure your incentive has the pulling power to get the target market to act. For example, we have found in many retail promotions "10 to 20 percent off" does not move the consumer. It must now be 20 percent or more!

3. *Build the necessary awareness for the offer.* So many marketers do well in promoting what the target market wants with a meaningful incentive, but then they do not make enough of the target market aware of the promotion to garner the participation required to make the promotion successful. Staging a promotion means very little if you don't tell enough people about it.

4. *Limit the barrier(s) to promotion participation.* To reduce the liability or cost of promotions, many promotions are overly constrained. Review what barriers or requirements you put in front of the target person in terms of amount of purchase, time made available to participate in the promotion, and incremental behavior required to participate in the promotion. For example, is it too much of a hassle for your target person to participate in your promotion? You can remove many barriers by looking at the promotion from the target person's viewpoint rather than a company viewpoint.

5. *Develop optimum value perception at minimum investment.* Finally, keep in mind that there are two parts to the promotion equation: company cost and target market participation. Accordingly, a promotion should attempt to provide the

perception of optimum value to the target market at the minimum of investment to the marketer.

ESTABLISHING SHORT-TERM PROMOTION SALES OBJECTIVES

Prior to developing promotion objectives, strategies, and executions, you need to set short-term promotion sales objectives for the promotion time period. In our development of a marketing plan, *promotion is the only marketing mix tool for which we develop specific sales objectives,* because promotion is both exclusively short term in nature and affects customer behavior. Customer behavior is affected through tangible incentives, resulting in incremental sales generation and/or an incremental association with the product. With promotion, the marketer will incur short-term expenses in the form of incentives and communication of the incentives in order to achieve the desired short-term consumer response.

The marketer needs to establish promotion sales goals for two reasons. One reason is that the promotion can be evaluated against projected payback both prior to and after execution. This will help determine if the expected incremental sales from the promotion are greater than the incremental costs (incentives and marketing costs associated with communicating the incentives). The second reason is to set a definite sales goal that the promotion must fulfill.

In the sales objective chapter you were urged to develop both annual and short-term, monthly sales goals. In most cases, your promotion sales goal will be a portion of the corresponding month's or week's sales goal. This is because promotions are executed to reverse a downward sales trend or provide necessary incremental sales in any given short-term period.

HOW TO DEVELOP YOUR PROMOTION OBJECTIVES

Promotion Objective Parameters

Promotion objectives and marketing objectives are very similar in that both are designed to affect consumer behavior. The difference is that promotion objectives should be designed to affect *specific incremental* behavior over a *short period of time.* Therefore, promotion objectives must

- *Induce incremental consumer behavior* over what was anticipated with no promotion.

- Be *specific.* The objective should focus on one goal only.

- Be *measurable.* The results must be quantifiable.

- Relate to a *specific time period.* However, because promotion objectives are short term in nature, the time period can be from one day to several months.

- Provide direction as to the *geographical* focus of the promotion.

- Include *budget constraints* or *profit parameters.* Remember, promotion is a marketing mix tool with its own sales objectives.

■ Focus on *affecting target market behavior* to: retain current users, increase purchases from target market, increase trial from new users, obtain repeat usage after initial trial, and affect attitudes through association with an event.

Promotions should be viewed as one method to help execute marketing strategies. In order to develop promotion objectives, you must first review the marketing objective and strategy section of your marketing plan and then restate your marketing strategies in quantifiable promotion objectives.

Task 1
Review Your
Marketing Strategies

Review your marketing strategies, paying particular attention to those listed under the promotion category and those for which the implementation tool of promotion might be appropriate. A marketing seasonality strategy such as "increase sales during the weaker selling months of May through August" could be implemented through promotion. Obviously, a marketing promotion strategy such as "develop in-store promotions during peak selling seasons to encourage purchases of weaker-selling product categories" should be addressed in the promotional plan. Thus, the first task requires isolating those marketing strategies that you feel promotions can help implement.

Task 2
Review the Selected
Marketing Strategies
and Corresponding
Marketing Objectives

This task involves reviewing each marketing strategy selected to be implemented through promotions in Task 1 and its corresponding marketing objective. In order to form promotion objectives, the marketer reviews the marketing objective to determine *what* needs to be accomplished and *who* is being targeted. Then, rely on your marketing strategy to guide you on *how* to develop a promotion objective. By linking your promotion objective to your marketing objective and strategy(ies), you ensure greater probability of developing promotions that will accomplish your marketing strategies and fulfill the marketing objectives established earlier in the plan. Assume the following situation:

Marketing Objective: Increase the number of total users/trial among the current target market by 10 percent.

Seasonality Marketing Strategy: Increase the purchasing level during the off-season while maintaining purchasing rates during the peak selling seasons.

Other Marketing Strategies: Note that there would typically be other marketing strategies to achieve the above marketing objective. However, assume that only the seasonality strategy is being implemented through promotion and that the other marketing strategies would be accomplished using other marketing mix executional tools.

In this example, the marketing objective will provide what the promotion objective should achieve and to whom the promotion should be targeted.

Increase number of users (marketing goal, *what*)

From the current target market (target market goal, *who*)

Continuing, the market strategy will help determine how the promotion objective is developed.

Increase purchasing during the off-season (method of achievement, *how*)

Task 3
Create Quantifiable
Promotion Objective(s)

In combining what, who, and how, the marketing objective and strategy can be restated into a quantifiable promotion objective as follows:

Increase the number of users from the current target market 25 percent during the off-season of May and June in all markets, with a positive contribution to overhead.

Note that geography and timing considerations and a measurable target market behavior are incorporated into the objective statement to make it as specific as possible. Geography and timing in the promotion objective would be consistent with the geography and timing constraints developed in the marketing strategy section of the plan. Also, note that a budget constraint is mentioned. In this case, the objective has to be achieved in a manner that contributes positively to fixed overhead. In a different situation, the objective of new trial might outweigh any short-term profit requirement, because the company would be investing in new customers or trial for future profits; however, there would be a budget constraint at the end of the promotion objective to limit the amount of the investment in new trial. The promotion objective might be "increase the number of new users 25 percent during the off-season with a promotion budget not to exceed $500,000."

The measurable amount in the promotion objective (in this example, 25 percent) must be realistic. Past experience provides the best assistance in deciding just how much you will affect target market behavior through promotions. Remember that promotion is just one of the marketing tools you will be using to achieve your marketing objectives. If promotions were the only tool, then the measurable goal in the promotion objective would have to equal the measurable goal in the marketing objective. In this example, the goal would have to be to add enough incremental new users during May and June to increase the total new user base for the year 10 percent above last year's results. This is highly unrealistic and points out why there are usually multiple marketing strategies for any given marketing objective. In addition, promotion is most often only partially responsible for the implementation of any given marketing strategy. Other marketing tools, such as advertising, distribution, pricing, and merchandising, might be used in conjunction with promotion to implement a specific marketing strategy.

In going through the above process, you may develop several promotion objectives, as there may be several marketing strategies that can be implemented and accomplished through the use of promotions. Each promotion objective will require one or more promotional strategies.

Promotion Strategy and Execution Considerations

Promotion Strategy Parameters

Once the promotional objectives are established, promotion strategies must be formulated demonstrating how to accomplish the promotion objectives. Promotion strategies should include:

- The type of promotion device.
- The promotion incentive.
- Whether to implement a closed or open promotion.
- The delivery method.

Type of Promotion Device

The marketer has to determine which promotional device (sampling, premiums, etc.) will best meet the promotion objective. The ten most common promotion categories were listed earlier in this chapter. Further details and the advantages and disadvantages of each of these promotion vehicles is presented in the Appendix to this chapter.

The Promotion Incentive

The promotion incentive must include a basic reward for the consumer. Since promotions are responsible for affecting target market behavior, the incentive needs to stimulate demand. The promotion incentive must be strong enough to move the market to participate in the promotion/event and/or purchase the product.

Keeping in mind profitability goals, the promotion incentive should be broad in scope in most instances. This means that the incentive must appeal to a broad category of consumers. Avoid spending substantial promotion dollars on promotion incentives that affect only small segments of the target market and thus have limited payback potential. A footwear retailer found that it was much more effective to promote a 20 percent discount on all athletic shoes than to promote price reductions on five individual running shoes. The broader nature of the 20 percent discount on all athletic shoes (court, running, fitness, walking) message appeals to a much larger cross section of consumers. The result is more interest in and trial of the store, greater sales of athletic shoes, and ultimately, more sales in nonathletic departments because of the increased traffic.

One exception is when an individual product or a narrow group of products is promoted with substantial incentives. The larger the individual incentive, the greater the impact of the promotion. The strongly promoted individual product often acts as a loss leader. A loss leader is a product intended to build trial for the product or traffic for a store. Another exception to the principle of developing broadly targeted promotion incentives is when the marketer is targeting a narrow target market. In this situation, an incentive that appeals to a select group of consumers might be very appropriate. Accordingly, you should expect a more limited response.

Finally, as a counter to the broad scope incentive parameter discussed above, the cost of the incentive must also be considered in conjunction with the promotion budget parameter. A half-price sale or a free premium would certainly be broad and appeal to a large cross section of consumers, but the cost in terms of reduced margins must also be considered and weighted against the anticipated increase in sales generated from the promotion. The key is to develop promotion rewards that are perceived to have high value by the consumer but provide adequate margins given the anticipated volume of sales, to ensure profitability.

The end result is that the promotion incentive must achieve the promotion objective. If the promotion objective is to increase purchases among existing customers nationally by 20 percent over the first quarter with a positive contribution to profits, then the promotion can't just generate additional purchases; it must do so profitably. The incentive must be enough to generate additional purchases, yet it cannot be too costly or the promotion will not be profitable. However, if the promotion objective is to increase new trial nationally by 20 percent among the target market with a budget of $500,000, then the strategy doesn't need to address a profit constraint, only a budget parameter. This promotion objective might be used by a company concerned with generating new trial as an investment for future profits. In this example, the budget constraint makes certain that a realistic investment is made and that the promotion is developed in a fiscally responsible manner.

Closed versus Open Promotions

A promotion can be open or closed. There are also degrees between these two extremes. An *open promotion* is one where the company offers an added incentive to purchase, with no specific behavior required to take advantage of the offer. A good example of this would be a 20 percent off sale at the retail level. In order to take advantage of this incentive or offer, consumers merely have to shop at the store. Anyone can participate with no restrictions.

Open promotions have the ability to generate maximum participation. Our experience has shown us that any restriction will reduce the consumer's interest, propensity to respond, and, ultimately, the effectiveness of the promotion. In retail, the sales results between an open sale (one where 20 percent off is advertised with no restrictions) and a closed sale (one where consumers are required to bring a coupon to receive 20 percent off) is substantial. However, because of the increased potential participation, open promotions are more costly, since consumers who were going to purchase at regular price will also receive the discount. But remember, greater promotional cost doesn't necessarily mean less profit; greater sales volume can make up for a loss in margin. We ran a promotion for a client that reduced overall margin by six points but added $500,000 to the bottom line. An open promotion also means greater trial and potentially more repeat purchases in the future.

With a *closed promotion,* an added incentive to purchase is offered to consumers, but they are required to do something in order to take advantage of the offer. An example would be a coupon that must be redeemed at purchase or a refund that requires ten proof-of-purchase validations.

There are degrees to the extent that a promotion is open or closed. Consider the example of instant coupons. In this case, the requirement of the individual consumer, beyond simply shopping, is very minimal. The customer has to tear a coupon off the package and present it at the checkout counter. However, a promotion such as a refund requiring multiple proofs-of-purchase may prove to be very restrictive. This type of promotion requires a great deal of purchase commitment on the part of the consumer before the incentive is received.

Closed promotions are used when the marketer wants to target a specific target market group or limit the cost of the promotion. When Chalet Ski entered the Twin Cities market, it staged a grand opening promotion offering a free pair of ski goggles to shoppers who redeemed a coupon at either one of their two new stores. The ski shop wanted to limit the cost of the promotion, and it wanted to make sure that the people who visited the shops and received the goggles were skiers who would be potential future customers. The promotion was delivered via direct mail coupon to a targeted list of skiers in the Twin Cities area. The closed promotion allowed Chalet Ski to achieve its objective of developing trial of the two new ski shops among existing skiers.

Delivery Method

Promotions can be delivered by three basic methods or combination thereof:

1. *Media*—There are multiple forms of media-delivered promotions. Direct mail, magazines, and newspapers are the most common media delivery methods for package goods and business-to-business firms, while television, newspaper, direct mail, and radio are the most common media delivery methods for retail firms.

2. *On, in, or near package*—For manufacturers, promotions can be delivered on the package itself, in the package, or near the package via a point-of-purchase

display. For retailers, the promotions can be delivered in-store through signage and point-of-purchase displays.

3. *Salespeople*—Many companies, especially manufacturers such as package goods or business-to-business firms that sell to intermediate markets, use salespeople to deliver a promotional offer. If the target market is not a major consumer group but a more limited purchasing group, direct personal communication of an offer can be efficient and very effective.

HOW TO DEVELOP PROMOTION STRATEGIES AND PROGRAMS

Now comes the fun part; the process of actually establishing promotion strategies is fairly simple and allows for a great deal of creative flexibility.

Task 1
Review Your Promotion Objective(s)

Review your promotion objective(s) to make certain you are focused on what you are trying to accomplish. Be particularly cognizant of who you are targeting and the measurable result that is expected.

Task 2
Review Your Problems and Opportunities

Review the listing of your problems and opportunities, as these are your knowledge base and will provide insights and ideas on what direction you should pursue in developing your promotion strategies. As you are reviewing your problems and opportunities, refer to your idea page (discussed in the Introduction of this book) and write down any ideas you may have. Refer to this later when you are actually formulating your strategies.

Two purchase rate/buying habit problems might be:

The average shopper is extremely brand loyal.

The Southwest consumes the product category at below average rates on a per capita basis, and your company has poor sales in this region of the country.

These two problems will affect your promotional strategies in the area of what incentive to offer. Knowing that the category is extremely brand loyal means that it will be very difficult to induce trial, so the incentive will have to be greater. And if you are going to target the Southwest, the challenge will be even greater, since it is a low consumption area where your company has poor sales.

These are examples of how your problems and opportunities will provide direction and insights concerning development of your promotion strategies. Study your problems and opportunities very carefully. They will help you in developing intelligent, data-based promotion strategies.

Task 3
Finalize Your Promotion Strategies

A promotion strategy must incorporate each of the issues outlined in the section on strategy parameters:

- Type of promotion device
- Promotion incentive
- Closed or open promotion
- Delivery method

Assume the following situation:

Marketing Objective: Increase usage rates among the target market nationally over the next year by 20 percent.

Marketing Strategy: Expand alternative uses of the product from exclusively a hot drink to include acceptance as a cold served beverage.

Promotion Objective: Obtain initial trial of 100,000 new customers nationally for the product as a cold beverage during the months of April and May. Achieve initial trial with a budget of $2,000,000.

Note that with this situation there would probably be an alternative promotion objective aimed at stimulating trial from among the existing customer base. This objective would have separate promotion strategies and executions.

The following promotion strategies could be utilized to accomplish the promotion objective. (A worksheet is provided in Appendix C.) Each of four strategy parameters will be addressed. The cost parameter is addressed only indirectly through the choice of an incentive amount. It will be covered in more detail in Task 5.

Utilize sampling of the product in-store to soft drink purchasers.

Provide coupons to potential customers in-store worth 50 cents off the purchase price the day of the sampling.

Incorporate a trade program offering price incentives as a way to induce shelf space and merchandising support.

Task 4
Develop Alternative Promotion Program Executions

The next task is to develop alternative executions for each promotion strategy. Then, choose the most appropriate execution for inclusion in your program. Multiple executions can be developed for each promotion strategy. Be creative and think of as many as you can. Some alternative promotion executions are presented in Exhibit 13.1. These alternatives were developed to meet two of the strategies: "Utilize sampling of the product in-store" and "Provide 50-cent coupons to potential customers in-store." A worksheet to help you channel your thinking and stay consistent from one execution to another is provided in Appendix C.

Note that there is a sales objective included. Since promotions are a short-term marketing tool affecting customer behavior, there will be short-term sales results generated by the promotion. Thus, it is a good idea to establish a sales goal along with the promotion objectives, strategies, and executions. When you analyze your promotion results, you will then have two results against which to gauge your success—the sales goal and the quantitative promotion objective.

Task 5
Calculate the Cost and Payback Potential of Your Promotions

Expenses must be projected for each promotion in your promotional plan. All costs associated with communicating and delivering the promotion to the target market should be included. This includes the media costs associated with delivering the promotion. (This does *not* include the media costs associated with your normal non-promotion/image advertising.) In addition, you must also estimate the cost of the offer or incentive. If you use 25-cent coupons, you must estimate the redemption number and multiply this by 25 cents plus handling costs to calculate a dollar cost of the coupon incentive.

Cost Calculation for Closed Promotion

In order to calculate the cost and potential payback of closed promotions, you need to accurately project redemption rates for your offer.

Exhibit 13.1 Alternative Promotion Program Execution

Program Theme
"Have one on us."

Sales Objective
Develop sales of $20,000,000 over a two-month period.

Promotion Objective
Obtain initial trial of 100,000 new customers nationally for the product as a cold beverage during the months of April and May. Achieve the initial trial with a budget of $2,000,000.

Promotion Strategies
Utilize sampling of the product in-store to soft drink purchasers.

Provide coupons to potential customers in-store worth 50 cents off the purchase price wherever the product is sampled.

Description
Display a giant self-serve beverage bottle with product being served hot from one side and cold from the other in grocery stores carrying the product.

Offer free samples in paper cups to all shoppers during four weeks in April and May, effectively leading the summer selling period.

Provide a 50-cent instant coupon to all consumers who sample the product.

Support
In-store signage and display.

Rationale
The promotion will build trial and exposure for the new cold drink. Serving the cold drink with the established hot drink will show customers alternative uses for the product and link the new brand to an established and accepted product. April and May were chosen as the time to sample because the time period effectively bridges cold and warm weather months.

The instant coupon will encourage immediate purchase after trial. The 50-cents incentive will be strong inducement and, along with the sampling, will lower the risk of trying an unknown product.

Note: Alternate executions would be developed for the same objectives and strategies. You could then choose the execution that most effectively and efficiently meets the objectives.

Exhibit 13.2 Average Redemption Range

| | Average Redemption Range | |
Promotion Technique	Low	High
Instant coupon	15.0%	55.0%
In product	7.5	17.5
On product	6.0	15.0
Electronically dispensed in-store	4.0	21.0
On-shelf distributed	4.0	16.0
Cross-ruff or cross-packs	2.0	6.0
Direct mail	1.0	9.5
Free standing insert	0.7	3.0
Magazine on page	0.5	4.5
Refunds	0.5	4.5
Newspaper (ROP)	0.5	2.5
Newspaper co-op	0.4	1.7
Self-liquidating POS premium	0.3	1.0

The participation estimates shown in Exhibit 13.2 are based upon a combination of our client experience and redemption averages published by industry sources. These are ballpark estimates for participation or redemption rates using different

Exhibit 13.3 Calculating Cost of a Coupon Promotion

	High	Medium	Low
Redemption Costs			
Value of coupon	50¢	50¢	50¢
Number of coupons distributed	500,000	500,000	500,000
Estimated redemption rate	4.0%	2.0%	0.5%
Number redeemed	20,000	10,000	2,500
Dollar value or offer			
(number redeemed × value of coupon)	$10,000	$5,000	$1,250
Advertising and Media Costs			
Printing of coupons (500,000 × 0.01)	$5,000	$5,000	$5,000
Mailing cost/envelopes (500,000 × 0.19)	$95,000	$95,000	$95,000
Total cost of promotions	$110,000	$105,000	$101,250

closed-promotion vehicles. Actual participation rates should be individually adjusted as they are a function of the following:

- *The offer*—Greater incentive and fewer restrictions equal greater participation.

- *The delivery method*—The closer the delivery method is to the product itself, the greater the redemption. For example, on-pack/in-pack will have higher redemption.

- *The timing*—Immediate incentives such as instant coupons will have higher redemptions. Also, promotions run when the target category is purchasing (bicycles in spring) will have greater participation than those run when category purchasing is at a low level.

- *The product category*—Health and beauty aids, for example, have average redemption rates lower than those of household products or beverages.

- *The price of the product*—The higher the purchase price of the product, the lower the participation. However, a higher promotion incentive can have some positive effect on participation if the high price of the product is not out of the economic reach of the majority of your target market.

Exhibit 13.3 demonstrates how to calculate the cost of a promotion. (A worksheet is provided in Appendix C.) We used a coupon promotion as an example because it has applications to retail, package good, and business-to-business firms. Three different redemption rates were used in order to provide the marketer with a range of expected responses. The cost of this promotion would be somewhere between $110,000 and $101,250, with a medium estimate of $105,000. This cost will be used, along with incremental sales and profits, when calculating potential payback for a closed promotion.

In addition, if you are a consumer goods firm with coupon redemption in grocery and other stores, there are handling charges to be included. If you are utilizing a clearinghouse, you must pay a charge for each coupon handled. Also, the retailer charges for each coupon handled. At press time of this book, the average total cost was approximately 23 to 25 cents per coupon redeemed.

Additional promotion administrative costs to consider are:

- *Costs of employing fulfillment houses*—For example, there is an incremental cost for fulfillment regarding refunds, sampling, premiums, and sweepstakes/games. Most companies aren't equipped to adequately fulfill promotion programs.

Exhibit 13.4 Payback Calculation Example for Open Promotion

Situation
Promotion: 20 percent off women's department merchandise
Estimated storewide margin decrease from 50 percent to 45 percent during promotion
Time period: First three weeks of March
Geography: All three stores in Madison, WI.

Sales	
Estimated sales for period without promotion	$300,000
Estimated gross margin dollars for period without promotion ($300,000 × .50)	150,000
Estimated sales with promotion	360,000
Estimated gross margin dollars with promotion ($360,000 × .45)	162,000
Estimated net margin dollar increase with promotion ($162,000 − $150,000)	12,000
Media and Advertising Cost	
Estimated ongoing advertising and media costs with or without promotion*	15,000
Total advertising and media costs with promotion	20,000
Incremental advertising and media costs due to promotion	5,000
Payout	
Incremental margin sales	12,000
Incremental advertising and media expenditures	5,000
Contribution to fixed overhead	7,000

*What would have been spent in regular, mainline advertising and media.

- *Cost of production*—For example, production lines are often slowed to accommodate on-pack/in-pack incentives.

- *Packaging costs*—For example, with bonus packs there will be cost to reconfigure the package.

Finally, the cost of the promotion must be compared to the incremental sales the promotion is expected to generate. This can be determined through a payback analysis.

Payback Analysis

Before you execute any planned promotion, you should make sure to review the numbers to determine if the promotion makes sense from a payback analysis standpoint. We recommend calculating the contribution to fixed costs,[1] as this method isolates the promotion and takes into account any incremental variable cost associated with the promotion. In using this method, incremental costs of the promotion (communication of the promotion and incentive costs) are subtracted from incremental sales generated from the promotion.

Exhibit 13.4 presents an example for a retailer considering a 20 percent off sale as an open promotion. A worksheet is provided in Appendix C. The retailer had experience with similar sales in the past and had a rough estimate on the incremental sales that could be generated by the promotional offer. This method looks at incremental sales and costs to calculate what the promotion will generate in terms of a contribution to fixed overhead. The incremental margin sales are sales above and beyond what would normally be expected for the time period. In this case, the retailer

[1]This method is commonly used by retailer, service firms, and manufacturers. However, manufacturers also utilize a gross margin to net sales method that is detailed in Chapter 18, Budget/Payout/Calendar.

had a good idea of what to expect. If you haven't run the promotion before, make a high, medium, and low estimate based upon similar company promotions run in the past and promotion experiences for the product category. This provides best and worst case estimates.

Note that the cost of the promotion (reduction in gross margin dollars) was calculated directly into the projected incremental sales figure. In some cases you may want to break this step out to show what the promotion costs were, particularly if you are a package goods marketer and you wish to show redemption projections.

Remember, the promotion must stand on its own. The only way to determine its potential success or failure is to weigh the projected incremental sales against the expected incremental expenses of the promotion. If the promotion contributes a meaningful positive dollar figure to fixed overhead (expenses that occur no matter what happens—e.g., rent) and meets the promotion sales goals, then the promotion should be executed. If the payback analysis shows that there is a negative contribution to fixed overhead, then you should consider another promotion, or rework the promotion with less incentive or a different product mix. The exception to this is the case in which there is no payback parameter specifying that the promotion must contribute to profits. If the firm is simply trying to gain trial, which it feels will translate into future profits, then the major constraints will be the budget parameter and the amount of desired trial.

Task 6
Select the Most Appropriate Promotion Executions

You have developed promotion objectives and strategies, created promotion execution alternatives, and analyzed costs and paybacks for each execution. Now it is time to select those executions that will best achieve the promotion objectives within the established budget constraints. When choosing your promotion executions, try to make sure the executions complement each other and work together through the year. Two consecutive premium offers would probably be ineffective as compared to other combinations of promotions. The best method to determine if your promotions properly interface with each other is to list the promotions in calendar form according to when they will be executed. This will allow you to make judgments on whether you have selected promotions that complement each other. It will also be useful when you are transferring your marketing tool executions to one master calendar, as is detailed in Chapter 18, Marketing Budget, Payback Analysis, and Marketing Calendar.

HOW TO APPROACH EVENT MARKETING

While we have discussed in detail most of the promotion categories, one important category into which we have not delved is events. Event marketing, sometimes known as "event sponsorship" or "lifestyle marketing," is a rapidly growing area. Event marketing expenditures by U.S. companies are in the billions annually and are showing double-digit growth each year. The largest portion of these expenditures is devoted specifically to sports sponsorships, although event marketing as a whole certainly encompasses much more than just sports marketing.

The growing popularity of event marketing can be attributed to its ability to cut through the advertising clutter and reach consumers (as well as other important audiences) in impactful ways. Well-planned and well-orchestrated events also integrate two or more communications objectives for maximum effectiveness. For example, an event that is promotional in nature may also achieve media publicity and/or build relationships with dealers or distributors.

What is the Goal?

Although events can be "leveraged" so that they accomplish several communications objectives, it is best to begin your planning with one central goal. This will keep your planning and execution focused, helping you choose from among the myriad of options that are open to you in event marketing.

Events can make a strong element in the marketing mix when any of the following is your goal:

—Launching a new product

—Introducing your product to a new market or target audience

—Increasing product trial

—Positioning your product or company

—Building personal relationships with the product and people associated with it

—Differentiating your product or company from the competition

—Building brand loyalty

—Establishing your company as a good corporate citizen

—Educating and informing the target audience

—Strengthening relationships with distributors, retailers, or other partners

—Recruiting, training, or motivating employees.

The event you select, and the features you give it, should grow naturally out of your primary goal. As an example, if increasing product trial is a key objective, you should choose an event that reaches the maximum number of people in your target audience and gives them an incentive to try the product via on-site trial or couponing. Also, remember to make every effort to quantify your specific event objective(s) such as providing a specific number of people you want to attract to try the product on-site.

Selecting an Event

Event selection and design is the most critical component in ensuring an event that will meet your marketing objectives. Successful events share the following characteristics:

1. There is a clear and meaningful connection between your product or company and the event itself. A shoe retailer, for example, can reinforce its area of business and convey corporate citizenship by giving away discontinued shoe styles to low-income children in the area. An event for the same retailer that is focused on building brand identity might tie an important product line, such as running shoes, with sponsorship of a marathon.

   At the same time, the presence of your product or company message should not be so intrusive that it interferes with people's enjoyment of the event itself. The sincerity of your company's commitment to the event or cause must be apparent, or the target audience may feel that they are being manipulated into buying a product.

2. Your company or product identity comes through clearly. This is particularly critical in sponsorship situations, where your company may "own" an event exclusively or "share" the event with other sponsors, media partners, or charities. You need to be sure that your identity is not lost on the target audience.

3. There is a compelling appeal to the target audience. Events are costly and time-consuming to stage, and nothing is worse than discovering that your event

has attracted low participation. You must select an event with clear appeal to those you are trying to reach and integrate features that will ensure maximum interest from your target audience. This includes everything from pre-event promotion and advertising to selecting a high-traffic location for an event designed around public participation.

4. The event has news value. Virtually every event can be enhanced with the addition of media coverage. Your event may have an element of "hard news" (i.e., a happening that merits coverage), or it may offer publicity opportunities in the form of human interest features or photo opportunities. When designing your event, you should give consideration to including features that will make the event more newsworthy, such as unusual contests or record-breaking events.

   There will be occasions when media publicity is not vital to your objective. For example, you might hold a seminar to educate a narrow group of prospects about a new technology that only they are in a position to use. While media coverage in a technology-oriented trade journal could be a helpful enhancement, the event would be a success without media coverage as long as it attracts a good number of attendees and generates their interest in the technology.

5. You can incorporate related communications elements that support the event and further your marketing objectives. What are the opportunities for tie-ins with sales promotions, direct mail, advertising, point-of-purchase displays, and/or dealer programs? These elements can be used to bring additional attention to the event and, in some cases, to extend the reach of the event to members of the target audience who may not experience it personally.

   Our client, Famous Footwear, did this when they designed a promotion to donate one dollar to charity for every pair of shoes sold. These same charities were benefiting from the Famous Footwear Criterium, which took place at the conclusion of the promotional period. As a result of this promotion, communicated primarily through outdoor advertising and point-of-purchase displays, even those consumers who were not spectators at the bicycle race became aware of the race and Famous Footwear's sponsorship of it.

Questions to Ask Yourself When Planning an Event

- Do you have the resources (time, money, manpower, connections, etc.) to create your own event, or are you better off "piggybacking" onto an existing and already established event?

- Can you establish a tie with a timed event such as an anniversary, sporting event, or designated week or month (e.g., June is Dairy Month)?

- Are there opportunities to localize the event? Any event that relates to the community in an integral way will be more meaningful to the target audience. If you are creating a new event, you can survey the community to determine issues and concerns that are important to people's lives.

- Are there opportunities to affiliate with a suitable charity or cause? If you and a nonprofit organization share a common interest, you can form a mutually beneficial relationship. The charity receives exposure and the implied endorsement of your company, while you receive the legitimacy and additional media coverage that come from being associated with a charity.

- Can you ally with a media partner who becomes a cosponsor? For many years, we helped plan and execute young adult events for Coors Beer, with contemporary radio stations cosponsoring the event. With a media cosponsor, you can negotiate a regular schedule of media coverage prior to, during, and after the event. This is a commonly used technique for charitable events, fairs, telethons, and sports sponsorships. Bear in mind, however, that news coverage from competing media is far less likely when one or more media are linked to your event as sponsors.

- Can you ally with other business partners who can provide resources and add an extra dimension to your event without overshadowing your involvement? For example, a local food manufacturer could be invited to serve free samples of their food at your event. This stretches your budget and enables the food company to reach consumers. Regardless of how you choose your cosponsors, make sure both parties benefit.

- Is there a theme or creative concept? A "big idea" that is attention-getting and has appeal to the target audience makes it easier to leverage your event with promotions, direct mail, point-of-purchase, and more. In the 1980s, it was the Coors Downtown Beach Party.

- Is a celebrity or expert spokesperson a possible draw? Celebrities with recognizable names (whether they are local or national in stature) can help attract attendance at your event and generate additional media coverage. If your event is a seminar or convention, the most appealing speaker may be one with strong credentials in the field, even if he/she is not a recognizable name outside of his/her own field.

- How can your company or product identity be reinforced? Signage, banners, giveaways, displays, clothing, and equipment are just some of the ways you can add your identity to the event. If media coverage from television and/or newspaper is expected, make sure your identity is positioned where it will be picked up by the camera.

- What is the timetable? Building a realistic and detailed timetable is a critical step in any successful event marketing program. Extremely long lead times are often required to plan, promote, and implement a successful event. Remember, detailed planning is the key to successful events.

- What is the budget? Budget is another factor that should be planned for in advance. A realistic budget can help you evaluate, while still in the planning phase, whether the event you are designing is likely to be worth the investment. Naturally, careful budgeting also helps ensure that you have the resources to execute the event of your choice. Usually, it is best to use the task method in budgeting and then pare back accordingly on a priority basis.

- How will the success of your event be evaluated? Consider evaluation methods during the up-front planning, so that you can build in any appropriate success measures from the start. Evaluation methods can range from simple counts of attendance, product sold, coupons distributed, and the like. Or, evaluation can incorporate primary market research for measurement of pre- and post-event target market awareness, perceptions, attitudes, and behavior.

Types of Events

A wide variety of events are available as marketing communications tools. This list will serve as an idea-starter.

Announcement of a new entity or product

News conference

Celebrity appearance

Spokesperson tour

Contest/competition

Professional sporting event

Amateur sporting event

Walkathon/bikeathon

Grand opening/open house

Product couponing/sampling event

Remote broadcast

Dedication/groundbreaking

Commemorative ceremony

Award presentation

Carnival

Parade

Street festival

Vehicle appearance or rides

Community cleanup

Cultural fair

Science fair

Concert

Book release

Telethon

Lecture/demonstration/exhibit

Information display

Seminar

Meeting or convention

Research presentation

DOS AND DON'TS

Do

- Utilize promotions to encourage incremental target market behavior.
- Make sure promotions are measurable.
- Utilize specific promotions for short-term durations.
- While promotions are effective in increasing sales in the short term, remember that they also can have long-term attitudinal and behavioral consequences.
- Try to utilize promotions that are consistent with and will enhance your positioning.

- Plan your promotions so that they complement the use of the other marketing mix tools. (An example of this would be national image advertising complemented with co-op in ad features of the product and point-of-sale displays in the stores. All advertising would also incorporate the same basic selling theme and tone.)

- Make sure you determine the cost and the potential payback of your promotions before implementing them.

- Evaluate the success or failure of each promotion to help in developing stronger promotions in the future.

- Promotion can be a very powerful, but expensive, marketing tool. Plan and evaluate carefully.

- Be aware of an ever-growing promotion problem—promotion fraud. Specifically, learn about coupon fraud among consumers and retailers, as well as refund/premium fraud among consumers where promotion offers require proofs of purchase.

- Whenever possible, test new promotions before making a major investment and using them on a broader scale.

- Use incentives that appeal to your target market and that are realistic for a vast majority of the target market to obtain. A sweepstakes will not pull as strongly as a percent-off coupon because the reward is not as obtainable. Only a few lucky people win the sweepstakes, but everyone is eligible for the coupon.

- Remember, successful promotions have optimum value perception among the target market with minimum monetary investment by the marketer.

- To have a successful promotion, remember that you need broad target market appeal for the product, a strong promotion incentive, high promotion awareness, and minimum restrictions for participation.

- Remember, 90+ percent of an event's success is in the preplanning of the event itself.

Don't

- Don't expect promotions to solve long-term sales declines or create a loyal consumer franchise among those who purchase the product for its inherent benefits—leave that to such other marketing tools, as packaging, product improvements, and image advertising.

- Don't rely on only a few promotional devices. Consider all the promotional tools available to you, but only use those that are appropriate to your product.

- Don't overuse or develop a dependence on promotions. This may cause an erosion of value and image.

- Don't schedule promotions without reviewing the entire marketing calendar and the specific promotion schedule. Consecutive use of similar promotions will diminish the success of the second promotion.

- Don't run promotions just because you ran them last year. Think strategically about what you are trying to accomplish.

- Don't give deals unless you can document that it builds the business.

- A promotion should not replace other tools of the marketing mix; use this marketing tool for its inherent strengths.

APPENDIX OF PROMOTION VEHICLES

Definition of Promotional Vehicles

Couponing	A type of promotion involving the distribution of a coupon that has a value upon redemption.
Newspaper ROP (run of press)	A method for delivering promotion incentives that involves the printing of an incentive in the newspaper, usually in an ad, on regular newsprint, with no special paper or inserts.
Magazines and supplements	A method for delivering promotion incentives, commonly coupons, printed on the page as part of an ad. Two variations are the pop-up coupon, printed on separate card stock and inserted into the magazine's binding, and tip-in coupons, which are glued to supplement inserts.
Cross-ruff coupons	An execution method for couponing that involves taking the consumer from one product, store, or department, carrying the coupon to a different product, store, or department for which the coupon is redeemable.

Sampling	A type of promotion that involves the free trial of a product.
Premiums	A type of promotion involving a product (gift) of perceived value that is given away, or made available, with the purchase of the product.
Self-liquidating premiums	An execution method for premiums, where the customer is required to cover the cost of the premium via payment.
Proof-of-purchase	An execution method for premiums, where the premium is sent to the customer in return for proof of one or more purchases.
Sale priced reduction or cents-off label	A method for executing the price reduction promotion; it can be in the form of advertised sales prices, prepriced goods, labels on the product that flag the price reduction, or price packs, which are specially priced make ups of different size than the regular package.
Free standing insert (FSI)	An insert with coupons or other promotional offers that are loosely inserted in a carrier such as the newspaper. Co-op FSI's carry multiple coupons for different product categories.
Instant coupon	A method of coupon delivery where the coupon is attached to the outside of the package. The consumer can pull it off in-store and utilize it during purchase.
Bonus pack	A method for executing the price reduction promotion. It involves providing bonus product for the price or close to the price of the original product.
Refunds	A type of promotion offering money back after the purchase and usually requiring some proof of purchase.
On pack/in pack	A method of promotion delivery where the offer is either flagged on the package or included in the package.
Stamps	Stamps may be redeemed for some item of value once specific levels have been accumulated.
Contests and sweepstakes	Games and events in which customers participate for the chance of winning a prize.

Evaluation of Promotional Vehicles

Promotion	Objectives	Execution/Delivery Methods	Advantages	Disadvantages
Couponing	Stimulate trial	Sales force	1. Allows pinpoint targeting of customers 2. Creates a value-added sales call	1. Very high delivery costs per coupon 2. Distribution of coupons limited
	Increase frequency of purchase	Direct mail	1. Higher redemption rates 2. Permits selective customer targeting	1. High delivery costs per coupon
	Increase multiple purchases	Newspaper ROP	1. Low delivery cost per coupon 2. Permits limited geographic distribution 3. Offers flexibility in timing, size, and layout of coupon ad	1. Lower redemption rates 2. Clutter and competitive advertising 3. High potential for misredemptions
		Magazines and supplements	1. Low delivery cost per coupon 2. Permits mass distribution to segmented audience 3. Allows some geographical selectivity through regional editions of national magazines 4. Allows high quality reproductions for creative appeal	1. Loss of flexibility in timing due to long lead times for insertion 2. Lower redemption rates relative to other vehicles
		Free standing inserts (FSI)	1. Higher redemption rates than ROP coupons 2. Lower delivery cost per coupon than direct mail 3. Permits limited geographic mass distribution 4. Permits more creativity than with ROP	1. High potential for misredemptions 2. Needs longer lead time to print and insert than with ROP
		In package/on package coupons	1. Draws attention to package at p-o-p 2. Higher redemption rates 3. Lower delivery cost per coupon	1. Limited stimulus for trial by new category users 2. Customer may seek simultaneous redemption of

Promotion	Objectives	Execution/Delivery Methods	Advantages	Disadvantages
			4. Effective stimulant of repeat purchase	coupon on package and previously distributed coupon 3. Distribution limited to users of the product category
		Cross-ruff coupons	1. The product the coupon is promoting receives implied endorsement from brand carrying coupon 2. Package with coupon perceived as value added 3. Can obtain trial of promoted brand by new users with demographics similar to carrier brand 4. Strong selling brand can cross-sell for weaker selling brand 5. High redemption rate if promoted brand has natural relationship to carrier brand 6. Low delivery cost of coupon	1. Effectiveness of coupon is a function of the effectiveness of carrier product 2. Limited distribution and target market reach
		Instant coupon	1. Very high redemption rate 2. Very low distribution cost per coupon	1. More likely to appeal to current users rather than create new trial 2. High gross redemption rates
		On-shelf instant coupon machine	1. Simple to use 2. High redemption rates	1. Limited distribution of in-store machines 2. Costs per redemption high due to the technology investment
		Coupons generated electronically at checkout lane	1. Based on consumer profile generated by purchases	1. Shopper must hold on to coupon until their next visit to retailer

Promotion	Objectives	Execution/Delivery Methods	Advantages	Disadvantages
			2. High redemption rates	2. Coupon is restricted to the retailer that issued it
Sampling	Develop initial trial of new products	In pack or on pack	1. Low distribution costs 2. Sample receives implied endorsement of carrier brand 3. Pack with sample increases trial of carrier brand 4. Selective distribution of pack with sample permits testing of sample's promotional effectiveness	1. Distribution limited to buyers of carrier brand 2. Trade may reject package if unusual size creates special handling requirements 3. Expensive because of cost of the sample and delivery of product 4. High cost of sample
		Direct mail	1. Selective customer permits a variety of creative and product presentations 2. Delivery may be timed to tie in with other promotions and advertising 3. May create consumer interest forcing the trade to carry the product 4. Permits mass distribution	1. Some products' size, weight, or fragility prevents mailing 2. High delivery costs per sample 3. Any wasted coverage due to inaccuracies in mailing list is very expensive
Premiums	Provide added value to the purchase of your product thus increasing trial Create impulse trial Develop continuity of purchases and multiple purchases	Self-liquidating premiums	1. Potential value added to product at minimum cost to the marketer 2. Premiums of value often get trade display 3. Image of brand may be enhanced through association with quality premium or premium consistent with brand's positioning 4. Repeat purchases can be increased by requiring multiple purchases for premium eligibility	1. Typically unused premiums cannot be returned forcing testing of consumer response rates. Even then an unpopular premium may result in an inventory of costly and unwanted premiums 2. Stimulates sales less than free premiums because consumer must make cash outlay

Promotion	Objectives	Execution/Delivery Methods	Advantages	Disadvantages
			5. Permits geographic and creative flexibility	
		In pack or on pack	1. May force increased shelf space and merchandising support from the trade	1. Premium should be tested to accurately predict consumer response
			2. Provides added value to the consumer	2. Physical size of premium may cause trade to refuse to handle product due to space limitations
			3. Premiums can be targeted to specific consumer segments	3. Poor quality or inappropriate premium may detract from brand's image
			4. Promotes trial and repeat purchase	
			5. Permits geographic selectivity	
		Bonus pack	1. Increases perceived value at p-o-p	1. Potential trade resistance to larger pack without profit incentives
			2. Stocking up takes customers out of market for competitors' products and habituates them to using your product	2. Customers may feel cheated when package returns to original size
		Proof-of-purchase	1. Encourages multiple purchases and continuity of purchases	1. Lack of immediate reinforcement reduces consumer interest
			2. Low redemption rate permits use of higher value premium	2. Impulse sales weaker than with instant premiums
			3. Consumer can be encouraged to trade up to larger size or more expensive item	3. Supporting advertising often needed to promote longer-term purchasing commitment
Price reductions	Stimulate incremental purchase/trial Influence purchase decision/increase purchase ratio at P-O-P Increase purchases per transaction Increase dollar amount per transaction	Sale price reduction	1. Greater profits may result if expected increase in sales exceeds effects from margin decrease	1. Continued price reductions can erode brand image over time
			2. Can counter competitors' activities encouraging repeat purchases by current users	2. Potential for price wars
				3. Too frequent price reductions makes reduced price the expected norms so consumers won't

Promotion	Objectives	Execution/Delivery Methods	Advantages	Disadvantages
		Cents-off label	1. Increased attention from flagging of package can influence purchase decisions at p-o-p 2. Increased trade support results from anticipated increase in product demand 3. Sales force provided with opportunity to increase sales to the trade	purchase at full price 1. Some stores will not accept flagged or prepriced packaging
Refunds	Develop trial and continuity of purchase Encourage multiple purchases (where multiple proofs of purchase required)	Same methods as for couponing	1. High perceived value by consumers 2. Relatively low cost promotion because large percentage of nonredemption 3. Can extend buying period of seasonal products with multiple purchase requirement 4. Flagging package with refund offer increases p-o-p and impulse sales 5. Multiple purchase requirement limits number of successful redemptions	1. Lack of immediate gratification reduces incentive to buy 2. Tends to reward current users rather than creating new trial
Repeat purchase offers	Develop repeat and continuity of purchases Increase purchases per transaction Encourage seasonal purchases Reduce competitive purchases	Refund program On pack or in pack premium program Stamps	1. Continuity programs help to create brand loyalty and establish consumer purchasing habits 2. Repeat purchase requirement often creates multiple purchases, temporarily taking the consumer out of the market for the product class and	1. Requires consumers to make a long-term commitment to the product 2. Thrust of repeat purchase program is to maintain current users not to develop new trial

Promotion	Objectives	Execution/Delivery Methods	Advantages	Disadvantages
			reducing chances of success for competitors' programs	
Contests, games and sweepstakes[1]	Develop multiple purchases Enhance brand image and develop attention through excitement of contest	Product in store, p-o-p media	1. Contest can be built around inherent drama of the product and communicate specific product attributes 2. Contest can be directed to specific target audiences 3. Contest's excitement can help generate trade support and p-o-p displays	1. Impact is limited since there is no guarantee of reward. Participation is less than that of price incentives, bonus packs, and other instant gratification promotions 2. Contest targets current users more than they develop new trial 3. There are many legal issues which must be considered before execution
Trade promotions	Increase trial by new customers Create multiple purchases Increase distribution Increase shelf space Obtain p-o-p merchandising support Introduce new or improved products to the trade	Price reductions or incentives Refunds Contest aimed at the trade P-o-p displays	1. Promotions to the trade help insure the product's availability for consumers and results in favorable merchandising 2. Limited target market for promotion makes it easier to implement 3. Promotion easily tailored to meet specific needs 4. Can limit competition's in-store efforts.	1. Trade can come to expect deals 2. Can take away funds from consumer advertising and promotions so that even if the trade stocks the product the ability to generate consumer demand is diminished

[1]While in some sweepstakes, games, or events, purchase of the product is not required, association with the product is usually necessary to participate. For example, the law in many states makes purchase an illegal requirement for participation in a sweepstakes game card promotion. While the consumer is not forced to purchase to receive a game card, he or she must visit the retail establishment or write the company to receive a game card. And, in the case of mass participation events (e.g., a brand-sponsored concert), association usually equates to attending the event.

14

ADVERTISING MESSAGE

Now that you have decided how to market, position, price, distribute, sell, and promote your product, you are ready to prepare the advertising segment of your marketing plan. This is another key learning chapter, because it deals with the translation of marketing objectives and strategies into advertising, which is usually the most visible communication to your external and internal targets. While developing the advertising message portion of your plan requires strategic and innovative thinking, the most fun will come when you and/or your agency actually get into developing the advertising executions. Because this is a "how to" for marketing plan preparation, this chapter will not review how to develop the advertising executions.

This chapter will discuss how to provide the direction for the advertising message for both consumer and business-to-business advertising. In most cases the major strategic differences between the two types of advertising occur not in the message but in the type medium used to deliver the message. In this book, advertising will refer to the message and media will refer to the message delivery method.

From This Chapter You Will Learn

The definition of advertising.

How to use a disciplined process that will lead to creative advertising that sells.

How to arrive at and write advertising objectives.

How to develop an advertising strategy that will be a catalyst for attention-getting advertising that clearly communicates and sells.

Criterium for the ideal advertising strategy.

Executional elements to consider before preparing the actual advertising.

How to select an advertising agency that will best execute the advertising program and your marketing plan.

OVERVIEW

Definition

Before discussing how the communication elements are factored into a marketing plan, it is necessary to understand the differences between these communication elements. It is a common error to bunch advertising, public relations or publicity, promotion, and merchandising together as one and the same. In fact, all of these forms of communication are very different from each other in terms of what they are capable of doing and what role they each play in the marketing plan. For this marketing plan discussion, we will define advertising as that which informs and persuades through *paid* media (television, radio, magazine, newspaper, outdoor, and direct mail).

What Is Expected of Your Advertising?

Before you begin developing the advertising section of your marketing plan, you must decide what your advertising can realistically accomplish. We know that advertising can build awareness and positively affect attitude. For your product, advertising can build recognition, help create a positive image, and differentiate it from the competition. Advertising can also build store traffic, assist in introducing new products and line extensions, feature products improvements, and announce promotions. Specifically, in the business-to-business category, advertising can also generate customer leads ("please send me more information") and open doors for the sales force. You must make sure you know what you expect advertising to accomplish for your product.

In addition to building awareness and positively affecting attitude, advertising can sometimes also move the target to action and to buy your product through direct response advertising. Direct mail is a good example of this. However, in the majority of situations, advertising cannot make the sale unless the product is on the shelf, there is a conveniently located store to visit, the wholesaler carries your product line, and/or a sales call is made to detail the product and close the sale. Remember, advertising alone usually cannot initiate behavior, the behavior element should be included as a marketing objective previously presented in the plan.

THE DISCIPLINED PROCESS FOR ADVERTISING

Because of its tremendous attention-getting power and inherent creativity, advertising is continually on stage for everyone to critique. Accordingly, nearly everyone thinks they are experts on advertising, because it is a marketing tool that has much subjectivity associated with it. Therefore, it stands to reason that the more subjective it is as a marketing tool, the more necessary it is to use a disciplined process to arrive at advertising that sells. This is basically a 1-2-3 process:

1. Define your advertising objectives.

2. Write your advertising strategy.

3. Detail what will go into the execution.

By now you have no doubt come up with a number of advertising ideas. However, before proceeding to the actual execution of your creative ideas, go through this disciplined process. Use of this disciplined approach will assure that the final advertising will be effective or at least more effective than if you had gone with the first ad idea that came to mind. Also, it should be pointed out that, given the choice between non-marketing-based advertising and advertising based on sound marketing, the latter will win most often. It will win because it is data-based and relates to the real marketplace, communicating the meaningful product attributes to the right target market. Accordingly, great advertising is usually based on great marketing. Further, bear in mind that your market positioning is the key to effective advertising. It is, in essence, the bridge from the more objective marketing to the more subjective advertising.

Task 1
Advertising Objectives

Advertising Awareness and Attitude Objectives

Advertising objectives deal with what you want your advertising to accomplish. The objectives are quantifiable, while the advertising strategy is not. Your advertising objectives will nearly always define *awareness* and *attitude* goals as they relate to the target market. The strategy deals primarily with describing the message communication needed to fulfill the advertising objectives.

Refer back to the marketing communication goals and the specific values goals you set for the advertising segment of your plan. You will want to use these value goals as a starting point in setting your advertising objectives. In addition to unaided awareness objectives, you might also want to add "first mention" or "top-of-mind" awareness objectives if you did not previously use them as advertising message value goals in the value strategies segment of this plan. Or you might want to include very specific advertising awareness goals under advertising objectives. Advertising awareness usually refers to that percentage of the target market that has read, seen, or heard advertising for your product. Unless the respondents who were asked about the advertising can actually identify a portion of the advertising message, they should not be counted as having advertising awareness.

Before you begin, check to see that you did *not* include advertising objectives in your marketing objectives and strategies section. The tendency is to deal with communication issues such as recall and understanding under marketing, but they belong under advertising.

Measurable Advertising Objectives

Even if you are not planning, or cannot afford, to implement a research program to measure the effectiveness of the advertising, setting measurable advertising objectives will force you to objectively evaluate the advertising challenge. Further, if your time period to achieve the advertising objectives differs from the time period set for the marketing objectives, indicate the time period with the advertising objectives.

Exhibit 14.1 presents some examples of how to define your advertising objectives. It is easier to set your advertising objectives if you have primary research. However, in many cases you will not have done market research that establishes a benchmark from which to measure awareness and attitude changes. Nevertheless, it is a good learning process to estimate (even if you can only make educated guesses) what percent of unaided awareness is necessary to affect a predisposed attitude to buy that then translates to a specific percent of the target market that will purchase.

You should also include a rationale for the advertising awareness and attitude objectives based on available awareness and attitude research. With or without this type of research, your rationale should include a discussion of the competitive share of market and the strength of your communications program versus that of the competition's past and anticipated marketing activity, particularly their advertising program.

Exhibit 14.1 How to Write Advertising Objectives

Awareness Objectives

Increase unaided awareness among the target market from 18 percent to 25 percent.

Establish among the target market an unaided awareness percentage equal to twice the number to purchase the product.

Increase advertising awareness from 8 percent to 12 percent.

Attitudinal Objectives

Establish a leadership image with 25 percent of the target market.

Move the product quality attitude ranking among the target market from fourth to third place.

Task 2
Advertising Strategy

The advertising strategy, also referred to as the creative strategy, is the catalyst of effective advertising. It provides direction on what should be communicated in the advertising message and how it should be communicated. It is a big part of the *means* that gets the desired product perception into the mind of the consumer. This strategy is the guide for development of creative and communicative advertising; the goals are to gain attention, be remembered, positively affect attitudes, and help move the target market to purchase your product. It becomes a guide for those (possibly yourself) who will actually create the advertising. Further, the advertising strategy describes the personality of the advertising and the parameters of the creative environment in which the advertising must perform. Without this guide, the final advertising could very well be exceptionally entertaining but not necessarily effective. Although we may like the advertising, it might not communicate the benefits of your product that will fulfill the needs and wants of the specified target market.

Not only a guide for creative development, the advertising strategy is also the basis against which creative work is evaluated to make sure that advertising communicates effectively. Usually, you want to develop alternative creative approaches for the advertising strategy and then identify the approach that best executes the strategy. Also, if you are having an advertising agency execute the creative, both the client and the agency should have input into and mutually agree on the written strategy before it is executed. This strategy agreement is necessary so that, when the advertising work is presented, there is no confusion or disagreement in terms of the description of the product, specific benefits, claims made, and feeling of the advertising. Further, having agreed upon a strategy up front will save time in creative development and help eliminate frustration for all involved.

The advertising strategy should include:

- *Promise:* Define the reward/benefit for the specific target market in solving a problem or taking advantage of an opportunity.

- *Support for this promise:* Substantiate the promise or provide reasons to believe it.

- *Tone:* Describe the feeling of the planned advertising that is consistent with the personality of the product. The tone must be appropriate not only for your product but also for the target market of the advertising.

Look to your positioning statement for direction when writing the advertising strategy, because it will be the key to developing an advertising strategy that differentiates your product from the competition. Make sure your advertising strategy directly conveys the image you want to instill in the minds of the target market.

Don't expect to complete an advertising strategy on the first attempt. Plan to rewrite each segment of the advertising strategy a number of times until you arrive at a strategy that clearly states what you want your final advertising to communicate. Each word in your advertising strategy is critical; therefore, make sure it communicates the intended meaning. Keep the strategy simple, clear, and single-minded in focus. Make sure your strategy conveys the inherent personality of your product that can come alive in your advertising and play to the needs and emotions of the target person.

The advertising strategy that has been reworked and included in your marketing plan should be the strategy that reflects the positioning and provides the *overall direction* for a *unified advertising campaign*. However, it might be that your marketing plan calls for additional, separate advertising strategies, such as for specific products within a company line. For example, an advertising strategy for Green Giant Corn would be a modification of the overall campaign strategy for Green Giant Canned Vegetables. Also, you may need separate strategies for special geographic and demographic markets, promotions, or trade advertising.

Although it is likely that you will need substrategies, it is important that your overall advertising strategy is written to be a campaign strategy to guide all of your advertising. Your primary strategy should lead to an advertising campaign in which all the individual advertisements continually reinforce your positioning. This is very important, because the advertising campaign will create a unified image and will provide a consistency for all of your creative executions. Obviously, there are always exceptions to this, particularly if you are marketing very different products to very different target markets.

An effective, strategic advertising campaign will incorporate similarities. The more similarities, the stronger the campaign. The advertising within a campaign should include as many common properties as possible, such as a similar look, sound, and/or feel/tonality, in order to convey a consistent personality. Further, in most cases, each advertisement will include a unified, basic selling idea (theme line), such as "Fly the Friendly Skies" or "Marlboro Country."

The rewards of developing a campaign are many. It will become cumulative in scope, with each advertisement reinforcing the others for a multiple effect, making your advertising work harder and maximizing your advertising investment.

Remember, before moving on to execution, include a brief rationale for the advertising objectives and advertising strategy(ies), defining why the objectives are attainable and why the strategies are appropriate. The rationale should include specific reasons for what is included in the strategy.

Exhibit 14.2 presents two examples of an advertising strategy. The first is a business-to-business example for a national printing company that wants to create an image for itself as the best printer for high-end quality work. The second, a retail example, is for a fabrics and crafts retail chain that wants to create an image of being the do-it-yourself home decorating store for women.

Criteria for the Ideal Advertising Strategy

The following is an eleven-point criteria to review both before and after you prepare your advertising strategy.

1. *It makes a promise to the customer.*

   For example, people are always tuned into the radio station WIFM. Why? What's In It For Me? Can your creative strategy answer this question for your product? For Northwest Fabrics & Crafts, the promise is "the best store for

Exhibit 14.2 How to Write Advertising Strategies

Strategy Against Users of High-End Printing

Promise
Convince the purchaser of high-end printing that Royle is the high quality printer for mid-run, high-end jobs because Royle has expert press people and special printing capability to provide sheetfed quality with the economy, efficiency, and versatility of the Web presses.

Support for This Promise
1. All major customer segments rated Royle's print quality high relative to the competition.
2. Royle utilizes a Total Quality Program in its pressroom to ensure consistent quality.
3. Royle's Heidelberg Web 8 and Web 16 presses have the capabilities to deliver the best of high-end printing.

Tone
The tone of the advertising should be preemptive and professional, confident (inspiring trust), and project a quality nature that reflects the best of all printing.

Rationale
Results of the survey research, including feedback from the focus groups, indicated that print buyers are involved in the print-buying process not on a personal level but on a purely professional level, particularly given that they often have a wide variety of responsibilities beyond print buying. Further, Royle's efforts to build trial among the target will require establishing a credibility and trust that they truly offer the quality and service they claim.

Strategy Against Women Who Decorate Their Homes

Promise
Convince women 25–54 with children who decorate their homes that Northwest Fabrics & Crafts (NWF&C) is the best store to shop to help decorate their homes because NWF&C is *the* Do-It-Yourself Home Decorating and Activities Center with both fabrics and craft materials for the home.

Support for This Promise
NWF&C has the ideas, the fabrics, and craft materials—from florals to custom framing, along with the experienced help of the store's staff—to make the customer's home decorating creativity come to life, enabling her to make a more comfortable and beautiful home for her family.

Tone
The tone of the advertising should be warm, helpful, creative (full of ideas), and identify with the unique personality and self-expression of each home decorator.

Rationale
No fabrics or crafts retail chain has positioned itself against the do-it-yourself home decorator, making NWF&C singular in its preemptive claim. Research and experience have shown creativity and self-expression to be important.
—Having both the craft materials and the fabrics is an important point of difference for NWF&C.
—The experience element comes into play both with the in-store help available (at the beginning and throughout a project) as well as in the availability of classes.

---

decorating your home," and for Royle it is "the high quality printer for mid-run, high-end jobs."

2. *It's brief.*

Ideally your strategy can be reduced to one word: the *safe* car, the *caring* hospital. Your promise should be easy to understand. The reason? Whether it is a billboard or a television commercial, people will make a judgment about whether they are interested in the first four seconds...or less. You must get to the point.

3. *It's unexpected.*

   People expect all food to taste good. They expect all shoes to fit. What is so unexpected about your promise that it will draw attention?

4. *It is based on an unexpected consumer insight.*

   Moms don't have time to shop anymore. More people are single and childless and pets are substitutes for children. People drink milk because it makes other things taste better, not because it's just good for them. Adults are looking for alternatives to alcohol and cigarettes. Women expect doctors to be competent, but they prefer a doctor who will treat them like a human being with feelings. All of these insights have led to great advertising strategies.

5. *It passes the "So what" test.*

   Most people don't wake up in the morning thinking about your product or your company. What is so *important* about your promise? Why should someone care? For example:

   "Introducing the new carbon monoxide detector."

   So what.

   "It can save your life."

   I'll take two.

6. *It answers one of three questions.*

   a) What does the product, company, or retail chain do?

   (Brand name shoes for less)

   b) Who's it for?

   (The do-it-yourself home decor store)

   c) How is it different from the competition?

   (Twice the sugar. Twice the caffeine.)

7. *It's believable.*

   People don't believe their own priests or government or news media anymore. Why should they believe someone like you who is trying to sell them something? You need hard proof. The more unexpected your promise, the more critical the believability of your strategy.

8. *It is relevant to a particular target market.*

   If you are selling a toy to parents, you may want to stress it's educational value. If you are selling the same toy to kids, you may want to stress how fun it is. Different strokes for different folks. It doesn't matter what you want. It doesn't matter what you think customers should want. All that matters is what your customers want. Make sure the inherent drama or uniqueness of your product will come through in your strategy as the something your target customers want.

9. *You can own the strategy.*

   People's existing perception of your company or product leads them to believe that you are the best company to own the promise of this strategy. It will be difficult for your competitors to copy immediately—giving you a head start. You have the media firepower to hold and own share of mind against the competition. You can own the strategy even when imitators appear.

10. *It leads naturally to great creative in all media.*

Creative people find it much easier to create great advertising when they are working with a great strategy—clear, simple, real, believable, and unexpected. They find the strategy easy to communicate in all media, not just print or television.

11. *It works for a long time.*

The Marlboro Man is still riding through Marlboro Country and United Airlines is still flying the friendly skies.

It is almost impossible to devise a single strategy that meets all these criteria, but it pays to review the strengths and weaknesses of various strategies against these tests.

**Task 3
Consideration of
Executional Elements**

Most often the execution segment of the advertising section is not included in the marketing plan but is detailed in what is sometimes referred to as an advertising implementation plan. This plan includes all of the information needed by those responsible to create the advertising. An example of an implementation plan format is provided in Appendix C.

In this separate document you might want to include additional copy or product information that is important to know, but that, in order to maintain strategic focus, is not included in the advertising strategy. For example, along with potential legal considerations (in this separate plan), you might include advertising requirements, such as:

- How the company and product name/logo must be used in the advertising

- How the theme line must be used in all advertising

- Product line/store location to be included

- Preproduction copy test requirements, production cost parameters, ad size, etc.

HELPFUL HINTS

**Review "How To
Create Advertising"
Sources**

With this advertising segment written, you are halfway to achieving creative advertising that will motivate. This book's aim is to show how to write a marketing plan, not how to create advertising. Therefore, you may want to refer to a number of "how to create advertising" sources. These books are available in your local library or nearby bookstore and are useful even if you do retain an advertising agency.

**How to Select an
Advertising Agency**

Once you have completed your marketing plan, you might find you need additional expertise to help in the execution of the advertising and other elements of the marketing plan. If this is the case, here are some things to keep in mind when selecting an advertising agency:

1. Do not select an advertising agency before comparing a number of different agencies.

2. In order to arrive at a number of different agencies to evaluate you can:
   - Solicit agency referrals from fellow business associates.

- Review advertising in various media and ask the management of the particular media vehicle (magazine, newspaper, station, etc.) for the name of the agency that placed the specific advertisement(s) that impressed you. Also, ask the media management for their agency recommendations.
- Check out the *Standard Director of Advertising Agencies* (referred to as the Red Book). It is probably available in your local library, and it lists agencies by geographic areas, along with each agency's clients, size, and key personnel.

3. Once you have arrived at a number of agencies to evaluate, interview them and make a selection. Or if you have a large list of agencies (five or more) to evaluate, have each agency complete a questionnaire. An advertising agency questionnaire is shown in Exhibit 14.3. After reviewing the completed questionnaires, select three or four agencies for personal presentations. Involve others in your company when reviewing the agencies to provide both more perspective and consensus.

4. The agency you select should:
   - Be genuinely honest and not promise miracles.
   - Sincerely care about you and your business and work with you as a partner, not just a vendor.
   - Provide the optimum in personal attention, experience, and expertise. The agency people must have real credentials.
   - Be a leader and not a follower. You should not have to tell the agency what to do with your advertising; they should provide sound recommendations.
   - Not consistently turn over staff and clients.
   - Be looking for a long relationship, not quick fixes.
   - Develop good advertising but also thoroughly understand good marketing.
   - Provide a real value (good advertising at competitive rates) and be able to document it.
   - Have financial strength, accurate accounting systems, and a billing program to fit your needs.
   - Have full-service capability. The agency should be able to provide real expertise in assisting you with your creative (including campaign development) and media needs, along with some assistance in marketing, promotion, merchandising, public relations, and perhaps even research.
   - Have the right ingredients to match your organization's needs in terms of size, consumer/business-to-business experience, staff personalities, and level of expertise. Is your advertising account/budget too small/big for them? There must be a match between agency ingredients and client needs in order for both to find the right chemistry for a mutually rewarding relationship.

5. Before making a selection decision, it is also a good idea to give the agency finalists a real product problem to solve in order to assess their strategic thinking and execution abilities.

6. Before making the final decision on an agency, actually visit their offices and check with a few of their current and past clients. It's amazing what you will learn. How many quality people does the agency really have? Do clients receive the agency's account supervisor's personal involvement? Does the agency come up with big ideas that can be affordably implemented? Does the agency pay attention to details?

Exhibit 14.3 Advertising Agency Questionnaire

Your Business Strategy
1. What objectives is your agency, as a business enterprise, pursuing?
2. What business strategy has your agency adopted for achieving these objectives?
3. What do you consider to be the principal product sold by your agency? What is the main competitive advantage it has over that of other agencies?
4. What method do you have for controlling the quality of your agency's service (specifically in the areas of marketing counsel and creative development/execution)?

Your Marketing and Advertising Philosophy and Practice
1. What is good marketing?
2. Do you prepare marketing plans and, if so, what is your approach?
3. What makes advertising effective? Include three examples of your most effective advertising.
4. How do you measure the effectiveness of advertising?
5. What is the method you use for developing effective advertising?
6. What are your attitudes/opinions on the role of research in advertising?
7. To what extent do you feel an advertising agency should or could act as a marketing support function?
8. To what consumer/business-to-business marketing successes has your agency recently contributed in a major way? When were they completed? On what basis do you judge them successful? Please limit your examples to no more than three.

Factual Information About Your Agency and Its Services
1. What was the total billing of your agency office (and of the entire agency if applicable) for each of the previous five fiscal years?
2. Which 12 months make up your fiscal year?
3. What percent of your billing is in each of the major media?
4. What is the amount of your largest account billing? Your smallest? Please submit a list of your current clients.
5. Describe the stability/longevity of your relationships with your clients in some way that will be more meaningful than a single average number of years figure.
6. What accounts have you added and what accounts have you lost in the past three years? Why? What is/was their approximate annual billing? (This can be a total figure if confidentiality is required.)
7. What experience does your agency have with consumer goods/retail/service/business-to-business, and which of these accounts do you believe would be of distinct value to our business?
8. Who are the senior general management and department management executives in your office? *Briefly*, what is the background of each one, including length of service and experience with your agency and other agencies or client organizations?
9. To what extent, if any, would these key executives participate in work on our business?
10. Does your agency have a good history of profitability? Are you currently financially sound?
11. Briefly describe your standard billing policies. What services would be covered by commissions earned. What would be billed net (and at what rate)? What would be marked up?
12. If your prefer fee, how do you compute the fee?
13. Are you willing to negotiate a compensation plan?
14. Describe your agency's research capabilities and how they have contributed to one or more of your clients successes.
15. Describe the interaction of the research department with the account service, creative, and media departments.
16. Describe your agency's media capabilities, including information on the following: planning, execution, and post analysis for national and local broadcast and print media; marketing and media measurement/planning sources; and media planning and experience.
17. Briefly discuss how the agency's media expertise has contributed to the successful marketing of one or more of your client's products.
18. Include a brief discussion of your media departments organization/operational structure.
19. If available, describe your promotion, merchandising, and publicity capabilities and experience.

New Product/Concept Development
1. What role do you think your agency could play in the development of new product ideas?
2. Do you have a specific system for product idea generation? If so, please describe it.
3. What are some of the major contributions you have made to the development of new products for your clients? Have these new products been successful?

DOS AND DON'TS

Do

- Make sure marketing leads the advertising.

- Use positioning as the bridge to effective advertising.

- Use the disciplined step-by-step process in developing creative advertising.

- Remember the awareness, attitude, and action sequence as you are developing your advertising program. Review the tactical value goals you set for the advertising tool in Step Six, Communication Goals.

- Make sure your advertising objectives are measurable.

- Make sure your advertising strategy has focus and provides the direction that will lead to advertising that fulfills the emotional as well as rational needs of the target person.

- Develop and evaluate alternative creative executions for the agreed upon advertising strategy.

- Ideally, prepare actual advertising messages that fulfill the desires of the target market, client, and advertising agency, in that order. Remember the target market's needs always come before those of the client and the agency.

- Develop specific advertising objectives and strategies for each target market if you are advertising to more than one.

- Make sure that before and after you develop the advertising strategy you review it against the Criteria for the Ideal Advertising Strategy.

- Develop campaigns, not just ads.

- Make sure your advertising communicates and is creative, which means it should be attention getting and relevant.

- Before producing the final advertising, ask others not directly involved with developing the advertising executions what the advertising says to them and what feeling they get from it.

- If you plan to use an advertising agency, do a thorough agency search and screen.

Don't

- Don't confuse advertising with other communication tools.

- Don't expect advertising to make the sale by itself.

- Don't advertise if you cannot deliver the product as advertised.

- Don't expect to sell anything without first making the target market aware of what you are selling.

- Don't begin creating any advertising until you have agreed upon a written objective(s) and strategy.

- Don't accept any creative approach (whether your idea or the agency's) unless it is on strategy.

- Don't create advertising that you cannot afford to produce.

- Don't create advertising that is so expensive to develop that you can't afford adequate media to deliver the message.

- Don't make your advertising different just to be different but to better sell your product.

- Don't drop a campaign because you and/or your agency become tired of it; do this only if it doesn't communicate and motivate. Most likely your target market has not tired of the advertising.

- Don't create advertising that pleases a boss or committee. Create advertising that you believe will sell.

- Don't begin creating an advertisement until all the executional details are clearly spelled out.

15

ADVERTISING MEDIA

Now that you have an understanding of what promotional and/or image messages need to be externally communicated, the next step is to prepare a media plan that will most effectively and efficiently deliver these messages. Make sure the advertising media fulfills its value goal, because it plays a major role in affecting the marketing communication goals of awareness and attitude. It is also critical that this tactical tool deliver on the plan expectations, because media most often represent the largest single dollar marketing investment. It is also the marketing mix tool that is probably the least understood from the technical standpoint. Accordingly, you will find that learning how to plan media is one of the most challenging, complex experiences you will encounter as you write your marketing plan. Finally, as you make your media plan decisions, keep in mind that you should use hard data whenever possible, but that you must also apply basic common sense.

From This Chapter You Will Learn

The marketing and media background data needed to prepare a media plan.

What media objectives are and how to set them, particularly in determining "how much media is enough."

How to develop media strategies that meet the objectives.

How to evaluate specific media and media vehicles, as well as overall plans.

How to construct a media plan in written and graphic form.

How to summarize a media budget.

The trends in the evolving personal media of relationship marketing.

OVERVIEW

Media can be divided into two parts: planning and execution. The overall goal of media planning and execution is to deliver the optimum number of impressions (messages) to the target audience at the lowest cost and within the most suitable environment for the message.

Planning consists of arranging the various media in combinations and support levels designed to most effectively and efficiently help fulfill the marketing, advertising, and promotion objectives and strategies. In essence, it is the process of refining probabilities in a step-by-step, disciplined manner.

Execution, on the other hand, encompasses negotiating, purchasing, and placing the media once the media weights, types, and budgets have been determined. Another part of media execution is the evaluation of the purchased media's performance once it has run, which is referred to as the postbuy. Depending upon the size and structure of your organization, you may have an outside agency assist in both planning and execution. This chapter concentrates only on media planning. Refer to a text on media buying if you intend to purchase your own media.

The actual media plan segment included in the marketing plan consists of three basic elements:

1. Media objectives

2. Media strategies

3. Media plan calendar and budget summary

Because preparing a media plan is a long, complex process, and because this chapter will be challenging to grasp, it is wise to review this chapter and its step-by-step media planning process and then refer to it as you develop your own media plans. A format to use in developing your media plan is provided in Appendix C.

DISCIPLINED APPROACH TO MEDIA PLANNING

Task 1
Review of Information Needed to Write a Media Plan

Before you can begin to prepare your media plan, you must first review all of the pertinent marketing and media data. Most of this information should be included in your business review. Below is a list of marketing and media data to be reviewed over a three- to five-year period, with five years of history preferred. Attempt to gather and review all of the items, depending on the data and time available to you.

- Review of the size and growth of the marketplace in dollars and units

- Analysis of the competitive market (including your product)
  —If available, sales history of each major competitor by size, share, and growth
  —If available, competitive media review of each major competitor
    Level and share of media spending/weight
    Spending and weight levels by medium, seasonality (quarterly if possible), and market
    Media spending as a percentage of sales
  —If available, review of unaided awareness, advertising awareness, and attitudes of the potential users/purchasers, on both a national/system-wide and market-by-market basis

- Analysis of your product(s)'s sales, marketing, and media history
  —Sales history by product, market (CDI & BDI), seasonality, and store/distribution channel

　　　—Your media target market

　　　—If available, unaided awareness, advertising awareness, attitudes, and behavior/usage

　　　—Historical media review of your product

　　　　Overall media weight delivery and spending

　　　　Spending and weight levels by medium (quarterly) and market

　　　　Media spending as percentage of sales

　　　—Results of media schedules run

　　　　Changes in awareness, attitudes, and behavior

　　　　Impact on overall sales, promotions, events, and media tests

　　　—Review of dollars allocated to media versus the other marketing mix tools

■ Review of the problems and opportunities section

■ Review of this marketing plan, from sales objectives to communication goals and tactical tools through advertising message.

This information will provide direction and insight as you develop your media plan.

Task 2
Set the Media Objectives

Your media objectives must provide a clear and definitive direction in the following critical areas:

■ To whom the advertising is to be directed (target audience)

■ Where the advertising is to go (geography)

■ When the advertising is to appear (seasonality)

■ What are the weight and impact goals for optimum communication?

　　—How much advertising is deemed sufficient to achieve the advertising objectives?

　　—What media environment will provide the impact to meet the advertising strategies in helping to communicate the message?

■ Determination of whether there is an initial set budget allocated for media spending or if a task method approach will be applied to arrive at a media budget.

If there is a set media budget allocation, it should be included up front in the media plan as a media objective. A task-derived media budget is dependent on the media support necessary to meet the awareness and attitude levels that will stimulate adequate usage to meet the sales objectives. In this case, the media budget is finalized and presented at the end of the media plan.

■ Determination of whether or not your marketing plan calls for testing of media

If so, you will include media test objectives in this section of the media plan.

Target Audience

To arrive at a target audience, simplify the target market you have already detailed earlier in the plan by listing the key strategic and segment descriptors.

The *strategic target* relates to purchasing and usage. Mothers purchase powdered soft drinks for their children, while their children who consume powdered soft drinks are the users. Then the question regarding your target market is do you go

Exhibit 15.1 Media Audience and Cost Sources*

Medium	Audience Data	Cost Data
Television	Nielsen Research Services (NTI, NSI)	Network/station representatives Media Market Guide Spot Quotations and Data, Inc. (Costs are negotiable)
Radio	RADAR—Network Arbitron Research—Spot	Network/station representatives Media Market Guide Radio SRDS (costs are negotiable)
Magazines	Audit Bureau of Circulation (ABC) Simmons Market Research Bureau (SMRB) Mediamark Research Inc. (MRI) Individual magazine representative	Magazine SRDS Magazine representatives (ad position is usually negotiable, but cost usually is not
Newspapers	Simmons/Scarborough Report Newspaper Association of America Local newspaper representative	Newspaper SRDS (space costs for national products) Local rate cards via newspaper representatives (lower cost for local business advertising than national products)
Outdoor	Traffic Audit Bureau (TAB) Local representative	Outdoor SRDS Outdoor representatives (costs are sometimes negotiable and board position is usually negotiable depending on availability)
Direct Mail	Direct Mail SRDS Dun's Marketing Services	Direct mail SRDS Dun's Marketing Services

*A handy and portable reference to current media rates, data, and demographics for most consumer media updated quarterly is *Adweek's* "Marketer's Guide to Media."

against the purchaser, the user, or both? The *segment target* audience should parallel the segmentation breakouts provided by syndicated media services that measure audience media habits and media vendors such as direct mail houses, broadcasting stations, and catalog publishers. If you have key submarkets, such as the trade (wholesalers, retailers, etc.) for a package goods product, that cannot be accommodated in one media plan, a separate media plan should be prepared for these target markets.

The media target audience should be limited to those descriptors that can be readily and effectively used in the planning, measurement, and evaluation of the various media. Review your target market sections in the plan and the audience sources listed in Exhibit 15.1 to arrive at meaningful descriptors. Also included in this exhibit are sources for the current media costs.

Some target audience objective examples:

For a company that sells copiers and fax machines:

> Primary—"Decision Makers" at small to midsized companies—3 to 5 million dollars (President and General office manager)

> Secondary—"Decision Influencers" at those same companies (senior level project managers)

For a company selling children's cereals:

> Primary—Kids 6–11

> Secondary—Mothers (women 25–49)

Geography

Once you have determined your specific media target audience, you must decide where and with what emphasis you want to place your media. Geographic media variation depends on the marketing strategies, as well as sales potential and profitability differences on a market-by-market basis or within a market and budget.

Geographic weighting of media levels by market is based on many factors. A few of the geographic factors to be taken into consideration when developing geography media objectives are:

Sheer geographic size and physical makeup of your trading area

Growth potential of the market

Competitive media activity

Media available to support your product

Concentration of potential users of your product

Concentration and trending of your product sales

The last two of these geographic factors can be taken into account by evaluating on a market-by-market basis the sales of the product category and the sales of your product. The market-by-market variations should have been detailed in your business review as a comparison of markets in two ways: category development index (CDI = percent category sales/percent households in a given market) and brand development index (BDI = percent product sales/percent households in a given market). You most likely will place some media weight where you have a set minimum level of sales and even greater weight where there is an above average concentration of category sales and, very importantly, an above average concentration of sales for your product. Accordingly, you will develop a media objective that takes into consideration the CDI, the BDI, and the relationship between the two. (For more detail on CDI and BDI analysis, see the Distribution task in the Product and Market Review step of your business review.)

Before finalizing your geographic media objectives, you should decide, on a market-by-market basis, whether your strategic marketing thrust is defensive (spend in markets to protect your business) or offensive (spend where there is potential but where sales have not been solidly built). This offensive strategy is also referred to as investment spending.

A beginning BDI/CDI guide for a defensive versus offensive approach might be:

High BDI/High CDI = Higher media spending to protect share; Defensive

High BDI/Low CDI = Media maintenance unless competition increases media weight; Defensive

Low BDI/High CDI = Investment media spending to capitalize on opportunity markets via new advertising, additional promotion, improved product/distribution/store penetration, etc.; Offensive

Low BDI/Low CDI = Limited, if any, media support

In additional to BDI/CDI considerations, you must also consider the trending of sales on a market-by-market basis. You might place additional media weight in markets with positive sales trends, while in markets with negative sales trends you might reduce the weight until a nonadvertising problem is fixed or add media weight to support promotional advertising to reverse the sales trend.

The remaining factor regarding geography that comes into play is the budget. If the funds necessary to implement an effective program across all key markets are not available, priorities must be established and the market list pared down. Advertise only where you reasonably believe you can achieve your objectives. Otherwise, you risk a diluted, ineffective program across all markets.

Some examples of geography objectives follow:

For a national package goods product:

Provide national media support.

Provide incremental local media weight in high BDI markets that cumulatively account for a minimum of one-third of sales.

	Percent Volume	BDI
Los Angeles	8.3%	119
New York	8.0	123
Chicago	7.7	125
Philadelphia	6.5	121
San Francisco	4.4	118
	34.9%	122

For a business-to-business company:

Provide broad-based media support of the full line of existing equipment.

Provide full introductory media support in addition to base support of the east, north, and central divisions for the new equipment introduction as soon as service commitment has been confirmed.

For a local retailer:

Provide marketwide media coverage.

Provide incremental media weight within one mile of store that accounts for 50 percent of current customers.

Seasonality

As important as it is to advertise to the right person in the right place, it is also important to advertise at the right time. Accordingly, to arrive at the right seasonality media objective(s), you must review the seasonality of your product and category sales to determine when sales for your product and the category are at their highest levels. The general media practice is to plan your greatest media weight support for periods of high sales volume.

Most products have sales skews. When the monthly sales index nears 110 or greater, you would most likely heavy-up (increase) your weight levels. Sometimes the seasonality of your product might differ from that of the category, with the category's heavy sales season beginning earlier or later than that of your product. After reviewing the reason(s) for this seasonal sales difference (e.g., special promotion or different competitive weight levels), you will probably want to concentrate your media weight when the target market is most likely to purchase.

Where affordable, advertising should *lead* the natural buying season, placing higher levels of media just prior to heavier sales periods. This is done to presell the consumer, building awareness and putting the consumer in a positive mode to purchase your product when the natural buying season arrives. With minimal media dollars, however, the first priority should be to concentrate media weight at the beginning of the heavy buying season. It is most efficient to reduce your media weight just before the end of the increased sales period so that you are not investing media dollars against a diminishing market; let the established awareness you built carry the latter portion of the sales period.

Another factor to consider in setting a media seasonality objective is what the competition has done in the past and what you anticipate they will do in the coming year. You may want not only to lead the peak selling season but also to be the first into the media arena, preempting the competition.

Some examples of seasonality objectives:

For a public transit company:

> Concentrate media in the adverse, winter weather (highest usage) months of January/February/March and the back-to-school period of August/September, while maintaining a media continuity throughout the year.

For a retail fabric chain:

> Provide media continuity support throughout the year, with a concentration of media effort in the heavy selling seasons of August through October and February through April.

Media Weight and Impact Goals

Having determined your media objectives of target audience, geography, and seasonality, you must next determine what your media weight and impact goals will be in terms of the quantitative and qualitative media delivery necessary to meet the awareness and attitude goals that will lead to projected sales.

Review of Rating Points, Reach, Frequency, and GRPs

Determining quantitative communications goals is very difficult even for the most experienced media planner because of the ever changing marketing environment in which there is a lack of definitive benchmarks, an uncontrollable competitive marketplace, and the continually changing needs and wants of the potential target market. The problem of accurately determining how much communication is received by the target market and its effectiveness in stimulating action makes this determination even more difficult.

Before discussing how to arrive at quantitative communication goals to provide media direction, you must have an understanding of some basic media terms: rating point, GRPs (gross rating points), reach, and frequency.

A *rating point* is defined as 1 percent of the universe being measured. A universe could include households, companies, women, men, adults, kids, purchasing agents, etc., in a single market or region or in the total United States. On a total U.S. household basis, a one rating (measured against households) for a commercial or ad means that an impression or exposure is made against approximately 970,000 homes nationally (1 percent of 97,000,000 homes). On a single market basis for Chicago, a one rating equates to approximately 31,000 homes (1 percent of 3,100,000 homes).

GRPs (also referred to as TRPs, or target rating points, when measured against a universe other than just households such as women 25–49 or kids 2–11) provide a common term of measurement to determine how much media weight is going into a defined marketplace and to make comparisons among different media. When we buy 100 home GRPs via multiple ad insertions, we are in fact buying a number of household impressions equal to the number of homes in that universe. Chicago has approximately 3,100,000 homes. A schedule of 100 GRPs would generate 3,100,000 household impressions. Please note that these 3,100,000 household impressions will not necessarily be made against 3,100,000 *different* homes in the market.

In actuality, when a schedule of ads and/or commercials is run, some homes will be exposed to the ad a number of times and others will not be exposed to it at all. This leads to two other important media estimate concepts:

Reach—how many different homes/persons we have reached at least once (expressed as an absolute or percentage)

Frequency—how often, on average, they have been exposed to one message

Reach, frequency, and GRPs are tied together mathematically as follows:

$$\text{Percent Reach} \times \text{Frequency} = \text{Total GRPs.}$$

Therefore, to reach 80 percent of a target market with a frequency of 10, you would need a schedule of approximately 800 GRPs of support.

We normally estimate reach and frequency on a four-week basis, but we can also provide reach and frequency figures for schedules ranging from one week to a full year.

Through research and experience, we have been able to establish standard reach levels for given GRP levels. Using the graph in Exhibit 15.2, you can approximate what each medium would generate in reach as a particular GRP level, as well as the average frequency. If your local market media plan calls for 300 GRPs in radio to support a two-week promotion, it would build an approximate 50 reach and an average frequency of 6 (300 ÷ 50 = 6). Or, if you determined a monthly magazine reach of 50 was required, then your schedule would have to approximate 125 GRPs. At this level, your frequency would be about 2.5 (125 ÷ 50 = 2.5). Exhibit 15.2 provides an overall GRP summary for television, radio, and magazine. For more accurate GRP data specific to your market, check with the appropriate media representatives.

To arrive at a rough approximation of reach and frequency data for each medium (other than television and radio), you can compute your own GRP data for magazines, newspaper, outdoor, and direct mail. However, for more precise data, you should contact your specific media representative. For your rough calculations use the following formulas.

Magazine: Use percent coverage for reach (circulation ÷ total market households or target readers ÷ target persons); number of insertions for frequency.

Newspaper: Use percent coverage for reach (circulation ÷ total market households or target readers ÷ target persons); number of insertions for frequency.

Syndicated sources (SMRB or MRI) or magazine readership studies can provide the necessary data to figure coverage of a specific target.

Outdoor: For a standard four-week showing estimate:

50 showing = 85 reach and 15 frequency

100 showing = 88 reach and 29 frequency

Direct Mail: Use percent coverage for reach (number mailed ÷ total market target households or target persons); number of mailings for frequency.

Exhibit 15.2 Relationship of Reach, Frequency, and GRPs

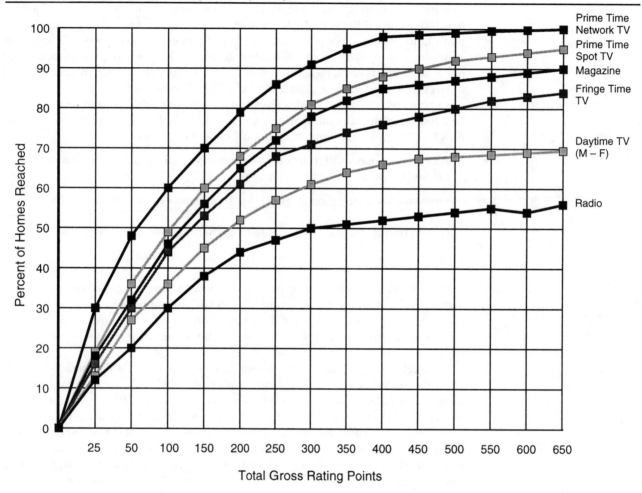

Source: Michael L. Rothschild, *Advertising, From Fundamentals to Strategies,* Lexington, Massachusetts, D.C. Heath and Company, 1987.

Once you have estimated reach and frequency for a single medium, you may want to combine media weights with another medium. Although not an exact method (but good enough for approximation), you can use the grid in Exhibit 15.3 to arrive at combined weight levels across media. For example, 300 GRPs of radio and 800 GRPs of magazines are planned (1,100 GRPs total) yielding reaches of 50 and 80, respectively. Then, using the grid, the planner can see that the combined reach is approximately 86 (86 is at the intersection of row 50 and column 80); therefore, average frequency for the combined 1,100 GRPs must be 12.8 (1,100 ÷ 86 = 12.8). Although neither the graph nor the grid is perfectly accurate, each gives a good approximation for planning purposes.

How to Arrive at Quantitative Media Weight Goals

Now that you have an understanding of media measurement, we can review three different methods of arriving at a communication weight level goal(s).

Micro Target Market Method   This approach is goal, or task, driven. It is based on moving a specific target market to action. With this approach you attempt to deter-

Exhibit 15.3 Accumulated Reach Levels Across Media

		All Media Combinations (Homes and Individuals)																
		5	10	15	20	25	30	35	40	45	50	55	60	65	70	75	80	85	90
Reach	5	10	14	19	24	28	33	38	43	47	52	57	62	66	71	76	81	85	90
	10	14	19	23	27	32	36	40	45	50	54	59	63	68	72	77	81	86	91
	15	19	23	27	31	35	39	43	48	52	56	61	65	69	73	78	82	86	91
	20	24	27	31	35	38	42	46	50	55	59	63	67	71	75	79	83	87	91
	25	28	32	35	38	41	44	48	53	57	61	64	68	72	76	79	83	87	92
	30	33	36	39	42	44	47	51	55	59	63	66	70	73	77	80	84	88	92
	35	38	40	43	46	48	51	53	58	62	65	68	71	75	78	81	84	88	92
	40	43	45	48	50	53	55	58	60	64	67	70	73	76	79	82	85	88	92
	45	47	50	52	55	57	59	62	64	66	69	72	75	77	80	83	86	89	93
	50	52	54	56	59	61	63	65	67	69	71	74	76	79	81	84	86	89	93
	55	57	59	61	63	64	66	68	70	72	74	76	78	80	82	85	87	90	93
	60	62	63	65	67	68	70	71	73	75	76	78	80	82	84	86	88	90	94
	65	66	68	69	71	72	73	75	76	77	79	80	82	83	85	86	88	91	94
	70	71	72	73	75	76	77	78	79	80	81	82	84	85	86	87	89	91	94
	75	76	77	78	79	79	80	81	82	83	84	85	86	86	87	88	89	91	95
	80	81	81	82	83	83	84	84	85	86	86	87	88	88	89	89	90	92	95
	85	85	86	86	87	87	88	88	88	89	89	90	90	91	91	91	92	92	95
	90	90	91	91	91	92	92	92	92	93	93	93	94	94	94	95	95	95	95
	95	95	95	96	96	96	96	96	96	97	97	97	97	97	97	98	98	98	98

Reach

Source: Michael L. Rothschild, *Advertising, From Fundamentals to Strategies*, Lexington, Massachusetts, D.C. Heath and Company, 1987.

mine what percent of the target market must be reached and how often. You want to reach this target with the frequency necessary to build the product awareness and understanding that will lead to a positive attitude toward the product and eventual purchase. In essence, you are attempting to determine the amount of GRP media weight you will need in order to effectively reach or communicate with a large enough portion of your target market and generate the required sales.

A good place to start when determining the desired reach and frequency is to review your marketing objectives and review what percent of the target market you have estimated will try your product, make repeat purchases, and become regular users in order to meet the sales objectives. Then review the overall communication goals and examine the advertising objectives to determine the percent of target market you projected must have specific unaided awareness of your product and a predisposed attitude toward your product.

It is also wise to review the media weight levels supporting your product over the past year, along with the level of media support for any promotions that may have been run. Based on these past supporting media weight levels, attempt to correlate sales results in order to determine what reach, frequency, and GRP levels are needed for this year's plan to help meet the estimated advertising and promotion objectives.

Every situation is different when setting reach goals, depending on the type of product you are selling and its awareness and acceptance by the target market. But as a suggested starting point, based on the authors' experience, you should consider a 60 to 90+ reach of the target market. For a meaningful impact, it is usually necessary to reach well over one-half of the target market with your message. This is sometimes difficult to accomplish, particularly with short-term promotions and when the appropriate media vehicles are not readily available.

Once you have estimated your specific reach goal(s) for the year, new product introduction, promotion, event, grand opening, etc., you must now estimate the frequency needed against the target in order to generate the effective reach necessary to elicit a specific response. In setting frequency goals, the frequency required to move the desired portion of the target market from product recognition to purchase is really a guesstimate. However, a potential range of frequency to make this happen is from a three to ten frequency. To determine whether you need more or less frequency depends upon the following:

More frequency	**Less frequency**
New product	Established product
New campaign	Established campaign
Complex message	Simple message
Nonuser prospects (trial objective)	User prospects (repeat objective)
High competitive advertising levels	Low competitive advertising levels
Nonloyal user category, especially with short purchase cycle	Stable/loyal user base
Promotion/sales event	

It has been the experience of the authors, specifically with retail clients who need immediate results, that it is usually more successful to reach a smaller percentage of the target market with greater frequency than to reach a larger percentage of the target market with minimum frequency. It is better to have a smaller audience understand and remember your message than to have a large audience that does not thoroughly understand or remember the message.

To help you determine the frequency needed to effectively communicate the message, you can estimate the number of times the individual target person must be reached by determining the necessary frequency for the anticipated response, as shown in Exhibit 15.4. To help you, we have included an estimated frequency range for each response. While the potential frequency range in this exhibit runs from one exposure for recognition to 10+ exposures to achieve the response of getting the sale, it could take many more exposures for recognition and merely one exposure to make a sale. The authors acknowledge that these ranges are very subjective and will vary dramatically with your specific product and current marketing situation.

Once you have determined the required reach and frequency to set a media weight goal, simply multiply your estimated reach by the total needed frequency for your total GRP level. For example:

$$\text{Reach } 80 \times \text{Frequency } 9 = \text{GRPs } 720$$

Keep in mind that, with this methodology, the frequency of message exposure is based on average frequency. Some people within the target market will be exposed once and others will be exposed at multiples of the average frequency number.

Exhibit 15.4 How to Determine Frequency Goals

Potential Frequency Range	Response	Definition	Judgmental Probability of Producing Response with Advertising Alone
1 to 3	Recognition	Recalls advertising when shown/mentioned product	Least difficult
3 to 6	Unaided awareness	Names product when asked about category	Difficult
4 to 7	Recall	Recalls advertising and identifies product	More difficult
5 to 8	Learning	Associates information about the product with the name	Very difficult
6 to 10	Attitude	Prefers the product, positive attitude	Extremely difficult
10+	Sales	Purchases	Most difficult

Exhibit 15.5 Media Weight Guidelines

Product/Service Type	Target Audience GRP Weight Levels		
	Minimum Weekly	Seasonal/Event 4-Week Period	Annual
Consumer			
Package goods			
Established	75–150	300–600	1,000–3,000
Introductory/Promotional	150–250	600–1,000	1,800–5,000
Retail/Service			
Established	100–200	400–800	2,000–5,000
Introductory/Promotional	175–350	700–1,400	3,000–10,000
Business-to-Business			
Established	25–50	100–200	600–1,600
Introductory/Promotional	50–150	200–600	1,200–3,600

You probably have surmised from this discussion of setting media weight goals that there is no one hard and fast rule for determining the optimum media weight level for your product; rather, there is a composite of many factors that you must consider. In Exhibit 15.5 we present some guidelines for you to consider and, we hope, modify (possibly very dramatically) as you determine the media weight goals for your product. These very rough media weight guidelines are based on some quantitative data, but are primarily based on the personal experience of the authors. Therefore, they are very subjective in nature and must be used with extreme caution.

In the package goods area, the 2,500 to 5,000 annual introductory GRP level on the average can generate *aided* brand awareness of 60 to 80 percent and trial rates of up to 20 percent. In the retail environment, the 5,000 to 10,000 GRP level on the average can generate an *unaided* store awareness of 20 to 40 percent and trial rates of up to 20 percent. The trial rate in the retail environment is very dependent on store penetration (or the number of stores you have in the market).

Some examples of media weight goals would be:

For a nationally marketed package good:

Provide a reach of 90 to 95 and a minimum of average frequency of four over five media flight periods. This will need approximately 2,000 GRPs on a national basis for the fiscal year.

For a package good marketed in the local opportunity markets of Chicago, Los Angeles, and Philadelphia:

> Provide a reach of 90 to 95 with a minimum frequency of six for the five four-week, heavy-up periods. This will take an additional 1,100 GRPs locally across the year.

For a business-to-business manufacturer:

> Reach a minimum 80 percent of the target market a minimum of eight times annually.

Macro Methods of Determining Media Weight Goal   With the macro methods described here, one of the first steps involves the establishment of a working media budget. With the micro (task) method, the communication goals were the driving factors. With the macro method, priorities are established, and the plan reflects the number of objectives that can be accomplished at a predetermined budget level. One macro method establishes the budget as a percent of sales based on industry averages, and the second macro method uses a comparison of share of media to share of market sales. Both are market-based approaches.

Percentage-of-Sales Method   This method begins with a review of the percent of sales allocated to advertising by the product category/industry in which you are competing. You could then use a similar percentage of your projected sales for your media budget after reducing this dollar budget by 10 to 15 percent to cover the cost of production to develop the ads and/or commercials. For example:

Percent advertising of sales for category	3%
Product's projected sales	$100,000,000
Ad budget (3% × $100MM)	$3,000,000
Ad production of 10 percent (10% of $3MM ad budget)	$300,000
Available media budget ($3MM − $300M)	$2,700,000

Now that you have established the budget, you must next use this budget to determine a media weight goal.

To arrive at a rough GRP weight level for your product, contact your media representative to arrive at a very approximate cost per rating point (CPP) by medium. For example,

> Cost of average insertion or broadcast spot/Average rating = CPP

Or,

> Average radio :60 commercial spot cost of $36/Average rating of 2 = $18 CPP

You can then divide the total media budget by the CPP for each medium to arrive at an approximate idea of how much media weight you can afford by each potential medium. For example,

$$\$27,000/\$18 \text{ CPP} = 1,500 \text{ GRPs}$$

Although the above example is for a consumer medium, you could use a similar approach for business-to-business media using an average cost per point for each medium such as trade publications and direct mail.

The percent-of-sales approach to advertising is not very sophisticated, but it does challenge you to maximize the dollars in your media budget. However, keep in mind that, because this approach is so broad in application, it does not take into consideration your current marketing situation or the competitive marketing environment.

Advertising as a percent of sales is only one method of arriving at the optimum media weight goal and should, in most situations, be a means for comparison.

Share of Media versus Share of Market Method   Another method of determining your media weight goal is the share comparison of media activity to sales—the *share of media versus share of market* method. This method compares your product's share of media voice (SOV) (in GRP media weight or media dollar expenditures as a percentage of total media advertising in your industry category or marketplace) to your product's share of market sales (SOM).

Organization	SOV		SOM	
	$M	**Percent**	**$MM**	**Percent**
A	$370	48%	$94.1	39.1%
B	230	29	70.0	29.1
C	69	9	38.6	16.1
D	105	14	38.0	15.7
Total	$774	100%	$240.7	100.0%

If you are using media dollar expenditures, take the media spending for each competitor, including your own product, from the business review and compare it to the corresponding share of market. Is your share of media spending above or below that of the competition? Is your share of media spending above or below that of your product's share of market? Based on the direction of your marketing strategies and this SOV to SOM comparison, you can determine media weight goals.

As a very rough guide and a starting point in using the SOV to SOM media weight determination, consider the following:

Share of voice should approximate share of market.

Usually the greater the share of market, the greater the share of voice.

If you want to increase your share of market, you most often should increase share of voice.

If your share of voice is below your share of market year after year, your sales share will eventually decease if everything in the competitive market environment and your marketing mix remains constant.

In using this method, keep in mind that there is no guarantee that there always will be a direct cause and effect between an increase/decrease of SOV and a similar increase/decrease in SOM. However, while there is not always perfect correlation, there is a direction cause-and-effect relationship between SOV and SOM. Broad-based studies and the authors' media experience with clients have also shown this cause-and-effect relationship during recessionary periods when there is a shrinking of the market and a decrease in total market sales for an industry. On the whole, companies that maintain or increase their media weight during recessionary periods realize an increase in share of sales and better profits than those companies that reduce ad budgets and corresponding media weights.

Summary of Methods to Determine Media Weight Goals   The micro and macro methods all have their merits. You might apply a combination of methods or decide to use one method that best fits your current planning situation. The important point is that you have an understanding of how these different methods are employed to determine the media weight for your product.

Qualitative Impact Media Goals

The qualitative delivery goals relate to the *impact* of the exposure within the particular medium in which it is run. This relates to the effectiveness of medium in providing an optimum environment for the product advertised and the message to be delivered. The media environment must also be consistent with and appropriate to the projected product image. The direction for this goal comes from the product positioning and creative strategy.

The qualitative media goal, while a guide, is also a safeguard. It ensures that the media selected not only provide the necessary impact for the target market but also enhance the reception of the actual message. An advertisement selling the advanced technology of a new car might best be placed in *Car and Driver*, while an advertisement that sells emotional benefits of the new car (such as the feeling of exhilaration one experiences while driving the car) might be best suited for television.

A qualitative media goal for a new product that represents a technological breakthrough might be: "Provide a media environment that is authoritative, credible, and has news value." This could eventually translate to placement in "60 Minutes" or local television news.

If your message introduces a chain of new high-fashion women's apparel stores, your communication goal might be: "Provide a media environment that is conducive to the display of quality, high-fashion apparel and is relative to a lifestyle of women who purchase this type of clothing." This could eventually translate to the placement of commercials in glitz television shows, where the wardrobes are watched with as much interest as the plot. This same goal could also translate to a high-fashion ad in the fall fashion edition of an upscale city publication.

Optional Media Objectives for Your Plan

Media Budget

It is usually best to use the task method when building a media plan, as you thereby arrive at a media budget that is the direct result of the type and amount of media required to fulfill the communication goals. Based on the cumulative marketing plan budget considerations, this type of media budget is then further refined to implement all of the elements of the market mix. However, if there are specific financial media parameters for the media plan, they are often included as part of the media objectives.

Some examples of media budget objectives would be:

Maintain total media expenditures at 3½ percent of total projected sales.

Execute an annual media plan at the $300,000 budget level.

Media Test Objectives

If the marketing plan calls for a media test(s), a brief statement of the test objectives should be included in this section. Some examples of media test objectives would be:

Test the impact on sales of increasing the media spending from 2 percent to 4 percent of sales.

Test the impact on sales of adding consumer media to the current use of business publications and direct mail to effectively reach new business-to-business clients.

Test the payout effectiveness of adding broadcast to the previously all print media plan.

Task 3
....
Prepare the Media Strategy

Under media strategy you should include:

- A brief summary of the *media mix*, or the different media to be used—magazines, direct mail, radio, etc.

- *The specific use of each medium.* This is a description of how each of the specific media is to be used, such as magazine types, ad size, broadcast programming/daypart type, and length of commercials.

- Description of the *scheduling* of the media in terms of when and at what levels each medium is used.

This strategy section is really the heart of the actual media planning process. It is an evolving and very fluid process, because you will be evaluating media elements for each of the strategy points. You will also be combining different media elements and evaluating these combination alternatives on a quantitative basis (delivery and efficiency) and on a qualitative basis (which media environment will best communicate the message). You will also want to include a rationale as part of the media strategy section, once you have decided on each of the specific strategies.

Keep in mind that, because of possible revisions of the sales objectives, marketing strategies, promotional program, budget, etc., you might revise the media strategies as the marketing plan evolves. Nevertheless, if changes to the media strategies are required, they are relatively easy to implement if you understand and have actually gone through this disciplined media planning process.

Finally, there are many new developments in the media arena that reach the target market on an individual basis. Two of these are based on interactive and direct marketing. For background on these developments, please refer to the Appendix of Evolving Personal Media at the end of this chapter.

Media Mix Strategy

Description and Value Comparison

Before you write a media mix strategy, you must first review and evaluate which media will best fulfill the media objectives. This evaluation should compare the media on both a quantitative and qualitative basis.

To begin your evaluation process, do a quick initial screen of the different media, determining which have a possibility of use in a media plan that will meed the objectives. It is a good idea to do this quick screen of *all* media to ensure that you do not automatically rule out a medium based on your preconceived notions or without determining if it could meet the objectives.

As a quick media review and handy reference guide, Exhibit 15.6 provides a general description and a comparison of media values based on quantitative data and the authors' experience. If you require more indepth background information on each medium, you can review an advertising or media text or check with the appropriate media representatives.

Arriving at the Right Media Mix

In order to arrive at the appropriate mix of media you must screen out the obvious inappropriate media. Do a quantitative and qualitative analysis of the potential media candidates, and consider how your media selection will impact the target market in comparison to the competitive media environment.

Exhibit 15.6 Handy Media Guide: General Description and Values of Various Media

Medium	Size/Length		Cost Comparison	
	Units Available	Recommended Size/Unit	Standard Unit	Relative Efficiency*
Television				
Network or spot	:60/:30/:15/:10 (spot :15 not regularly available)	:30	:30	Overall above average
Prime				Most costly
Day				Least costly
Early fringe				Average
Late fringe				Above early fringe
News				Network: Average
				Spot: Close to prime
Sports				Most costly
Cable	:60/:30/:15/:10	:30		Low national but high spot CPM
Radio				
Network ⎱ ⎰ AM drive / Midday	:60/:30/:10	:30	:30	Very efficient vs. TV
Spot ⎱ ⎰ PM drive / Evening		:60	:60§	Generally efficient vs. TV
Local Newspapers	Various	¼ to ½ page	⅓ page	Average/various
Sunday Supplements	Various	½ to full page	⅔ page four color	Par with many magazines
Magazines—Consumer General Editorial Special Interest News Weeklies Shelter Books (Ex. men/women) Etc.	Various	½ to full page	Page four color bleed	Generally more efficient than TV
Magazines— Business-to-Business/Trade Vertical (targeted via specific industries) Horizontal (targeted via job function)	Various	1/2 to full page	Page b/w	Expensive but less than direct mail
Outdoor/Out of Home	25/50/100 showing	50=	50 to 100 showing	Most efficient
Direct Mail	Up to 6⅛" × 11½" × ¼" thick, 1 oz. or less#	Larger than smaller, B/W plus one color	Various	Most expensive on a pure CPM basis, but very targeted with a lower out-of-pocket cost

*Represents normal relationships of cost efficiency among media types. Individual variances occur frequently.
§A :30 on network radio is half the price of a :60. In the case of spot radio, a :30 spot can cost from 80 percent of a :60.
=A 50 showing means approximately 50 percent of the market will pass one of the locations each day.
#Acceptable size and weight with no incremental postage cost.

Exhibit 15.6 continued

Clutter		Reach/Target Audience Pinpointing	Communication Values
% Advertising/ Total Time or Space	Noticing Value†		
		Somewhat precise	Pros: Audiovisual impact; most intrusive; demands less active involvement relative to print; immediate impact; quick reach and good frequency; relatively homogenous national coverage; broad homogenous local coverage as well as beyond metro areas
16% to 23%‡	65	Broad total audience	
27	45	Housewives, kids	
27	45	Housewives, kids	
27	55	Adults	Cons: Limited to commercial length constraints; one exposure per expenditure
27	60	Adults, somewhat older	
27	45	Men Most precise of TV	
17 to 20 per hour	35	Fairly precise in terms of age/sex demographics only and for ethnic targets	Pros: Good frequency medium; demands less active involvement; good localized spot coverage for city/metro area
20 to 30 per hour	35		Cons: Audio impact only; low ratings; limited to commercial length time constraints; one exposure per expenditure; reach builds slower than TV and newspaper
70	55	Broad total audience	Pros: Immediate impact; very high reach potential; coupons get redeemed more quickly; very timely Cons: Low readers per copy; very little pass along; very short life span; limited in production quality
60 to 65	55	Broad total audience	Pros: Immediate impact; very high reach potential; good coupon carrier; better production quality than newspaper Cons: Low readers per copy; very little pass along; very short life span; not as flexible in timing as newspaper
40 to 60	50	Very precise in terms of many demographics	Pros: No time constraints per message, potential for multiple exposures per expenditure; indepth product description potential; generally upscale demography; pass along readership; coupon/promotion delivery vehicle; good production quality Cons: Visual impact only; requires active involvement; less immediate impact; lower reach and local market coverage than TV, radio, and newspaper
40 to 60	65	Precise by industry or job function	Pros: In-depth product description potential; reaches relatively small but targeted audience; ads and editorial are highly read; coupon carrier; low cost per inquiry Cons: Visual impact only
None to some (varies by area)	30	Imprecise	Pros: Good for product/package identification; good reach; high frequency; good directional vehicle; local geographic concentration Cons: Visual impact only; limited copy development potential; very high total monthly cost for anything approaching national coverage
All ad/no editorial	70	Most precise	Pros: Extensive copy development potential; very selective; easy to track response; excellent coupon carrier; flexible in terms of timing and types of inclusions per mailing; can be kept for future reference Cons: Visual impact only; easy to discard

†Estimated percent of audience who noticed advertising (the probability of the advertising being noticed by the medium's audience). Percent notice based on :30s in television, Page 4 color in magazines/supplements, ½ page in newspaper, :30s in network radio, :60s in spot radio, and 30-sheet in outdoor. The 70 percent notice value for direct mail is based on the estimated percentage that open the direct mail piece. (Noticing values for television are for spot TV.) For further explanation of noticing values, review the discussion under the heading "Arriving at the Right Media Mix."
‡Nonnetwork television station affiliates.

Screen Out Inappropriate Media   After reviewing the strengths and weaknesses of each medium in terms of its appropriateness for meeting the media objectives, screen out those media that logically could not meet the objectives. If you are marketing a new product to a broad, general market that required emotional image advertising, you would not use direct mail; if the product was very technical and required detailed explanation, you would not use outdoor; if you were grand opening one, 1,000-square-foot ice cream shop in a suburb of Chicago, you would not use television.

Evaluate Each Medium on a CPM Quantitative Basis   After eliminating those media that will very obviously not meet the objectives, compare the remaining media on a quantitative, cost-per-thousand (CPM) basis to determine media efficiency. A CPM is used as a common denominator for media comparison.

To arrive at a CPM for a medium, you can either divide target audience into the medium cost multiplied by 1,000 [Cost ÷ (Audience × 1,000) = CPM] or move the decimal point of the audience three places to the left and divide into the medium cost [Cost ÷ (Audience ÷ 1,000) = CPM]. If a network prime-time television :30 commercial cost is $124,000 and the number of the target persons reached is 6,264,000, then $124,000 ÷ 6,264 = $19.80 CPM.

You want to evaluate each of the potential media in your marketplace that you have screened and deemed appropriate for your product on a CPM basis. In order to do your CPM efficiency analysis, you will need both audience and cost information. A listing of some sources for generating audience and cost data is included in Exhibit 15.1.

To more easily compare medium CPMs, you might want to rank order each medium from the lowest to highest CPM. The chart in Exhibit 15.7 provides an example of a national media CPM comparison.

After you have ranked by computed CPM, you might want to weight the gross audience by the probability of the advertising being noticed. This is an important consideration, because the number of target market persons *receiving* the media as reported by audience research services and the media vehicles (station, newspaper, magazine, etc.) is usually much higher than the actual number *seeing and/or hearing* the advertising message. Based on a computation of media data and the experience of the authors, a rough estimate of the *noticing value* for the various media is included in Exhibit 15.6. It must be mentioned, however, that these estimates of noticing values are quite subjective. Further, the research data that provides some objective substance for these estimates is continually changing.

Keeping this in mind, you can apply these noticing values to each medium's gross audience to arrive at a lesser (and hopefully a more realistic) adjusted audience from which you can derive an *adjusted* CPM:

Prime time audience	10,415,000
Noticing value	× .65
Adjusted prime time audience	6,769,750
Average unit cost	$88,245
Adjusted prime time CPM	$13.04

As indicated in Exhibit 15.7, you can then rerank the media CPMs based on the noticing value after adjustments are made.

Having reviewed the ranked media CPMs, you can begin to eliminate those media with high CPMs. However, you cannot automatically assume that those with the lowest CPMs should be included in your media mix. You must also consider the qualitative factors of each medium and the competition's use of the media. In the

Exhibit 15.7 Media Mix Cost Comparisons

Medium/ Unit Size	Average Unit Cost	Average Rating W25–54	Women 25–54 (000)	CPM	Rank	Noticing Value	Adjusted CPM	Rank
Network TV (:30s)								
Daytime	$14,350	4.0	2,257	$6.36	2	45	$14.13	2
Prime-time	$124,000	11.1	6,264	$19.80	10	65	$30.46	9
Early Evening News	$49,325	6.2	3,498	$14.10	7	45	$31.34	10
Late night	$24,100	3.0	1,693	$14.24	8	65	$21.90	4
Network Radio (:30s)								
6A-7P Scatter Plan	$2,175	0.8	454	$4.79	1	35	$13.69	1
Magazine (1/2 Page, 4/c)								
Women's service	$68,900	16.1	9,060	$7.61	3	50	$15.22	3
Newspaper								
Sunday comics (1/3 page, 4c)	$440,120	51.2	28,921	$15.22	9	55	$27.67	8
Sunday supplements (1/2 page, 4c)								
Parade	$315,500	44.1	24,871	$12.69	4	55	$23.07	5
USA Weekend	$164,710	20.9	11,774	$13.99	6	55	$25.44	7
Sunday Magazine Network	$138,296	18.8	10,637	$13.00	5	55	$23.64	6

final analysis, it is not always the lowest CPM but the lowest cost per sale (CPS) that proves most important. What may appear to be too costly based on a pure CPM evaluation might be the most effective medium in terms of selling goods. In the much more narrowly defined business-to-business marketplace, the use of mass consumer media such as television, with its higher gross cost and CPM, has proven successful for such companies as Federal Express (overnight mail) and IBM (small business computers). These same types of comparisons can be made using cost per point (CPP) in place of CPM.

Evaluation on a Qualitative Basis   Having done your quantitative analysis of the media, you must still consider the qualitative factors of each medium. The following questions will help you determine those characteristics unique to your product, service, or store that you need to take into account when assessing each medium's ability to enhance the advertising message.

- What is required of the creative execution: demonstration, package registration, appetite appeal, technical explanation, consumer offer?

- What is required of the medium as related to the creative execution: sight, sound, and/or motion?

- How is the environment of the medium important to communicating the advertising message: news value, editorial compatibility (e.g., food preparation, home improvement)?

- To what extent is the audience interested in the product category/brand: very, somewhat, mildly?

- How important is immediacy (speed of audience accumulation) to the advertising objective: very, somewhat, mildly?

Competitive Media Mix Considerations   You must consider the competition's use of the media mix. What is their media mix selection? When do they use each medium? At what levels? How do they use each medium in relation to the others? If a competitor with a considerably larger media budget dominates the medium that would have been your first choice, you might decide to concentrate all of your media dollars in your second choice where you can dominate and where you will not have your media effort diluted.

With or without competition, it is usually better to concentrate your media dollars in a few media rather than to dilute your media dollars over many different media, thereby fragmenting your media effort. Plus, the more competition you have in the media, the more it becomes necessary for you to do a good job in one medium before placing weight in another. Make sure that each additional medium added to the media mix is used with weight levels that will have competitive impact and generate effective reach. In business-to-business media, you are usually better off concentrating your media in the top two or three publications by industry or job classification; doing so, you have the potential to generate a 75+ reach with the necessary frequency to have competitive impact, while maximizing your media dollars.

Media Mix Strategy Examples

After you've evaluated the media alternatives from quantitative, qualitative, and competitive points of view, you must now write your media mix strategy. Below are some examples for a national package goods client:

> Use a combination of network television for national coverage and spot television in the designated high opportunity markets of Chicago, Los Angeles, and Philadelphia.

> Use women's service magazines for selective reach against the primary target market and to carry cents-off coupons.

Some examples for a business-to-business crafts manufacturer are:

> Use national trade publications across a minimum of two top craft magazines to broaden reach potential of both primary and secondary target audiences.

> Take advantage of all available extras from trade publications, such as new product references, direct response cards, and use of publication mailing lists, when placing orders to increase awareness and obtain new dealers.

> Use frequency mailings to merchandise new products to large/key accounts.

Specific Usage of Each Medium

Within this media strategy section, define the specific tactical usage of each medium to be employed, based again on the media objectives. Include the following medium specifics where they apply.

Television and Radio: Daypart TV—Day, Fringe, Prime Time, News, Sports; Daypart Radio—AM Drive, Mid-Day, PM Drive, Night—program types; length of commercial

Magazines: List magazine type (news weeklies, sports, etc.) and/or specific magazines by name; ad size, position; black and white; one-, two-, three-, or four-color

Newspaper: Daily, weekly, and shopper (nonpaid); ad size; section of paper; black and white; one-, two-, three-, and four-color; day of the week

Outdoor: Level of showing (25/50/100), special location or directional requirements, size (if not 30 sheet), other specifics—painted, rotary, etc.

Direct Mail: Size (height/width), number of pages, quantity, black and white/color specifics

Medium Usage Strategy Examples

Some examples of media vehicle strategy/tactic statements would be:

For a package goods food client:

Use full-page, four-color ads in:

Women's service magazines—*Women's Day, Family Circle, Ladies Home Journal,* and *Good Housekeeping*

General interest magazines—*People* and *TV Guide*

Regional/lifestyle magazines—*Sunset* and *Southern Living*

For a regional retailer:

Use a :30 television daypart mix of 30 percent daytime, 30 percent general fringe, 20 percent prime time, and 20 percent late news.

Use ⅓-page newspaper ads for continuity and ½- to full-page ads to support major promotions on Thursdays in the main news section.

Use a targeted mailing in the trading area of each store.

For a business-to-business firm:

Use four-color, full-page ads in *Food Processing,* and use black-and-white, ½-page ads in *Food Engineering.*

Use black and white plus one-color, 6- by 11-inch postcard for frequency against the 1,000 key accounts.

Scheduling Strategy

Along with the selection of the optimum medium, media vehicle, and ad size/commercial length, you must also determine how the media should run. While the seasonality media objective provides guidelines for when to advertise throughout the year, the scheduling strategy provides specific direction of how the media is to be run.

Scheduling Approaches

There are a number of different strategic approaches to scheduling.

Continuity schedules are just that, continuous, and run at a relatively fixed, even level to help sustain nonseasonal/nonpromotion programs.

Heavy-up schedules incorporate incremental media weight to support periods of higher market activity, new product or campaign introductions, grand openings, and promotions.

Pulsing schedules run in a continuous on/off pattern; for example, the media runs two weeks, then is off two weeks, on two weeks, off two weeks, etc. The on/off pattern is repeated on a regular basis. The pulsing schedule provides more media support when advertising, which helps cut through the media noise level in the market, making the advertising stand out from that of the competition.

Flighting-in scheduling is generally three to six weeks of continuous advertising followed by hiatus periods or periods of no advertising. Flighting is used for short-term promotions and events, product introductions, and during periods of high seasonal sales.

Front loading is the running of heavier weight levels with the commencement of a media schedule when you kick off seasonal advertising, new advertising campaigns, new product introductions/grand openings, promotions, or trade show announcements.

Scheduling Strategy Examples

Once you have written your scheduling strategies, make sure you include a rationale as well.

Some examples of scheduling strategies for a package goods product are:

To quickly generate awareness, schedule a high level of television support (approximately 300 TRPs/week) during the new creative introductory period.

After the introductory period, schedule support at a minimum of 100 TRPs/week to maintain awareness.

Schedule support in flights of three weeks on, two weeks off, to maintain continuity across the year.

Some scheduling strategies for business-to-business advertisers are:

Schedule magazine advertising to run alternating months to maintain awareness across a greater portion of the year.

Schedule direct mail drops in months when magazine ads do not run to maintain a higher level of awareness against the primary segments of the target market.

Combine magazine ads and direct mail in each of the two months prior to the spring trade show.

Media Testing Strategies

If your media objectives call for a media test, then you want to include a media test strategy. This media test strategy should include a strategy statement on media mix, media vehicles/tactics, and scheduling, along with a listing of test markets and a description of how the test is to be evaluated.

However, keep in mind when testing media that you must include control markets for comparison. These control markets would be very similar to the makeup of your test markets and represent your normal, base media schedules. Make sure you test only one media variable at a time so that you can read or evaluate the effectiveness of the media change being tested. Because media testing is a rather involved process, you should refer to a text that provides information on the testing of media.

<table>
<tr><td>

Task 4

Development of the Final Media Plan with Calendar and Budget

</td><td>

Prepare and Review Alternative Media Plans

At this point, having already set media objectives and strategies, you should have so-lidified your media thinking. You are now ready to rough out a graphic representa-tion of at least two potential media plans in calendar form. Exhibit 15.8 presents a calendar for a retail store media plan. A blank planning calendar is provided in Ap-pendix C. You should prepare alternative plans in terms of different media included, usage of each medium, scheduling, total media weight levels, and budgets. Then, compare the alternative plans to each other in terms of total weight placed against the target market (reach, frequency, and GRPs). Also, compare corresponding costs to determine which plan meets the media objectives, maximizing the delivery of the message to the target audience at the lowest cost.

Finalize the Media Plan

After reviewing the alternative plans, you still might not be satisfied. Add to and/or delete from the best plan alternative to meet your media weight and cost require-ments. Even if you have a predetermined media budget, you will most likely have to revise your media plan once the first rough draft of the marketing plan is complet-ed. You will revise your media plan in terms of the weight levels, type of media used, and timing in relation to the other elements of the marketing plan. If you do not have a predetermined media budget, you will most likely revise the media plan to ar-rive at a media budget that will fit into a fixed marketing budget or a marketing budget developed through a task basis.

Prepare a Complete Media Calendar

Once you have finalized the media plan, make sure you have a complete media cal-endar in your media section. A good calendar is complete by itself. If your marketing plan dictates a different media plan for each market or grouping of markets, or if you have test markets, make sure each is represented on your calendar. Or, you can in-clude a calendar for each market or grouping of markets. Exhibit 15.9 shows items that should be considered for inclusion in your media calendar.

Prepare a Media Budget Summary

Along with a finalized media flow chart calendar, also include a media budget that you can exhibit in a number of different ways depending on the needs of your mar-keting plan. Two media budget examples are presented. One details spending for each medium by quarter (see Exhibit 15.10). If you want to present more spending detail, you can break out your dollars for each medium by month using a similar budget format. If you want to show both weight levels and spending, you can detail GRPs/TRPs and dollars for each quarter or month using a similar format.

If you have included a number of different products or markets in the marketing plan that require specific media support, you should also include a media budget that details media spending by product/market and medium. This example is shown in Exhibit 15.11. (Worksheets for both formats are presented in Appendix C.) It is best to show your media budget summary in the media section and then include media totals as part of the total marketing plan budget, which is included at the end of the marketing plan document (discussed in Chapter 18).

</td></tr>
</table>

Exhibit 15.8 Graphic Calendar for a Retail Store Media Plan

Media Calendar

1998
Monday (Bdcst) Dates

Example
Retail Store
Tier 1 Markets
December 1, 1997

Media	January	February	March	April	May	June	July	August	September	October	November	December	Schedule
	29 5 12 19 26	2 9 16 23	2 9 16 23	30 6 13 20 27	4 11 18 25	1 8 15 22 29	6 13 20 27	3 10 17 24 31	7 14 21 28	5 12 19 26	2 9 16 23 30	7 14 21	

Advertising Program
Women 18–49

Grand Opening — Sustaining — Back-to-School — Sustaining — Holidays

Madison, Milwaukee, Detroit and Columbus

Spot Television :30s (18 weeks) — 275 / 175 ... 275 / 175 ... 275 / 175 — **4,050 TRP's**
Women 18–49 TRP's Per Week
20% Day, 50% Fringe, 30% Prime

Newspapers—Thursday Main News — 1 Insertion Per Week — **39 Insertions** / **1,755 TRP's**
1/3 Page—B/W

Direct Mail: 1 Mile Radius of Store — **11 Mailings** / **110 TRP's**
Approx. 10% of Target/Mailing

Media Test—Madison Only

Spot Radio :60s (21 Weeks) — **3,675 TRP's**
175 Women 18–49 TRP's per week
1/3 AM, 1/3 Mid Day, 1/3 PM
Approx. 4 stations
20 spots per station per week

Total Rating Points (Milwaukee, Detroit & Columbus):   5,915
Total Rating Points (Madison Test):   9,590

Exhibit 15.9 Media Calendar Inclusions

Flow Chart Headings	Product/service/store name
	Market(s) name
	National
	Regional (describe)
	Group of markets that receive the same schedule.
	Example: Tier I, Tier II, etc. (List markets on calendar or attach a list of markets by tier if there are too many markets for inclusion on the calendar.)
	Individual market name
	Time period of plan
	Date prepared
	Program/Season (across top—optional)
All Media	Target audience
	Total GRPs/TRPs
	Cost(s) of medium and grand total (optional)
Television	Daypart mix
	GRPs/TRPs per week and total weeks and weight
	Length of spot
Radio	Daypart mix
	Number of spots and GRPs/TRPs per week and total weeks and weight
	Length of spot
	Number of spots per station (optional)
Magazine	Name of publication(s) (attach list of magazines if extensive)
	Size of ad/color
Newspaper	Name of newspaper(s) (attach list of newspapers if extensive)
	Size of ad/color
	Edition
Direct Mail	Number of mailings
	Quantity per mailing
Outdoor	Showing
	Number of boards

Exhibit 15.10 Media Budget: Spending by Medium and Quarter

Product: **Hot Dogs**
Year: **1998**
Date: **10/1/97**

Medium	1st Quarter ($000)	2nd Quarter ($000)	3rd Quarter ($000)	4th Quarter ($000)	Total ($000)	Percent
1. TV	$5,250.1	$2,361.0	$3,648.1	$4,430.1	$15,699.3	51.4%
2. Newspaper	2,341.0	1,060.7	1,678.0	1,876.4	6,956.1	22.8
3. Magazine	1,960.2	900.2	1,005.8	1,246.7	5,112.9	16.8
4. Direct Mail	1,102.3	534.2	542.7	580.4	2,759.6	9.0
Total	$10,653.6	$4,856.1	$6,874.6	$8,133.6	$30,517.9	
Percent	34.9%	15.9%	22.5%	26.7%		100%

As in the media objectives and media strategies sections, you should include a rationale for the final media plan. This rationale should include a brief discussion of the alternate plans considered and why this final plan fulfills the needs of the total marketing program. Alternative plans and budgets discarded can be included in a marketing plan appendix.

Exhibit 15.11 Media Budget: Spending by Market and Media

	Product:	Apparel
	Year:	1998
	Date:	11/1/97

Market	Newspapers		Television		Yellow Pages		Spending by Market	
	$M	Percent	$M	Percent	$M	Percent	$M	Percent
Buffalo	$113.4	12.3%	$50.5	14.9%	$1.1	7.0%	$165.0	13.0%
Des Moines	106.6	11.6	19.7	5.8	1.9	12.1	128.2	10.1
Ft. Wayne	49.7	5.4	18.8	5.5	0.9	5.7	69.4	5.5
Grand Rapids	46.6	5.1	36.6	10.8	1.1	7.0	84.3	6.6
Kansas City	114.0	12.5	51.5	15.2	2.9	18.5	168.4	13.2
Lincoln	50.4	5.5	14.9	4.4	1.2	7.7	66.5	5.2
Madison	55.6	6.1	19.8	5.8	0.8	5.1	76.2	6.0
Minneapolis	258.9	28.2	82.8	24.4	2.8	17.8	344.5	27.1
Omaha	62.7	6.8	21.8	6.5	2.2	14.0	86.7	6.8
Spokane	59.9	6.5	22.8	6.7	0.8	5.1	83.5	6.5
Spending by Medium	$917.8	72.1%	$339.2	26.7%	$15.7	1.2%	$1,272.7	100%

Final Check of the Media Plan

As a final check of the media plan, ask yourself the following questions:

- Are the media objectives and strategies consistent with the marketing objectives and strategies (particularly those relating to target audience(s), geographic allocations, seasonality/scheduling, weight levels, and the product positioning)?

- Is the media plan complementary and synergistic with advertising objectives, creative strategies, and execution?

- Is the media plan complementary and synergistic with promotion plans?

- Does this media plan demonstrate significant improvements over the previous year's plan?

- Does the plan provide a competitive advantage?

- What are the principal vulnerabilities of the plan, and how can they be addressed?

- Have alternative media plans been evaluated, and do these alternatives represent meaningful strategic differences?

- Have extra steps been taken to enhance the overall impact of the plan—tactical innovations, merchandising support, etc.?

- Are all media strategies and tactics actionable and stated specifically enough to facilitate execution?

- Does the media plan provide for a realistic financial commitment and flexibility? Do the financial media commitments extend for an entire year? Are they noncancellable?

- Does the plan include test proposals that can contribute important knowledge and are actionable?

- Does this media plan make common sense and meet with your real-world experience?

DOS AND DON'TS

Do

- Remember to ask yourself the who, where, when, and how questions to determine media objectives before you select and schedule the media.

- Make sure you strive for a basic understanding of the reach, frequency, and weight levels necessary to sell your product.

- Make sure the media you select not only fully reach the target audience effectively and efficiently but also enhance the message and are appropriate in terms of affordable advertising production cost.

- Remember our golden media rule: more than less and sooner than later.

- Attempt to dominate your medium of first choice before adding another medium to the mix.

- Use cost per thousand or cost per point in evaluating media, but remember, the end result is cost per sale.

- Quantify the media before you use it and evaluate its effectiveness after it runs.

- Concentrate on generating enough frequency to fully communicate the message and sell the product.

- When you have a small share of market and a limited media budget, the key term is media focus. Focus media by demographics, geography, time, and/or medium.

- Remember: If you are a retailer with very low per-square-foot occupancy cost versus the competition, you most likely will need greater media weight to attract customers.

- If you have a product with intangible benefits that requires imagery, it most likely needs heavier media weight than other more tangible-type products.

- Maximize your media investment with smart scheduling.

- Remember: the shorter the promotion period, the heavier the media schedule.

- Use heavier media weight in larger markets where the noise level is greater.

- The smaller the target market, the greater the need for awareness among this target to generate meaningful response.

- There is a greater need of unaided awareness for retailers who are *not* located in large, traffic-generating malls. A high level of unaided awareness is necessary among the target market to consider this type of retailer as a choice before the actual shopping experience.

- The more competition within a category, the greater the need to use heavier media weights to differentiate your product from the competition.

- If at all possible, determine your media budget by need, not by what you have in terms of budgeted dollars.

- Once you place your media schedule, make sure it runs and you receive what you paid for.

Don't

- If possible, don't use only advertising media as a percent of sales to determine the media budget.

- Don't underspend in your media plan, particularly for new product introductions, grand openings, test products, and promotions.

- Don't rely on preconceived ideas regarding media selection; thoroughly review alternative media before making a final decision.

- Just because you have a quality product does not mean it will sell itself. In fact, the higher the quality, typically the greater the need for media weight to build awareness for the quality product's features.

- Don't fragment media dollars over many media, thereby diluting your effort.

- If you can't evaluate media with available data, don't guess which media is best...test!

- Don't exclude a medium from your plan without objective consideration and analysis.

- Don't let high gross medium costs scare you off—check out the CPM and CPS.

- Don't use guesswork to develop a media plan—use discipline.

- Don't expect the competition to stand still while you execute an aggressive media plan. Think as if you were the competition and then prepare a contingency media plan for both the short and long term.

- Don't just consider the traditional media such as newspaper, radio, and television; consider all viable mediums, including interactive and direct response media.

Appendix of Evolving Personal Media

The area we call evolving personal media deals with the trend towards more one-on-one marketing, also referred to as relationship marketing. As competition increases, lifestyles change, media continues to become even more fragmented, and as the cost to reach consumers through the mass media vehicles continues to rise, the role of one-on-one, or relationship marketing will become increasingly more important in the overall marketing plan. Two of the elements that fall within the area of evolving personal media are direct marketing and interactive media.

Direct Marketing

Most of this section on media has focused on mass media vehicles. For many new product introductions, as well as in any instance where a strong market presence and awareness is needed, the more mass media vehicles would probably still be the most appropriate. However, there are also situations where you do not need or want to reach a very broad target market or where the potential "wasted" coverage is too costly. For these products or services, a very targeted direct marketing program, taking the message directly to the most likely prospect or decision maker, would be the better course of action. The most important element of any direct marketing program is the list of names. The more focused this list, the more efficient the program.

Your current list of customers would be the best place to start. Since they have already purchased something from you, they are good candidates for repeat purchases. If you don't have an accurate list of your customers, it might be a good idea to begin one through checks, credit cards, warranty cards, etc.

If you need to expand your current list, there are a number of outside sources from which you can rent names. Keep in mind, however, that if you have not already begun to develop your own base of names, you should make that one of your priorities. Once again, that base of names will be the best and most targeted for future direct marketing programs.

As to renting names from an outside source, there are many different ways that the marketplace can be segmented. For example:

- The marketplace can be segmented by demography and by ZIP code. For example, names can be rented for Women 18–49 who live in certain ZIP codes or who live within a certain distance from a retail store.

- A market can be segmented by hobby or lifestyle. For example, names are available for people who like to sew, go skiing, are avid book readers, etc. Companies like Claritas and Strategic Mapping, Inc., through their PRIZM and Cluster-Plus systems, have clustered the U.S. population into approximately 60 groups, based on a combination of factors that includes demographics, lifestyles, attitudes, and product usage patterns. Companies like Donnelley Marketing have their database names PRIZM and ClusterPlus coded. You can, therefore, rent a list of names of people who are in a certain lifestyle cluster.

- The names of subscribers to most magazines (general editorial and specific-interest publications) can be rented (in total or by geographic area).

- Lists of company names by segment and personal names by job title or function can be obtained through various list brokers and publications.

- In some cases, you can rent the names of people who have purchased a specific product. For example, through Donnelley Marketing, names are available of people who have purchased a CD player in the past 6 months.

- Newcomers to a market or newlyweds are just two more of the many ways that people can be segmented and identified for direct marketing programs.

Many different list brokers or list managers can be found in the SRDS Direct Mail edition, grouped by categories of interest.

On a cost basis, the price to rent one-time use of a list can range from $20 per thousand to over $150 per thousand, depending on how specific the list must be. Postage and printing can add another 75¢ to each piece. At that rate, it can become costly if you are using a large list of names. However, one of the goals of a good direct marketing program is to narrow down the list to the most likely prospects. With effective targeting, direct marketing truly becomes more efficient, especially when measured on a cost-per-sale basis.

Similar to the approach with the more mass media, testing is another crucial element in the development and maintenance of a good direct marketing program. Current lists can soon become outdated, and it is important to continually look for ways to update as well as add to the current list. Aside from using the same sources for updating lists of names, new sources of lists should be tested as a means of finding new customers. For example, if you sell high quality whole bean coffee, you might consider testing a list of subscribers to a publication which editorially focuses on gourmet food, such as *Gourmet,* or *Bon Appetit.* For a local retailer, periodically renting the names of newcomers to the area would be good way to introduce themselves to these new area residents. Another element to test is the actual message or offer. You should consider varying the offer as a means of determining which type of message or offer results in the greatest rate of response or sale.

Developing a "prime" list of target prospects, coupled with a focused message, can result in a very effective marketing tool.

INTERACTIVE MEDIA

In the 1950s, the new medium was television. In the 1980s, the buzzword was cable TV. In the 1990s, the spotlight is on interactive media.

What differentiates interactive media most from the more traditional forms of advertising is that it is more buyer initiated. The communication process basically begins when the consumer requests some specific information about a product or service. The consumer now plays a direct part in the communication process, choosing both when the message is delivered and, to some extent, the actual content of the message. Instead of an advertiser developing one message, sending it out to the masses, and hoping that it is the right message delivered at the right time, the advertiser can send out a wealth of information, letting consumers select what they feel is most important. Interest and attentiveness are at very high levels, since this is information that has been specifically requested.

There are many advantages and opportunities in the interactive world, some of which are:

- The advertiser is not limited to a page in a magazine or a 30-second time frame in which to communicate the key product benefits to a broad segment of the target market.

- The consumer can potentially find answers to specific questions at a time of their own choosing.

- The advertising has the potential to be significantly more effective, due to the higher interest and attentiveness levels.

Much of what was initially viewed as the interactive world of the future had all of this interactivity taking place through the television set. That, however, is still a few years away. The more immediate future (and to some extent, the present) has this taking place through our personal computers. The mechanics of this have already been in place for a number of years. Basically, all you need is a computer and a modem with which to connect to another computer.

Home computers have already become a way of life for many people. Currently, about 34 million homes have computers (approximately 30 percent of all U.S. households). Modems, once an add-on piece of hardware, are now being bundled with most new computer packages and are now in about 14 million homes (40 percent of all homes with computers). The number of homes with computers and modems should continue to increase. In addition, most computer packages also come with access to one or more on-line service, such as a Compuserve, Prodigy, or America On-line. These services, as well as others, will also provide access to the Internet and the World Wide Web, at which point you really can begin to travel the information superhighway about which so much has been written—all at just the stroke of a key.

Add to all this the fact that we have a society that is becoming increasingly more comfortable with using computers for more than just word processing and balancing checkbooks. The stage has been set, therefore, for the development of more effective ways to communicate with our target consumer.

Currently, there are already well over 30,000 different sites that marketers of various products and services, as well as just information providers, have already set up on the World Wide Web. Most are just experimenting with this new medium, looking for the most effective ways to get even closer to their target consumers.

For advertisers looking to begin experimenting with this new medium, there are basically two ways to get started:

1. *Establish your own site.* Going this route, you would design your site, or contract with someone to do that for you, and then rent space on a computer that is already connected to the high speed networks on the Internet. A listing of several companies in your area that will rent space on their computers, as well as those that can help in the design, can be found on the Internet itself.

The next step would be to develop a marketing program that would let your customers know:

- That you are on the Internet.

- How they can find you.

- What type of information they can expect to get at your site.

2. *Become part of an existing site.* Under this scenario, you would just pay to be included on someone else's site. You would still have to provide all of the data to be included at your particular site, but you would not have to rent computer space or do nearly as much marketing. You would be at a site that already has people coming to it. For example, a marketer of boating accessories could become part of a site geared to boating, one that has an established user base. An analogy might be the difference between developing, producing, and marketing your own magazine versus running ads in publications that already have a targeted, established readership base. Obviously, the least costly way to find out if print advertising worked would be to run ads in existing publications as opposed to starting your own magazine.

Accountability

As the Internet develops and matures, an element critical to it's long-term success will be accountability. There will have to be some form of system in place (just as there is with television, radio, and print) that will measure the extent to which consumers are actually being reached through this form of interactive media. Currently, companies such as A.C. Nielsen and Internet Profiles Corporation (I/PRO) are in the early stages of developing a system to measure how many people are coming to specific sites, who they are, and how much time they spend at that site. That type of information will be important when comparing the actual effectiveness/value of this type of interactive media to other forms of communication.

The next few years should be very exciting years, as more advertisers begin to experiment with this new medium. It will be very interesting to see what direction this new medium takes and to find out if we are both smart enough and creative enough to take advantage of the opportunities this new medium offers.

16

MERCHANDISING

Now that you have developed advertising and promotion plans and decided how to deliver their message through your media plan, it is time to focus on how non-media communication can enhance the effectiveness of your overall marketing program. Don't overlook the sales generation potential of this very basic, but effective, marketing tool.

Start by reviewing the marketing strategies which apply to merchandising and the related problems and opportunities. Then, when you are developing your merchandising objectives and strategies, remember that your merchandising program can effectively support and complement your more broadscale marketing and communication efforts. Further, remember the need to develop a merchandising program that will deliver the awareness and attitude levels required to fulfill the merchandising communication value goals.

Merchandising is a tangible communication link between your product and the consumer. Therefore, you need to make sure that this marketing tool is used in a manner which is consistent with the positioning and that it will complement the other tactical tools.

From This Chapter
You Will Learn

The definition of merchandising.

The issues affecting your merchandising plan.

How to develop your merchandising objectives and strategies.

OVERVIEW

Definition of
Merchandising

We define merchandising as the method used to communicate product information, promotions, and special events and to reinforce advertising messages through *nonmedia communication* vehicles. Merchandising is a way to make a visual or written statement about your company through a medium other than paid media with or without one-on-one personal communication. Merchandising includes brochures, sell sheets, product displays, video presentations, banners, posters, shelf talkers, table tents, or any other nonmedia vehicles that can be used to communicate product attributes, positioning, pricing, or promotion information.

Issues Affecting Merchandising

Merchandising Delivery Methods

Merchandising communication can be delivered through the following methods:

Personal Sales Presentation: Brochures, sell sheets, catalogs, and other forms of merchandising are often used to enhance a personal sales visit. The material can guide the sales visit, provide visual and factual support of the sales presentation, and serve as a reference that can be left behind for the customer or prospect.

Point-of-Purchase: In many product categories, over two-thirds of the purchase decisions are actually made at the point of purchase. For this reason, merchandising is a useful tool at the point of purchase to help affect purchase decisions that are made in-store. Merchandising materials can also be utilized at the point of purchase in the form of shelf talkers, table tents in restaurants, product displays, banners, etc. Merchandising at the point of purchase allows the marketer to make an impact on the purchaser above and beyond what can be expected from a product's packaging. Point-of-purchase (p-o-p) communication may be in the form of permanent product displays that enhance the presentation of your product or provide additional information. Point-of-purchase may also be of a more temporary nature. Such p-o-p often supports a special promotion, new product launch, and sales.

Merchandising, especially p-o-p, often requires another channel member (most often a retailer) to devote some resources for implementation of the program to be a success. These resources may include shelf or floor space, labor to set up and stock a display, etc. The question is, how do you sell the merchandising to the channel? Accordingly, it is often necessary to include a trade incentive to help ensure successful implementation of the program. These incentives may, for example, be in the form of special pricing or discounts during the program period, special advertising support, or participation in a sweepstakes.

Events: Merchandising is utilized through special events or company functions where contact with the target market occurs through sales meetings, conventions, mass participation events, concerts, etc. Banners, product displays, or fliers are commonly used at mass participation events to communicate brand name and product benefits to the target market.

Geography

Your merchandising plan should address where your merchandising programs will be executed. Will they be national, regional, local, or even in selected stores within a market?

Timing

The timing of your merchandising programs is also important. Therefore, the timing of the merchandising execution in relation to the other marketing mix elements must be decided. For example, your plan may require a brochure to be delivered prior to sales visits or after the advertising campaign kick-off. Or, you may want a retail store's featured inventory displayed for the duration of an advertising media blitz.

Merchandising's Purpose

Also address what the merchandising is being used to accomplish. You need to describe what marketing tool the merchandising will be assisting. Will you be merchandising product attributes, a new or lower price, a promotion, an advertising message, a personal sell-in presentation, etc.? In summary, you must decide upon the communication focus of the merchandising prior to writing this merchandising segment of the marketing plan.

How to Develop a Merchandising Plan

Task 1
Establish
Merchandising
Objectives

Your merchandising objectives should include:

- The number of merchandising pieces delivered or displayed at specific target location(s)

- The geography

- The timing

- The merchandising's purpose: the communication focus of the merchandising

The following merchandising objectives might be established to help achieve your marketing strategies:

Achieve placement of the new product display, which communicates the product's benefits, in 40 percent of the grocery stores carrying the product line nationwide in the month of September.

Obtain placement of price promotional tents from June through August in 50 percent of the current accounts in the top ten markets.

Display four product banners at each event during the concert series in all markets.

Task 2
Establish
Merchandising
Strategies

Your merchandising strategies should detail how to achieve your objectives in the following areas:

- The delivery and display method that should be used

- How to achieve placement of the merchandising elements and what trade incentives are necessary

- Description of creative parameters for development of the merchandising materials

Examples of merchandising strategies include:

Use the personal sales force to deliver the new product brochure during sales presentations.

Obtain placement of the shelf talkers by offering a competitive discount on each case in return for participation in the shelf talker program.

Obtain placement of the brand identification banners by the sales force. Employ a weekly monitoring system to assure that the banners remain in place for the four-week period.

The shelf talkers should incorporate visible brand identification and highlight the rules of the sweepstakes. An entry pad should be included.

A worksheet for you to use in developing your merchandising objectives and strategies is provided in Appendix C.

DOS AND DON'TS

Do

- Review your marketing strategies and your problems and opportunities prior to developing your merchandising plan.

- Think of more than one way to use merchandising. There are multiple uses, and there should be multiple merchandising executions in your plan.

- Tie in existing creative from advertising, promotion, and publicity to your merchandising. An overall look provides for a unified communication effort and allows one marketing mix tool to reinforce the other.

- Find out from the field what merchandising tools are needed to help them increase their selling effectiveness.

- Make sure the merchandising materials sent to the field are properly utilized. All too often, there is a great deal of time and effort put into producing merchandising materials only to have them receive limited attention or not be used at all.

- Make sure the merchandising materials that you develop are designed to fit into the retailer's store/shelf format.

- Make sure your distributors and retailers are provided adequate incentive to participate in and effectively execute the merchandising program.

Don't

- Don't ignore the importance of execution and persistence as the keys to a successful merchandising program.

- Don't think of merchandising at the last minute. Strategically incorporate this powerful tool into your mix.

- Merchandising materials are expensive. Don't be wasteful; make sure they get used.

- Don't expect your merchandising materials to be readily accepted by the trade. Develop a well-thought-out program that will assure acceptance.

- Don't overlook the many new ways to communicate via merchandising using new media and advanced point-of-sale techniques.

17

PUBLICITY

Publicity can play a unique role as a tool in your marketing plan. It is especially valuable in a wide range of situations where public awareness and/or public opinion is critical to your marketing success. For example, marketing objectives and strategies that call for introducing a new product; building brand loyalty; enhancing company image; educating a target audience; countering misperceptions; responding to societal trends; or generating community, industry, or legislative/regulatory support are often well supported through a publicity program.

As with all the other marketing tools, review the problems and opportunities section for specific input, the pertinent marketing strategies for direction, and the communication value goals in terms of awareness and attitudinal levels requirements before writing this plan segment.

From This Chapter You Will Learn

The definition of publicity.

The issues affecting your publicity plan.

How to develop your publicity objectives and strategies.

OVERVIEW

Definition of Publicity

In this book, we will define publicity as *nonpaid media communication* that helps build target market awareness and positively affects attitudes toward your product or firm. In a publicity program, your organization provides information to the news media that is used for its news value.

Publicity provides your firm or product with benefits not found in any other marketing mix tool. Since publicity utilizes noncommercial communication through independent news media, it adds a dimension of legitimacy that can't be found in advertising. Unlike paid advertising, publicity also provides the means to tell your story in greater depth and in a manner that tends to be informational rather than promotional. This can be a tremendous asset when you need to educate your target market about a new product or technology or build awareness and understanding of an issue that is key to your product's and your firm's success.

Obtaining publicity for your firm or product can be difficult, and there are no guarantees regarding the placement of your message, when it appears, or what is ultimately communicated. As publicity is nonpaid, it is to a large degree uncontrollable. But there are some things you can do to help generate positive publicity for your firm. These are discussed in the issues section of this chapter.

Before incorporating a publicity segment in your marketing plan, you should ask yourself these questions:

- Do your objectives, marketing strategies, and subject matter lend themselves well to publicity?

- Do you need and want the added dimension of legitimacy to your overall communications effort?

- Do you need additional media weight without media dollar investment, knowing that there is no certainty to the amount (if any) and type of publicity you will receive?

- After careful consideration of your product, your target audiences, and the external environment in which you operate, are you confident that there is minimal (or manageable) risk of unfavorable publicity?

- Are you willing to view publicity as a long-term investment that contributes to positive image and to use other, more controllable marketing tools to generate short-term sales?

- Are you willing to make the investment in time either through your company staff or an outside agency to generate publicity, knowing its benefits and limitations? Is there a likelihood that this investment will be worth it?

Also, keep in mind that publicity is only one facet of public relations. Public relations is a broad discipline that seeks to develop and maintain mutually beneficial relationships between an organization and its various publics. Public relations builds good will by affecting public opinion issues and by ensuring that the organization meets its responsibilities to customers, shareholders, employees, suppliers, the community, and others. The resulting goodwill helps an organization succeed in the marketplace and can be a key competitive advantage in a crisis situation. If you need in-depth information on public relations, refer to a text exclusively devoted to this subject.

Issues Affecting Publicity

Publicity Planning

Publicity doesn't just happen. In most instances, positive publicity is the result of a written, well-thought-out plan and a hands-on execution program. Included in the publicity section of the marketing plan should be target markets, objectives, and strategies. Before planning your annual publicity program, make sure you review the relevant problems, opportunities, and marketing strategies.

There are usually two distinct types of publicity target markets—the media, which needs to be made aware of the news story, and the target market or markets to whom you wish to communicate. When preparing your strategies, it is important to understand the interests of your *product's* target market and those of the *media* target market.

Your product's target market looks to your firm to provide certain product benefits and meet certain consumer needs. The media target market, on the other hand, is interested in providing their readers, viewers, or listeners with information they will find useful or informative. Some media representatives are also interested in distinguishing themselves from their competition by being the first one to "land" a certain news story. You will be more successful in placing stories with news editors and writers if you help them do their jobs more effectively.

Finally, before you prepare your publicity plan, make sure you have clearly delineated in your mind what you want to accomplish with this marketing tool.

Publicity Is Contingent on What Is Newsworthy

A major task in generating publicity is to attract the attention and interest of newspeople so that, eventually, your story can be communicated to the target market. The media are "gatekeepers," in that they decide what your ultimate target audience will read, see, or hear in the various news outlets. Your first approach to these gatekeepers should be carefully planned, because you often can't go back to the news media a second time with a publicity item or story idea that has already been rejected.

To obtain publicity you must have an angle of interest (hook) for the targeted public above and beyond the selfish interest of promoting your company. The news media has no desire to turn its editorial copy into advertising. The press *does* have a need to provide newsworthy stories of interest to the public.

An estimated 80 percent of news releases are thrown away by newspeople because they are not deemed worthwhile to the medium's audience. Publicity potential was one reason we developed a Downtown Beach Party event for the Coors Young Adult department. The unusual twist of creating a beach party with a million pounds of sand in the middle of a downtown area as a major charity fundraiser enabled us to develop extensive television, newspaper, and radio publicity for Coors beer.

When evaluating the newsworthiness of your material, bear in mind that different types of media have different needs, because they serve distinct audiences. For example, *Restaurant Business,* a trade journal for restaurant operators, might run a feature article on trends in kitchen equipment. If you represent a kitchen equipment manufacturer, you would benefit from a mention in this issue and should contact the appropriate editor. Yet, the same material you send to *Restaurant Business* would be of no interest to the news assignment editor at a television station or to the local daily newspaper. A truly successful publicity effort begins with an understanding of each media outlet you are targeting, including who they serve, their editorial style, and what types of publicity materials they consider newsworthy.

Publicity Should Generate Added Awareness for Your Company, Product Name, and Key Product Attributes

Make sure that the publicity you receive creates positive awareness for your firm and its products. Think carefully about the information you have available for release and how you can enhance its presentation so that the positive attributes of your product or firm come through loud and clear. When publicizing the Diaper Genie®, the diaper disposal system that controls odor by encasing each individual diaper in a plastic film, it was important for both the news media gatekeepers and the consumer to understand exactly how the product works. To accomplish this, we provided a news release (Exhibit 17.1) and a cut-away illustration in our press kit showing exactly what goes on inside the Diaper Genie when a diaper is inserted and the lid is twisted. The illustration enhanced the believability of the odor-free claim by proving

Exhibit 17.1 News Release

February 1994   Contact: Susan Morris
                                                                The Hiebing Group, Inc.
                                                                (608) 256-6357

ODOR-FREE DIAPER DISPOSER
STORES SOILED DIAPERS FOR FUTURE DISPOSAL

The Diaper Genie®, a compact diaper disposal system, provides a modern solution to the age-old problem of diaper odor.

The system eliminates odor by individually wrapping soiled disposable diapers in an odor- and germ-resistant film and storing them in an odor-free container for disposal at a convenient time.

"The Diaper Genie uniquely improves upon the conventional diaper pail by wrapping each soiled diaper, eliminating odor each and every time a baby is changed," explained John Hall, president of Ohio-based Mondial Industries, Limited, manufacturer of the Diaper Genie. "It is truly the only odor-free diaper disposal system available."

Introduced in the U.S. in the spring of 1993, the Diaper Genie already has been recognized for excellence and innovation in industry competitions in two countries. In October 1993, the Diaper Genie was named a winner of the "Show Off" Product Competition at the 24th Annual International Juvenile Products Show, sponsored by the Juvenile Products Manufacturers Association (JPMA). In 1991, after just three months on the market in England, the Diaper Genie won the Gold Award for being the most innovative product at the U.K. Child and Nursery Fair.

"We're seeing signs that the Diaper Genie could largely replace the conventional diaper pail in home nurseries," said Hall. He reports that registered owners include both first-time parents and those who've discarded their previous diaper pails, as well as grandparents and day-care center operators.

The Diaper Genie is operated by removing a twist-cap on the container, inserting a soiled diaper, replacing the cap, and twisting it to wrap the diaper in an odor- and germ-resistant film. It requires neither batteries nor electricity. "Because of its special design, the Diaper Genie remains odor-free even with the insertion of the next soiled diaper," Hall said. Once diapers are sealed away in the disposer, they cannot be tampered with by children or pets.

As diapers are added, the container produces an odorless chain of up to 20 tightly wrapped diapers that can safely and hygienically be disposed of. "Because it separates diapers from other trash, the Diaper Genie additionally offers a first step toward the recycling of disposable diapers," Hall noted.

The compact Diaper Genie stands 18 inches tall, making it smaller than most diaper pails and easier to transport.

The Diaper Genie usually sells for about 30 dollars. Refills, which wrap up to 180 disposable diapers each, retail for approximately five dollars.

The product is available in the U.S. at many retail chain stores and baby specialty stores. National chains that carry the Diaper Genie include Kmart, Sears, Target, and Toys 'R' Us. It is also available through The Right Start, One Step Ahead, and The Safety Zone catalogs. In Canada, the Diaper Genie can be purchased at Sears and Toys 'R' Us.

For information on the Diaper Genie, call Mondial Industries, Limited, at (216) 467-4443.

that each diaper is wrapped separately. Some newspeople printed the illustration in their publications, while others used it to gain knowledge of the product and decide that it was worthy of positive mention.

Ideally, the information that comes through in your publicity should be positive, and it should also reinforce the key messages in your marketing communications program. One way to accomplish this type of communication is to tie your product to a newsworthy happening or event that is consistent with the product's positioning or will highlight its product attributes. For example, a ski manufacturer who sponsors the winning skier in the race has the implied endorsement of the champion and is communicating a great deal about the performance of its skis.

If you are sponsoring an event, try to have visual identification in the form of banners, hats, T-shirts, etc., visible the day of the event. Don't forget to get your company's identification on all potential spokespeople. These forms of identification are likely to appear in news coverage of the event, reinforcing your company or product name before a large audience.

Always Consider and Prepare for the Potential Downside of Publicity

One of the disadvantages of publicity is that you lack control over the content. The news media is entitled to print or air virtually anything they choose about your company or product (as long as it is not considered libelous). In fact, their right to do this is protected by the First Amendment to the U.S. Constitution, which guarantees both free speech and freedom of the press.

As a result, your quest for publicity may inadvertently result in negative exposure. This does not necessarily mean that you should avoid a publicity effort altogether. However, you should make an assessment of the potential downside as part of your planning process.

Some organizations or products are more susceptible to negative publicity than others. These include companies working in controversial areas such as environmental issues; industries that regularly come under public scrutiny, such as financial institutions and telecommunications; any regulated or recently deregulated industry; and products or services related to "hot topics" such as the rising costs of health care. Even products that are not normally susceptible to negative publicity can suddenly find themselves in an unfavorable spotlight. Johnson & Johnson's Tylenol scare, in which pills tainted with poison killed several consumers, is a renowned example.

Given the unpredictability of the content of publicity, virtually every marketer should have some type of contingency plan in place for responding to negative publicity. If you anticipate problems due to the nature of your product or your industry, try to minimize such negative exposure by releasing information in a manner that directly addresses public concerns. Have honest, informative answers prepared for challenging questions you may be asked by newspeople preparing balanced pieces on an issue or industry. And don't forget that an infrequent negative comment in the media does not necessarily erase the positive effects of all the other publicity you receive. Keep it in perspective.

Look for Connections Between Publicity and the Other Tools in Your Marketing Program

Every publicity effort you devise should also be examined for its potential value elsewhere in the marketing program. For example, favorable coverage received in an important magazine can be reprinted in quantity (with the publication's permission) and distributed to salespeople or dealers for use as a sales tool, as well as to employees. Important news releases may be mailed directly to customers or dealers; this is an effective technique when used discriminately. Also, favorable product reviews from leading media may be cited on packaging or in advertising.

The reverse is also true, in that some other aspect of your marketing program may provide you with an occasion for publicity. Some companies generate publicity worth thousands (or even millions) of dollars when they create advertising campaigns that are newsworthy because they use a celebrity spokesperson, generate controversy, or break the traditional advertising mold in some dramatic and unusual way. Apple Computer's famous Orwellian "1984" television commercial, which aired during the 1984 Super Bowl, would be an example. Or, perhaps your promotional program includes some type of consumer contest or event that the news media might cover.

Always examine all of the tools in your marketing mix to identify ways your publicity activities and results can support these other efforts possible sources of publicity ideas.

Types of Potential Articles or News Stories

Several types of articles and stories will generate publicity, if newsworthy.

Standard News Release

Announcement of newsworthy events that are happening whether reported or not (opening new offices, new services, a new product, etc.) are of potential interest to the general public or specific groups. Other newsworthy events are manufactured, in that they are created and staged at least partially for their publicity value. Examples of these events include workshops or seminars for businesspeople or customers, celebrity appearances, contests, and public events. In addition to distributing a standard news release to the media, you can find additional value in distributing the news release to in-house company newsletters, customers, dealers or distributors, and employees.

Feature Stories

While the standard news release is a simple announcement of a future or current event, the feature article explores a subject of interest to the target audience in greater depth. Unlike standard news items, which are typically time sensitive, the feature story may appear at any time or during a broad time period of relevance, such as the winter season. Ask yourself, "What do I know that the general public would like to, or should, know?" Then develop meaningful feature article ideas to pitch to the appropriate news media.

A successful how-to feature article must be genuinely instructive, providing a benefit to the reader. The benefit to the firm comes in subtly establishing the firm as a leader with particular expertise. In some cases, such as specialized publication for a particular group of consumers, the name of your product and its attributes may also receive mention.

Exclusives

The exclusive is a type of feature story that is offered to only one media outlet and not to competing media. This type of opportunity can be attractive to newspeople because it allows them to offer readers or viewers a story no one else can offer. However, nothing angers competing news media more than when a company withholds information they have a right to receive. Never use exclusives for "hard news" or "breaking news" developments on which all relevant media should be informed. Also, never promise one media outlet an exclusive and then give the same story to another, competing media outlet.

Concept Articles

These are articles describing the basic concept of your business and why people should take advantage of the offering. An accounting firm might develop a concept article on why businesses should make use of a full-service accounting firm. The concept article stresses the importance of doing things in a particular way and the benefits to be derived from doing it in that manner. However, the reader cannot escape the unstated message that the people who wrote the article or who are quoted in it are the experts in the field.

Opinion Pieces

Where controversy exists, so does the opportunity to reinforce a leadership image by taking a stand and communicating that stand. A variety of story formats can fall under the category of "op/ed" (opinion/editorial). They can be as brief as a well-written letter to the editor or as detailed as a point-of-view article in local dailies, commentary in television news programs, testimony before legislative committees, etc.

Opinion pieces that carry the byline of a someone at your company position the author and author's company as experts in the field. Another alternative is to use the op/ed format to achieve a form of third party endorsement, by going to the editorial boards of newspapers or televisions and urging them to write or air a story advocating your point of view. When you use either approach, the media may come to rely on you for input concerning other issues relevant to your field. If you are cited in the media repeatedly, you will be perceived as a spokesperson for your industry, helping your company to be viewed as a leader in the field.

Photo Opportunities

Some company activities may not merit a full story but would make an excellent photo opportunity for the print or television media. Wire service photos of this type can even receive broad distribution throughout the country or the world. Companies and products have received wide exposure in the news media for everything from look-alike people and pet contests to the exhibiting of a visually exciting new product at a trade show. If you have something that is visually appealing but without much informational content, consider offering it as a photo opportunity rather than a feature story. In general, media representatives will prefer to take their own photos in these cases; supplying photos to them is not recommended.

Public Service Advertising/Announcements (PSAs)

PSAs are advertisements run free of charge by the media. Although public service advertising is not a true form of publicity because you do control message content, it is very much like publicity because you do not control where, when, or how much the message will run in the media. The time or space for these ads is donated to non-profit organizations, government agencies, and other groups judged worthy by the broadcast, print, and outdoor media.

The number of available PSAs is often a function of supply and demand for the medium's time or space. Television and radio stations, and to a lesser degree outdoor companies, usually provide more PSA support than newspapers and magazines. The broadcast media have a set number of commercial minutes to fill each hour, and if the time is not purchased, they will often run public service announcements. The chance of getting PSA time is often greatest during the post-holiday period of January and February, when demand for broadcast time and outdoor advertising is at a minimum. Summer months can also be a good PSA time, particularly for television.

It should be mentioned that it is difficult to generate print PSAs. Your efforts will be much better spent focusing on placement of broadcast and outdoor PSAs.

The Timing of Your Publicity Efforts Is Important

Whether you are using a pure publicity effort or PSA program, the timing of placement is critical. When is the consuming target in the mode to purchase? When is the specific media in need of newsworthy information? Does your story rely on a time-sensitive hook such as reference to a holiday or the start of a certain season? What is the lead time for the various news media you are contacting (which can vary from three to five months for magazines to days or even hours for daily news media)?

The weekends are usually slow news times for the broadcast media and may be easier times to place a story with a television and radio station. However, the price you may pay is reaching a smaller audience at those times. If you are releasing what you consider to be "breaking news" (for example, an announcement of a business development that is clearly newsworthy), you stand a much higher chance of reaching a weekday audience in the broadcast media.

Timing is also a critical question when conducting phone contacts, whether initial contacts or follow-up calls, with the news media. All journalists have times when they are on tight deadlines. If they need something from your company at those times, immediate handling of that inquiry is critical. Contacts that are not time sensitive, such as follow-up calls to media contacts who have been mailed your materials, should not be made to newspeople who are on deadline and too busy to talk. Deadlines vary by medium (magazines usually observe monthly deadlines, while daily broadcast media face multiple deadlines a day), so it is incumbent upon you to learn what those deadlines are and to respect them. If you are unsure, simply ask.

HOW TO DEVELOP A PUBLICITY PLAN

Task 1
....
**Establish Your
Publicity Objectives**

Similar to your marketing, advertising, and promotion objectives, your publicity objectives should be specific, measurable, and relate to a specific time period. However, since publicity is not a paid, controlled message, it does not usually focus on affecting a target market behavior directly; rather, it focuses on making the target market aware of the product or company in a positive light. In this manner, publicity "softens" the market so that prospects are more likely to respond to your advertising or promotional offers. Sometimes publicity does generate inquiries directly from your prospects, though the source of those inquiries may or may not be easy to measure.

Your publicity objectives should address the following:

- The specific purpose of the publicity effort (i.e., announce a grand opening, gain additional exposure for a new product, generate PSA support, etc.).

- The specific target market (medium and audience)

- The time period and marketplace

- The expected level of exposure, by medium, to be generated from the publicity effort

- The basic message or messages you would like to get across about your company or product, including the product positioning you would like to communicate.

An example of a publicity objective would be:

In the next year, achieve maximum exposure among people who sew for the grand opening events through the television, radio, and newspaper media in each of the 20 DMA markets.

Obtain coverage from a minimum of two television stations and a minimum of three radio stations.

Obtain coverage from a minimum of one newspaper before and after the event.

Build understanding of the fact that even busy people can find time to sew due to new convenience products and the emergence of simpler patterns and lines in both clothing and home fashions.

<table>
<tr><td>

Task 2

Establish Your Publicity Strategies

</td><td>

Publicity strategies describe how to achieve the media coverage delineated in the publicity objectives. Address the following in formulating your strategies:

</td></tr>
</table>

- What newsworthy material you have and how the material aligns with the interests of both your media targets and your product targets

- Types of news releases or stories to use

- Coverage via interviews and/or news conferences with television, radio, newspaper and magazine editor representatives

- Participation in talk shows and local interest programs

- Possible use of on-line services or the Internet to reach specialized audiences or the media

- Visibility at conventions, seminars, and public events

- Public service announcements (if you are a nonprofit organization or can develop a joint effort with a nonprofit organization)

- Ways to maximize the value of your publicity by incorporating it elsewhere in the marketing program

In developing your publicity strategies, also consider the following:

Make sure the news media is thoroughly aware of the event or product's news. For example, you may write news releases and deliver them in a memorable way. The Coors Downtown Beach Party news releases were delivered by local personnel equipped with flippers, scuba masks, and surfboards.

Detail a specific follow-up procedure to make certain the news releases weren't forgotten or lost and, most importantly, to ensure that they will be used in some manner.

Develop ways to tie the media into the publicity event itself, or obtain a third party to help legitimize your requests for publicity support. For example, provide cosponsorship packages to media and charities in return for publicity. The media and charity cosponsors become cosponsors on all paid, printed advertising in return for pre-determined publicity requirements both prior to and during the event.

Provide a unique twist to interest the media in providing publicity. This can be communicated in a news release or by phone to the media to pique their interest. This technique worked very well for our Famous Footwear client. Major news media were offered the chance to interview All-Pro football player Al Toon of the New York Jets in return for publicity surrounding the opening of a new Famous Footwear store.

Where possible, *include memorable but appropriate product identification.*

The following is an example of publicity strategies that could be developed to achieve a publicity objective. Assume you are developing publicity strategies for the following publicity objectives:

Achieve maximum radio and newspaper exposure in each market among young adults 18 to 24 for the five concerts to be staged within the next year in five to-be-determined DMA markets.

At a minimum, obtain coverage from two of the top five young adult radio stations.

At a minimum, obtain coverage from a major daily before and after the event.

Potential publicity strategies would be:

Prepare four different news releases, each with a different newsworthy slant on the event, to be delivered via mail and personally before and after the event.

Stress the various benefits to the charity in the news release, particularly how important the event is in regard to the charity's yearly fundraising.

Have the local press interview the concert performances and the local charity spokesperson, incorporating company identification at the interview site.

A worksheet to use in developing your publicity objectives and strategies is provided in Appendix C.

DOS AND DON'TS

Do

- Plan your publicity effort. It doesn't just happen. Be as detailed as possible. Thoroughly review your target markets and their needs prior to developing the publicity plan.

- Approach publicity knowing its limitations but also understanding the potential it provides.

- Examine the other sections of your marketing plan to determine how the results of your publicity efforts can be incorporated into other parts of the program. Also, look for possible newsworthy stories or events that are inspired by elements of the marketing plan themselves.

- Be willing to persevere and be persistent with the key media people in order to achieve results.

- Distinguish between material that is "hard news" and publicity material that is more feature oriented. "Hard news" is any newsworthy announcement that the news media and the audience will want to know—an actual happening of importance rather than a manufactured event. Each type of news requires its own publicity techniques.

- Adopt an outsider's view of your material and do an honest assessment of its news value.

- Provide the media with a meaningful benefit for featuring your firm, product, or event, such as a unique and/or timely story for their audience or a chance to cosponsor a program/promotion that is of interest to the local community.

- Work through or with another organization such as a charity or service group to provide credibility with the media and assistance in staging and publicizing the event.

- When possible, include a photograph or illustration with your news release (as eye catching or unique as possible), as this sometimes increases the chance of getting your story covered. In addition, offer the media's own photographers easy access to your event or company if appropriate.

- Localize your material to the target media and target audience whenever possible. This might include geographic localization for the daily news media or customization to the particular audience addressed by a certain trade journal or consumer magazine.

- Provide a compelling yet credible lead to your news release. Your theme and/or angle should be readily apparent in the headline and the first paragraph.

- Provide a contact name and phone number to media representatives for further questions. Make sure this is someone who is both qualified to answer questions and readily available to respond to media inquiries.

- Select the distribution method(s) most appropriate for the media you are targeting and the level of urgency to the information you are disseminating. Distribution methods include hand delivery, phone, fax, regular mail, express mail, paid wire services, commercial on-line services, and the Internet. Make sure the media you are targeting can be reached via the distribution method you choose.

- Plan your follow-up contacts carefully and be prepared to answer any questions—or even pitch your story again—when your follow-up call is made.

- Remember that there are no guarantees in nonpaid media coverage. Even if a reporter has already expressed interest in your material or attended your event, a more compelling news story can "bump" your story right up until the last minute. If your story is not out-of-date by then, you can follow up on the possibility of later use of the material.

- Record and evaluate the publicity received to determine if the objectives were met and to improve your future publicity programs.

- Generating meaningful publicity is hard work. Do it right or not at all.

Don't

- Don't look at publicity as a substitution for advertising. You can't control the content or the amount of exposure, and you usually can't include a call to action asking the prospect to buy.

- Don't confuse publicity with public relations. Publicity generates nonpaid media exposure for your product or company. Public relations is more encompassing and seeks to manage your company's relationships with its key constituency groups, including how those relationships affect the long-term image of your company, product, and industry.

- Don't assess potential stories from a company perspective; evaluate them from a news editor's position. The media has a responsibility to stay objective and fulfill the needs of their audience.

- Don't assume all media vehicles are the same. Take time to know the media vehicle and the kind of stories in which its editors are interested.

- Don't write your firm or product's whole life story in a press release. Give only the basic facts in one to three pages of double-spaced copy. If a significant amount of background information is needed to understand the content, put the background on separate fact sheets that are provided as addendums to the main news release. Where there are a number of individual pieces (e.g., news release, backgrounders, and photos), enclose them in a press kit.

- Don't expect attention-getting delivery or creative packaging to compensate for a lack of news value. Creative delivery of your information can get a reporter's attention, but this alone doesn't guarantee coverage. You must also offer information of usefulness of interest to the media target's audience.

- Don't overcommercialize your message. Try to provide needed information. If you are too self serving, it will be difficult to obtain publicity.

- Don't state opinions or interpretations as if they are facts. Any information that is not objective and factual should be attributed to a qualified and verifiable source. Often, such material is provided within a quotation from a spokesperson. Independent sources who do not have a company bias are the most credible and should be used when available.

- Don't expect competing media to run stories about your event if it being cosponsored by a particular media outlet (such as a newspaper, television station, or radio station). Only rarely are competing media willing to devote any space or time to an event that promotes one of their own competitors; in those cases, they will make their stories as brief as they can while still meeting their obligation to provide news to the community.

- Don't argue with editors or reporters who have decided not to use your material. If their understanding of your story pitch is clear and they still don't want to use it, ask them what types of news releases or story leads they prefer to receive. Use rejection of this one idea as an opportunity to learn how to do better next time and to establish mutual respect between you and the editor.

- Don't expect publicity efforts employed on a sporadic, hit-and-miss basis to be effective. Use publicity in a planned, continuous manner.

- Don't launch your publicity program without first evaluating the likelihood of adverse publicity of any kind. Prepare for that possibility and, if necessary, develop publicity materials that address possible public concerns and make your company's point of view on the issues clear.

- Don't generate publicity without considering its impact on your overall positioning.

Step Eight   Marketing Plan Budget and Calendar

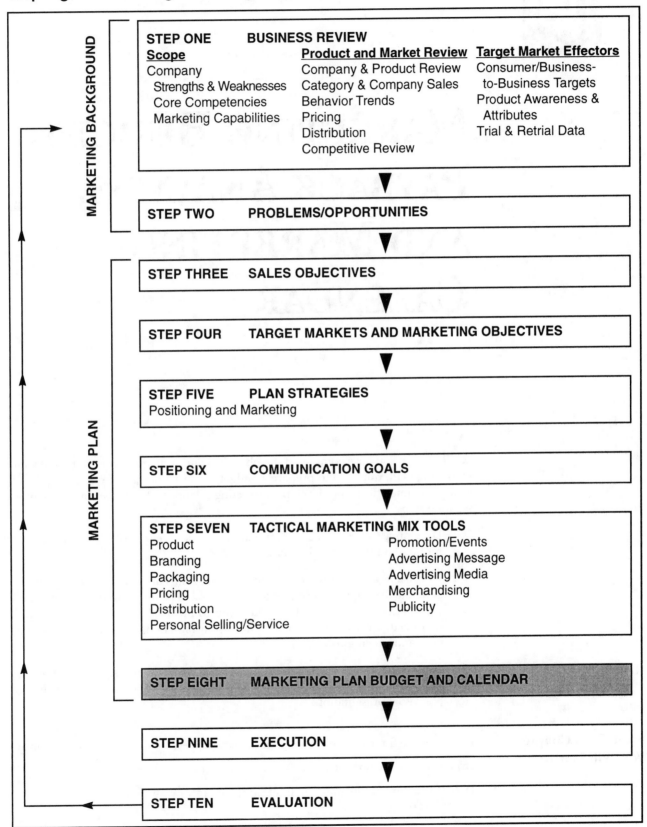

MARKETING BUDGET, PAYBACK ANALYSIS, AND MARKETING CALENDAR

Now that you have completed the objectives and strategies for each tool of your marketing plan, you need to prepare a budget, project a payback from the results of your marketing effort, and develop a marketing calendar. This process involves three separate steps:

1. Develop a *budget* to provide estimated costs associated with each marketing tool used in the marketing plan.

2. Utilize a *payback analysis* to determine if the results of your marketing plan will generate the required revenues to meet sales and profit goals. If the payback indicates that your plan will not allow you to meet sales and profit goals, you may need to revise your budget and/or your marketing plan objectives, strategies, and executions.

3. Once you have reconciled your budget and payback analysis, a *marketing calendar* should be developed to provide a summary of all marketing activities in one visual presentation.

From This Chapter You Will Learn

How to utilize three basic budgeting methods: task, percent-of-sales, and competitive.

How to develop a payback analysis.

How to develop an integrated marketing calendar for your marketing plan.

BUDGETING OVERVIEW

Based upon our experience, it seems there are never enough marketing dollars regardless of which budgeting approach is employed. For this reason, the marketer needs to determine priorities for the plan, along with corresponding executional costs for the various marketing activities. Then, based on the priorities and associated costs, pare back the activities to meet the predetermined budget level, striking a balance between what needs to be accomplished and what you can realistically afford. Ideally, you will be able to develop a budget that is realistic from a total spending standpoint and yet will provide the necessary resources to support a successful marketing plan.

HOW TO DEVELOP YOUR BUDGET

Task 1
Task Method

The authors recommend that you begin your budgeting process using the task method as the first step, because with this method you set a budget (without bias) based not on what the industry category or key competition is spending but on what needs to be accomplished for your product. This method attempts to develop a budget that will adequately support the marketing mix activity in your plan to achieve the sales and marketing objectives. To arrive at the total dollar budget, you must estimate the costs for each marketing tool execution involved in the plan. The assumption is that, through a disciplined planning process, challenging yet realistic sales objectives were established, along with a marketing plan to meet those objectives. Thus, the budget will allow the objectives to be met in an efficient manner. An aggressive marketing plan will result in a more aggressive budget utilizing this method. However, there is no *real* test of affordability or profitability, which is why a payout analysis is presented in the payout section of this chapter.

Task 2
Percent-of-Sales
Method

The second step in developing a budget for your marketing plan is to benchmark your marketing budget total as a percent of total sales. You can review the amount spent on advertising/media, promotion, and total marketing by other firms in your industry as a percent of sales. Usually, an industry standard exists that will provide the average percent of sales that will account for the advertising/media budget, the promotion budget, and sometimes even the total marketing budget.

The major disadvantage with this method is that it creates a situation where sales determine marketing expenditures. However, the whole idea behind a disciplined campaign development is the belief that marketing affects sales. When sales decline and there are problems to be solved, there is less money available to solve them with the percent-of-sales method.

The percent-of-sales method makes most sense if used as a way to determine whether your task method budget is realistic. Additionally, if your firm has no real history with the effects of marketing and specific tactical tools, then the percent-of-sales method will act as a way to allocate expenditures that should be fairly consistent with industry standards. You can find the industry advertising-to-sales ratios for the standard industrial classifications (SIC) codes within a published report by Schonfeld and Associates. *Advertising Age* also publishes the advertising-to-sales ratio of the top 100 advertisers each year. Another source is *Fairchild Fact Files*, a publication which provides information on individual consumer industries. Annual reports and 10-Ks are another excellent source for this information.

Task 3
Competitive Method

The final method is to estimate the sales and marketing budgets of the leading competitive firms and compare those estimates to your sales and marketing budget. This method might allow your firm to match or beat specific competitive expenditures, helping to assure that you remain competitive in the marketplace. The advantage of this method is that it provides the potential for an immediate response to competitive actions. The disadvantages are that it is difficult to estimate competitors' budgets and it does not take into consideration the inherent potential of your firm based upon data developed from the business review. Utilizing this method alone, you may be restricting the actual potential of your firm based upon your competitors' lack of insight and marketing ability. However, like the percent-of-sales method, you can use the budget derived from this method as a means of comparison to the task method to arrive at your final budget.

USING A COMBINATION OF THE THREE TASKS TO FINALIZE YOUR BUDGET

If the data are available, we recommend using a combination of all three steps in finalizing your marketing budget. First, use the *task method*. This will provide you with a budget that will be your best chance to achieve the stated objectives in your own marketing plan. As the budget is derived based solely upon what is required to provide for the success of your individual marketing plan, the task method is not as biased or as limiting as other methods. Product history and industry averages play a lesser role in the budgeting process. However, if the task method budget varies substantially from the percent-of-sales method budget, you need to review the reasons why your plan requires either substantially more or less expenditures than the industry average. If, for example, you are introducing a new product, you may be required to spend at greater levels than the industry average to obtain initial trial of the new product and still maintain sales of your existing lines.

Second, use the *percent-of-sales method* to provide a guideline or rough, ballpark budget figure based upon the historical spending of your product and of the marketplace. Used properly, the percent-of-sales budget will help provide insight into whether your task-generated budget is too low or too high based upon the experiences of other similar companies in your industry.

Finally, consider using the *competitive budgeting method* as a device to help you respond to competitive pressures in the marketplace. If your company is consistently spending less than a major competitor and is losing market share while this competitor is gaining market share, then you might want to develop a budget that allows you to be more competitive from a spending standpoint. There is not much any marketer can do, no matter how sophisticated, if continually and dramatically outspent by the competition.

HOW TO DEVELOP YOUR BUDGET FORMAT

When preparing your budget, you should begin with a rationale that outlines what the budget is designed to accomplish. The rationale covers:

- Restatement of the sales goals

- Marketing objectives
- Geography parameters
- Plan time frame

Following the rationale is a breakout of planned expenses by line item under each expense category. The budget line item categories include all applicable marketing mix tools and any other miscellaneous marketing expense items, such as research. The example shown in Exhibit 18.1 can serve as a prototype for your budgeting process. The only difference between this budget and one you may develop is that your budget may have more line item expense categories. (A worksheet is provided in Appendix C.) If you are going to be developing new products, there will be a new product development expense category. If you include publicity in your plan, this marketing tool will also have a budget line item. Exhibit 18.2 shows how you can compare your budget to that of the previous year, industry average, and the competition.

PAYBACK ANALYSIS OVERVIEW

An important part of any budget is the payback analysis. The payback analysis provides the marketer with a projection of whether the marketing plan or specific marketing programs in the plan will generate revenues in excess of expenses. The payback analysis should review both short-run and long-run projected sales and associated costs to estimate the initial program payback in the first year and the projected payback in the second and third year.

Reconciling Your Budget and Payback Analysis

If the payout analysis determines that the marketing plan dollar investment cannot be justified, a rethinking and adjustment of sales objectives and marketing plan objectives, strategies, use of the marketing mix tools, and budget expenditures is needed. After this is accomplished, another payout analysis is needed to determine if the new plan will meet payout expectations.

How to Develop Your Payback Analysis

We recommend using one of two payback methodologies: the contribution to fixed cost or the gross margin to net sales.

Contribution-to-Fixed-Costs Payback Analysis

Retailers, service organizations, and sometimes manufacturers use a contribution-to-fixed-cost payback method. It focuses on two sets of figures:

1. Sales and revenues
2. All direct marketing costs associated with the sale of the product to the consumer

Contribution-to-fixed-costs payback results are determined by first calculating estimated gross sales and then subtracting cost of goods sold to derive a gross profit on sales figure. Next, all variable selling expenses directly associated with the sales of the product (selling costs, advertising and media expenditures, etc.) are subtracted from the gross profit figure to provide a contribution to fixed cost figure. This method can be utilized to analyze individual marketing programs or a whole year's plan.

Exhibit 18.1 Heartland 1998 Marketing Plan Budget

Rationale

The budget for the fiscal year is designed to:

1. Provide support necessary to meet the aggressive sales goal of increasing store for store sales 15 percent over the previous year.
2. Provide support necessary to meet the systemwide marketing objectives of:

    Increase existing customer purchasing rates from 1.2 to 2 purchases per year.

    Initiate new trial, increasing the customer base 20 percent above current levels of 5,000 active customers per store.

Marketing Mix Tool (Nov 5, 1997)	$M	Percent of Total Budget
Media		
Television (6 markets)	$350.0	31.8%
900 TRPs :30s		
900 TRPs :10s		
Newspaper (12 markets)	202.0	18.3
30, 1/3 page insertions		
Direct mail (12 markets/24 stores)	120.0	10.9
10,000 per store per drop		
Postage (4 drops per year)		
Media total	$672.0	61.0%
Production		
Television	$100.0	9.1
2:30 and 3:10 spots (to be used for two years)		
Newspaper	18.0	1.6
Type, photography/illustration for 30 ads		
Direct mail	100.0	9.1
Four direct mail drops, 240M pieces per drop		
Photography, type, printing		
Production total	$218.0	19.8%
Promotion		
Redemption cost	$120.0	10.9
Redemption cost of $5 off coupon in two of the four mailings.		
Estimated response of 5 percent		
5 percent × 480,000 mailing = 24,000		
24,000 × $5 = $120,000		
Media		
Media costs calculated in media section		
Production		
Product costs calculated in production section		
Promotion total	$120.0	10.9%
Merchandising		
Store signage	$30.0	2.7
20 signs per store per month to support planned media promotions and in-store promotions		
Point of purchase displays	10.0	0.9
Two p-o-p displays per store to support the April and December promotions		
Merchandising total	$40.0	3.6%
Selling Costs		
Sales incentive programs	$20.0	1.8
Sales total	$20.0	1.8%
Research Costs		
Market research	$32.0	2.9
Market wide $20.0		
In-store $12.0		
Research total	$32.0	2.9%
Total budget estimate	$1,102.0	100.0%
Total sales estimate	$24,000.0	
Marketing budget as a percent of sales	4.6 percent	

Exhibit 18.2 Heartland Marketing Plan Budget Comparison

Marketing Mix Tool	$M	Percent of Sales
Total Budget Compared to Industry Average and Previous Year		
Marketing as a percent of sales per plan:	1,102	4.6
Marketing as a percent of sales per industry average:		4.0
Index company budget percentage to industry average:	115*	
Index company budget to previous year ($1,102M/$1,000M):	110	
Total Planned Budget Compared to Competition†		
Total planned budget for Company:	1,102	4.6
Total estimated budget Competitor A:	2,000	4.5
Total estimated budget Competitor B:	1,000	5.5

*In this example the planned budget would be 15 points above the industry average for marketing as a percent of sales and 10 points above the previous year's plan.

†If the data exists, we recommend that this analysis be accomplished on an individual market basis and a national basis. This will help demonstrate localized geographic spending policies of competitors.

The contribution-to-fixed-cost method is utilized because it accurately demonstrates the results of the marketing executions. Only the revenues and expenses directly attributed to each marketing effort are used in the analysis. By doing this, the marketer can judge each marketing program on its own merits and on the basis of whether it will contribute to help cover the company's fixed costs.

The short-term objective is to make sure that the marketing programs generate enough sales to adequately cover the direct marketing costs necessary to generate the sales. The longer-term objective is to develop programs that cover both direct marketing costs and fixed overhead, resulting in a profit to the firm.

Exhibit 18.3 provides a contribution-to-fixed-cost payback example for a start-up, direct mail/response program for an existing firm. A worksheet is provided for your use in Appendix C.

There are few limitations to this methodology for most companies. However, the question of capacity needs to be addressed. If, for example, you brew beer and you are at full capacity, the marketer would need to make sure that the revenues from *all of the marketing programs* together cover both total variable marketing expenses and total fixed overhead. However, unless there is the issue of full capacity, *individual marketing programs* should be judged only on their ability to cover variable expenses and contribute to fixed overhead. The overhead will be there whether the program is executed or not. Thus, *if there is excess capacity,* it is always better to execute an additional program that covers the variable costs associated with the program and contributes some additional revenue toward covering some of the fixed costs.

The payback analysis shown in Exhibit 18.4 is for a retail chain considering the implementation of its yearly marketing plan. (A worksheet is provided in Appendix C.) The analysis determines whether projected sales will cover marketing expenditures and allow for a contribution to fixed costs and overhead.

Gross-Margin-to-Net-Sales Payback Analysis

With package goods marketers, payback calculations are sometimes analyzed slightly differently than for retailers. The gross margin is often defined as covering advertising, promotion, and profit, and it is referred to as gross margin to net sales or, sometimes, as advertising, promotion, and profit (AP&P). For example, if there is a 40 percent gross margin, 40 percent of all sales would cover advertising and promotion costs (consumer and trade) and provide the profit. Furthermore, 60 per-

Exhibit 18.3 Contribution-to-Fixed-Overhead Payback Analysis for a Direct Response Marketing Program

	Estimated Response		
Projected Mailing to 10,000 Customers	Low 1 Percent	Medium 2.5 Percent	High 5 Percent
Responses	100	250	500
Gross sales ($26 per order)	$2,600	$6,500	$13,000
Less refunds (5 percent of sales)	130	325	650
Less cancellations (2 percent of sales)	52	130	260
Net sales	2,418	6,045	12,090
Less cost of goods sold (40 percent)	967	2,418	4,836
Gross profit	1,451	3,627	7,254
Less selling expense			
Catalog production mailing (@ 20 cents per piece)	2,000	2,000	2,000
List rental	N/C	N/C	N/C
Photography	N/C	N/C	N/C
Type	N/C	N/C	N/C
Boxes, forms, supplies (2 percent of gross)	52	130	260
Order processing ($3.20/order)	320	800	1,600
Return postage	N/C	N/C	N/C
Telephone	10	10	10
Credit card (30 percent credit card sales with 3 percent charge from store's bank)	23	59	117
Total Expenses	$2,405	$2,999	$3,987
Contribution to Fixed Costs	$ (954)	$ 626	$3,267

Exhibit 18.4 Contribution-to-Fixed-Overhead Payback Analysis for a Retail Marketing Plan

Assumptions

The plan will result in a 10 percent store-for-store increase in sales over last year.
Cost of goods sold will average 50 percent throughout the year.

Nine stores	$M	$M
Sales	$7,920.0	
Less cost of goods sold	3,960.0	
Gross profit		$3,960.0
Less variable costs:		
Media	$316.8	
Production costs	31.7	
Promotion costs	50.0	
Merchandising	30.0	
Selling	25.0	
Research	20.0	
Public relations/miscellaneous	5.0	
Total marketing mix tools		478.5
Contribution to fixed costs		$3,481.5
Fixed costs		3,081.5
Profit before taxes		$ 400.0

cent of the sales would cover all allocated fixed costs (plant, equipment, etc.), as well as the variable selling costs (selling costs, salaries, raw material needed to produce product, etc.).

The example shown in Exhibit 18.5 utilizes the gross-margin-to-net-sales payback methodology. We are assuming a 40 percent margin on a new product. The pay-

Exhibit 18.5 Gross-Margin-to-Net-Sales Payback Analysis for a New Package Goods Product

Assumptions:
$100MM product category, with growth rate of 10 percent per year.
Three competing brands in the category and miscellaneous private labels.
Introduction of new product at an expected margin of 40 percent.

	Year 1 Projections	Year 2 Projections	Year 3 Projections
Net sales	$10.0MM	$12.0MM	$13.0MM
Gross margin (40%)	4.0	4.8	5.2
Less promotion	3.0	2.5	1.5
Less advertising	2.0	1.5	1.5
Profit/(loss)	(1.0)	0.8	2.2

back analysis is projected for three years in order to determine both the short-term and the longer-term profitability for the new product. In this example the product is projected to payback sometime early in year three. (A worksheet is provided in Appendix C.)

Use Your Finance Department for Help

If you are using the contribution method, you should review your financial operating statements to determine the amount needed to cover fixed costs. Or, your finance department can provide you with further details specific to your company, which will allow you to arrive at the sales needed to cover fixed costs and provide a profit for your company.

Furthermore, if you are using the gross-margin-to-net-sales method, your finance department should be able to again provide you with an accurate margin figure as defined in this chapter.

MARKETING CALENDAR OVERVIEW

After the marketing plan budget and payback have been completed, it is time to summarize the plan on a single page. This summary should be in the form of a marketing calendar. When completed, the marketing calendar will serve as a visual summary of the marketing plan for the specific designated period or, more likely, for the coming year.

A marketing calendar should contain the following elements:

- Headings, including product/service/store name, time period, date prepared, and a geographic reference (national, regional, group of markets or tier) or individual market name

- A visual summary of the marketing program week by week, outlining all marketing tool executions and including all other marketing-related activities such as research

- A visual summary of media weight levels by week

- A separate marketing calendar for markets with substantial geographic differences and for test markets

Exhibit 18.6 Marketing Calendar for a Retail Chain

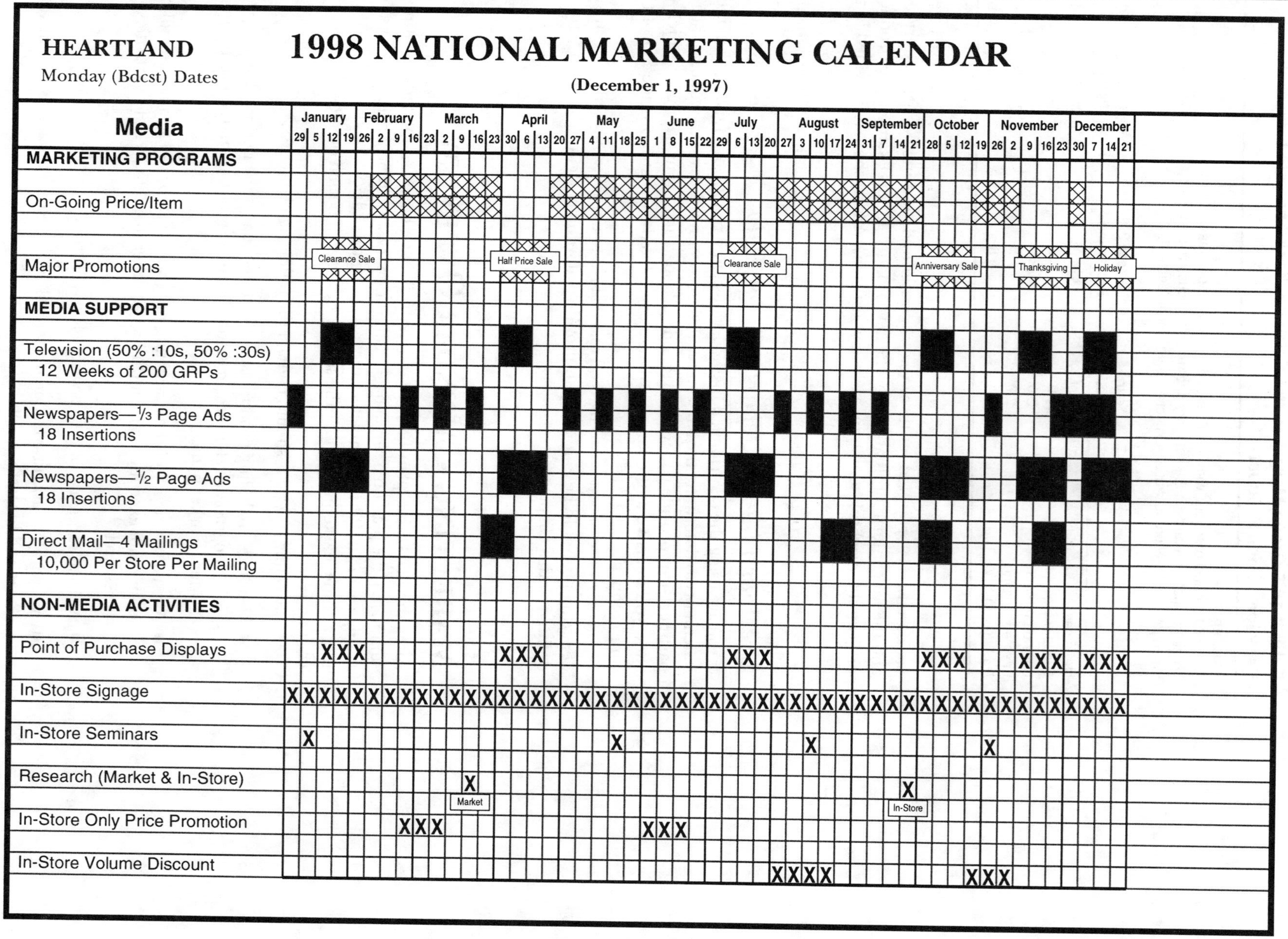

HEARTLAND — **1998 NATIONAL MARKETING CALENDAR** (December 1, 1997)

Monday (Bdcst) Dates

Exhibit 18.6 shows a prototype for you to follow when developing your own marketing calendar. A retail chain plan is used for the example. A blank calendar is provided in Appendix C.

DOS AND DON'TS

Do

- Develop marketing budgets utilizing the task, percent-of-sales, and competitive budgeting methods.

- Be prepared to change your budgets and/or your marketing plan after the payback analysis is completed if you are either over your predetermined budget or if you determine that your plan is not paying back at the expected rate.

- Visually show your entire year's marketing plan activities on a single page in calendar form. Always date when this marketing calendar was prepared.

Don't

- Don't substantially reduce your budget without rethinking your sales objectives and marketing activities.

- Don't prepare a payback analysis that gives the results for which you are looking. If your plan will not generate sufficient sales to cover expenses, change your plan.

- Don't forget to continually update your marketing budget and calendar whenever changes are made in your marketing plan.

PART THREE

EXECUTION

Step Nine   Execution

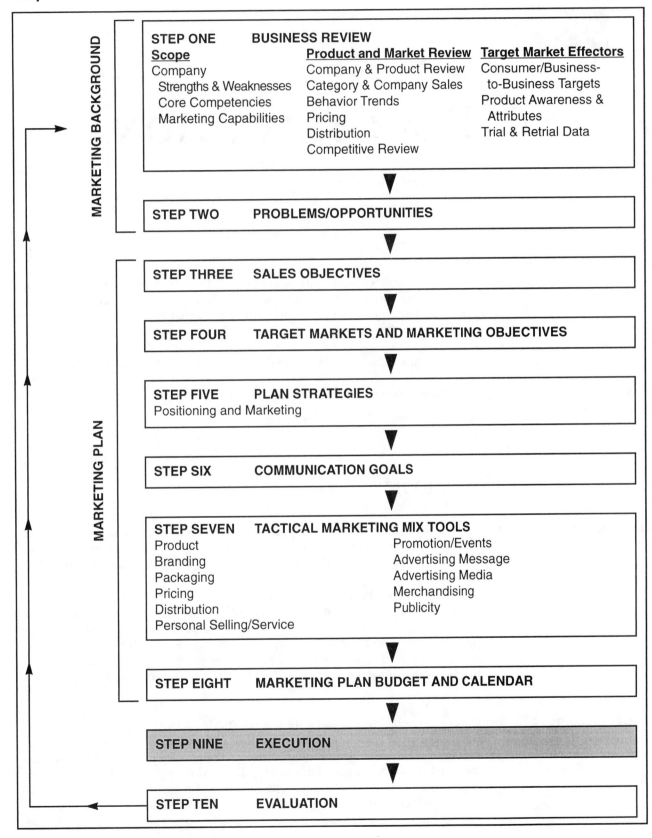

PLAN EXECUTION

Y ou've completed your marketing plan. It's been reviewed, approved, and the budget is authorized. What may have seemed like a daunting task has been successfully completed. But the plan is only half of the equation; thorough execution is the other half. Remember:

Disciplined Marketing Plan + Thorough Execution = Successful Marketing

From This Chapter You Will Learn

What thorough execution encompasses and why it is important.

Key steps to successful execution.

OVERVIEW

Definition of Execution

Webster's defines execution as "to carry out *fully;* to put *completely* into effect" (italics added). By its very definition, execution implies comprehensiveness and thoroughness—attention to details. The genius of successful marketing plan execution is in those details.

A truly integrated marketing plan is greater than the sum of its parts, as the effect of each element is enhanced by the impact of the other elements. A salesperson has a greater chance of success calling on a prospect who has already heard of his company through advertising because part of the selling has already begun—awareness has already started to build. It is attention to detail in every aspect of implementation that helps assure that the synergistic effect of all the marketing plan activities will take place.

The Importance of Thorough Execution

A marketing plan, unless and until it is effectively executed, is nothing but a comprehensive list of good intentions. All of the work and resources that went into the business review, identification of problems and opportunities, and development of the plan itself are a substantial investment. The return on that investment and an accurate evaluation of the plan's activities for use in future planning can be realized only if you follow through with thorough execution of all the plan elements. A very good promotional idea may not give very good results, not because the idea was bad, but because the execution was poor. Unless you've given each marketing plan activity the best opportunity to work through careful execution, you won't be able to accurately evaluate it. If you can't evaluate your marketing activities, they are of little use in planning for the following year.

Most important of all, successful execution is the key to maximizing the dollars allocated to each of the marketing mix tools, with the ultimate goal of positively impacting sales and profits. For example, a well-targeted direct mail campaign does the job of generating qualified leads. If these leads are not followed up on in a timely manner through personal selling, the dollars and effort of that campaign have been essentially wasted. Worse yet, prospect expectations have not been fulfilled, so a negative impression has been created.

Successful marketing plan execution generally requires the coordination of many people and resources. Participation and support will be required of many areas both within and outside the company. Ongoing follow-up with all participants is essential to ensure that they:

1. Understand their role and the importance of their contribution to the overall marketing effort.

2. Have what they need to do their part in "making things happen."

3. Are actually doing what needs to be done.

4. Receive feedback on the results of their activities, as well as the overall marketing effort.

Without diligent follow-up and ongoing communication, execution will fall short and marketing objectives will be compromised. Moreover, these people will be far less enthusiastic the next time they are asked to participate. Like the prospect example above, a negative impression may be created.

KEY STEPS TO SUCCESSFUL EXECUTION

Review and Understand All Elements of the Plan

No doubt some time will pass between submission of the marketing plan document for review and approval and the point at which you receive the go-ahead and budget authorization. No matter what this interval is, you should review the plan to be sure you

1. *Have adequate resources in place and are committed to carrying out each plan activity.*

Allocation of supporting resources will have been addressed in the planning and budget approval process. (In the planning process, you will have asked for—and hopefully received—input from appropriate personnel, both within and outside the company. Issues brought up by these key players—problems to be solved and opportunities to be taken advantage of—will have been addressed in the plan. Key participant involvement helps to make the plan their own and make them more committed and enthusiastic.) So, as execution begins, the marketing plan activities are not a surprise; rather, they are confirmation of specific tactics designed to respond to the input received. This check is to be sure that those commitments have not been changed and that your need for them remains a high enough priority to accomplish the objectives within the time frame called for by the plan.

For example, if the communications program will require establishing or updating a customer database, is your MIS department adequately staffed and scheduled to provide this service? If no, other resources will have to be used. If telemarketing is to be a major component, will assignments need to be changed or should more staff be added?

2. *Understand the lead time necessary for everyone who needs to participate in each executional element.*

Generally, more time is better. However, beware the danger (rare though it is) of too much lead time for a project. This can allow other, more pressing assignments to interfere. Also, maintaining energy and enthusiasm for the work over an extended period of time can be difficult and may lead to inefficiencies and "re-starts."

A good guideline is that you should always begin working *at least* three to six months in advance of the date on which a program or tactical project must be implemented; six months (or more) in advance for major executional programs and communication campaigns. And the three-month or six-month lead time needs to take into account the time necessary to presell and inform all those who need to participate. A promotion developed for consumers that will be executed by the trade target market or a dealer network needs to be developed in time to allow communication to the dealers, giving them time to plan and stock accordingly.

3. *Understand completely and in detail what each department, vendor, etc., needs in order to execute the element(s) of the plan for which they are responsible and the time they will require.*

As you review each activity, if you can't answer the executional needs and time requirements with certainty, you must address them immediately. Even if you're confident about the processes and timetables, you will want to confirm these when you communicate with those involved.

Develop Activity Lists For The First Six Months

Begin with a summary list of all the major activities covered during the first six months of the marketing plan. You will already have prepared an annual marketing calendar showing these activities. A format like the following can be used to begin to provide more detail.

MAJOR MARKETING ACTIVITIES
JANUARY–JUNE 1996
IDENTIFICATION, RESPONSIBILITY, AND DUE DATE

Activity	Responsibility of	Due Date
1. Develop marketing information system	MIS	01/02
2. Assign Marketing Services Staff	Mktg Dir.	01/02
3. Assign key accounts for phone contact	Mktg Dir.	02/15
4. Develop and implement a survey for customer service and sales staffs regarding customer service	Mktg Mgr.	02/15
5. Develop three inserts for publication advertising	Mktg Mgr./Agency	03/15

For each of the major activities, develop a detailed list of all the tasks that need to be completed to accomplish the given activity, along with due dates. Update this list on a monthly basis so that it always covers at least six months (or longer as projects dictate).

Always operate against specific due dates. Just as nothing gets under way until you actually start the activities, call the first meeting, or detail the parameters of each activity, nothing will be finished unless specific due dates are set, communicated, and agreed to by everyone involved (see Communication, below). Without a specific date for the marketing activity, it can easily be postponed by any other task that the individual responsible for that activity has to do.

Setting specific dues dates also provides momentum and a sense of urgency. Breaking down each major activity into its various segments and assigning due dates offers two important advantages. You not only help assure that all the necessary details are covered but you also are breaking down into manageable pieces activities which, if taken as a whole, could seem overwhelming.

Segmenting in this way also forces you to think through the project in a step-by-step, detailed manner. Also, meeting a number of interim dates provides a sense of accomplishment for those involved.

Once these activity lists are completed, you have the structure and outline for the next steps—communication with all those involved.

Communicate the Plan

Just as you have consumer and end-user target audiences with which you ultimately need to communicate, you also have a number of important internal and external target groups that you must communicate with in order to execute the marketing plan. Many of the same considerations that you will give to develop end-user communications should be given to the communications with each of these groups—message content, tone, communication vehicle, and frequency. Your audiences for these communications fall into two general groups: key individuals within your organization (company) and those within the distribution channels (noncompany).

Key Company Staff

You will need the cooperation of various departments throughout your company to implement the marketing plan, including field sales, telemarketing, and MIS groups. Key personnel will include home office as well as field staff.

Ideally, you would have an initial personal meeting with key individuals, and subsequently with their staff members as needed, to review the activities with which you need their help and involvement and that they have the authority to accomplish. The activity lists discussed above give you the basis for these discussions. In each case it's important to present the key plan elements and then relate how the specific area is important and integral to the effective execution of these elements. For example, in the discussion with MIS, details of the advertising are not critical, but how the advertising is expected to generate information for a prospect database is. The goal is to gain understanding of what needs to be done, why it needs to be done, when it needs to be done, and how each area's contribution is important to the overall marketing effort. These meetings also give you an opportunity to confirm what information each area will require and the time necessary to complete the tasks being discussed. It's essential that these communications be clear, specific, and concise and that everyone understand and agree to what is expected of them and when.

Company Staff Overall

Everyone within an organization, either directly or indirectly, impacts the company's marketing efforts, since everyone contributes in some way to delivering the products or services being marketed. So, the staff as a whole must understand what the overall marketing program is, what their role is in its execution, and why it is important. There are a variety of ways to communicate with staff, depending on the size of your organization. Personal meetings with each department, group meetings, company newsletters, and bulletin boards are all methods that can be used effectively to gain interest and enthusiasm for the plan. The goal is to provide an overview of the marketing plan in easily understood terms and gain commitment from each staff member to do his part according to the timeline and guidelines developed.

Distribution Channels

Noncompany staff, such as wholesalers, dealers, brokers, franchisees, and retail trade, are the other group which must be included in marketing plan communications. Without commitment from these channels to participate in the marketing program through carrying product, promoting in-store, etc., effective marketing execution isn't possible.

These individuals, because they are not part of your company, need to be persuaded that what you're asking them to do will enhance their business and will do so better than your competition—and certainly better than doing nothing at all. Communications with this group need to focus on the contribution your product or service will make to the profitability of their enterprise. Presentations at dealer/franchisee meetings, either regional or national, provide good opportunities to address these groups. Written and, possibly, phone follow-up will be required for those who do not attend such meetings and will serve as reminders to those who do. Dealer/trade newsletters provide another vehicle for these communications. Telemarketing and customer service phone support are other direct methods for communicating with these groups.

Clearly, commitment to carry and promote your product, participate in a given promotion, etc., carries with it the obligation on your part to deliver product and promotional materials, as well as other services like field support, when promised and as needed.

Ongoing Follow-up

A disciplined system of regular, ongoing follow-up is necessary to ensure successful implementation of the marketing plan. Again, going back to the activity lists above, you have determined specific due dates for all personnel involved in implementation. In addition, you need to determine interim dates at which you will follow up with each area to be sure progress is being made, obtain specific data on that progress, help to solve problems which have developed or take advantage of opportunities, and gain assurance that the projects are being given the priority needed. This needs to be done early and often enough in the timeline to allow for remedial action if needed. You can never assume that, if you hear nothing, everything is going as planned. Odds are, it isn't going at all.

In addition to following up, you must also communicate results of the marketing efforts to the groups above. This allows you to show your appreciation for their help and contribution and to build cooperation in the future.

Stay Committed to the Plan

It's very easy to make decisions and do things without regard to the plan. The plan must be looked upon and embraced as a *working document,* guiding all of the marketing decisions you make during the period of the plan. If opportunities or ideas are brought up throughout the year (and they will be), they should be evaluated based on the plan that's being executed, which was designed to achieve very specific objectives.

A staff member brings up a media opportunity based on a "good deal" on the media cost. This "opportunity" must be evaluated against the target audience identified in the plan. Is it a valid plan supplement? It is needed? Where will the money come from? If additional funds aren't available, what won't get done as a result of doing this? Go back to the plan.

The plan may already have tests built into it and, very possibly, dollars budgeted for contingencies or opportunities throughout the year, but even these dollars should be used only after consideration of the goals of the plan.

Focus is the key to keeping resources and attention committed to the task at hand—achieving the objectives detailed in the marketing plan. Review the plan and, particularly, the positioning frequently.

Top Management Support

If you have completed a thorough, comprehensive marketing plan, odds are you did so through providing strong, ongoing leadership and the driving energy to complete the task. And, you had the support of your organization's leadership. Top executive involvement, support, and visibility is equally essential in the implementation of the plan. All those involved, both inside and outside the organization, need to know and understand that the marketing plan, and therefore its implementation, is a critical, integral part of the management of the organization. It is not something imposed on the organization but, rather, something developed out of the need to more effectively and efficiently operate and grow the business by those ultimately responsible for the success of the enterprise.

Top management's support and sponsorship needs to be visible when the implementation is kicked off and throughout the year in the form of regular reports on status and evaluation of efforts. As discussed above, implementation requires efforts and contributions from a number of different departments throughout a company. Management's involvement and active endorsement helps assure that the cooperation and support needed from the other areas will be provided in a timely and effective manner. Without this leadership support, successful execution will be very difficult, if not impossible.

DOS AND DON'TS

Do

- Be sure you have adequate, committed resources in place to carry out each plan activity.

- Be sure you understand the lead time necessary for everyone who needs to participate in each executional element.

- Be sure you understand completely and in detail what each department, vendor, etc., needs to do and what information and lead time they will require in order to execute the element(s) of the plan for which they are responsible.

- Develop a list of major activities for each six-month period of the plan, including individual(s) responsible for each activity and the due date.

- Break down each major activity into the essential steps necessary to accomplish it; identify the individual(s) responsible for the activity and the due date.

- Communicate plan elements with key company personnel, detailing responsibilities and due dates.

- Gain commitment from company staff and noncompany distribution channels to execute the marketing plan.

- Consider message content, tone, communication vehicle, and frequency when developing communications about the marketing plan to internal and external participants.

- Follow up with status reports and results of marketing plan activities with all of those responsible for execution.

- Review the marketing plan and the positioning frequently to stay focused on the objectives and means of accomplishing them.

- Enlist top management's endorsement of the marketing plan throughout its execution.

- Initiate every element of the plan; nothing will happen until you make it happen.

- Always operate against specific due dates.

Don't

- Don't consider any executional detail too small. Make sure it's being taken care of.

- Don't accept that activities are going according to plan unless you have specific, concrete information to show that they are.

- Don't use the same communications regarding the marketing plan to audiences with different roles and different levels of marketing expertise.

- Don't communicate just once with those individuals enlisted to execute the marketing plan.

- Don't allow the calendar to slip away from you. Once major components of the plan are delayed, the entire system can unravel, negating the cumulative effect of the plan elements.

- Don't neglect internal issues in lieu of external communication efforts. For example, preparations must be made for the sales and inquiry activity generated by advertising and other efforts.

- Don't ever *assume* that the plan is being implemented without personally checking on it.

PART FOUR

EVALUATION

Step Ten   Evaluation

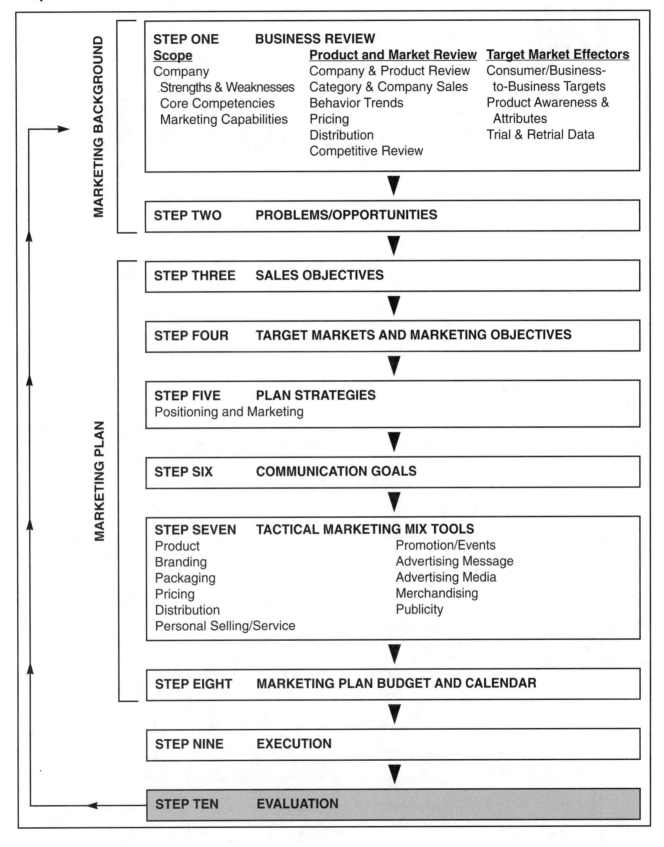

MARKETING BACKGROUND

STEP ONE   BUSINESS REVIEW

Scope	Product and Market Review	Target Market Effectors
Company	Company & Product Review	Consumer/Business-
Strengths & Weaknesses	Category & Company Sales	to-Business Targets
Core Competencies	Behavior Trends	Product Awareness &
Marketing Capabilities	Pricing	Attributes
	Distribution	Trial & Retrial Data
	Competitive Review	

STEP TWO   PROBLEMS/OPPORTUNITIES

MARKETING PLAN

STEP THREE   SALES OBJECTIVES

STEP FOUR   TARGET MARKETS AND MARKETING OBJECTIVES

STEP FIVE   PLAN STRATEGIES
Positioning and Marketing

STEP SIX   COMMUNICATION GOALS

STEP SEVEN   TACTICAL MARKETING MIX TOOLS

Product	Promotion/Events
Branding	Advertising Message
Packaging	Advertising Media
Pricing	Merchandising
Distribution	Publicity
Personal Selling/Service	

STEP EIGHT   MARKETING PLAN BUDGET AND CALENDAR

STEP NINE   EXECUTION

STEP TEN   EVALUATION

PLAN EVALUATION

After completing your marketing plan, you need to evaluate the results. An evaluation methodology should be established to assess the success of the marketing plan itself and to ensure ongoing evaluation of the marketing plan executions. In addition to providing a database from which to make strategic decisions for next year's plan, this information also provides invaluable feedback from which to make modifications during the execution of this year's plan.

From This Chapter You Will Learn

How to evaluate the effectiveness of the marketing plan.

How to evaluate your marketing plan execution(s) using two alternative methods: sales trend comparison and pre- and post-execution research.

OVERVIEW

Upon execution completion of a year-long plan and specific marketing activities through the year, such as an individual advertising campaign, a promotion, a pricing change, or the use of a new media vehicle, there should be an evaluation of the results.

Evaluation of the Marketing Plan and Its Components

If you were able to prepare your marketing plan via the Disciplined Marketing Planning methodology, you will be able to thoroughly evaluate your marketing plan to determine what was and was not successful and to incorporate your learning into the marketing background section for the preparation of next year's plan.

On an *overall* plan basis, you can evaluate the success of your plan by the level of achievement of the following:

Sales and profit objectives

Marketing objectives

Marketing plan communication awareness and attitude goals

Sales and profit data should be readily available for evaluation. You should also have measurable target market behavior information to evaluate marketing objectives, such as customer retention, new customer trial, store visits, dollars per transaction, etc. Survey research is required to evaluate target market behavior (for the marketing objectives) and target market awareness and attitude (for the communication goals).

On a specific, *tactical tool* basis, you can evaluate the success of each tactical tool in fulfilling its function within the marketing mix. You should be able to accurately measure each tactical tool's performance, because each tactical segment in your plan has an objective(s) against which you can measure the tool's performance. For example, for publicity—achieve placement of one feature article in one of the two leading trade magazines. In addition, although difficult, attempt to measure (most likely through interpolation) in a directional manner whether each tool fulfilled its individual awareness and attitude communication goals. In order to make this tactical tool evaluation, it's important that you diligently collect the pertinent performance data for each tool. The tendency is to get caught up in the day-to-day fires of plan execution and ignore the plan evaluation. Subsequently, it will be difficult to plan for next year because you don't have the necessary data. It's critical that you evaluate the effectiveness of each tool. While you can evaluate the overall plan's success to tell you "how well you did," the tool evaluation will help tell the "why" in terms of what generated the bulk of the success or caused the plan not to achieve the predetermined sales and profits.

Sales Trend Comparison

While the previous evaluation was *plan* based, this sales evaluation method compares current sales with the previous year's sales *prior* to, *during*, and *after* any given marketing execution. Sales are analyzed prior to the promotion period to determine if there was a downward, upward, or flat sales trend as compared to the previous year's sales. Sales are also compared to last year's both during and after the execution period. In analyzing the preperiod, the execution period, and the postperiod separately, added insight is provided on the affect of the individual test or marketing execution. Sales might have been trending down prior to the marketing execution. Even a small increase during the marketing execution period would mean that the marketing execution might have helped reverse a negative trend. Then, in analyzing sales after the marketing execution period, the marketer can begin to determine if the marketing execution had any long-term effect on sales. If the marketing execution was designed to gain new users or trial of the product, the sales results in the months after the execution will help determine if repeat purchase or continuity of purchase was achieved.

There are two types of methods for comparing sales trends: with control markets and without control markets.

Sales Trend Analysis with Control Markets

This methodology utilizes control markets (markets with no marketing execution or markets receiving a mainline marketing execution) to compare against test markets receiving a new marketing execution or the marketing execution you want to analyze. Control and test markets should be similar in terms of sales volume, sales trending, distribution levels, penetration/marketing coverage, size, demographic profile, and other market and media characteristics. Also, there should be a minimum of two test and two control markets to guard against any anomalies.

In summary, control markets serve as a benchmark to determine whether the specific marketing execution was responsible for sales increases in the test markets. If the analysis demonstrates that sales and profits in test markets that received advertising were substantially above control markets that received no advertising, then the decision should be made to consider expanding advertising to other markets.

Sales Trend Analysis Without Control Markets

Whenever possible, we recommend using the sales trend analysis with control markets. However, for many businesses, control markets are not available because the business is located solely in one market, in a minimal number of markets, or there are no control markets comparable in their make-up to the test markets. In other situations, the marketer needs to analyze results of a marketing execution that was implemented across all markets. In these situations, a sales trend analysis without control markets is used. Sales are analyzed before, during, and after the execution to determine if the period during the marketing execution received greater total sales and greater percentage sales increases or decreases over last year. Without control markets, the marketer can't be sure that the sales results are totally a function of the marketing execution. The results could be the effect of other market factors that caused marketwide sales increases or decreases not only for your company but for the competition as well. However, even without control markets, the analysis of sales trends provides general insight into the success or failure of individual marketing executions.

Sometimes test market performance is compared to national or total company sales. In this case, the national or company total is used as a benchmark. The method is not as accurate as a comparison of test versus control markets but it does provide a basis for evaluation.

Pre- and Post-execution Research

Pre- and post-execution primary research is implemented both before and after the execution of the plan of activities. Most pre- and post-execution research involves awareness, attitude, and behavior tracking studies. These studies can measure the movement of awareness, attitude, and behavior both before and after the marketing plan was executed and measure movement of specific plan executions, such as promotions, campaigns, and merchandising programs.

While increased sales is a very valuable indicator of the success of a marketing execution, it is not the only one. Many times, though sales remain relatively flat, there is a significant movement in awareness and attitudes. These shifts signal the probability of future increases in sales. As has been proven time and time again, with increase in awareness there is a good probability that there will be an increased level of purchases.

Pre- and post-execution research can also serve as a diagnostic tool to help explain why sales went up or down. Research can identify changes in consumer awareness of your product, attitudes about your product, changing purchase behavior patterns, or competitive strengths and weaknesses as reasons for increases or decreases in sales. Thus, the research evaluation method has the ability to providing more in-depth information than the sales trend comparison method.

In summary, research allows the marketer to evaluate the success or failure of the overall marketing plan and communication programs. For example, research can determine whether you met your communication awareness objective of "increasing awareness from 50 percent to 70 percent."

Research can help evaluate the success of the behavior objectives such as "increasing trial (percent of first-time purchasers) from 30 percent to 40 percent." Research can also help you measure whether you met the tactical objectives or specific executions. Above all, research is an evaluation tool which helps determine *why* your sales goals were or were not achieved.

The example in Exhibit 20.1 demonstrates the ability of pre- and post-execution research to evaluate the results of an advertising program. In this example, a utility was evaluating the effectiveness of its campaign to persuade consumers that it was a better source of energy information and was more concerned about energy conser-

Exhibit 20.1 Advertising Awareness/Attitude Indices

	No Advertising Control Markets			Advertising Test Markets			
	Pre	Post	Difference	Pre	Post	Difference	Net Gain
Advertising awareness	(100)	(105)	+5	(100)	(152)	+52	+47
Better source of energy information	(100)	(82)	-18	(100)	(135)	+35	+53
More concerned about energy conservation	(100)	(84)	-16	(100)	(127)	+27	+43
More concerned with the environment	(100)	(100)	—	(100)	(115)	+15	+15

vation and environmental issues. The numbers have been indexed for confidentiality. The results clearly provided the utility with insights into the effectiveness of the campaign.

HOW TO STRUCTURE THE SALES EVALUATION PROCESS

The following method demonstrates how to measure the sales performance for your marketing activities. This method utilizes the growth rate of improvement (GRI) process, which is one specific type of sales trend comparison. A retail example is used; however, a similar procedure could be established for any business type.

The only changes needed to make the method applicable to any business would be in the evaluation categories. These would be made consistent with the business. A manufacturer would use product sales and units sold. A retailer could use such measurements as visits, transactions, dollars per transaction, units sold, and product sales. A service firm would use sales and people served.

You should plan to use a similar method for your evaluation system. A worksheet is provided in Appendix C. However, wherever appropriate, we suggest that the pre- and post-execution research evaluation method also be utilized and that the research be executed by a professional research firm.

Growth Rate of Improvement (GRI) Sales Trend Method Example

The following provides retail examples of evaluation objectives and strategies along with an execution format for the GRI sales trend evaluation process.

Example Evaluation Objective:

Develop a data feedback methodology to monitor and determine results of marketing test program and executions.

Example Evaluation Strategies:

Implement a disciplined data feedback system in order to quickly and easily evaluate sales activity for marketing planning and execution.

Utilize the growth rate of improvement (GRI) method.

Execution

Each test market is compared against a control market of similar type and number of stores and per store sales averages. The test markets receive the test activity and the control markets receive the regularly scheduled marketing activity. If you don't have control markets, the test market can be compared against your national system or all other markets.

Task 1

A *preperiod* is analyzed to determine sales trending prior to the test period.

Task 2 .... For the *test period,* the period during which the marketing program is executed, data are analyzed to determine sales trending.

Task 3 .... For the *postperiod,* the period immediately following a test period, data are analyzed to determine sales trending.

Task 4 .... Finally a *growth rate of improvement* is determined by analyzing the difference between visits, transactions, and sales dollars per store in the preperiod, the test period, and the postperiod. The data enables the marketer to determine incremental visits, transactions, and sales during the test period for each market and to evaluate the rate of success.

Whenever feasible you should utilize the growth rate improvement method to compare the preperiod to the test period, test period to postperiod, and the preperiod to the postperiod. The preperiod is compared to the test period to determine if the test altered expected behavior. If the preperiod showed that sales were flat and the test period demonstrated a marked increase in sales, a determination would be made that the marketing program executed during the test period was effective. The test period is compared to the postperiod to determine if the marketing execution had a lasting affect and to gain knowledge on how much, if any, sales drop off after the test period. Finally, a very important long-term analysis is the comparison of preperiod to postperiod. This comparison shows if the marketing execution had a positive affect on sales after the test as compared to sales trending before the marketing execution or test period.

Examples of Preperiod to Test Period Comparisons

The following examples demonstrate a comparison of preperiod to test period. Exhibit 20.2 compares a test market to a control market, and Exhibit 20.3 compares a test market to the national system average.

DOS AND DON'TS

Do
- Evaluate using the overall plan objectives and tactical tool objectives of your marketing plan.
- Use what you learned from the evaluation process in the development of your plan for next year.
- Use primary research to help evaluate the "why" of the sales numbers in terms of awareness, attitude, and behavior.

Don't
- Don't just evaluate your total year's results. Whenever possible, evaluate each promotion, each campaign, and the effectiveness of each of your marketing tactical tools, Then, apply what you have learned.
- Don't wait until the plan's completion to begin to evaluate. Evaluate the specific plan executions as they are completed to determine their success.
- Don't implement a marketing execution without first determining an evaluation methodology.

Exhibit 20.2 Test versus Control Market Dollar Sales Analysis: Test Period 2/24 to 3/30 (Weekly per Store Average)

	Last Year Dollars (000)	This Year Dollars (000)	Percent Change Dollars
Preperiod 1/20–2/23			
Test market—Detroit (2 stores)	$121.0	$185.1	+53%
Control market—Indianapolis (2 stores)	$118.0	$159.3	+35%
Test Period 2/24–2/30			
Test market—Detroit (2 stores)	$29.0	$53.4	+84%
Control market—Indianapolis (2 stores)	$26.0	$25.7	−1%

	Preperiod Percent Change	Test Period Percent Change	Percent Point Gain/Loss
Growth Rate Improvement (GRI)			
Test market—Detroit (2 stores)	+53%	+84%	+31%
Control market—Indianapolis (2 stores)	+35%	−1%	−36%
Net percent point difference	+18%	+85%	+67%

Incremental Sales: GRI: +67 percent × Test Period Sales $53,400 = Net Weekly Gain $35,778.

Note: The same method would be used for visits and/or transactions if the data are available.

Exhibit 20.3 Test versus National Dollar Sales Analysis: Test Period 2/24 to 3/30 (Weekly per Store Average)

	Last Year Dollars (000)	This Year Dollars (000)	Percent Change Dollars
Pre Period: 1/20–2/23			
Test market—Detroit (2 stores)	$121.0	$185.1	+53%
National system average	$120.0	$144.0	+20%
Test Period: 2/24–3/30			
Test market—Detroit (2 stores)	$39.0	$53.4	+84%
National system average	$27.0	$31.6	+17%

	Preperiod Percent Change	Test Period Percent Change	Percent Point Gain/Loss
Growth Rate Improvement (GRI)			
Test market—Detroit (2 stores)	+53%	+84%	+31%
National system average	+20%	+17%	−3%
Net Percent Point Difference	+33%	+67%	+34%

Incremental Sales: GRI: +34 percent × Test Period Sales $53,400 = Net Weekly Gain $18,156.

Note: The same method would be used for visits and/or transactions if the data are available.

- Don't expect the same results of your test market experience when you roll-out the tested program to the other markets. Usually there is some fall-off from the test market results because its difficult to maintain the same attention to execution in all the markets as was done in the original test markets.

MARKETING RESEARCH AND TESTING (R & T)

Another step of evaluation includes how to evaluate plans and tools *before* broadscale execution. This is what we define as testing. As marketing is deemed to be as much art as science, there is much chance for failure. Accordingly, there will be no guarantee of success when you use new plans and plan elements, when going against new target markets and new strategy approaches, or when implementing new tactical tools. For example, it has been estimated that 90 percent of new products fail within their first full year of introduction. Attempting to try new marketing approaches on a broad scale will require a sizable outlay of dollars and have a significant impact on the effectiveness and success of your plan. Enhancing the success of these new marketing approaches requires marketing research and testing (R & T). Both testing and research are a means of staying ahead of the competition and avoiding costly errors. What follows is just the rudiments on this topic. Because research and testing are challenging and complex disciplines, we would recommend you seek professional assistance to help with their implementation.

From This Chapter You Will Learn

Why you need to test.

When to test and when not to test.

How to test within three different types of research and testing environments—exploratory, experimental, and in-market.

Examples of various testing programs—positioning, new products, branding, promotion, advertising message, and media.

Some thoughts about, limitations of, and examples of different testing techniques.

OVERVIEW

Why the Need to Test

Every business situation can be thought of as a test. Many small entrepreneurs do not spend any money on a formalized research and testing program. But they do "test" the market by posting a sign and setting up shop. Accordingly, the vast majority of them do not make it through their third year in business. With a research and testing program, one can significantly reduce the odds of failure. A testing program can be thought of as a form of risk management. You would not think about running your business without insurance. Why run your marketing plan without research and testing?

When to Test and When Not to Test

Not every marketing tool or tactical execution needs to be, or should be, tested. Testing every alternative would not be feasible from a cost or time standpoint. Thus, a prioritization approach should be considered. Some questions to consider when determining what to test include the following:

- What is the risk of not having this information? This is probably the most critical question. If one is sinking millions of dollars on a positioning strategy, then spending a few thousand dollars on research makes sense. However, to take the time and money to test a one-week, single-market media flight may not be worth the investment in research.

  As an example, one of our clients, Mercury Marine, was introducing a revolutionary new propeller. They were to spend major dollars against this introduction. There was little consensus on the name for this propeller. Thus, they tested branding alternatives against their consumer and dealer markets. In contrast, they also had a branding issues on another line of propellers. In this case, these propellers were a small part of a family of propellers geared toward a small target niche. It was decided to not spend the effort to test these names, since the downside risk was minimal.

- What is the cost of obtaining reliable information? This would appear to be somewhat obvious. For example, in order to test the effectiveness of an advertising campaign, you need to conduct an in-market test, matching several markets with different advertising messages. It may cost almost as much to develop and test the campaign as it would to implement the campaign without testing, in which case the decision may be to not test.

- What are the time constraints? If test results cannot be obtained in time to impact the decision-making process, then one must question the value of testing. However, the key here is to avoid this situation by planning for research and testing in the first year of your marketing plan, with a roll-out to all markets in years two and three.

- How valid and translatable is the testing environment? The marketer must be able to take the research results and apply them to his/her marketing situation. One cannot measure the "effectiveness" of advertising through a "forced-exposure copy testing" environment. (Copy testing of advertising will be discussed later in this chapter). Showing consumers a commercial once or twice in a research room and asking for their reactions will not assess the effectiveness of advertising. Advertising does not work in that way. However, you can measure in this environment the "communication value" of advertising. Did the commercial communicate the sponsor's name and intended message?

Types of Research and Testing Environments   For the purposes of this book, we can categorize marketing research and testing environments into three types—exploratory, experimental, and in-market.

Exploratory

Marketers should always base their marketing objectives and strategies on what their consumers need. Marketing tools should relate to how the consumers think, what are their attitudes, and how they behave. In many instances, exploratory research can provide help in the development process of marketing tool alternatives and in preliminary evaluation of alternatives. Focus groups are probably the most prevalent form of exploratory research.

A focus group is a discussion among target group respondents. Typically, group sizes range from 8 to 10 participants, although groups of 4 to 6 participants are also common. The group discussion is led by a moderator who follows an outline of topics to cover. Focus groups are an excellent way to generate ideas and obtain feedback from target respondents on complex attitudinal issues such as positioning, product concepts, and advertising messages; and increase understanding of the buying dynamics of a product or service category. When utilized early in the planning process, focus groups can help develop alternatives and provide initial qualitative feedback on alternatives. Focus groups are very qualitative in nature, although when done in numbers (six or more preferably), marketers can gain an enlightened, but not quantifiable, insight into the target market.

Experimental

When focus groups are used extensively for exploring the dynamics of the consumer attitudes and behavior, they are really a form of experimental research. Experimental research is any kind of research that is not an in-market testing situation under "real" conditions. Evaluating advertising copy via mall intercepts, testing pricing strategies via telephone interviews, and testing positioning concepts through a mail survey are all forms of experimental research.

With experimental research, you are generally forcing exposure of testing concepts onto your target market in an unnatural setting. This type of research is used for the reasons of control, cost, and time constraints. In order to isolate and understand consumers reactions and preferences to product, positioning, and marketing mix tools, the researcher needs to control the test environment. In this way, only one variable (e.g., product feature, advertising message, brand name, or positioning alternative) is changed from one test exposure to the next. In this way, the researcher can determine that the differences in consumer preferences are due to the change in the one variable. If multiple variables were changed, then the researcher would not know to what to attribute the consumer's preference. Marketers need feedback in a short amount of time (days to weeks) for decision-making purposes. Experimental research allows this to happen by controlling the exposure to different marketing alternatives. Compared to in-market testing, experimental research is also a more cost effective form of gathering information.

In-market Testing

In-market testing is really a small scale implementation of a specific marketing approach. The key to effective in-market tests is to match markets as much as possible, so that you are controlling for all variables except the one you are testing. The ability to accurately read test results relies heavily on the ability to match test markets as closely as possible.

Considerations for matching markets would include sales trends, competitive situation, penetration/distribution, media options, and geographic and demographic issues. In-market testing is used most notably for new product introductions, before rolling out nationally. Many companies with well-known brands will use in-market testing before rolling out package, product formulation, or positioning changes. In-market testing also can be used effectively for testing alternative media programs.

EXAMPLES OF HOW TO DEVELOP TESTING PROGRAMS

You can literally test anything related to your marketing plan. Also, there is no one absolute right way to test marketing alternatives. The following examples outline some parameters for research and testing of various marketing plan elements.

Positioning Concepts

Positioning is the heart of the marketing plan. All marketing mix tools are developed to support the product's or service's positioning, which in turn is the link to the consumer's relationship with the product or service. Positioning concepts generally consist of complex attitude structures, which require a sensitive means of testing.

The objectives of testing positioning alternatives are to evaluate the connection between the target market relative to the product and competition. Important issues would include identifying the relevance of the positioning to the target, the importance of the positioning to the target, and the likelihood that the positioning would encourage trial. Positioning can be tested through many forms, including focus groups, mall intercepts, or mail surveys. Generally a "positioning concept board" is created. The concept board has a visual element and copy points to convey the benefits and positioning elements. Targeted consumers can be shown the concept board and then be asked to respond to a short survey covering attitudinal and intention-type questions.

One limitation to the concept board approach is that consumers tend to be very literal in research settings; they begin to be copywriters rather than focusing on the positioning "idea." An approach developed to counteract this tendency is the audio concept "board." Here, the positioning is stated on an audio tape that is played to respondents. Since they cannot read the concept, respondents are less likely to be quite so literal. They must take away the key positioning from what they heard. This method is very effective for positioning with a strong emotional appeal, as the tone of the audio can impart the desired emotion more easily than the writing on a concept board.

Product Testing

Probably the most amount of testing dollars are associated with research for new product development. Product concepts are explored and formulated through numerous focus groups. Concepts are refined through more consumer testing using all of the methods discussed above. There are also simulated test models that produce expected market shares when fed with market and benefit criteria. Much of the research on new product development is conducted to determine the ideal bundle of benefits, both rational and emotional, that a product should contain. The ultimate test of a new product is putting it into a real market situation.

Branding Testing

The target market will recognize your offering through the brand name of your product. But what is the best brand name? And how do you determine the best brand name? The process for brand testing is to first develop alternative names for testing (see Chapter 9). As a rule, the number of names for consumer testing should not be more than about seven names. A number beyond seven creates respondent fatigue and results in a lack of name discrimination.

The objectives of branding research is to narrow the list of alternative names and to identify the strengths and weaknesses of each name alternative. There are factors other than consumer preferences to be considered in branding. Creative consideration is one example. If some names can be eliminated through branding research, then other factors can be considered in the final decision-making process. When evaluating brand alternatives, three areas of questioning are utilized to achieve the above objectives.

1. *Word association:* What connotations does the name elicit? Are they positive or negative? For example, when testing name alternatives for a merged pair of hospitals, one of the test names generated for our client was Meriter. Through word associations, two common themes were Merit cigarettes and the word "merit" (to be worthy). The word association was done out of context of a hospital name. Thus, when put in context of a hospital, the cigarette association would be expected to disappear, while the merit—to be worthy—definition could be used in an advantageous way.

2. *Ratings on product/service benefits:* Each name is rated against various product/service benefits to ascertain strengths and weaknesses. In the hospital example, the names were rated on leadership, caring, professional, state-of-the-art, and quality.

3. *Preference scores:* Respondents are asked for their name preferences, given a concept statement read to them. Reasons for their preferences are also obtained.

All three types of measurement—association, ratings, and preferences—are analyzed to determine viable names. This type of testing can be conducted through telephone interviews or mall intercepts.

Promotion Testing

Promotion testing can be performed at the idea development stage or at the execution stage. The key objective in evaluating promotions is to determine the effectiveness of the promotion in generating incremental sales, new trial, or brand loyalty. At the idea generation stage, focus groups can be a useful tool for obtaining ideas and feedback. Mall intercepts can also be used to evaluate the stopping power and selling power of alternative promotions in an advertising context. At the execution stage, in-store exit surveys can be used to determine consumers buying habits and profiles. For example, this type of survey can determine if the promotion was a specific reason that consumers shopped at a store. The profile of the customers can also be checked to determine first-time shoppers, improved purchase ratios, or higher average transaction amounts.

Advertising Message Communications

Advertising is probably one of the most difficult marketing tools to measure. This is due, in part, to the long-term and cumulative effects of advertising and to the difficulty of isolating advertising effects. This is one of the most discussed and controversial research topics. The closest one can come to truly measuring the "effectiveness" of advertising is through in-market testing. However, controlling for all other variables is very difficult with in-market testing, and the necessary time and budget are seldom available for this type of measurement. However, assessing the communication value of advertising can be done more readily and efficiently.

Copy testing is a means of measuring the communication value of advertising. As a diagnostic tool rather than an evaluative tool, copy testing can be instrumental to the creative development process. There are two key objectives in a copy testing framework. One objective is to determine whether the advertising can cut through the clutter and make people stop and notice the ad. The second is to assess whether the ad communicates the intended message. There are several means of copy testing ads, many through syndicated research sources that can provide norms to compare the test results with other products in the same category or format. The basic principle is common through most techniques. Respondents are shown the ad or commercial, often with other advertising clutter, and then asked questions pertaining to communication playback, negative/positive diagnostics, and feelings. Persuasion scores and purchase intentions can also be part of the questioning. Copy testing can be conducted on both broadcast and print forms of advertising.

Media Tests

Which medium or media mix is the right one? How much media weight do I need? How many media dollars do I need to spend? Media testing can help answer these questions.

In testing media there are two key variables to evaluate—media mix and media weight. Testing the impact of alternative media or weight levels is very difficult to accomplish in a forced-exposure experimental design. In-market tests are typically used for media mix and weight tests. Market tiers are derived which receive different weight levels of similar messages. Or, the variable may be different types of media such as TV versus newspaper. There may be many combinations to consider, with markets and dollars available for testing being the limiting factor. The key is to control for all variables except for the media weight or mix. The typical measurement tool would be sales analysis. Survey research can also be utilized to determine awareness levels affected by the alternative media plans. Telephone research is generally utilized for this purpose.

DOS AND DON'TS

Dos

- Access the risk factor of *not* conducting research and testing on the various plan elements.

- Conduct research when the cost of implementing the marketing execution is high.

- As much as possible, control for all variables except the one test variable.

- Match the research technique with the type of information you want to obtain.

Don't

- Don't implement research if you intend to pursue the same path no matter what the research results say.

- Don't use research as the only tool for determining alternatives. Research is only one of many decision-making tools.

- Don't attempt a major new approach by trying it in all of your markets or across the country. In other words, don't make it a national test. It's expensive and you may never have another chance because it may be a national failure.

- Don't implement the test yourself unless you are willing to pay the consequences. Use a professional to design and evaluate the results.

IDEA STARTERS BY MARKETING SITUATION

Across the top of the following pages, you will find eleven column headings, each one corresponding to a different marketing situation you may encounter as you prepare and execute this marketing plan. The leftmost column contains idea starters grouped by marketing mix tool. To use this idea grid, simply choose the marketing situation in which you find your product and the marketing mix tool with which you are currently working, selecting the best ideas for the specific situation.

For example, if you are looking for promotional event ideas for a store opening, check under the marketing situation column head "New Product/Store Intro/Grand Opening" in the Promotion/Events section of idea starters. Then follow the column down and evaluate the suggestions that seem most appropriate.

| | Marketing Situations | | | |
Idea Starters for Each Marketing Mix Tool	Flat/Continual Decline in Sales	Increase Small User Base	Poor Repeat/ Limited Loyalty	Need to Build Amount Purchased
Product/Service/Store				
Offer product in more convenient, smaller/ larger sizes	•	•	•	•
Make store easier to shop				•
Test new department/product extensions	•	•		
Provide follow-up repair/maintenance program			•	
Reformulate/update product/retail concept	•	•	•	
Add new products to line	•	•	•	
New product for emerging market for specific need/use	•	•		
Test new shops/boutique/services within store	•	•	•	•
Provide home delivery/shop at home service	•	•	•	
Provide product/service at home or on location	•	•	•	
Offer money-back guarantee			•	•
Develop new products with existing products/materials or equipment/ technology	•	•		
Develop new/more/varied uses for your product	•	•		•
Develop private store brand/label and sell at value			•	
Develop a different product by price segment in same category		•		•
Develop product for special uses/time of year (i.e., McDonald's Shamrock Shakes)		•		
Develop special trial sizes	•	•		
Do primary research for the product/retail concept with potential target market/ consumer customers	•	•	•	
Reposition product for alternative target market(s)	•	•	•	
Bundle products together	•			•
Develop brand extensions and flankers	•	•		
Expand hours of store	•			
Offer longer/lifetime warranty	•	•	•	
Branding				
Change name to reflect repositioning of store	•	•		
Brand for direct association with target market				
Brand for credibility		•	•	
Brand by price category (i.e., Budget Rent-A-Car)				
Brand for suggestion of quality or function				
Brand for communication and/or benefit				
Develop unique brands for each product line			•	

Marketing Situations

New/ Greater Competition	Low Awareness	Need to Improve/ Change Image	New Product/ Store Intro/ Grand Opening	Seasonal Sales Problem/ Opportunity	Need Support From Intermediate Markets/Channels	Regional/ Local Market/ Store Problem
			•			
•				•		•
•		•				
•			•			•
•			•			•
•		•	•			
•		•	•			•
•			•			
			•			
•		•	•			
			•			
			•	•		
•		•				
•						
•			•	•		•
•			•			•
•	•	•			•	•
	•	•				
•			•	•	•	
•			•	•		
•		•				
			•	•		
	•		•	•		
		•	•			
•	•	•	•			
	•	•	•			
	•	•	•			

	Marketing Situations			
Idea Starters for Each Marketing Mix Tool	Flat/Continual Decline in Sales	Increase Small User Base	Poor Repeat/ Limited Loyalty	Need to Build Amount Purchased
Branding—continued				
License use of brand for additional/ supplementary products				
Provide different brand name in different markets				
Develop alternative brands of product for various targets				
Put subliminal benefit in name (i.e., ACURA Integra [integrity]; Legend [legendary])				
Packaging				
Update packaging/signage for changing target market		•		
Package multiple units of same item together			•	•
Package different products together (i.e., shampoo with conditioner)		•		•
Include handy feature on package (i.e., spout, carry handle, etc.)		•		
Include usage information inside or on package (i.e., recipe, additional uses, etc.)		•	•	•
Include contest on package		•	•	
Redesign package or store to serve secondary benefit		•	•	•
Develop package for disposability, and/or increase shelf life		•	•	
Develop permanent reader board inside and outside store that changes daily		•		•
Package for visual sampling of product (see product through package window)		•		
Build in additional feature for after use (i.e., package container becomes drinking glass)		•	•	
Make package easy to stock for trade			•	
Make package and display piece one in the same/dependent on each other		•		•
Research brand/package alternatives				
Provide on-pack toll-free number to provide assistance/tips			•	
Develop package that increases shelf life				
Develop package that takes less shelf space				
Introduce packages at various sizes/amounts for various targets/channels (i.e., individual, travel)	•	•		•
Develop environmentally-friendly package (i.e., recyclable)		•	•	
Pricing				
Set up customer panel that monitors competitive pricing				

Marketing Situations

New/ Greater Competition	Low Awareness	Need to Improve/ Change Image	New Product/ Store Intro/ Grand Opening	Seasonal Sales Problem/ Opportunity	Need Support From Intermediate Markets/Channels	Regional/ Local Market/ Store Problem
						•
•		•				
•	•	•	•			
		•				
•						
•						
			•			
•						
•						
			•			
•					•	
	•			•		
•		•	•			
•		•			•	
•					•	
			•		•	
•		•	•			
•						
				•	•	
					•	
•			•		•	•
•	•	•				•
•						

	Marketing Situations			
Idea Starters for Each Marketing Mix Tool	**Flat/Continual Decline in Sales**	**Increase Small User Base**	**Poor Repeat/ Limited Loyalty**	**Need to Build Amount Purchased**
Pricing—continued				
Employ volume discount program				●
Vary price points by seasonality and market differences				
Price to skim (introduce at high price, then reduce price to broaden consumer base)				
Price at lower level to steal share	●	●		
Match price to intended perceived quality of product (i.e., high price to support premium image)			●	
Penetration pricing—introduce at low price and hold		●		●
Cream pricing—introduce at high price and hold				●
Employ flexible pricing, negotiate with each customer from highest to lowest price				●
Price based on replacement cost, not what was paid for product		●		
Product line pricing (maintain similar price range for all products in line)				
Test higher/lower prices in various markets	●	●	●	●
Fit product to price ranges		●		●
Price all merchandise at one price		●		
Parity price but regularly feature lower price specials for lower price perception	●	●		
Provide renewal/repurchase discounts	●		●	●
Price by distribution channel				
Good, better, best pricing	●	●		
Price some items as loss leaders				●
Distribution/ Store Penetration				
Fully distribute product/penetrate each market before rolling out to other markets		●		
Employ new channel(s) (i.e., sell product in new/different retail outlets; retail through direct mail)	●	●		
Use exclusive/selective distribution				
Use extensive mass market distribution	●	●		
Establish minimum distribution levels prior to use of other marketing activities (i.e., advertising)				
Continually monitor distribution/out-of-stock versus competition to understand performance	●		●	
Letter/printed piece/sample/premium to purchasing agent, trade, etc.			●	●
Concentrate store penetration in markets with high product usage and low media cost		●		

Marketing Situations

New/ Greater Competition	Low Awareness	Need to Improve/ Change Image	New Product/ Store Intro/ Grand Opening	Seasonal Sales Problem/ Opportunity	Need Support From Intermediate Markets/Channels	Regional/ Local Market/ Store Problem
•					•	•
				•		•
			•	•		•
•			•			•
		•	•			
•			•			
		•	•			
						•
•					•	
			•		•	•
•			•		•	
•		•				•
•						
•						
						•
					•	•
•				•		•
•	•				•	
•		•	•		•	•
		•	•		•	•
•						
			•			•
			•			•
•					•	•
•	•		•		•	•

	Marketing Situations			
Idea Starters for Each Marketing Mix Tool	Flat/Continual Decline in Sales	Increase Small User Base	Poor Repeat/ Limited Loyalty	Need to Build Amount Purchased
Distribution/Store Penetration —continued				
Develop limited service satellite outlets in outlying areas to feed main facility		•	•	
Intensive distribution employing trade discounts				
Send sample of product to home of buyer/ purchasing agent or spouse				
Optimum distribution/inventory for new product introduction/grand opening		•		
Offer merchandise on consignment or guarantee return		•		
Provide co-op advertising program		•		
Offer exclusivity to outlets by market or within certain radius				
Locate your "mini-store" within a larger store	•	•		•
Use electronic/vending machines	•	•		•
Just In Time (JIT) delivery				
Close unprofitable stores and relocate to better trading areas/locations/markets	•	•		
Test larger "super"/mini stores for a greater selection/convenience, respectively	•	•		•
Personal Selling/ Service				
Institute/strengthen sales commission programs	•	•	•	•
Institute highly visible peer recognition program with reward	•	•		•
Research and then fulfill vocation and avocation needs of staff—graduated dollar incentive program; free vacation/prizes for winning sales contest	•			•
Change method of selling product, (i.e., direct versus manufacturer's representative)	•			•
Continuous sales training/seminars	•			•
Sponsor all company events (convention, banquet, dinner, sales meeting, etc.)	•			•
Institute on-going feedback program from field on promotion, selling, merchandising, product, inventory, etc.		•	•	•
Initiate on-going internal competition among sales staff/districts/stores		•		•
Incentives/prizes for number of sales contacts and selling ratio	•	•	•	
Develop lead qualifying program to provide best prospects to sales staff	•			
Establish sales contests between regions and within regions	•			

Marketing Situations

New/ Greater Competition	Low Awareness	Need to Improve/ Change Image	New Product/ Store Intro/ Grand Opening	Seasonal Sales Problem/ Opportunity	Need Support From Intermediate Markets/Channels	Regional/ Local Market/ Store Problem
•	•					•
•					•	•
			•		•	•
			•		•	
•			•		•	•
•	•		•	•	•	•
			•		•	•
•	•	•				•
•	•				•	•
•			•		•	•
	•					•
•		•				•
					•	•
					•	•
					•	
•					•	•
					•	•
•			•		•	•
			•		•	•
•			•	•	•	•
					•	
•			•		•	
•			•			•

Marketing Situations

Idea Starters for Each Marketing Mix Tool	Flat/Continual Decline in Sales	Increase Small User Base	Poor Repeat/ Limited Loyalty	Need to Build Amount Purchased
Personal Selling/Service—continued				
Adjust commission rate for current customers to emphasize retention			•	
Allow sales staff limited free product for sampling to gain new customer trial		•		
Establish service standards	•		•	•
Follow-up sales call after personal visit or direct mail drop	•		•	
Provide 24-hour toll-free expert troubleshooting	•	•	•	•
New product seminars	•			•
Inventory control/services			•	•
Promotion/Events				
Half-price sale (buy one, get second at half-price)	•	•		•
Sampling—free product/gift/service; on pack/in mail		•		
Free goods with purchase	•	•	•	
Media carried coupon	•	•		•
Salesperson carried coupon	•	•		•
Bounce-back coupon	•		•	•
Multiple coupon for greater redemption	•	•	•	•
Instant coupon redeemed when product purchased	•	•		
Gambler's sale (everyone receives discount but discount amount is left to chance)	•	•	•	
Cross-ruff package couponing by similar demographic targets	•	•		
Stage "Let's Make A Deal" auction on selected/sale merchandise	•		•	•
Tie-in offer with non-competitor in-store, on pack, in ad		•		
Offer free/lower cost financing	•	•		•
Trial sizes	•	•		
Low price as loss leaders	•	•		
Use trial-to-loyalty continuity program	•	•	•	
Free product with series of purchases via punch/validation card	•		•	•
Sweepstakes that require some show of product knowledge to enter				
Value packs	•	•		•
Premiums	•	•	•	•
In-store/department couponing	•		•	•
In-store demonstration with sampling		•		
Iree samples to the trade/buyers at office and home				

Marketing Situations

New/ Greater Competition	Low Awareness	Need to Improve/ Change Image	New Product/ Store Intro/ Grand Opening	Seasonal Sales Problem/ Opportunity	Need Support From Intermediate Markets/Channels	Regional/ Local Market/ Store Problem
		•	•			
•		•	•			•
			•			
•		•				•
•	•	•	•			•
•		•		•		
•			•	•		
	•	•	•		•	
			•	•	•	
•	•		•	•	•	•
•			•	•	•	
•			•	•	•	•
•			•	•	•	•
•			•		•	•
•			•	•	•	•
•				•	•	•
				•		•
•	•	•		•		•
•						•
•						•
•						•
•			•			•
			•			
	•	•	•		•	
•						
•						
			•		•	
			•		•	
						•
			•		•	•

	Marketing Situations			
Idea Starters for Each Marketing Mix Tool	**Flat/Continual Decline in Sales**	**Increase Small User Base**	**Poor Repeat/ Limited Loyalty**	**Need to Build Amount Purchased**
Promotion/Events—continued				
Discounts for special groups (seniors, students, etc.)	•	•	•	
Sweepstakes—on/in pack; in-store; in ad		•	•	•
Game with many/all instant winners and few big winners	•	•	•	
Continuous specials on specific days/hours	•	•	•	•
Use a grand opening of one store to sell all market stores for month(s)	•	•		
Tie promotions to timely local, regional, and national events				
Free goods/discount for bringing/referring friend	•	•		
"2 for 1" special	•	•		
Provide a free service to bring customers to outlet	•	•		
In/on pack coupon	•	•	•	•
In-store/other retailer cross-ruff couponing	•			•
Graduated open or coupon sale (i.e., 10 percent off one item, 20 percent off two, etc.)	•			•
Premiums—free with purchase, self-liquidating; continuity (i.e., set of glasses)	•	•	•	•
Bonus pack (i.e., 20 percent extra product at no extra cost)	•	•	•	•
Refunds—mail-in for cash/coupons; rebates	•	•	•	•
Stamps			•	
Volume discounts—reduced price; free item with multiple purchases (punch card); free case with multiple purchases	•		•	•
Make coupon as large as the page it is printed on		•		
Free appealing gift to first 50 to 500 customers	•	•	•	
Establish customer club (i.e., free coffee breakfast club)			•	
Coupon turn-about—promote acceptance of competitors' coupons	•	•	•	
Pre/post clearance sales/specials	•	•	•	
Develop value added specials by packaging items together at special price		•	•	•
Contest		•		
In-store display allowance		•		
Discount allowance for product feature in retailer ad		•		
Free new product with purchase of an established product	•	•		

Marketing Situations

New/ Greater Competition	Low Awareness	Need to Improve/ Change Image	New Product/ Store Intro/ Grand Opening	Seasonal Sales Problem/ Opportunity	Need Support From Intermediate Markets/Channels	Regional/ Local Market/ Store Problem
•						
•	•	•	•	•	•	
•				•	•	
•				•		
•	•		•	•		•
	•			•		•
•				•		
•			•	•		•
			•			•
•			•			•
•			•			
•						
			•	•	•	
•					•	
•					•	
•					•	
•				•	•	
•	•		•			
•			•			•
		•				•
•						•
•				•		
			•	•		
	•	•	•			
•	•	•	•		•	•
•	•				•	•
•			•		•	

	Marketing Situations			
Idea Starters for Each Marketing Mix Tool	**Flat/Continual Decline in Sales**	**Increase Small User Base**	**Poor Repeat/ Limited Loyalty**	**Need to Build Amount Purchased**
Promotion/Events—continued				
Premiums/prizes with contest for trade based on their knowledge of your product				
Have charity sell product/dollar savings certificate	•	•		
Stage election/contest for naming the best local, regional, and national sports team		•		
Celebrate customer's birthday with free good/services			•	
Sell gift/dollar certificates (generates positive slippage)	•	•	•	
Free gift with purchase of dollar certificates	•	•	•	
Dollars-off purchase with donation to charity (i.e., bring used coat for needy, receive dollar discount)	•	•		
Double coupon—instant and bounce back coupons for immediate and subsequent purchase	•	•	•	
Cross-ruff coupon from high to low volume and complimentary brands	•	•	•	•
Retailers solicit co-op promotion support and tie-in with manufacturers and industry groups				
Build a promotional event around a recognized celebrity or spokesperson				
Develop a contest or award that shows real people using your product	•	•	•	•
Create a mascot, character, or vehicle (hot-air balloon, auto, etc.) that can tour parades, fairs, etc.				
Create an event for employees that builds motivation and excitement for marketing initiatives				
Off-hour/VIP customer sale	•		•	
Have a grand open house to draw people and expose all areas of store	•	•		•
Use store as deposit center for charity drive		•		
Use store as meeting place for groups/clubs			•	
Advertising Message				
Stress product's quality/inherent drama/ uniqueness		•	•	
Stress brand name			•	
Emphasize profitability of product to trade				
Feature consumer advertising to trade that will be supporting the product				

Marketing Situations

New/ Greater Competition	Low Awareness	Need to Improve/ Change Image	New Product/ Store Intro/ Grand Opening	Seasonal Sales Problem/ Opportunity	Need Support From Intermediate Markets/Channels	Regional/ Local Market/ Store Problem
•			•		•	
		•		•		•
	•	•		•		
		•				
				•		
				•		
		•		•		•
•						
		•	•	•		•
•	•	•	•	•	•	•
	•				•	
		•		•	•	•
			•	•		•
•			•			•
		•	•	•		•
		•	•			
			•			
•			•			•
•	•		•			
			•		•	
			•		•	

Marketing Situations

Idea Starters for Each Marketing Mix Tool	Flat/Continual Decline in Sales	Increase Small User Base	Poor Repeat/ Limited Loyalty	Need to Build Amount Purchased
Advertising Message —continued				
Use problem/solution approach when building market		•		
Use band wagon (everyone is doing it) approach		•	•	
Testimonial by authority/celebrity figure				
Comparative product/pricing	•	•		
Feature alternative product uses	•	•	•	•
Use music for mood, entertainment, emotion, continuity, attention				
Use emotion to create difference for personalized commodity type product like beer, cigarettes				
Educational/editorial type advertising (advatorial) to help build/preempt the market		•		•
Use company spokesperson				
Use animation for greater interest/ entertainment value				
For :30s use two integrated :15s/three :10s for different messages				
Provide key decision information to encourage purchase		•		
Borrowed interest/familiarity for imagery and/or memorability with established music, sound, phrase				
Make sure audio and video in TV sync together for most effective communication				
Make sure you have adequate name identification—early and late product identification in broadcast commercials				
When logical and possible, "new"/"grand opening" and "free" are powerful words to use in your advertising	•	•		
Use teaser campaign to build interest prior to introduction	•	•	•	•
Use an involvement device (i.e., a puzzle)	•	•	•	•
Reduce your message to a single word or picture	•	•	•	•
Copy test advertising before running				
Advertising Media				
Increase media weight	•	•		
Use heavy television	•	•		
Use direct mail in store's trading area	•	•		
Use direct mail against competitor's customer trading area				

Marketing Situations

New/ Greater Competition	Low Awareness	Need to Improve/ Change Image	New Product/ Store Intro/ Grand Opening	Seasonal Sales Problem/ Opportunity	Need Support From Intermediate Markets/Channels	Regional/ Local Market/ Store Problem
	•					
		•	•			
	•	•				
•						
•						
	•	•				
	•	•				
	•	•	•			•
•		•	•			•
	•	•				
•	•		•			
	•	•	•			
	•	•	•			
	•	•				
	•	•				
•	•	•	•		•	•
•	•	•	•			•
•	•	•	•			•
•	•	•	•			•
	•	•	•			
•	•	•	•			•
	•		•			•
	•		•			•
•			•			•

	Marketing Situations			
Idea Starters for Each Marketing Mix Tool	**Flat/Continual Decline in Sales**	**Increase Small User Base**	**Poor Repeat/ Limited Loyalty**	**Need to Build Amount Purchased**
Advertising Media—continued				
Build and use direct mail customer list for all heavy users	•		•	
Test direct mail to new target markets	•	•		
Use multiple, smaller ads in same issue of newspaper/magazine				
For target market impact, test medium never used before	•	•		
Use cable TV for specially targeted groups by usage, demographics and geography		•	•	
Roadblock same time period/news on all TV stations				
Target outdoor/transit around store, in concentrated area, near company buying office, competition		•		
If available and efficient, use :10s/:15s for additional frequency				
Provide radio station tie-in promotion in return for free spots				
Sponsor high rated/memorable television special once/twice a year if budget is limited				
Local/suburban newspapers to target selected areas	•	•		
Stage periodic media blitz in TV/radio with spots every hour on all TV/top radio stations	•	•		
Use :10/small space ads as teasers with frequency for product intro, grand opening, promotion				
Follow-up direct mail with telemarketing for increased response	•	•	•	•
Negotiate free radio bonus spots, remote broadcast, etc., when purchasing radio spots from stations				
Use heavy radio schedule for high frequency	•			
Sponsor community events, local sports events (high school)			•	
Place multiple spots within the same program for immediate message reinforcement				
Use broadcast medium/large print ads to attract new customers/build the market	•	•		
Use unique coupon insert in print medium (i.e., bag, cut-out game, toy, etc.)	•	•		
Frequency trade mailings to office and home				
Free-standing insert (FSI) in newspaper (good coupon carrier)		•		
Ethnic media to expand the user base	•	•		

Marketing Situations

	New/ Greater Competition	Low Awareness	Need to Improve/ Change Image	New Product/ Store Intro/ Grand Opening	Seasonal Sales Problem/ Opportunity	Need Support From Intermediate Markets/Channels	Regional/ Local Market/ Store Problem
	•				•	•	•
				•			
		•		•			
	•	•	•	•			•
		•		•			•
		•		•			
				•			
	•	•		•		•	•
	•	•		•			•
		•		•			•
			•	•			
	•		•	•			•
	•	•	•	•			•
		•	•	•			
							•
		•	•				•
		•	•	•			•
			•				•
		•		•			
		•		•			
		•	•	•			•
			•				
				•		•	
	•	•		•		•	
		•	•	•			•

	Marketing Situations			
Idea Starters for Each Marketing Mix Tool	Flat/Continual Decline in Sales	Increase Small User Base	Poor Repeat/ Limited Loyalty	Need to Build Amount Purchased
Advertising Media—continued				
Develop trade-out agreement with broadcast station exchanging advertising for your product/service				
Use bag around home-delivered newspaper as medium	•	•		
Use colored comics to reach whole family (adults, teens, kids) for cost of black and white		•		
Use direct mail/outdoor around new store in large multiple store market				
Manufacturers develop disciplined, aggressive media co-op program for dealers/retailers for added, efficient media weight				
Test alternative media mix and support levels		•		
Put a home page on the Internet	•	•	•	
Create an interactive CD-Rom	•	•	•	
Bathroom stall messages (captive audience)				
Use in-store communication services (i.e., electronic reader board, grocery carts, etc.)	•		•	•
Merchandising				
Use cross-ruff display to sell other products/ departments	•	•		
Use buttons to suggestive sell				•
Do tie-in display with non-competitor		•		•
Announce timely specials in store via P.A. system				•
Feature new/add-on products at checkout				•
Use same window signs to sell inside as well as outside store				•
Tie-in all trade and in-store display materials to advertising				
Flyer/handouts in high traffic areas, on neighborhood bulletin boards				
Communicate guarantee of product/lowest price in store to enhance sale	•	•	•	•
Kids play area in store		•	•	•
Decorate store with unique mobiles/balloons				•
Distribute coupons in store	•	•	•	
Aisle, point-of-purchase (p-o-p) displays to sell/sample product/distribute coupons		•		•
Use in-store advertising for point-of-sale (p-o-s) awareness (i.e., grocery cart, video reader board)		•		•

Marketing Situations

New/ Greater Competition	Low Awareness	Need to Improve/ Change Image	New Product/ Store Intro/ Grand Opening	Seasonal Sales Problem/ Opportunity	Need Support From Intermediate Markets/Channels	Regional/ Local Market/ Store Problem
	•		•			•
•	•		•	•		•
	•					
	•		•			•
	•		•		•	
	•					
	•					
•	•	•	•	•	•	•
•	•	•	•	•	•	•
•	•		•			•
			•	•		•
•		•	•			•
			•			•
	•					
		•	•			
	•	•	•		•	
•	•	•				
•		•	•			
	•	•	•			
•	•		•			•
			•			•
	•		•		•	•

Idea Starters for Each Marketing Mix Tool	Marketing Situations			
	Flat/Continual Decline in Sales	Increase Small User Base	Poor Repeat/ Limited Loyalty	Need to Build Amount Purchased
Merchandising—continued				
Provide demonstrations/lessons on how to use product and expand its uses (i.e., use of fabrics for home decorating, not just for sewing clothes)	•	•	•	•
Make display compatible with product and target market (i.e., in-store shoot a basket display for athletic shoes)			•	
When purchasing radio, newspaper, and magazines ask for free merchandising such as on-air contest and/or product merchandising to the intermediate/ consumer markets				
Bag stuffers with useful and changing message including specials	•	•	•	
Use TV monitor or large screen for in-store information, sales, entertainment			•	•
Answer store phone with special message			•	
Customer newsletter with timely information, promotion announcements, cross-ruff/ discount coupons			•	•
Shelf talkers whenever possible		•		
Put information of product on video cassette for review by purchasing agent at convenient time in home or office				
Use shopping bag as walking billboard/ reminder			•	
Merchandise future sales	•		•	
Place product information/coupons at point of purchase		•		•
Hold a product display contest for dealers/trade				
Provide sales staff with ad/direct mail reprints for in-person distribution				
Develop turnkey point of sale materials for retail outlets				
Develop video demonstration with TV/VCR incentive for retailers/dealers				
Provide removable signage for seasonal displays				
Publicity				
Tie-in with radio/TV station and charity to sponsor event		•		
Contribution to charity for every product sold		•	•	•
Tie-in with charity and secure free PSAs from broadcast stations		•		

Marketing Situations

	New/ Greater Competition	Low Awareness	Need to Improve/ Change Image	New Product/ Store Intro/ Grand Opening	Seasonal Sales Problem/ Opportunity	Need Support From Intermediate Markets/Channels	Regional/ Local Market/ Store Problem
				•			
	•		•	•	•		•
		•		•		•	•
			•	•		•	•
			•				
			•		•		
	•	•	•	•			•
	•	•		•			•
				•		•	
		•	•		•		
	•			•		•	•
			•	•		•	•
		•		•		•	
		•		•	•	•	•
		•		•		•	•
		•	•	•			•
		•	•	•	•		•
			•				•
		•	•	•			•

	Marketing Situations			
Idea Starters for Each Marketing Mix Tool	**Flat/Continual Decline in Sales**	**Increase Small User Base**	**Poor Repeat/ Limited Loyalty**	**Need to Build Amount Purchased**
Publicity—continued				
Request PSA support from media public affairs directors, salesperson, and station manager		•		
Sponsor community events (i.e., fairs, community interest programs, etc.)				
Market by market visits by company representative with local news media people		•		
Charity tie-ins on special day(s) and gift giving times of year		•		
Provide game contest with prizes and coupons for spectator participation at sporting events, concerts, etc.		•		
Sponsor celebrity market tour/in-store appearance				
Feature representatives for various companies in retail outlet			•	
Provide news media with periodic stories on high interest topics relative to product/ store/company				
Volunteer program for community activities (i.e., team physician for high school sports)				
Tie publicity events to introduction/grand opening				
Send/deliver news release to news/editorial staff with free product/premium and/or in unique manner				
Establish company speakers bureau to make presentations to key target groups				
Place a feature story that shows how your product benefited a particular user	•	•	•	•
Place a feature story profiling a company executive/employee			•	
Issue a news release announcing new product/ new store/grand opening for the public and/or for charity				
Publicize a newsworthy advertising campaign or promotion				
Publicize a seasonal use for your product	•			•
Offer to be a source of industry expertise for the media			•	
Develop and publicize a seminar or educational event for your specific target			•	
Take an action that conveys image (i.e., donate product to charity, support employee volunteerism) and publicize it			•	

Marketing Situations

	New/ Greater Competition	Low Awareness	Need to Improve/ Change Image	New Product/ Store Intro/ Grand Opening	Seasonal Sales Problem/ Opportunity	Need Support From Intermediate Markets/Channels	Regional/ Local Market/ Store Problem
		•	•		•		•
		•	•				•
		•	•	•			•
		•	•		•		
		•	•				•
		•	•	•			•
				•			•
		•	•	•	•		•
			•				•
		•	•	•			•
		•	•	•			•
		•	•				
	•	•				•	•
	•	•	•				•
				•		•	•
		•	•	•		•	
		•	•		•	•	•
	•	•	•			•	
	•	•			•	•	•
	•	•	•	•		•	•

Marketing Situations

Idea Starters for Each Marketing Mix Tool	Flat/Continual Decline in Sales	Increase Small User Base	Poor Repeat/ Limited Loyalty	Need to Build Amount Purchased
Publicity—continued				
Develop and place features with a local interest angle				
Submit an opinion piece on a local/ regional issue				
Editor briefing tours		•		
Get industry expert advice on use of your product and pass along to consumers		•	•	

Marketing Situations

New/ Greater Competition	Low Awareness	Need to Improve/ Change Image	New Product/ Store Intro/ Grand Opening	Seasonal Sales Problem/ Opportunity	Need Support From Intermediate Markets/Channels	Regional/ Local Market/ Store Problem
•	•	•	•			•
	•	•			•	•
	•	•	•			•
•	•	•				

B

Worksheets for the Marketing Background

The following worksheets correspond to the Tasks in Chapter 2 of the Business Review. The purpose of the charts is to provide the marketer with a guide on how to assimilate data in order to answer the questions listed in each step of the Business Review. Note that there are three business review sections and several tasks within each section. However, due to the nature of some material or where company-tailored charts would be more useful, charts are not provided.

Also included at the bottom of each chart is material to use as reference on where to find the information necessary to complete the chart.

Worksheets for Chapter 3, Problems and Opportunities, are also included in this Appendix.

WORKSHEET

Company Strengths

- Target market needs, wants, and consumption trends

- Value the organization brings to the target market

- Product and technological

- Operational

- Distribution

- Pricing

- Promotion/marketing communications

Definition of strength:
Capability or resource that the organization has which could be used to improve its competitive position (share of market or size of market) or improve its financial performance.

Where to find this information
Internal company data/survey of employees and management

WORKSHEET

Company Weaknesses

- Target market needs, wants, and consumption trends

- Value the company brings to the target market

- Product and technological

- Operational

- Distribution

- Pricing

- Promotion/marketing communications

Definition of weakness:
Exists in any capability or resource that may cause your organization to have a weaker competitive position or poorer financial performance.

Where to find this information
Internal company data/survey of employees and management

WORKSHEET

Identify Your Company's Core Competencies

1.

2.

3.

4.

Core competencies must meet the following criteria:

- Makes a significant contribution to the perceived customer's benefit of the end product.
- Are difficult for competitors to imitate.

Where to find this information
Internal company data/survey of employees and management

WORKSHEET

Identify Your Organization's Marketing Capabilities

1.

2.

3.

4.

A marketing capability must meet the following criteria:

- A unique ability to provide access to target markets versus the competition.

Where to find this information

Internal company data/survey of employees and management

WORKSHEET

Alternative Scope Options

1.

2.

3.

4.

Where to find this information
Internal company data/survey of employees and management

WORKSHEET
Analysis of Options

Option 1 _____   Organization Rating
What's needed to succeed for the above option

	Strength	Weakness
1.		
2.		
3.		
4.		
5.		
6.		
7.		
8.		
9.		
10.		

Option 2 _____   Organization Rating
What's needed to succeed for the above option

	Strength	Weakness
1.		
2.		
3.		
4.		
5.		
6.		
7.		
8.		
9.		
10.		

Option 3 _____   Organization Rating
What's needed to succeed for the above option

	Strength	Weakness
1.		
2.		
3.		
4.		
5.		
6.		
7.		
8.		
9.		
10.		

Where to find this information
Internal company data/survey of employees and management

WORKSHEET

Core Competencies Needed To Succeed

Correlation to your
organization's core competencies?

Option 1 _____

	Yes	No
1.		
2.		
3.		
4.		

Correlation to your
organization's core competencies?

Option 2 _____

	Yes	No
1.		
2.		
3.		
4.		

Correlation to your
organization's core competencies?

Option 3 _____

	Yes	No
1.		
2.		
3.		
4.		

Where to find this information
Internal company data/survey of employees and management

WORKSHEET

Marketing Capabilities Needed to Succeed

Correlation to your
organization's capabilities?

Option 1 _____

Yes	No

1.

2.

3.

4.

Correlation to your
organization's capabilities?

Option 2 _____

Yes	No

1.

2.

3.

4.

Correlation to your
organization's capabilities?

Option 3 _____

Yes	No

1.

2.

3.

4.

Where to find this information
Internal company data/survey of employees and management

WORKSHEET

Risks and Opportunities

OPTION 1 _____

RISKS

1.
2.
3.
4.
5.

OPPORTUNITIES

1.
2.
3.
4.
5.

OPTION 2 _____

RISKS

1.
2.
3.
4.
5.

OPPORTUNITIES

1.
2.
3.
4.
5.

OPTION 3 _____

RISKS

1.
2.
3.
4.
5.

OPPORTUNITIES

1.
2.
3.
4.
5.

Where to find this information
Internal company data/survey of employees and management

WORKSHEET

Corporate Philosophy/Description of the Company and Product

- Corporate goals and objectives

- General company history

- Organizational chart

Where to find this information:
Internal company data

WORKSHEET

Product Analysis

- Identify products sold in the industry category and within the scope of your business.

   Industry   Category

   1.   1.

   2.   2.

   3.   3.

   4.   4.

   5.   5.

- Describe your product's history. What developments over the past years make it special today?

- Describe company and product strengths and weaknesses.

- Describe competitive product strengths and weaknesses.

- Highlight product trends within your product category(ies) from both an industry and company perspective.

Where to find this information:
Internal company data

WORKSHEET

Sales Growth Analysis of Company Product Categories Relative to Industry Trends

The purpose of this chart is twofold—first, to track growth of total company sales relative to total industry sales, and second, to track growth of company product/brands as compared to industry category against which the company products or brands compete.

	1996		1995		1994		1993		1992		% Change 1992–1996	
	Units	$	Units	$	Units	$	Units	$	Units	$	Units	$
Industry Sales												
Product Category												
Product Category												
Product Category												
Company Sales												
Product/Brand												
Product/Brand												
Product/Brand												

Where to find this information:
U.S. Bureau of the Census, current industrial reports.
Fairchild Fact Files
Trade research
Trade publications
Sales and Marketing Management Survey of Buying Power
U.S. Bureau of the Census, current industrial reports
Company data
Annual reports/10-K reports from public companies

WORKSHEET

Industry Category Sales Compared to Company Sales Resulting in Market Share Estimates

The purpose of this chart is to calculate market share trends. Calculate total industry category sales (e.g., all athletic shoe sales), your company's product sales (e.g., your athletic shoe brands), and the resulting market share.

Year	Total Industry Sales M	Change	Total Company Sales M	Change	Your Company's Market Share
	$	%	$	%	%
1991					
1992					
1993					
1994					
1995					

Estimated Sales By Competitor	Sales 1996	Market Share	Sales 1995	Market Share	Sales 1994	Market Share	Sales 1993	Market Share	Sales 1992	Market Share
		%		%		%		%		%
Competitor A										
Competitor B										
Competitor C										
Total Market Sales										

Where to find this information:
Industry research reports
Trade publications
Fairchild Fact Files/Government census reports
Annual reports/10-K reports from public companies
Company data
Similar chart for transactions and profits (margins)

WORKSHEET

Company Sales Trends—Store-for-Store Sales

Market	Sales Volume (M)	Change from PreviousYear	Number of Stores	Per Store Average (M)	Change from Previous Year	Per Store Average Indexed to System Average ($	M)
City A							
City B							
City C							
City D							
City E							

(M = $000)

Note: Make sure your year-to-year analysis of per store averages includes comparable stores that have been open for the full year.

Where to find this information:
Company data

WORKSHEET

Sales Seasonality by Month for Industry Category and Company

Month	Company Percentage of Sales	Company Index to Average ( )	Industry Category Percentage of Sales	Industry Index to Average ( )
January				
February				
March				
April				
May				
June				
July				
August				
September				
October				
November				
December				

Where to find this information:
Fairchild Fact Files
Company data

WORKSHEET

Product Brand Seasonality by Month for Industry Category and Company

	Base*	November Percent of Total Dollars	November Index to Total Year	December Percent of Total Dollars	December Index to Total Year	Etc.
		%		%		
Industry category sales						
Company Product/Brand Sales						
Major competitor Product/Brand sales						
Company Brand						

*Base equals total figures for the year.

Where to find this information:
Company data

WORKSHEET

Behavior Trends

- Demographic/target market trends

- Geographic trends

- Social/consumer trends

- Technological trends

- Media viewing trends

Where to find this information:
U.S. Bureau of the Census data—current population projections
The Popcorn Report—Faith Popcorn
Yankelovich Monitor Study
American Demographics Magazine

WORKSHEET

Distribution—Purchases by Outlet Type (5 Year Trend)

Distribution Outlet Type	Total Sales					
	1996		1992		Points Change (1996 to 1992)	
	Units	Dollars	Units	Dollars	Units	Dollars
	%	$	%	$	%	$

Where to find this information:
Fairchild Fact Files
Trade publications

WORKSHEET

Distribution—Store Penetration Analysis I

	Number of Stores	Sales Last Year (M)	Estimated Number of TV HHs (M)	Sales per HH	Current Advertising Plans		Future Advertising Plans			
					( )%* of Sales (M)	Target Market Media Weight Level	Average Sales per HH	Number of Stores Needed	( )%* of Sales (M)	Target Market Media Weight Level
Group 1 Markets (Weaker Markets)										
A										
B										
C										
D										
E										
F										
Subtotal										
Group 2 Markets (Stronger Markets)										
G										
H										
I										
J										
K										
L										
Subtotal										
Totals/Averages Groups 1 and 2										

Average per store sales Groups 1 and 2 $_____.
(M = 000)

*Fill in current percent of advertising spending and future spending based upon company records.

Where to find this information:
In-house sources/company data
SDRS
Nielsen Test Markets Profiles

WORKSHEET

Distribution—Store Penetration Analysis II

	Number of Stores	Existing Stores per 100M* HHs	Total Sales Last Year (M)	Advertising Budget: Percent of Sales
A				
B				
C				
D				
E				
F				
G				
H				
I				
J				
K				
L				
All Stores				

*Or whatever you determine to be the optimum.

			Penetration of 1 Store per 100M HHs		
	Estimated 1 Week Cost	Estimated Number Weeks	Minimum 1/100M HHs	$	New Estimated Number Weeks
A					
B					
C					
D					
E					
F					
G					
H					
I					
J					
K					
L					
All Stores					

(M = 000 or $000)

Where to find this information:
In-house sources/company data
SDRS
Nielsen Test Market Profiles

Market Coverage Chart

	Coverage for Your Product % ACV	Percent of Shelf Space Given Your Product in Store	Percent Shelf Space for Main Competitors in Product Category	
			Competitor 1	Competitor 2
Outlet A				
Outlet B				
Outlet C				
Outlet D				
Outlet E				
Outlet F				
Outlet G				
Outlet H				
Outlet I				

Note: An identical chart would be created for each key market.

Where to find this information:
Store checks/interviews with store managers
Nielsen
SAMI

WORKSHEET

Pricing—Price of Your Company's Product Relative to the Competition During Key Selling Periods

	Price 1st Quarter	Price 2nd Quarter	Price 3rd Quarter	Price 4th Quarter
Your Company				
Competitor A				
Competitor B				
Competitor C				
Competitor D				

Where to find this information:
Company data

WORKSHEET

Distribution of Sales by Price Point (5 Year Trend)

	Price Range Industry Product Category		Price Range Company's Product	
	Percent of Sale	Percent of Items	Percent of Sale	Percent of Items
1996				
$___ to $___				
$___ to $___				
$___ to $___				
$___ to $___				
$___ to $___				
$___ to $___				
1995				
$___ to $___				
$___ to $___				
$___ to $___				
$___ to $___				
$___ to $___				
$___ to $___				
1994				
$___ to $___				
$___ to $___				
$___ to $___				
$___ to $___				
$___ to $___				
$___ to $___				

1993, etc.

1992, etc.

Where to find this information:
Fairchild Fact Files
Company data
Trade publications

WORKSHEET

Marketing Communications Review—Company versus Competitive Spending

Annual Competitive Spending Analysis

Company	Total Dollar Expenditures	Share of Spending—Total Expenditures	Change from Last Year	Television			Newspaper		
				Total Dollar Expenditures	Percent	Change from Last Year	Total Dollar Expenditures	Percent	Change from Last Year
	$	%	%	$	%	%	$	%	%

Competitor	Magazine			Radio			Outdoor		
	Total Dollar Expenditures	Percent	Change from Last Year	Total Dollar Expenditures	Percent	Change from Last Year	Total Dollar Expenditures	Percent	Change from Last Year
	$	%	%	$	%	%	$	%	%

Note: The above information should also be obtained on a quarterly basis to track seasonality of spending. If available, total dollars for each category should also be obtained.

Where to find this information:
Media representatives from television stations, newspapers, radio stations, outdoor companies
LNA (Leading National Advertisers) for national companies
PIB
RADAR
Media records
BAR

WORKSHEET

Marketing Review—Competitive Analysis

Your Company	Competitor A	Competitor B	Competitor C	Competitor D

Market Share/Sales
Current
Growth/Decline Past 5 Years

Target Market
Primary
Secondary

Marketing Objectives/Strategies

Positioning

Product/Branding/Packaging
Strengths
Weaknesses

Pricing Strategies/Pricing Structure
Higher/Lower/Parity

Distribution/Store Penetration/Market Coverage Strategy

Geographic Sales Territory

Store/Outlet locations and descriptions of locations (e.g., for retailers strip center, mall, etc.)

Personal Selling Strategies

Promotion Strategies

Advertising Message

Media Strategies and Expenditures
TV
Radio
Newspaper
Direct Mail
Other

Customer Service Policies

Merchandising Strategies

Publicity Strategies

Testing/Marketing R&D Strategies

Summary of Strengths and Weaknesses

Where to find this information:
Your company's past experiences
Primary research
Fairchild Fact Files
Trade publications
Industry 10–K Reports
Media representatives
Field sales reps
Radio/TV reports

WORKSHEET

Industry and Company Review of the Consumer Target Market— Demographic Profile by Volume

Demographic Descriptor	Industry Category			Company		
	Total Number of Customers	% of Total Customers	% of Total Purchases	Total Number of Customers	% of Total Customers	% of Total Purchases
Age						
Under 18						
18 to 24						
25 to 34						
35 to 44						
45 to 54						
55+						
Sex						
Male						
Female						
Household Income						
$15,000 and Under						
$15,001 to $24,000						
$24,001 to $30,000						
$30,001 to $40,000						
$40,001 to $50,000						
$50,001+						
Education						
Did not graduate high school						
Graduated high school						
Some college						
Graduated college						
Occupation						
White-collar						
Blue-collar						
Farmer						
Employment						
Full-time						
Part-time						
Unemployed						
Family Size						
1						
2						
3 to 4						
5 to 6						
7+						
Geography						
Urban						
Suburban						
Rural						
Home						
Own home						
Rent						

Where to find this information:
SMRB (Simmons Market Research Bureau)
MRI (Mediamark Research, Inc.)
Fairchild Fact Files
Census data/county business patterns
Industry trade publications/research departments
Industry research studies (supplied through trade associations)

WORKSHEET

Industry and Company Review of the Consumer Target Market— Demographic Profile by Concentration

Demographic Descriptor	Percent of Industry Total Category that Purchases Product Nationally	Concentration Index*	Percent of Company Customer who Purchases
Age			
Under 18			
18 to 24			
25 to 34			
35 to 44			
45 to 54			
55+			
Sex			
Male			
Female			
Household Income			
$15,000 and Under			
$15,001 to $24,000			
$24,001 to $30,000			
$30,001 to $40,000			
$40,001 to $50,000			
$50,001+			
Education			
Did not graduate high school			
Graduated high school			
Some college			
Graduated college			
Occupation			
White-collar			
Blue-collar			
Farmer			
Employment			
Full-time			
Part-time			
Unemployed			
Family Size			
1			
2			
3 to 4			
5 to 6			
7+			
Geography			
Urban			
Suburban			
Rural			
Home			
Own home			
Rent			

*% of industry category that purchases/% of the total population that purchases (e.g., 10% of all people purchase, but 30% of the 18–24 year-olds purchase, or a 300 index—30 ÷ 10)

Where to find this information:
SMRB (Simmons Market Research Bureau)
MRI (Mediamark Research, Inc.)
Fairchild Fact Files
Census data/county business patterns
Industry trade publications/research surveys from trade publications
Your company records

WORKSHEET

Review of the Consumer Target Market—Demographic Description of Company Purchasers Compared to Industry Category Purchasers

Demographic Descriptor	Percent Purchasers of Industry Category Nationally ( )*	Percent Purchasers of Company Product ( )*	Index: % Company/% Industry
Age			
Under 18			
18 to 24			
25 to 34			
35 to 44			
45 to 54			
55+			
Sex			
Male			
Female			
Household Income			
$15,000 and Under			
$15,001 to $24,000			
$24,001 to $30,000			
$30,001 to $40,000			
$40,001 to $50,000			
$50,001+			
Education			
Did not graduate high school			
Graduated high school			
Some college			
Graduated college			
Occupation			
White-collar			
Blue-collar			
Farmer			
Employment			
Full-time			
Part-time			
Unemployed			
Family Size			
1			
2			
3 to 4			
5 to 6			
7+			
Geography			
Urban			
Suburban			
Rural			
Home			
Own home			
Rent			

*Provide total dollar volume in parentheses.

Where to find this information:
SMRB (Simmons Market Research Bureau)
MRI (Mediamark Research, Inc.)
Your company records
Primary research

WORKSHEET

Review of the Consumer Target Market—Heavy User Demographic Descriptors Compared to All User Demographics Descriptors

	Heavy User Demographic Profile	% of Purchases
Age		
Sex		
Household income		
Education		
Employment		
Family Size		
Geography		
Home ownership		

<u>Lifestyle description</u> of the heavy user compared to the average user

<u>Attribute preference</u>

<u>Geographic location</u>

Where to find this information:
SMRB (Simmons Market Research Bureau)
MRI (Mediamark Research, Inc.)
Your company records
Primary research

WORKSHEET

Business-to-Business Target Market—National Distribution of Businesses by Size Within SIC Category

This chart demonstrates the total number of businesses that exist nationally and categorizes those businesses by SIC segment. It also delineates the number of businesses by SIC within the employment and dollar volume segments.

SIC	Total Establishments		Percent of Establishments by Employment Size Class						Percent of Establishments by Dollar Volume					
	Number	% of Total Census	1 to 4	5 to 9	10 to 19	20 to 49	50 to 99	100+	$000–$1MM	$1MM–$10MM	$10MM–$50MM	$50MM–$100MM	$100MM–$500MM	$500MM+
Agriculture/ Forestry/ Fisheries														
Mining														
Construction														
Manufacturing														
Transportation														
Public Utilities														
Wholesale Trade														
Retail Trade														
Finance/ Insurance/ Real Estate Services														
Public Administration														
Percent														
Total Census (M = $000)														

Where to find this information:
County business patterns
U.S. Department of Commerce
Bureau of the Census
Dun's Marketing Service, a company of the Dun & Bradstreet Corporation

WORKSHEET

Business-to-Business Target Market—Company Distribution of Customers by Size Within SIC Category

This chart demonstrates the total number of customers a firm has and categorizes those businesses by SIC category. The SIC categories could be further broken out if necessary (e.g., sporting good retailers versus the overall category of retailers.) It also delineates the number of businesses by SIC within the size parameters of number of employees and dollar volume of the business. This chart can then be compared with the previous one to determine company penetration of each SIC category.

SIC	Company Customers		Percent of Establishments by Employment Size Class						Percent of Establishments by Dollar Volume					
	Number	% of Total Customers	1 to 4	5 to 9	10 to 19	20 to 49	50 to 99	100+	$000–$1MM	$1MM–$10MM	$10MM–$50MM	$50MM–$100MM	$100MM–$500MM	$500MM+
Agriculture/ Forestry/ Fisheries														
Mining														
Construction														
Manufacturing														
Transportation														
Public Utilities														
Wholesale Trade														
Retail Trade														
Finance/ Insurance/ Real Estate Services														
Public Administration														
Percent														
Total Census (M = $000)														

Where to find this information:
Company data

WORKSHEET

Business-to-Business Target Market—Revenue Distribution of Customers by SIC Category

SIC	Number of Customers	Total Company Sales per SIC Category	Average $ per Customer ($M)	Index to Average (Average $ per Customer/ Average all Categories)
Agriculture/ Forestry/ Fisheries				
Mining				
Construction				
Manufacturing				
Transportation				
Public Utilities				
Wholesale Trade				
Retail Trade				
Finance/ Insurance/Real Estate Services				
Administration				
Total				
Average All Categories (M = $000)				

Where to find this information:
Trade publications
Company records

WORKSHEET

Business-to-Business Target Market—Product Category Purchases by Outlet Type

Outlet Type	Where Consumers Purchase	Percent of Total Outlets

Where to find this information:
Trade publications
Industry sources

WORKSHEET

Product Awareness

- Unaided awareness relative to competition by target market segment

    Segment 1:

    Segment 2:

    Segment 3:

- Aided awareness relative to competition by target market segment

    Segment 1:

    Segment 2:

    Segment 3:

- Unaided awareness relative to competition by target market segment

    Segment 1:

    Segment 2:

    Segment 3:

Where to find this information:
Primary research data—telephone survey

WORKSHEET

Product Attributes

- Attribute importance by target market segments

  <u>Segment</u>   <u>Attribute Importance</u>
  1.

  2.

  3.

  4.

- Competitive ranking of attributes by target market segments
  (Your company's rank for each attribute relative to the competitors')

  <u>Segment</u>   <u>Attribute Ranking</u>
  1.

  2.

  3.

  4.

Where to find this information:
Primary research data—telephone survey

WORKSHEET

Behavior—National Category Development Index (CDI)

DMA	Percent of U.S. Population	Percent of Industry Category Dollar Volume	Category Development Index: CDI (Volume/ Population)	Population Number (000)	Dollar Volume of Industry Category Nationally ($000)	Per Capita Consumption
City 1	%	%			$	$
City 2						
City 3						
City 4						

Where to find this information:
Sales & Marketing Management Survey of Buying Power

WORKSHEET

Behavior—Company Brand Development Index (BDI)

DMA	Percent of Company Population	Percent of Company Dollar Volume	Brand Development Index: BDI (Volume/ Population)	Population Number (000)	Dollar Volume of Company ($000)	Per Capita Consumption
City 1	%	%			$	$
City 2						
City 3						
City 4						

Where to find this information:
Company data

WORKSHEET

Trading Areas by Store

Zip Codes Surrounding Store   **Percent of Customers over 1 Week Period**

_____   _____ %

_____   _____

_____   _____

_____   _____

_____   _____

Where to find this information:
Company store survey
Company mailing lists

WORKSHEET

Behavior—Brand Loyalty

Brand	All	Sole	Loyalty Index	Sole and Primary	Loyalty Index	All Users
	%	%		%		%

Where to find this information:
SMRB (Simmons Market Research Bureau)
MRI (Mediamark Research, Inc.)
Primary research

WORKSHEET

Behavior—Purchase Rates/Buying Habits

- Average # of purchases per <u>customer</u> in industry   _____

- Average # purchases per <u>company</u> customer   _____

- Average industry: $ per <u>consumer</u> purchase   _____

- Average company: $ per <u>customer</u> purchase   _____

- Average industry: number of items purchased per
  consumer purchase   _____

- Average company: number of items purchased for
  customer purchase   _____

- Company market share   _____

   $ market share   _____

   % of target market penetration
   (Percent of target market universe which is a customer)   _____

Note: The above should be completed for the aggregate consumer/customer and for each significant segment.

Note: A similar chart should be developed for the heavy user segment contrasting heavy users to all users.

WORKSHEET

Purchasing Rates/Buying Habits—for Retail

This chart provides examples of how to monitor heavy user purchase behavior through primary research. A "heavy purchasers" and "all purchasers" category is provided for each question.

Number of _____ (whatever the product category) purchased in one year.
Heavy purchasers _____.
All purchasers _____.

Number of stores usually visited to find what you want per purchaser.
Heavy purchasers _____.
All purchasers _____.

Amount purchased per visit (dollars and units).
Heavy purchasers _____.
All purchasers _____.

Visits to your store per month/year.
Heavy purchasers _____.
All purchasers _____.

Visits to all stores per month/year.
Heavy purchasers _____.
All purchasers _____.

Purchases at your store per month/year.
Heavy purchasers _____.
All purchasers _____.

Purchases at all stores per month/year.
Heavy purchasers _____.
All purchasers _____.

Average purchase ratio in percent or people who purchase versus those who do not with each visit to the store.
Heavy purchasers _____.
All purchasers _____.

Note: The above should be completed for the aggregate consumer/customer and for each significant segment.

Where to find this information:
In-store survey

WORKSHEET

Behavior—Trial/Retrial

	Percent Ever Used	Percent Used Last 6 Months	Loyalty Measure: Percent Used Past 6 Months/ Percent Ever Used

Company

1. Segment
   Product

   Product

   Product

2. Segment
   Product

   Product

   Product

Competition

1. Segment
   Product

   Product

   Product

2. Segment
   Product

   Product

   Product

Where to find this information:
Market Survey

FORMAT

Problems and Opportunities

Corporate Philosophy/Description of the Company

Problems   Opportunities

Sales Analysis

Problems   Opportunities

Distribution

Problems   Opportunities

Pricing

Problems   Opportunities

Historical Marketing Review of the Competition versus Your Company

Problems   Opportunities

Demand Analysis

Problems   Opportunities

Target Market

Problems   Opportunities

Product Awareness and Attributes

Problems   Opportunities

Purchase Rates/Buying Habits

Problems   Opportunities

WORKSHEETS AND FORMATS FOR THE MARKETING PLAN

The following worksheets correspond to the preparation of your marketing plan presented in Chapters 4 through 21 of this book. Their purpose is to provide the marketer with a strategic framework for efficiently preparing an effective, well thought out marketing plan. Use these worksheets to identify and compile material for each of the sections as well as to use as formats in completing your marketing plan.

WORKSHEET

Sales Objectives: Macro Method

Market and Share Data

	Market Sales Volume				Company Share Percent of the Market			
	$ ( )	Percent Change Previous Year	Units ( )	Percent Change Previous Year	$	Percent Points Change from Previous Year	Units	Percent Points Change from Previous Year
Previous 5 years								
1								
2								
3								
4								
5								
Projections Next 3 Years								
1								
2								
3								

Three Year Sales Projection for Company

	Dollars			Units		
Year	Market Sales $ Volume ( )	× Company Share Percent of Market	= Company $ Sales ( )	Market Sales Unit Volume ( )	× Company Unit Share Percent of Market	= Company Unit Sales ( )
1						
2						
3						

WORKSHEET

Sales Objectives: Micro Method

Projections from Top: Sales Forecast for Manufacturing, Service, or Retail Category*

	Company Sales Volume			
	$ ( )	% Change Previous Year	Units ( )	% Change Previous Year
Previous 5 years				
1				
2				
3				
4				
5				
Next 3 Years Projections				
1				
2				
3				

Note: Complete a worksheet for your company's total sales and a worksheet for each individual product or department.

*Based on your type of business, include in your sales projections dollars and units/transactions/persons served, and take into consideration new products, distribution channels, stores or services, and price changes.

Use net dollar sales to trade/intermediate markets.

Projections from Bottom: Sales Forecast by Distribution Channel for Manufacturers*

	Existing			New		
Channel	Number	Dollars (MM)	Units	Number	Dollars (MM)	Units

Total

Note: Develop projections for each year for a three-year period.

*In your sales projections, take into consideration new products, changes in distribution outlets, and price changes. Use net dollar sales to trade/intermediate markets.

Projections from Bottom: Sales Forecast by Store for Retailers*

	Stores	
	$	Transactions
Market	( )	( )
Name/Store number		

Market Total

Note: Develop projections for each year for a three-year period.

*In your sales projections, take into consideration new stores, products, and services along with price changes. Service organizations use service office/center in place of stores. Use dollar sales to ultimate purchasers. Service organizations use persons served in place of transactions.

WORKSHEET

Sales Objectives: Expense-Plus Method

Review of Historical Financial Data

			Expenses	
Previous 5 Years	Gross Margin Percent of Sales	Profit Percent of Sales	Percent of Sales	Dollars (MM)
	%	%	%	$

Method Calculations

Planned Margin	%
Planned Profit −	%
Operating Expense	%

Budgeted Expense Dollars of $ _____ /Operating Expense of _____ % = Sales Objective of

WORKSHEET

Sales Objectives

Reconciliation of Sales Objectives

	Macro		Micro		Expense Plus		Composite Sales Objectives	
	Dollars (MM)	Units (MM)	Dollars (MM)	Units (MM)	Dollars (MM)	Units (MM)	Dollars (MM)	Units (MM)
Short-term 1 Year								
Long-term 2 year								
3 year								

WORKSHEET

Qualitative Adjustment of Quantitatively Derived Sales

Qualitative Impacting Factors	± Point Change	Percentage Adjustment ×	Composite Sales Objectives =	Adjusted Sales Objectives

Total _____

Final Adjusted Average
(Total of adjusted sales objectives divided by number of calculated factors)

Note: 1. List the qualitative factors and to what extent they will impact on the previous numerically-arrived at
sales objectives. Adjust composite sales objective(s) accordingly to arrive at final sales objective(s).
2. Use qualitative adjustments for units, transactions, or persons served, as well as for sales dollars objectives.
However, percentage point adjustment may differ from dollars.

FORMAT

Sales Objectives for Manufacturers

Short-Term (One-Year)

1. Increase dollar sales _____% over previous year, from $_____ to $_____.

2. Increase unit sales _____% over previous year, from _____ to _____.

Long-Term*

1. Increase dollar sales _____% from year_____ to year_____, from $_____ to $_____.

2. Increase unit sales _____% from year_____ to year_____, from $_____ to $_____.

Rationale

Note: 1. Use this format for total company sales as well as for specific products.
        2. Include profit objectives as well, using a similar format.

*List two and three year sales objectives separately.

FORMAT

Sales Objectives for Retail and Service

Short-Term (One Year)

1. Increase total dollar sales _____% and transactions _____% over previous year, from $_____ to $_____ and from _____ transactions to _____ transactions.

2. Increase comparable store sales _____% and transactions _____% over previous year, from $_____ to $_____ and from _____ transactions to _____ transactions.

Long-Term[†]

1. Increase total sales _____% and transactions _____% for year _____ to year _____, from $_____ to $_____, and from _____ transactions to _____ transactions.

2. Increase comparable store sales _____% and transactions _____% for year _____ to year _____, from $_____ to $_____, and from _____ transactions to _____ transactions.

Rationale

Note: 1. Use this format for total company sales as well as for specific retail and service categories. Retailers might also want to use unit objectives as well. Service organizations use dollar and persons/companies served.
       2. Include profit objectives as well, using a similar format.

[†]List two and three year sales objectives separately.

WORKSHEET

Product Sales Volume for Development of Target Market

List the largest sales volume and fastest growth products from the category. Provide sales trends, profits trends, and percent of category sales. Provide company information (sales trends, profit trends, percent of category sales and market share) for the same leading products.

M=$000

Category 5-Year Trend

Category's Highest $ Volume Products	Sales					% of Category Sales					Profit					# Transactions/Purchases				
	Yr. 1	Yr. 2	Yr. 3	Yr. 4	Yr. 5	Yr. 1	Yr. 2	Yr. 3	Yr. 4	Yr. 5	Yr. 1	Yr. 2	Yr. 3	Yr. 4	Yr. 5	Yr. 1	Yr. 2	Yr. 3	Yr. 4	Yr. 5
1)																				
2)																				
3)																				
•																				
•																				
•																				

Company 5-Year Trend

Company's Highest $ Volume Products	Sales					% of Company Sales					Profit					# Transactions/Purchases				
	Yr. 1	Yr. 2	Yr. 3	Yr. 4	Yr. 5	Yr. 1	Yr. 2	Yr. 3	Yr. 4	Yr. 5	Yr. 1	Yr. 2	Yr. 3	Yr. 4	Yr. 5	Yr. 1	Yr. 2	Yr. 3	Yr. 4	Yr. 5
1)																				
2)																				
3)																				
•																				
•																				
•																				

Product	Market Share				
	Yr. 1	Yr. 2	Yr. 3	Yr. 4	Yr. 5
1)					
2)					
3)					
•					
•					
•					

Index Company to Category

$ Volume Products	Sales % Change Company (5-year trend) Yr. 1 to Yr. 5	Sales % Change Category (5-year trend) Yr. 1 to Yr. 5	Sales Index Company/Category Yr. 1 to Yr. 5	% of Sales Index Company/Category Yr. 1 Yr. 2 Yr. 3 Yr. 4 Yr. 5
1)				
2)				
3)				
•				
•				
•				

WORKSHEET

Target Market Descriptions/Target Market Behavior

List the target market description for the largest industry or company product category (based upon sales volume, sales growth, and/or profitability), the second largest, third largest, etc. Use a separate form for each target market description.

List the target market behavior rates for the category and company.

Target Segment Description #1

_____

_____

_____

Segment accounts for ___ of Total Category Sales	Segment accounts for ___ of Total Company Sales	Market Share
CATEGORY	**COMPANY**	**COMPANY/CATEGORY**
Growth Rate This Year Past 5 Years	Growth Rate This Year Past 5 Years	Penetration This Year
Number of users	Number of users	Number of users
Number of purchases	Number of purchases	Number of purchases
$ Customer	$ Customer	
Retrial rate	Retrial rate	

Target Segment Description #2

_____

_____

_____

Segment accounts for ___ of Total Category Sales	Segment accounts for ___ of Total Company Sales	Market Share
CATEGORY	**COMPANY**	**COMPANY/CATEGORY**
Growth Rate This Year Past 5 Years	Growth Rate This Year Past 5 Years	Penetration This Year
Number of users	Number of users	Number of users
Number of purchases	Number of purchases	Number of purchases
$ Customer	$ Customer	
Retrial rate	Retrial rate	

WORKSHEET

Awareness and Attribute Rankings

List the awareness of the target markets for the company and the leading competitors. List the top purchase attributes for the target markets and the relative ranking of the company versus the leading competitors.

TARGET SEGMENT AWARENESS RATINGS

Target Segment:

	Yr. 1	Yr. 2	Yr. 3	Yr. 4	Yr. 5

Company

Leading
Competitor

Leading
Competitor

Leading
Competitor

TARGET SEGMENT ATTRIBUTE RATINGS

Target Segment:

Top 5 Attributes	Company Ranking					Leading Competitor Ranking					Leading Competitor Ranking					Leading Competitor Ranking				
	Yr. 1	Yr. 2	Yr. 3	Yr. 4	Yr. 5	Yr. 1	Yr. 2	Yr. 3	Yr. 4	Yr. 5	Yr. 1	Yr. 2	Yr. 3	Yr. 4	Yr. 5	Yr. 1	Yr. 2	Yr. 3	Yr. 4	Yr. 5
1)																				
2)																				
3)																				
4)																				
5)																				

FORMAT

Target Market for Consumer—Short-term (Package Goods, Retail, Service)

Primary Market

Secondary Market (Where Applicable)

Rationale

FORMAT

Target Market for Consumer—Long-term Package Goods, Retail, Service)

Primary Market

Secondary Market (Where Applicable)

Rationale

FORMAT

Target Market for Business-to-Business—Short-Term

Primary*

Secondary* **(Where Applicable)**
Intermediate

End User

Other

Rationale

FORMAT

Target Market for Business-to-Business—Long-Term

Primary*

Secondary* **(Where Applicable)**
Intermediate

End User

Other

Rationale

FORMAT

Marketing Objectives

Short-Term Objectives

Rationale

Long-Term Objectives

Rationale

WORKSHEET

Positioning: Matching Product Differences to the Target Market's Needs/Wants

Key Competition

1

2

3

4

5

Key Target Market

Differences from Competitor
Product/Store/Service Attributes/Benefits

New Products/Improvements

Packaging/Store Appearance

Branding/Name/Reputation

Distribution/Penetration

Price

Advertising (Message/Media)

Promotion

Merchandising

Personal Selling and Service

Publicity

Characteristics—Needs/Wants
What

Where

When

Why (Benefit)

How Purchased/Used

How the Target and Its Needs/Wants Are Changing

WORKSHEET

Positioning: Mapping Product Importance by Competitive Ranking

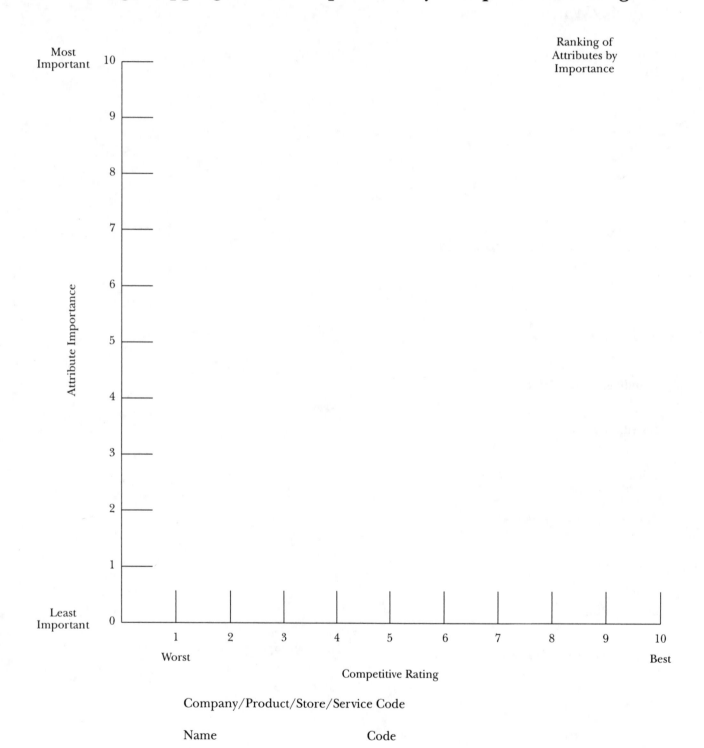

Ranking of
Attributes by
Importance

Company/Product/Store/Service Code

Name   Code

FORMAT

Positioning Strategy

Strategy Statement

Qualifier/Descriptors (Only if necessary)

Rationale

FORMAT

Marketing Strategies

Build the Market or Steal Market Share Strategies

National, Regional, and Local Marketing Strategies

Seasonality Strategies

Spending Strategies

Competitive Strategies

Target Market Strategies

Product Strategies

Packaging

Branding Strategies

Note: Provide rationale for each strategy.

Pricing Strategies

Distribution of Product/Store Penetration or Coverage Strategies

Personal Selling/Service/Operations Strategies

Promotion Strategies

Advertising Message Strategies

Advertising Media Strategies

Merchandising Strategies

Publicity Strategies

Marketing R&T (Research and Testing) Strategies

WORKSHEET

Locking Sales from Target Market to Marketing Objectives and Communication

<u>Total Sales</u>

<u>Total Target Market</u>

	Previous Purchasers				**Non-Purchasers**			
Segmented Target Sales Objectives								
Marketing Objectives	<u>%</u>	#			<u>%</u>	#		
Purchasers (via retention and trial)								
# of annual purchases								
Average $ purchase								
Purchase Intent	<u>%</u>	#			<u>%</u>	#		
Believe they will definitely purchase								

	Unaided Awareness		**Positive* Attitude**		**Unaided Awareness**		**Positive* Attitude**	
	<u>%</u>	<u>#</u>	<u>%</u>	<u>#</u>	<u>%</u>	<u>#</u>	<u>%</u>	<u>#</u>
Marketing Plan Communication Goals								
Tactical Tool Communication Goals								
Product								
Branding								
Packaging								
Pricing								
Distribution/Penetration								
Personal Selling/Service								
Promotion/Events								
Advertising Message								
Advertising Media								
Merchandising								
Publicity								

*List specific primary attitude to be affected for previous purchasers and non-purchasers:
Previous purchasers   _____
Non-purchasers   _____

FORMAT

Communication Goals Application

Target Market   _____ Total Target Market #

Purchasers   _____%

Definitely Purchase Intent   _____%

Specific Positive Attitude   _____%

Unaided Awareness   _____%

WORKSHEET

Communications Values Review

Tactical Tool	Activity	Results	Directional Implications
Product			
Branding			
Packaging			
Pricing			
Distribution/Penetration			
Personal Selling/Service			
Promotion/Events			
Advertising Message			
Advertising Media			
Merchandising			
Publicity			

WORKSHEET

Method to Set Marketing Communication Goals to Fulfill the Marketing Objectives

	Target Market		
	Current Purchasers	Non-Purchasers	Total
	%	%	%

Marketing Objectives

Purchase Intent

Marketing Communication Goals

Specific Positive Attitude

Unaided Awareness

WORKSHEET

Tactical Tool Importance Ranking

Tactical Tool	Awareness Purchaser	Awareness Non-Purchaser	Attitude Purchaser	Attitude Non-Purchaser
Product				
Branding				
Packaging				
Price				
Distribution/ Penetration				
Personal Selling/ Service				
Promotion/ Events				
Advertising Message				
Advertising Media				
Merchandising				
Publicity				

VI = Very Important
MI = Moderately Important
I = Important

░░ **FORMAT** ░░

Individual Tactical Tool Value Goals for Your Product by Awareness and Attitude

	AWARENESS		ATTITUDE	
	Purchaser	Non-Purchaser	Purchaser	Non-Purchaser
	% Point	% Point	% Point	% Point
Product				
Branding				
Packaging				
Distribution/ Penetration				
Personal Selling/ Service				
Promotion/Events				
Advertising Message				
Advertising Media				
Merchandising				
Publicity				
TOTAL*				

*Total % for purchaser and non-purchaser for awareness and attitude should sum to awareness and attitude communication goals previously set.

FORMAT

Product

Product Objectives

Product Strategies

Rationale

FORMAT

Branding/New Name

Branding Objectives

Branding Strategies

Branding Parameters

Rationale

FORMAT

Packaging

Packaging Objectives

Packaging Strategies

Rationale

FORMAT

Price

Price Objectives

Price Strategies

Rationale

WORKSHEET

Pricing Considerations

Consideration	Specific Situation	Pricing Implications	Potential Price Approach
Problems/Opportunities	_____	_____	_____
	_____	_____	_____
	_____	_____	_____
Marketing Objectives	_____	_____	_____
	_____	_____	_____
	_____	_____	_____
Positioning	_____	_____	_____
	_____	_____	_____
	_____	_____	_____
Marketing Strategies	_____	_____	_____
	_____	_____	_____
	_____	_____	_____
Price Communication Goals	_____	_____	_____
	_____	_____	_____
	_____	_____	_____
Break-even	_____	_____	_____
	_____	_____	_____
	_____	_____	_____
Price Elasticity	_____	_____	_____
	_____	_____	_____
	_____	_____	_____
Product Lifestyle Stage	_____	_____	_____
	_____	_____	_____
	_____	_____	_____
Product Differentiation	_____	_____	_____
	_____	_____	_____
	_____	_____	_____
Business Goals	_____	_____	_____
	_____	_____	_____
	_____	_____	_____
Competition Pricing	_____	_____	_____
	_____	_____	_____
	_____	_____	_____

FORMAT

Distribution

Distribution Objectives

Distribution Strategies

Rationale

FORMAT

Personal Selling/Service

Selling/Service Objectives

Selling/Service Strategies

Rationale

FORMAT

Promotion/Events

Promotion Objectives

Promotion Strategies

Rationale

FORMAT

Promotion Program Execution

Program Theme

Sales Objective

Promotion Objective

Promotion Strategies

Description

Support

Rationale

WORKSHEET

Calculating Cost of a Coupon Promotion

	High	Medium	Low

Redemption Costs

Value of coupon

Number of coupons distributed

Estimated redemption rate

Number redeemed

Dollar value or offer
 (number redeemed × value of coupon)

Advertising and Media Costs

Printing of coupons

Mailing cost/envelopes

 Total cost of promotion

WORKSHEET

Payback Calculation for Open Promotion

Situation

Promotion:

Time period:

Geography:

Sales

Estimated sales for period without promotion

Estimated gross margin dollars for period without promotion

Estimated sales with promotion

Estimated gross margin dollars without promotion

Estimated net margin dollar increase with promotion

Media and Advertising Cost

Estimated ongoing advertising and media costs with or without promotion*

Total advertising and media costs with promotion

Incremental advertising and media costs due to promotion

Payout

Incremental margin sales

Incremental advertising and media expenditures

Contribution to fixed overhead

*What would have been spent in regular mainline advertising and media.

FORMAT

Advertising Message

<u>Objectives</u>

Awareness

Attitudes

Rationale for Objectives

Advertising Strategy

Promise

Support for this Promise

Tone of the Advertising

Rationale for Strategy

<u>Advertising Execution (If no separate advertising implementation plan is prepared)</u>

Additional/Key Strategy Information

Specific Legal Considerations

Advertising Requirements

FORMAT

Advertising Implementation Plan

Date: _____

	Plan Approval		
	Name	Approved	Date

Product: _____ 1.

Job Title: _____ 2.

Prepared By: _____ 3.

Job Description: (including requirements/sizes) 4.

Advertising Strategy:

Due Dates:

Concept _____   Art/photography _____

Copy/layout/boards _____   TV shoot _____

Client OK _____   Mechanical _____

Preproduction (Print/TV/AV) _____   Ship to printer _____

Ship finished job _____

1st air date/insertion/use _____

Budget:

Total Project Cost:

$ _____

Estimate needed from:

☐ Art/Photography   ☐ Commercial Production

☐ Multi-image   ☐ Print Production

Estimate needed by: _____

Guidelines for Writing Implementation Plans

Follow general order of subjects listed, selecting those which apply to the current job. If pertinent information is not available, indicate date it will be available. Attach additional information to this planning form.

Print	**Radio/TV/ Multi-image**	**Copy**	**Art**	**Budget Limitations**
Quantity	Storyboards	Product/Service	Layout/	Internal
Stock	Medium (Film,	Objective/Strategy	Storyboard	Time/$
Size	Tape, Slides)	Target Market (Attached	Stage	Outside
Colors	Length	additional information	Art Reference	Suppliers/
Delivery, Mailing List/	Music	to this planning form)	Detail	$ Available
Labels		Benefits—Major	Information	
Proofs		Benefits—Minor		
Printing Process		Exclusives		
Preprints and Reprints		Buying Information		
Publication		Appeal		
Requirements		Emotion		
Releases		Limitations		
Art/Photography		Musts (Incl. Legal Requirements)		
Price Information		Research Info.		
Logo, Sig. Code/Ad #		Competitive Info.		

This copy for:

Name/Department

☐ _____

☐ _____

☐ _____

☐ _____

FORMAT

Media Plan

Media Objectives

Target Audience

Geography

Seasonality

Weighting/Impact Goals
Quantitative

Qualitative

Budget (Optional)

Media Test Objectives (if applicable)

Rationale for Objectives

Media Strategies

Media Mix

Specific Medium Usage

Scheduling

Rationale for Strategies

FORMAT

Media Calendar

YEAR: _____

BROADCAST MONTHS (WEEK BEGINNING MONDAY)

Media	January	February	March	April	May	June	July	August	September	October	November	December

FORMAT

Media Budget

Spending by Medium and Quarter

Company/Product/Service:

Year:

Date:

Medium	1st Quarter ($)	2nd Quarter ($)	3rd Quarter ($)	4th Quarter ($)	Total ($)	Percent %
Total	$	$	$	$	$	
Percent	%	%	%	%		100%

Spending by Product/Market and Medium

Company/Product/Service:

Year:

Date:

	Medium						Total Spending by Product/ Market
Product/Market	$( ) %	$( ) %	$( ) %	$( ) %	$( ) %	$( ) %	$( ) %
Total Spending by Medium	$ %	$ %	$ %	$ %	$ %	$ %	$ 100%

FORMAT

Merchandising

Objectives

Strategies

Rationale

FORMAT

Publicity

Objectives

Strategies

Rationale

WORKSHEET

Marketing Plan Budget (Date Prepared)

	($M)	Percent of Total Budget
Marketing Mix Tool		
Media		
Television		
Newspaper		
Radio		
Direct mail		
Outdoor		
Other		
Total		
Production		
Television		
Newspaper		
Radio		
Direct mail		
Outdoor		
Other		
Total		
Product/Branding/Packaging		
Total		
Personal Selling/Operations		
Total		
Promotion		
Redemption cost		
Media support		
Production		
Total		
Merchandising		
Production		
Total		
Publicity		
Total		
Research		
Total		
Miscellaneous		
Total		
Grand Total		

WORKSHEET

Marketing Plan Budget Comparison

	$M	Percent of Sales

Total Budget Compared to Industry Average and Previous Year
Marketing as a percent of sales per plan
Marketing as a percent of sales per industry average
Index company budget to industry average
Index company budget to previous year

Total Planned Budget Compared to Competition
Total planned budget for company
Total estimated budget for Competitor A
Total estimated budget for Competitor B
Total estimated budget for Competitor C

WORKSHEET

Contribution to Fixed Overhead

Payback Analysis
Assumptions

Sales
Less cost of goods sold
  Gross profit
Less:
  Media
  Production costs
  Promotion costs
  Merchandising
  Selling
  Research
  Public relations/miscellaneous
    Total marketing mix tools
Contribution to fixed costs
Fixed costs
Profit before taxes

WORKSHEET

Gross Margin to Net Sales
Payback Analysis
Assumptions

	Year 1 Projections	Year 2 Projections	Year 3 Projections
Net sales			
Gross margin			
Less promotion			
Less advertising			
Profit/loss			

FORMAT

MARKETING CALENDAR

YEAR: _____

Media	January	February	March	April	May	June	July	August	September	October	November	December

MARKETING PROGRAMS:

MEDIA ACTIVITIES:

NON-MEDIA ACTIVITIES:

WORKSHEET

Growth Rate of Improvement Sales Trending Method

Evaluation Objective

Evaluation Strategies

Evaluation Execution

Test Market versus Control Market Dollar Sales Analysis

Test Period _____

	Last Year	**This Year**	**Percent Change**

Preperiod versus
Test Period _____

Preperiod
   Test market
   Control market
Test period
   Test market
   Control market

Growth Rate Improvement	**Preperiod Percent Change**	**Test Period Percent Change**	**Point Gain/Loss**
Test market			
Control market			
Net percent point difference			

Incremental sales: GRI _____ x Test Period Sales $_____ = Net Weekly Gain $_____

	Last Year	**This Year**	**Percent Change**

Test Period versus
Postperiod _____

Test period
   Test market
   Control market
Postperiod
   Test market
   Control market

Growth Rate Improvement	**Test Period Percent Change**	**Postperiod Percent Change**	**Point Gain/Loss**
Test market			
Control market			
Net percent point difference			

Incremental sales: GRI _____ x Test Period Sales $_____ = Net Weekly Gain $_____

Growth Rate of Improvement Sales Trending Method—continued

	Last Year	This Year	Percent Change

Postperiod versus Preperiod _____

Postperiod
  Test market
  Control market
Preperiod
  Test market
  Control market

Growth Rate Improvement	**Postperiod Percent Change**	**Preperiod Percent Change**	**Point Gain/Loss**
Test market			
Control market			
Net percent point difference			

Incremental sales: GRI _____ x Test Period Sales $_____ = Net Weekly Gain $_____

Test Market versus National System Average Dollar Sales Analysis

Test Period_____

	Last Year	This Year	Percent Change

Preperiod versus Test Period _____

Preperiod
  Test market
  National system average
Test period
  Test market
  National system average

Growth Rate Improvement	**Preperiod Percent Change**	**Test Period Percent Change**	**Point Gain/Loss**
Test market			
National system average			
Net percent point difference			

Incremental sales: GRI _____ x Test Period Sales $_____ = Net Weekly Gain $_____

	Last Year	This Year	Percent Change

Test Period versus Postperiod _____

Test period
  Test market
  National system average
Postperiod
  Test market
  National system average

Growth Rate Improvement	**Test Period Percent Change**	**Postperiod Percent Change**	**Point Gain/Loss**
Test market			
National system average			
Net percent point difference			

Incremental sales: GRI _____ x Test Period Sales $_____ = Net Weekly Gain $_____

Growth Rate of Improvement Sales Trending Method—continued

	Last Year	This Year	Percent Change

Postperiod versus
Preperiod _____

Post period
  Test market
  National system average
Preperiod
  Test market
  National system average

Growth Rate Improvement	**Postperiod Percent Change**	**Preperiod Percent Change**	**Point Gain/Loss**

Test market
National system average
  Net percent point difference
Incremental sales: GRI _____ x Test Period Sales $_____ = Net Weekly Gain $_____

INDEX